THE SECRET DOCTRINE WÜRZBURG MANUSCRIPT

by

H. P. Blavatsky

The 1885-1886 Version with the Stanzas of Dzyan and H.P.B.'s Accompanying Commentaries

Eastern School Press

2014

© 2014 Eastern School Press
Cotopaxi, Colorado, U.S.A.
mail@easterntradition.org
ISBN 978-0-912181-05-9
ISBN 0-912181-05-2

TABLE OF CONTENTS

Introduction by David Reigle vii

VOLUME I
HISTORY OF SOME GREAT OCCULTISTS

To the Readers 3

Chapter I – On Eastern and Western Occult Literature 15

    Section I

        1. Explanation of the First Page of *Isis Unveiled* . . . 17
        2. Hermetic and Other Books of Antiquity 27

    Section II

        1. White and Black Magic – in Theory and Practice 37
        2. Hermes and the 32 Ways of Wisdom 43

    Section III

        1. Mathematics and Geometry – the Keys to the Universal Problems 53
        2. The Key of the Absolute in Magic – the Hexagon with the Central Point – or the Seventh key 57

    Section IV

        1. Who was the Adept of Tyana? 63
        2. The Roman Church Dreads the Publication of the Real Life of Apollonius 67

Section V

1. Confession and Property in Common 73
2. What the Occultists and Kabalists have to say .. 87
3. The Souls of the Stars – Universal Heliolatry ... 93
4. The Mystery "Sun of Initiation" 105
5. The Trial of the Sun-Initiates 111

Appendix I

The Star-Angel Worship in the Roman Church, Its
Re-Establishment, Growth and History 123

VOLUME II
EVOLUTION OF COSMOS

Part I (Archaic Period)
Chapter One

Pages From a Prehistoric Past 133

Stanza I 145
Commentary on Stanza I 147

Stanza II 155
Commentary on Stanza II 157

Stanza III 161
Commentary on Stanza III 165

Stanza IV 175
Commentary on Stanza IV 177

Stanza V 189
Commentary on Stanza V 191

Stanza VI 207
Commentary on Stanza VI 209

Stanza VII 217
Commentary on Stanza VII 219

VOLUME III
EVOLUTION OF MAN

Book II – Archaic Chronology, Cycles, Anthropology 249

    I. Calculation and Hypothesis of Geology and Anthropology; Conclusions and Modern Theories .. 253

Appendices

The Writing of *The Secret Doctrine*: A Chronology compiled by Daniel H. Caldwell 261

The Myth of the "Missing" Third Volume of *The Secret Doctrine*, by Daniel H. Caldwell 351

Introduction

by David Reigle

The so-called "Würzburg manuscript" is a partial copy of H. P. Blavatsky's early manuscript of *The Secret Doctrine*, written in 1885 and 1886 while staying in Würzburg, Germany, and Ostende, Belgium. A copy of her manuscript was made to be sent to India for review and correction by T. Subba Row. Of this copy, a portion estimated to be a third or fourth of the whole was found, and this is now known as the Würzburg manuscript. Only portions of this portion have ever been published until now. Here, at last, we have the full text of this valuable document as it is now extant. It tells us much. In it we have unrevised translations of the stanzas from the "Book of Dzyan," primarily on cosmogenesis (most of the anthropogenesis portions are lost), and Blavatsky's unrevised commentaries on them. In it we also have much of the material that was later published as "volume 3" of *The Secret Doctrine*. This shows us that, contrary to widely held Theosophical opinion, this material was indeed originally intended by Blavatsky to be part of *The Secret Doctrine*.

The copy of Blavatsky's manuscript was made by at least two different scribes. When copying the manuscript the scribes made scribal errors, as scribes do. In fact, these scribal errors are so extensive that they caused C. Jinarajadasa to give up on publishing it after a number of installments in *The Theosophist*. The point to be noted is that the Würzburg manuscript we have is a copy of Blavatsky's original manuscript, not the original manuscript itself. Moreover, it is a very incomplete copy. Only a portion of the material sent to India has so far been found.

The Würzburg manuscript may have been lost forever, if not for its chance discovery by C. Jinarajadasa. He mentions how this happened in a brief anecdote in his article, "H.P.B.'s Precipitated Teapot and Other Phenomena," published in the April 1952 issue of *The Theosophist* (vol. 73, no. 7, p. 13):

The original manuscript of the first *Secret Doctrine*, Vol. I, sent by H.P.B. to Colonel Olcott, was at Adyar. How it reached Dr. Besant's room in Banaras I do not know; but once when she was not present at Convention I happened to look into an empty bookcase in her room, and on one shelf, in a dark corner, lying flat, was this big foolscap volume. Who had forgotten it when emptying the shelves, I do not know. I brought it to Adyar and began publishing it.

This manuscript was discovered in 1921, as we learn from another comment made in passing by Jinarajadasa in his article titled, "A Unique Manuscript," published in *The Theosophist*, August 1923 (vol. 44, no. 11). The unique manuscript described in this article is not the Würzburg manuscript, but rather is an unpublished manuscript by J. Ralston Skinner that was presented by him to Blavatsky and was quoted by her in *The Secret Doctrine*. Jinarajadasa writes about them both (p. 565):

> Among the material which I found in Benares in 1921, there were two striking manuscripts. The first of these has already been mentioned; it is the first draft of the first volume of *The Secret Doctrine* which H.P.B. sent to T. Subba Row.

The first manuscript "has already been mentioned" in "On the Watch-tower," apparently by Annie Besant, opening the March 1922 issue of *The Theosophist* (vol. 43, no. 6). She there (p. 531) refers to "the original MS. volume of *The Secret Doctrine*, sent over here by H.P.B. from London." Then she elaborates a few pages later (pp. 533-534):

> Mr. C. Jinarajadasa has discovered among the records of the T.S. much interesting material. . . . Another interesting "find" is the first manuscript of the first volume of *The Secret Doctrine*, mentioned above. This evidently is the manuscript which H.P.B. sent from Ostend in 1886 to T. Subba Row. *The Secret Doctrine*, as we now have it, is an expanded version of this first manuscript, though in the later revision some sections are omitted which are in this original draft. Five of these sections, which were

discarded by her from Volumes I and II, appear in Volume III. Some of the Appendices referred to in this MS. of Vol. I similarly appear in Vol. III or elsewhere.

We will return to the material from the Würzburg manuscript that appeared in volume 3 of *The Secret Doctrine* shortly. First, let us continue the quotation from Annie Besant, where she brings in another find, and concludes by adverting to why all this early material is of great interest to students.

> One solitary page discovered of another draft—that beginning "Commentary on Stanza I"—shows that it is different from the first draft, and from that finally printed. H.P.B. wrote and re-wrote, correcting even when the final page-proofs were ready to be struck off. Mr. R. L. Christie, the Treasurer of the Scottish Section, T.S., is typing the MS. of the first *Secret Doctrine*, and the T.P.H. is arranging to publish the MS., in the same size as *The Secret Doctrine* as finally revised by H.P.B. The verbal changes, omissions and re-arrangement of her material by H.P.B. are of very great fascination to students.

The solitary page here referred to was published in facsimile in the October 1924 issue of *The Theosophist* (vol. 46, no. 1, p. 106) under the title, "The Secret Doctrine: A Solitary Page of the MS.," by C.J. [Jinarajadasa]. On the following page (page 107) was reproduced in facsimile "A Page from the First Draft of the Secret Doctrine"; i.e., from the Würzburg manuscript. Both of these pages were again published in 1925 in *The Golden Book of the Theosophical Society* (pp. 72, 112), and once again in 1978 in the "Historical Introduction" by Boris de Zirkoff to *The Secret Doctrine* (pp. 34, 36).

This solitary page has the three fundamental propositions of the Secret Doctrine in an early version, which differs not only from the version finally published in 1888, but also from the early version found in the Würzburg manuscript. So we have three different versions of the three fundamental propositions of the Secret Doctrine. These are so essential, that any and every help we can get in understanding them is most welcome.

The "solitary page" is in Blavatsky's own handwriting, and may well be from the actual first draft of *The Secret Doctrine*. Even by the time of the Würzburg manuscript copy we see that the three fundamental propositions of Secret Doctrine had been revised and are much closer to the version finally published in 1888. The actual first draft of *The Secret Doctrine* in Blavatsky's own handwriting seems to have almost entirely disappeared. Besides this "solitary page" (also reproduced in *The Theosophist*, vol. 52, no. 11, August 1931, p. 600), what is apparently one other page from it was reproduced in facsmile in Manly P. Hall's 1931 book, *The Phoenix* (p. 113). If it is a mystery how this "solitary page" got to Adyar, it is an ever greater mystery how another page came into the hands of Manly Hall in California. These are the only two pages from it now known to exist.

For the copy referred to as the Würzburg manuscript, the scribes were primarily Countess Wachtmeister, Mary Gebhard, and occasionally one or two others. Help in this needed task was accepted from whoever happened to be there and volunteered for it. From the time this manuscript was discovered in 1921 by C. Jinarajadasa, there was always the intention to publish it, as we see from Annie Besant's 1922 statement quoted above. What ever happened to the transcript then being typed by Mr. R. L. Christie, Treasurer of the Scottish Section of the Theosophical Society, is unknown. He may have abandoned this project not long into it, because when the first installment appeared in 1931 in the "H.P.B. Centenary Number" of *The Theosophist*, it was edited by C. Jinarajadasa. It was titled, "The Secret Doctrine [First Draft]" (*The Theosophist*, vol. 52, Aug. 1931, pp. 601-607). Then a little while later Jinarajadasa began publishing it serially as "The Secret Doctrine, Vol. I. Original Manuscript of 1885" (vol. 54, Oct. 1932, pp. 27-36; Nov. 1932, pp. 140-150; Dec. 1932, pp. 265-271; Jan. 1933, pp. 397-401; Feb. 1933, pp. 538-542; Mar. 1933, pp. 623-628; vol. 54, part 2, Apr. 1933, pp. 9-14; May 1933, pp. 137-143; June 1933, pp. 263-266; July 1933, pp. 391-395; Aug. 1933, pp. 505-509; Sep. 1933, pp. 633-637; vol. 55, Oct. 1933, pp. 12-16; Nov. 1933, pp. 143-146).

The publication of the Würzburg manuscript ceased with the November 1933 issue. Jinarajadasa there explains (p. 146):

Owing to the many difficulties constantly encountered in getting this Manuscript of Volume I of *The Secret Doctrine* ready for printing, its further publication will be suspended during my absence from Adyar. The amanuensis who copied from H.P.B.'s manuscript is chaotic in the use of capitals, dashes and quotation marks, though I suspect the real offender in the matter was H.P.B. herself. H.P.B. knew the Greek and Hebrew alphabets, but evidently not the amanuensis, who copied blindly—*hinc illae lachrymae*, for me. I have never come across such an irritating manuscript as this to get ready for the printer. We are still in the introductory part; naturally the real interest will begin when we come to the Stanzas of Dzyan.

Publication of the Würzburg manuscript did not resume. However, a transcription of the Stanzas of Dzyan found in it was published in the 1938 (and later) six-volume Adyar edition of *The Secret Doctrine* (vol. 1, pp. 101-107). Josephine Ransom was in charge of the preparation of this edition, and we probably have her to thank for this important inclusion. The Würzburg Stanzas were then published side by side with the 1888 Stanzas in George S. Arundale's 1939 book, *The Lotus Fire* (pp. 23-40). They were also included by Boris de Zirkoff in the 1978 edition of *The Secret Doctrine* (vol. 3, 1979, General Index and Bibliography, "Appendix III," pp. 514-520). Here we make available for the first time Blavatsky's unrevised commentaries on the Stanzas of Dzyan from the Würzburg manuscript.

As was observed by Jinarajadasa, the Würzburg manuscript is chaotic in the use of capitals, dashes, and quotation marks. So, for example, very often opening quotation marks are not followed by closing quotation marks, and vice versa. In these cases we have tried to find the quotation as later published by Blavatsky and have restored the relevant quotation marks. We have placed all of these in square brackets, since they were not always certain. Because square brackets have been used by us for our insertions, we have changed the few square brackets that were in the Würzburg manuscript to rounded parentheses. In this way our additions can always be distinguished, because only our additions are in square brackets.

Besides the problems in the Würzburg manuscript such as these of punctuation, Jinarajadasa also alluded to difficulties with the Greek and Hebrew alphabets. Words written in Greek and Hebrew letters occur in the manuscript. The amanuenses, not knowing these scripts, tried to copy these letters as well as they could. As a result of this, the identification of these terms is often uncertain. When the Theosophical Publishing House was still planning to publish the Würzburg manuscript as a book, this and the other afore-mentioned problems were brought out in explaining the reason for a delay in doing so. Jinarajadasa writes in "On the Watch-tower" for July 1931 in *The Theosophist* (vol. 52, part 2, p. 429-430):

> In connection with this centenary year, an announcement was made a few months ago that the T.P.H. at Adyar would publish for the first time the original draft of Vol. I of *The Secret Doctrine*, as completed by H.P.B. in 1885 and sent to Swami T. Subba Row for his endorsement. The aim of the T.P.H. was to issue this volume so as to be on sale before August 12th. This plan has undergone great modification, owing to the very great difficulty in getting the manuscript ready for the press, and correcting it page by page to make it as near the original as possible. Among the difficulties that the editor of the work finds is the utter absence of method in the manuscript in the use of quotation marks, so that sometimes a quotation is begun and not ended, or is ended without marking where it begins. In addition, Frau Gebhard, who copied the manuscript, evidently from sheets in H.P.B.'s handwriting, puts hyphens constantly, and the staff at Adyar have the greatest difficulty in deciphering whether these are meant for commas or dashes. Now and then a word in Greek appears, transcribed by an amanuensis who did not know Greek letters, and much consultation of Greek dictionaries is necessary to restore the original word.

Jinarajadasa in his student years in England had studied Greek for the "Oriental Languages Tripos" at the University of Cambridge (see his: "Trilingual Scholarship," in *Dr. C. Kunhan Raja Presentation Volume*, Madras, 1946, pp. 131-133), and it is apparently he who did the consulting of Greek dictionaries to restore the original words. For the portions of the Würzburg manuscript printed in *The Theosophist* we have much relied on his restorations. Like him, we have retained these words in the Greek script. For the portions found in *The Secret Doctrine* of 1888 we have relied primarily on the 1978 edition prepared by Boris de Zirkoff. For the portions found in the third volume of *The Secret Doctrine*, first published in 1897, and again published in H. P. Blavatsky's *Collected Writings* edited by Boris de Zirkoff, we have relied on the latter. We have also retained the Hebrew words in Hebrew script. For these words we have relied on the above-mentioned editions when possible. In the installments in *The Theosophist* Jinarajadasa did not attempt to reproduce these words in most cases, but merely gave a footnote saying that a word (or words) in Hebrew script appears here in the Würzburg manuscript. There are also a couple of Sanskrit words in devanāgarī script in the Würzburg manuscript. Again, these have obviously been copied there by an amanuensis who did not know this script. We have given these transliterated into roman script. I am responsible for deciphering and restoring these Sanskrit words.

There are many Sanskrit words in roman script used by Blavatsky in the Würzburg manuscript, and some of these have circumflex accents. We have left these as they are found for the most part, despite the fact that they are often erroneous. On a few occasions, when it seemed likely that these were merely a scribal error of the copyist (because they were correct nearby in the manuscript), we have corrected them.

We tried to retain the spellings, punctuation, capitalization, etc., of the manuscript. We of course had to add missing periods at the end of sentences. The one change we made was to put *Isis* in italics when it obviously referred to the book, *Isis Unveiled*.

Returning now to the issue of the material that appeared in volume 3 of *The Secret Doctrine*, this material is found in the first part of the Würzburg manuscript. It was clearly intended by Blavatsky to be the first part of *The Secret Doctrine*. This is also how Blavatsky's original handwritten manuscript was arranged when received by Bertram and Archibald Keightley in 1887 for editing. After reviewing it, they suggested that it be rearranged. It was they who suggested that the material found in the first part of Blavatsky's manuscript, originally intended as introductory, be moved and made into a third volume. Bertram Keightley writes:

> Further, instead of making the first volume to consist, as she had intended, of the history of some great Occultists, we advised her to follow the natural order of exposition, and begin with the Evolution of Cosmos, to pass from that to the Evolution of Man, then to deal with the historical part in a third volume treating of the lives of some great Occultists; ..."
> (In *Reminiscences of H. P. Blavatsky and "The Secret Doctrine,"* by Countess Constance Wachtmeister, London, 1893, p. 91.)

Blavatsky accepted their suggestion, and *The Secret Doctrine* was published as thus arranged. The first volume is on the evolution of the cosmos, and the second volume is on the evolution of man. The material for the third volume was held over, and not published until 1897, nine years after the first two volumes were published in 1888 (and which happened to be six years after Blavatsky's death in 1891). There arose controversy about it starting in 1922. Since then, many Theosophists have thought that this material was not part of *The Secret Doctrine*. Now, with the publication of the Würzburg manuscript, it will be easier to see that this material was indeed part of the original *Secret Doctrine*, the first or introductory part.

The relevant evidence on this issue had been gathered by Daniel H. Caldwell and reexamined in his article, "The Myth of the 'Missing' Third Volume of *The Secret Doctrine*" (*The American Theosophist*, Late Spring/Early Summer 1995, pp. 18-25; a 2004 revised edition was published on his website, blavatskyarchives.com). Daniel found that the key to the whole question, the Rosetta Stone, was the statement made by Bertram Keightley in 1890 and again in 1893 (quoted above), that the first volume became the third volume. After the controversy about the authenticity of the third volume arose in 1922, Bertram, upon being asked, confirmed its authenticity:

As regards the matter intended by H.P.B. for future volumes—besides the two first published under her own supervision—*all* this material has been published in the *third* volume which contains absolutely *all* that H.P.B. has left in manuscript.
(*O. E. Library Critic*, vol. 12, no. 24, July 4, 1923, unpaginated.)

Since Daniel had already done all this research, and since his article was not as widely known as might be expected, it seemed advisable to try to obtain permission from him to include it in this book. He kindly gave his permission for this, and added to it a newly prepared comprehensive chronology of the writing of *The Secret Doctrine*. Both are given here as appendices, the article being the revised and enlarged 2004 version. I thank him for these valuable additions to this book.

Preparing the Würzburg manuscript for publication was no small task. It required considerable labor and considerable expense. I was only one of four individuals involved in this task, the other three preferring to remain anonymous. It was they who did most of the work and bore all of the expense. I offer my sincere thanks to them.

The Secret Doctrine Würzburg Manuscript

[VOLUME I
History of Some Great Occultists]

The Secret Doctrine Würzburg Manuscript

TO THE READERS
"Strike but listen"
Epictetus

Error runs down on an inclined plane, Truth has to climb laboriously its way up hill. This is a reflection suggested by daily life experience. The old truism of guarding against such error would be to keep one's mind entirely free from all prejudice; and never to form a decisive opinion upon any subject under disputation before a thorough examination of it and from all its aspects.

This is said with regard to the largely prevailing mistake that by Esoteric *Buddhism* — the tenets of the religious system preached by Gautama Buddha are meant. Nothing more erroneous than that could be ever imagined, but the error has now become so universal that many persons — even among the Fellows of the Theosophical Society — have fallen victims to it. This has to be laid directly at the door of those who, having been the first to bring the subject under public notice have neglected to point out the difference between Buddhism — the religious system of ethics preached by Gautama and named after his title of Buddha, and Buddhi,[1] the Wisdom or the faculty of cognising, from the Sanskrit root "Budh" *to know*. The real culprits are we, the theosophists of India ourselves. To avoid the deplorable error was easy: the spelling of the word had only to be altered, and by common consent both pronounced and written — either Bud*h*ism or *Bodhism* instead of "Bud*d*hism."

The above remarks are more than necessary at the beginning of such a work as this one. "Wisdom-religion" is the inheritance of all the nations — the world over. ADI BUDDHA the One (or First) primeval *Wisdom*, is a Sanskrit term an appelation given by the earliest Aryans to Parabrahman, — the word "Brahmâ" not being found in the Vedas and Brahmanas as rightly told in John Dowson's "Classical Dictionary" (p. 57) — the absolute and secondless (Adwaita) Wisdom. Æons of untold

---

1. Moreover the planet Mercury is also called *Budha* (one *d*) and it is the name — meaning "wise, intelligent" of the son of Brihaspati's wife; Budha who married Ilâ, the daughter of Manu Vaivasvata, the progenitor of our race.

duration had, perhaps, elapsed, before the epithet of Buddha was so humanised, so to say, as to allow the term being applied to some mortals, and finally pronounced in connection with one whose unparalleled virtues caused him to receive the name of "Buddha of Wisdom unmoved." *Bodhi* means the acquirement of *divine* knowledge, Buddha — one who has acquired "bodhi"; and "Buddhi" is the faculty of cognising the channel through which knowledge reaches the *Ego*. It is also that plane of existence in which spiritual individuality is evolved and from which *personality* is eliminated. When "Buddhi" absorbs our EGO-tism and all its vikaras,[2] the pratyagâtma[3] or "Avalokitesvara" becomes manifested and Mukti[4] is reached. It was all this (and still is) before "Bodhi"[5] became simply "intelligence," the "intellect" and even "the holy fig tree" as defined by Dr. Eitel in his ["]hand book for the students of Chinese Buddhism."

Unwise are those and ungenerous — as the matter stands, who, in their blind and, in our age, untimely hatred of Buddhism — however right they may be from a personal standpoint to view it as a *heresy* — go against its esoteric teachings which are those also of the Brahmins, simply because the name reminds them of the (to the Monotheist) noxious doctrines.

---

2. Vikara is transformation or change.

3. Pratyagâtma is a compound word meaning "separation" and soul or "Spirit" when Maya and every wordly conception eliminated from the *inner* nature of man his spirit becomes one with the Ocean Spirit or Parabrahman.

4. Mukti — freedom, the same as *Nirvana*; freedom from the trammels of Maya.

5. Not "Bodhi" but the Bo-tree (aswattha); it is also the name of a particular state of *Samadhi* (bodhi) the trance in which the subject reaches the culmination of spiritual knowledge. The *Aswattha*-tree character of the Universe is realised. The small seed sends forth the big tree, which sends down from its branches the peculiar roots which reenter the earth and support the tree of knowledge (see Bhagavad Gita).

Unwise — is the correct term to use in their case. For alone the Esoteric philosophy is calculated to withstand, in this age of crass and illogical materialism its repeated attacks on all and every thing man holds most dear and sacred to him, in his inner spiritual life.

The true philosopher, the student of the Esoteric Wisdom, entirely loses sight of personalities, dogmatic beliefs, and special religions. As there cannot be two absolute Infinitudes, so there cannot be two true religions. Esoteric philosophy reconciles them all, strips every one of its outward, human garments, and shows the root of one identical with those of every other great religion. It proves the necessity of an Absolute divine Principle in nature. It denies Deity no more than it does the sun. Esoteric philosophy has never rejected God in nature, not even Deity, as the absolute and abstract *Ens*. It only refuses to accept any of the Gods of the so-called monotheistic religions — Gods created by man in his own image and likeness, a blasphemous and sorry caricature of the ever UNKNOWABLE. It is not, because the remnants of the once Universal Science and its occult literature are now claimed to be in the hands of the trans Himalayan Initiates of Tibet, that Esoteric *Buddhi* must necessarily be identified with Buddhism. The records we mean to place before the reader embrace the esoteric tenets of the whole world since the beginning of our Humanity, and Buddhistic occultism occupies in it only its legitimate place — and no more. Therefore even the alleged atheistical and materialistic Buddhism could be easily made to face the unmerited charge, were the task before us to give the public its esoteric doctrines alone, *which it is not*. Indeed the secret portions of the *Dan* or Dhyan of Gautama's metaphysics grand as they appear to one unacquainted with the tenets of the Wisdom religion of antiquity — are but a very small portion of the whole. The Hindu Reformer limited his teachings to the purely spiritual aspect of Wisdom-Religion, to the Soul Ethics and MAN alone, leaving "things unseen" and incorporeal Beings outside of our terrestrial sphere entirely untouched. Time and human imagination made short work of the purity and the philosophy of even that small portion, once that it was transferred from the region of the purely esoteric circle of his

Arhats to a soil less prepared for metaphysical conceptions than India. How its pristine purity was dealt with, may be found in studying some of the so called esoteric Buddhist schools of antiquity in their modern garb, in China, Japan and other Buddhist countries; also even among the lay laity and most of the uninitiated lamas of Tibet and Mongolia.

Thus the reader is asked to bear in mind the important difference between *Buddhism* and Bodhism and also — since we shall have to refer to it in the course of this work — that the SECRET doctrine preached by Gautama Buddha differs vastly from his exoteric or public teaching. The Buddha was a born Aryan, a Hindu, a disciple of the initiated Dwijas — the twice born. Unable to teach publicly *all* that had been imparted to him, he taught a philosophy built upon the ground work of the true esoteric *knowledge*, he only gave the world its outward material body and kept its SOUL for his Elect.

Unlike all other books this work could not stand alone on the authority of its own statements, and had to find allies, whether willing or unwilling. It has secured them in a long series of the well known names of a number of respected, often illustrious men of science. Though most of them have worked on entirely different lines and have made their researches with quite another object in view — they have, nevertheless, been made to help us in the propagation of more than one truth throughout the whole work.

Natural sciences, archæology, theology, philosophy — all have been forced to give their evidence in support of the teaching herein propounded. *Scripta manent* . . . their published admissions can be made away with — even by the opponent; they have been made good use of. Had we acted otherwise, the *Secret Doctrine* from the first chapter to the last, would have amounted to uncorroborated personal affirmations. Scholars and most of the latest discoveries in various departments of science being brought to testify to what might have otherwise appeared to the average reader as the most preposterous hypothesis based upon unverified assertions, the task proposed will now be made easier. Occult teachings will be examined in the light of both sciences — the physical as much as the spiritual and psychical. Although the reader is offered no more than the bare outlines of the Mysteries and hardly a few of the innumerable occult subjects taught in Esoteric philosophy, it would yet be the height of conceit and pride to come out in such a dangerous battle against prejudice single-handed. Nor could more be given in a work of such dimension as now proposed.

As already said, the *Secret Doctrine* is quite a new version of *Isis Unveiled* much of which could hardly be understood by theosophists in those days. It is in [an] *indispensable* corollary to the first work.

Concerned chiefly with our Humanity — that is to say from the commencement of the Fifth Root-race of the fourth Round up to our days — no more than a hurried glance can be thrown at present at the three antediluvian races that preceded the Atlantean family, or the *Fourth* Race. Nor can the vast catalogue of the Sciences taught by the Antediluvians — be treated in any other than a cursory way, especially when concerned with such tremendous problems as Cosmic and Planetary Evolutions, the age of our globe and its Humanities.

But even the little that can be given is better than complete silence upon those vital truths. The present world, in its mad career toward the unknown which it is too ready to confound with the unknowable, whenever the problem eludes the grasp of the physicist — is rapidly progressing on the earthly, material plane, and losing proportionately in the plane of spirituality. It has now become a vast λοφοςατης — the Valley of Death of the ancient Greek philosophers a *necropolis* wherein lie buried the highest, the most holy aspirations of our Spirit-Soul. That soul becomes with every new generation more paralyzed, and atrophy is rapidly setting in. The "amiable infidels and accomplished profligates" of society spoken of by Gresley, care little for the revival of the *dead* sciences of the past, little thinking that they have themselves become the "whitened sepulchres" of their Scriptures. These can hardly be galvanized *from within*. But there is a fair minority of earnest students who are entitled to learn the few truths that may now be given to them.

Before giving out the occult and hitherto concealed teachings an outline must be traced before the reader of the mechanical arrangement of the whole Doctrine, an extensive work as one can see. Much thought and labour have been bestowed upon the arrangement, such as would satisfy every reader — not only the student more or less familiar with the Occult Doctrine. If the work could have been published as a whole in so many volumes, the task might have been made easier. For reasons that would not interest the outside world, this could not be done and the writer had to conform to the original plan. The Secret Doctrine would come out in four distinct Parts — the *Archaic*, Ancient, *Medieval* and Modern Periods. Each part had to cover a period of 6 months to be issued in 2 chapters monthly, thus forming 48 and with additions 49 chapters in their two years duration, and the 4 glossaries (one to each Part) making at the end an additional, or 50th chapter. Should the writer find at the end of that period that the subjects with which she has to deal are not yet exhausted, that this work meets with the approval of her readers and that health and life are spared to her the Secret Doctrine may probably extend its present limits. Moreover there was the difficult problem at first proposed to so arrange the subject matter that the contents of no one part should infringe upon any of the three others, the Archaic period being forbidden to treat of that which belonged — say — to the middle Ages and the post and pre Christian centuries or the Ancient Period having to be shut out from the purely archaic age. How was this to be done? It was easy to fill Part I (Archaic Period) with a thesis which is but the verbal translation from the Catechisms and Elementary works of the Secret Doctrine on Cosmic and Planetary Evolution, the Birth of the Primeval Beings, "The Builders" the subsequent task the gradual formation of our Earth and its fellow-spheres of the chain, the progressive work throughout Aeons and Cycles of those "Heavenly Races" busy with the formation and the growth of our planet giving the impulse to the Kingdoms of the Earth, and finally the Birth of present Man, his gradual and irresistible Fall into Matter, then the four Races that preceded our actual fifth Race their history and development, the submerging of Atlantis — the real Cataclysm upon which were subsequently built all the legends of the Deluge etc. etc. etc. The writer has all this placed before her, to hear, to see and — to copy. What would be the results? And the reader's opinion there on — save that of a few students and chelas? A fairy tale, woven out of the abstruse problems, poised in and based on the air and soap-bubbles bursting at the slightest touch of serious reflection, with no foundation as would be alleged to stand upon — even the ancient *superstitions* and *credulous* classics having no word of reference to it, and the symbols themselves failing to yield a hint at the existence of such a system?[6] Such would be the criticism of the most benevolent among the critics, even of those desirous of learning something new and quite open to belief. Evidently the Archaic Period could not stand alone. Moreover before Part II could be read to its end the teachings of the Secret System, so new and unfamiliar to the European ear would have been half, if not entirely forgotten and the reader would have to turn back at

---

6. An instance may now be given as an illustration of what is said taken from the History of Freemasonry whether rightly or wrongly. J. M. Ragon, an illustrious and learned Belgian Mason — reproaches the English masons of having *materialized* and dishonoured Masonry once based upon the Ancient Mysteries, by adopting them owing to a mistaken notion of the origin of the craft, the name of *Free masonry* and Free Masons. The mistake is due, he says, to those who connect Masonry *with the building of Solomon's* Temple, deriving its origin from it. He derides the idea and says: . . . "The Francmaçon (which is not *maçon libre* or free masonry knew well when adopting the title, that it was no question of *building a wall* but that of *being initiated into Mysteries veiled under the name of Francmaçonnerie* (Free masonry); that his work was only to be the continuation or the renovation of the ancient mysteries and that he was to become a *Mason* in the manner of *Apollo* or *Amphion*: do not we know, that the ancient *initiated* poets when speaking *of the foundation of a city* meant thereby *the establishment of a doctrine*? Thus *Neptune* is a god of reasoning, and *Apollo*, the god of the *hidden* things, presented themselves as masons before Laomedan, Priam's father, to help him to build the city of Troy, that is to say to establish Trojan religion? . . . ." (*Maçonnerie Orthodoxe* p. 44.) Such *veiled* sentences with double meaning abound in the ancient classics and writers: Therefore, had an attempt been made to show that — say — Laomedan was the founder of a branch of archaic mysteries, in which the earth-bound, material soul (the 4th principle) was personified in Menelaus' faithless wife, the fair Helen — we might be told that no classic speaks of it, and that Homer shows Laomedan building *a city* not an *esoteric worship* MYSTERIES had not a Ragon, or some one else come to corroborate what was asserted.

every page of the second Part in order to be enabled to perceive and realize the ground upon which such or another symbol of later and esoteric systems was built, the root from which such or another shoot of some special religion has sprung from. This would never do. Thus it was thought best to preface each chapter with a stanza or two translated from the *Book of Dzyan* — barring such points that cannot be yet given out in this century. This book (see Chap — Sect) is the extensive compendium of the History of our present grand Period (Maha Kalpa) premissing [premising] with a superficial and short account of the re[-]evolution of Kosmos and our own planetary System and starting to give more definite outlines from the appearance of man on Earth to our own age. It ends in 1897 agreeably with our chronology. Such an arrangement of chapters beginning each in an uninterrupted sequel with a first quotation from the Book of Dzyan, the subjects permitted to be discussed being divided into 49 parts it becomes easy to explain that which most naturally would have appeared hazy when read independently; thus also the verses or stanzas given (as in the original) can be glossed and interpreted by, and in the light of many a remark made by ancient writers never correctly understood by the modern, and by pointing out to the equally misconceived symbols bearing on each question or subject as it presents itself along one after the other.

Such were the difficulties now overcome, as it is hoped in dealing with mysteries of such tremendous importance.

The Past could not be read with[out?] rending asunder the veil behind which it lies concealed, drawn down by too cautious hands to screen it from the profane and the inappreciative: therefore the necessity of often teaching upon subjects sacred to some readers and the dealing with which may as often give them pain. This being unavoidable is to be sincerely regretted but truth is the first and ought to be the *only* criterion of every religion. No human born dogma, no institution, however sanctified by custom and antiquity can compare in sacredness with the dogma of Nature. The key of wisdom that unlocks the massive gates leading to the arcana of the innermost sanctuaries can be found hidden in her bosom only, and that bosom is — in the countries pointed to by the great Seer of the past century Emanuel Swedenborg. There lies the heart of nature that bosom whence issued primeval Humanity and which is the cradle of man.

The writer is too well acquainted with human nature and the state of modern Society to hope for more than a few dozen of men who among the thousands will abstain from branding this work *a priori* as a fiction — perhaps an elaborately made up mystification. It will be called a tissue of unverified and unverifiable assertions at best superstitious legends and groundless traditions. We live in an age when everything which is not bluntly denied is at least strongly doubted; and History herself is dealt with by the so called Christians as brutally as legendary lore. If Niebuhr could with one stroke of his pen cross out from his work (though he could hardly hope to blot them out from his history) — the first five centuries from Roman empire and Lewis chose to begin with Pyrrhus and Schlosser — killing Cadmus, Donaus and Cecropes commence *his* history with Minos, let us hope that all such *historians* may one day perceive their error and regret it as sincerely as Augustin Thierry did. The latter has at any rate made *amende hons rable* if one may believe his biographers. He deplored the erroneous principle that made them all (the *would be* historiographers) lose their way and each presuming to correct tradition that *vox popoli* [*populi*] which nine times out of ten *is vox dei* — by their personal views and preconceived opinions; and he finally admitted that in legend alone rests real History; for legend his biographer makes him add is *living* tradition and three times out of four it is truer than what we call History.[7]

More dangerous even than the termites in one of Michelet's tales, the modern recorder[s] of Universal History are preparing for her the fate of most of the buildings in India. History will tumble down and break into atoms in the lap of the XXth century — devoured to its foundations by her annalists — who are the white ants of our Century the XIXth.

The very fact, that a work with pretentions to philosophy and an exposition of the most abstruse problems has to be commenced by tracing the evolution of mankind from what is

---

7. *Revue des deux mondes*, Littré, 1865, pp. 157-58.

regarded as supernatural beings — *Spirits*, will arouse the most malevolent criticism. Believers in and the defenders of the Secret Doctrine, will have to bear the accusation of madness and — worse as philosophically as the writer does. Whenever a theosophist is taxed with insanity he ought to reply by quoting from Montesquieu's *Lettres Persanes*: "By opening so freely their lunatic asylums to their supposed madmen, men only seek to make one believe that they are not themselves mad."

Nevertheless before proceeding to give out the translated stanzas from the Book of *Dzyan*, on Cosmic Evolution and the work of *Creative* Spirits a brief recapitulation must be made in Chapter I of the ideas upon Occult philosophy and Magic prevalent during the few centuries that preceded and followed our era. This was the last turning point in History, the period of the supreme struggle that ended by the throlling [throttling] of Paganism in the Western world. From that time the vista into the far distant Past, beyond the "Deluge" and gardens of Eden began to be forcibly and relentlessly closed by every fair and unfair means against the indiscreet gaze of posterity. Every issue was blocked up, every record that hands could be laid upon destroyed. Yet there remains enough among such mutilated records to warrant us in saying that there is there in every evidence possible proofs of the actual existence of a Parent Doctrine. Fragments have survived geological and political cataclysms to tell the story; and that very survival showing evidence that the now *Secret* Wisdom was once the one fountain head, the ever perennial source at which were fed, all its streamlets, the later religions of all nations — from the first down to the last. This period, beginning with Buddha and Pythagoras at the one end, and the New Platonics and Gnostics at the other is the only focus left in history wherein converge for the last time the bright rays of light unobscured by the hand of bigotry and fanaticism from the aeons of time gone by.

However superficially the Public has also to be made acquainted with the efforts of other World Adepts, and Initiates of those ages to benefit Humanity with their knowledge and thus preserve the mother-philosophy; as also now the modern Teachers made themselves acquainted with the lore of the Archaic Age.

The Initiate of 1885 would remain indeed incomprehensible and for ever an impossible myth were not like Initiates shown in every other age in history. This may be done only by naming chapter and verse where the mention of these great characters may be found who were preceded and followed by a long and interminable line of other great Antediluvian and Postdiluvian Masters in the arts. Thus only can be shown a semi traditional and semi-historical authority that the Occult knowledge and the powers it confers are not altogether fictions, but that they are as old as the world itself.

The *Past* however, shall help to realise the PRESENT and the latter to better appreciate the PAST. The errors of the day must be explained and swept away. It is more than probable since in the present case it amounts to certitude — that once more the testimony of long ages and history shall fail to impress any one but the very intuitional — which is equal to saying the very few. In such a case the *true* and the *faithful* may console themselves with presenting the skeptical modern Sadducee with the mathematical proof of his obdurate obstinacy and dullness. There still exists somewhere in the archives of the French Academy the famous law of probabilities. It was worked out by an algebraical process for the benefit of skeptics by certain mathematicians and runs thus. If two persons give their evidence to a fact and thus impart to it, each of them $5/6$ of certitude, that fact will have then $35/36$ of certitude; *i.e.* its probability will have become to its improbability in proportion of 35 to 1. If three evidences are joined together, the certitude will have become $15/16$. The agreement of ten persons giving each ½ of certitude will produce $1023/1024$ etc. etc. The occultist may remain satisfied — and care for no more.

NOTE. It must not be imagined from the subtitle of the advertisements "a new version of Isis Unveiled" that the Secret Doctrine is simply a rearrangement of old matter. It is an entirely new work with only occasional quotations and extracts from *Isis* to serve a double purpose. Because it has been often said (a) that the theosophical teachings clashed with the statements in the earlier work after the publication of Mr. Sinnett's Esoteric Buddhism and (b) to show that not only was the writer of the present familiar then with all the topics now given in the Secret Doctrine but that there is not a single contradiction if properly understood. When *Isis* was written only fragmentary portions could be given but now the reader will be instructed how to fit in the disjointed pieces so as to perfect the whole.

Note. In view of the multiplicity of subjects every chapter will be divided into sections (§) and whenever required into numbered sub-sections.

Chapter I
On Eastern and Western Occult Literature

Introducing the Reader and leading him to Chapter II. The evidence of Profane and Sacred History, to an Antediluvian Wisdom-Religion; Divine and Human,[8] or White and Black Magic and Adepts of the same. Old Fragments and manuscripts known and unknown.

---

8. "Human" means in esoteric parlance "evil" magic; being materiality.

The Secret Doctrine Würzburg Manuscript

§ I

Archaic Fragments and their Authors — Hermetic Books — Orphic Hymns — The Argonauts and their probable date — The Cainites and the Noachians — The two Teachers — Chemenesua-Zoroaster.

1 — Explanation of the 1ˢᵗ page of "Isis Unveiled" — The Teachers and The Doctrine of Self — The "Souls" of the Stars.

Volume I of *Isis* begins with a reference to an old Book — ["]so very old that our modern antiquarians might ponder over its pages an indefinite time, and still not quite agree as to the nature of the fabric upon which it is written. It is the only original copy now in existence. The most ancient Hebrew document on occult learning — the Siphra Dzeniouta — was compiled from it, and that at a time when the former was already considered in the light of a literary relic. One of its illustrations represents the Divine Essence emanatic [emanating] from Adam[9] like a luminous arc proceeding to form a circle; and then, having attained the highest point of its circumference, the ineffable Glory bends back again and returns to earth, bringing a higher type of humanity in its vortex. As it approaches nearer and nearer to our planet, the Emanation becomes more and more shadowy until upon touching the ground it is as black as night." Further on it is stated that — "A conviction founded upon *seventy* thousand years of experience as they allege, has been entertained by hermetic philosophers of all periods that matter has in time become, through sin, more gross and dense than it was at man's first formation; that at the beginning the human body was of a half-ethereal nature; and that, before the fall, mankind communed freely with the now unseen universes. But since that time matter has become the formidable barrier

---

9. The name is used in the sense of the Greek word ANTHROPOS.

between us and the world of spirits. The oldest esoteric traditions also teach that, before the mystic Adam, many races of human beings lived and died out, each giving place in its turn to another."

Not one word would be changed in the above statements. Only the few lines may grow into Chapters — the logical and scientific necessity for accepting these hermetic views having to be shown.

The short allusion to "the seventy thousand years of experience" has also to be vindicated and shown correct and the claims of the Kabalists and the Occultists more definitely stated. The Eastern Adepts claim most decidedly their science to be older than that; for they place its origin with the First Race of men "whose thoughts were objectively expressed in colour" as Speech descended later on, on Earth. The query in *Isis*: "Were these precedent types more perfect? Did any of them belong to the *winged* race of men mentioned by Plato in *Phaedrus*" — having remained unanswered, a reply has to be given now. A ten year old experience, however, having shown that Science is as unwilling as ever to solve problems of this nature, nor is the general public quite ready to follow the landmarks left by the old Occultists and accepted by those of our modern days — the present work is intended for neither of the two. It is offered to the students of Occultism alone. It is the special task of the writer to prove what was stated in *Isis* as true. For instance, the following sentence has to be explained.

"As the cycle proceeded, man's eyes were more and more opened, until he came to know 'good and evil' as well as the Elohim themselves. Having reached its summit, the cycle began to go downward. When the arc attained a certain point which brought it parallel with the fixed line of our terrestrial plane, the man was furnished by nature with 'coats of *skin*,' and the Lord God 'clothed them.'["]

The cycle having to follow its downward course for some yet, and man — though his eyes are still opening every day more and more owing to his alleged knowledge of "good and evil" — evidently preferring the latter, it has to be explained how it is, that ["]redemption of sin" and salvation notwithstanding, he has so little progressed in "good" and is actually becoming more sinful with every century since the year 33 A.D. — indeed, *worse than he ever was when a pagan*. This can be made plain only by *showing who* the "Lord *the Gods*" was (or were) who "clothed" men in Eden.

The problems will be solved, on the esoteric plane only now; for *Isis* was a first and cautious attempt to acquaint the public with Occultism. Having proved as unpalatable to many of those interested in psychic phenomena as to the skeptical, the present work will have in view the theosophists alone and those who have welcomed the first one.

Although the few lines cited from *Isis* have grown since into a volume known as "Esoteric Buddhism,"[10] the latter work might yet be very easily amplified into 24 such volumes and still the hundredth part of the subject not be exhausted.

The very "old Book" is the original work from which the many volumes of Kiu-te were compiled. Not only this, and the *Sepher Dzeniouta*, but even the *Sepher Jezirah*[11] attributed by the Hebrew Kablists to their Patriarch Abraham, and the book of *Shu-King*, China's primitive Bible, the sacred volumes of the Egyptian Thoth-Hermes, the Chaldean Book of "Numbers" and the *Pentateuch* itself — are all due to that small Parent Volume. Tradition tells us that it was taken down in Senzar, the secret sacerdotal tongue from the words of the Divine Being who dictated it to the Sons of Light in Central Asia at the very beginning of the 5th (our) Race. For there was a time when its language — the *Senzar* — was known to the Initiates of every nation, and that the forefathers of the Toltec understood it as easily as the inhabitants of the lost Atlantis who inherited it in

---

10. By A. P. Sinnett. *Fifth* Edition with annotations. Chapman & Hall, London.

11. Rabbi Jehoshua ben Chananea who died about A.D. 72, openly declared that he had performed "miracles" by means of the *Book of Sepher Jezirah*, and challenged every skeptic. Franck, quoting from the Babylonian *Talmud*, names two other thaumaturgists, Rabbis Chanina and Oshai (see "Jerusalem Talmud Synhedrin," c. 7, etc.; and "Franck," pp. 55, 56.) Many of the Medieval Occultists claimed the same and even our modern Kabalist — Eliphas Levi proclaims in print the same thing.

their turn from the sages of the 3rd Races the *Manooshis* [Manushis] who learnt it by heart from the *Devas* of the 1st and 2nd Races. The "illustration" spoken of, relates to the evolution of these Races in our "Vaivasvata Manvantara" composed of the Yugas of the seven periods of Humanity; four of which are now passed, and nearly the middle point of the 5th is reached. The illustration is symbolical. When it is said that as it approaches nearer to our planet the emanation becomes more shadowy, until upon touching the ground it becomes as black as night! Two facts are meant — the *falling of spirit into matter*, or that which always mars its purity, and the state of our present Humanity especially in *Kali-Yug* or the "Iron Age" we are in. The "old Book" having described Cosmic Evolution, and explained the origin of everything on earth including man, and given the true history of the Races — from the 1st down to the 5th Race goes no further. It stops short at the beginning of Kali-Yuga, just 4986 years ago at the death of Krishna — the bright *Sun-god* and the once living hero and reformer.

But there exists another book. None of its possessors regard it as very ancient as it was born with, and is only as old as the Black Age, namely about 5,000 years ago. In about 13 to 14 years hence, the first cycle of the first five millenniums that began with the great Cycle of the *Kali-Yuga* will end. And then the last prophecy contained in that Book, Volume I, of the prophetic Record for the Black Age will be accomplished. We have not long to wait and many of us will witness the dawn of the new Cycle, at the end of which not a few accounts will be settled and squared between the races.

Volume II of the Prophecies is nearly ready, having been in preparation since Gautama Buddha's time. But this work is really concerned only with the first one. It contains all and much more of that which is permitted to be known to the Humanities of our Fifth Root race, with the sole exception of its recorders — the INITIATES.

"What do they know — what *can* they know, those Initiates" — "more than any profane man of science knows," the reader is often asked [often asks]. "The imagery of the ancients, their mythology and theories are at best poetic fancies, imagination." Probably some of them are. But poetry — said

Campbell — is also "the eloquence of truth." It may sometimes be no doubt the natural language of excited feeling, and "a work of *imagination* wrought into form by art." But imagination [—] as Pythagoras justly expressed it — *is the memory of our preceding births.* And if "imagination" leads us, as it has led the Samian Sage, to discover and proclaim such great truths as he has — one of which (the heliocentric System) [—] then it may be not altogether empty of meaning. Furthermore it is complained — by those who do believe in both the teachers and their science — that the latter is withheld from the public. The reason for this secrecy was stated in *Isis Unveiled* and elsewhere.

Says *Isis*: ["]From the very day when the first mystic found the means of communication between this world and the worlds of the invisible host, between the sphere of matter and that of pure spirit, he concluded that to abandon this mysterious science to the profanation of the rabble was to lose it. An abuse of it might lead mankind to speedy destruction; it was like surrounding a group of children with explosive batteries, and furnishing them with matches. The first self-made adept initiated but a select few and kept silence with the multitudes. He recognized *his 'God'* and felt the great UNIT within himself. The 'Atman' the Self,[12] the mighty Lord and Protector, once that

---

12. This "self" which the Greek philosophers called Augoeides, the "Shining One," is impressively and beautifully described in Max Müller's "Veda." Showing the "Veda" to be the first book of the Aryan nations, the Professor adds that "we have in it a period of the intellectual life of man to which there is no parallel in any other part of the world. In the hymns of the 'Veda' we see man left to himself to solve the riddle of this world . . . . He invokes the gods around him, he praises, he worships them. But still with all these gods . . . beneath him, and above him, the early poet seems ill at rest with himself. There, too in his own breast, he has discovered a power that is never mute when he prays, never absent when he fears and trembles. It seems to inspire his prayers, and yet to listen to them; it seems to live in him, and yet to support him and all around him. The only name he can find for this mysterious power is 'Brahman;' for Brahman meant originally force, will, wish, and the propulsive power of creation. But this impersonal brahman too, as soon as it is named, grows into something strange and divine. It ends by being one of many gods, one of the great triad, worshipped to the present day. And still the thought within him

man knew him as the I 'am,' the 'Ego Sum' the 'Ahmi' showed is [its/his] full power to him who could recognize the 'still small voice.' From the days of the Primitive man described by the first Vedic poet, down to our modern age, there has not been a philosopher worthy of that name, who did not carry in the silent sanctuary of his heart the grand and mysterious truth. If initiated, he learnt it as a sacred science; if otherwise, then, like Socrates repeating to himself as well as to his fellow men, the noble injunction, 'Oh man, know thyself,' he succeeding in recognizing his God within himself. 'Ye are gods,' the king-psalmist tells us, and we find Jesus reminding the scribes that the expression, 'Ye are gods,' was addressed to other mortal men claiming for himself the same privilege without any blasphemy.[13] And as a faithful echo, Paul, while asserting that we are all 'the temple of the living God' cautiously adds, that after all these things are only for the 'wise,' and it is 'unlawful' to speak of them.["][14]

We must accept the reminder and simply add that throughout the mystic literature of the whole ancient world we detect the same idea of esoterism [esotericism] and of the *personal* God existing *within* nowhere *outside* of us. But that *personal* God is no vain breath or a fiction, but an immortal

---

has no real name; that power which is nothing but itself, which supports the gods, the heavens, and every living being, floats before his mind, conceived but not expressed. At last he calls it 'Atman' for Atman, originally breath or spirit, comes to mean Self and Self alone; *Self* whether divine or human; Self, whether creating or suffering; Self, whether one or all; but always Self, independent and free. 'Who has seen the first-born,' says the poet, [']when he who had no bones (form) bore him that had bones? Where was the life, the blood, the Self of the world? Who went to ask this from anyone who knew it?['] (RigVeda, 1, 164, 4.) This idea of a Divine Self once expressed, everything else must acknowledge its supremacy; Self is the Lord of all things. As all the spokes of a wheel are contained in the nave and circumference, all things are contained in this Self; *all Selves are contained in this Self*.["] (Ibid., p. 478; 'Khândogya Upanishad[']; viii, 3, 3, 4.)

13. John X, 34-35.

14. 2 Corinth. VI-16.

Entity — the INITIATOR of the Initiates now that the Heavenly or Celestial Initiators of primitive Humanity — the SISHTA of the preceding Cycles are no more among us. Like an undercurrent rapid and clear it runs without mixing its crystalline purity with the muddy and troubled waters of dogmatism, an enforced Anthropomorphic Deity and religious intolerance. We find the idea in the tortured and barbarous phraseology of the *Codex Nazareenes* [*Nazaraeus*], and the superb Neoplatonic language of the Fourth Gospel of the later religions; in the oldest *Veda* and in the *Avesta*, in the *Abhid[h]arma* and Kapila's *Sankhya*, in the *B[h]agavat-Gita* and in Pantanjali [Patanjali]. We cannot attain Adeptship and Nirvana, Bliss and the Kingdom of Heaven unless we link ourselves indissolubly with our *Rex Lux*, the Lord of Splendour and of Light, our immortal God *within* us. AHAM EVA PARAM BRAHMA. "I am myself a God" has ever been the one living truth in the heart and mind of the Adept,[15] and it is that, which helped him to become one. We must first recognize our immortality and then conquer it and "take the Kingdom of Heaven by violence" *offered* to our *material* selves — never reached by the latter. ["]The first man is of earth earthy; the *second* (inner) man from heaven. Behold, I shew you a mystery," says St. Paul in Corinthians (I, xv, 47).

It stands to reason, therefore, that in such a work as this one, the true meaning of expressions hitherto misinterpreted, such as "God, *the Gods*, the God of Gods" etc., should be given. They are met with in the symbolism of every great religion and nation. Moreover, truth has to be vindicated by showing also the distinction to be made — one that has always existed — between bodies and their souls or what we call the "informing principles" in nature. Saturn the "Father of the Gods" and Saturn, the planet with its *seven* moons and then rings, must be separated and yet shown *virtually* united — as man and his Spirit are two, yet only

---

15. Ye are "the temple of God" addressed by St. Paul to the Corinthians means precisely the same thing. Only the Vedantists who never refer to their *bodies* as being *themselves* formulate the idea still better, who then would identify himself with his house or lodging? And Paul adds: "Ye are God's *building* and the Spirit of God *dwelleth in you*." But fanciful interpretation will go a long way!

One. Thus with regard to the stars, as heavenly bodies, and the "host of the stars," *Sabaoth Elohim*;[16] or again, the stars of the Great Bear, the Riksha and the *Chitra* Sikhandina [Sikhandin] "the bright-crested," and the Rishis, the mortals and Sages who have appeared on earth during the *Satya-Yuga*. If all of these have been so closely united in the visions of the Seer of every age — the Bible Seers included — there must have been a reason for it. Nor need we go back so far into the periods of superstition and unscientific fancies, to find great men in our epoch sharing in them. It is well known that Kepler, the eminent astronomer, as many other great men who believed the heavenly bodies ruling favorably or adversely the fates of men and nations, fully credited besides this the idea that all heavenly bodies — even our own earth, are endowed *with living and thinking Souls.*

So far, the conquests achieved by astronomy in the domain of material infinitudes have only led the profane to the utter loss of any conception of spiritual infinitudes — in our present century at any rate. As remarked somewhere, by Baron du Potet, Spirit sees better than the eye.

Perchance the day is not far off when the spiritual telescope of the ancients may thus be shown superior for the increase of human knowledge — to its successor of wood, glass and brass.

With a view of preparing the reader to understand more clearly the teachings on Cosmic Evolution and the birth of man in Chapter II, we will show on the authority of numberless works, ancient, mediæval and modern, the actual existence of a WISDOM-RELIGION whose origin is lost in prehistoric periods. By introducing also to the Reader, for his reminder, some of the most celebrated proficients in the so-called "Magic art," whose existence and fame (the latter having crossed, in some cases, two millenniums) cannot be denied, though their *post-mortem* memory is still slandered, we shall pave the better

---

16. The meaning of Sabaoth or Tzabaoth from the Hebrew word Tzaba (army) shall be explained further on and the relation of the Hebrew Angelogogy [Angelology]— the Chaldaic and Magian rather — to the Dhyan-Chohans shown.

the way to what follows. If the independent and often unwilling testimony of modern historians and scholars is added to all this, the minds of the readers unacquainted, so far, with the archaic doctrine as propounded by the Teachers. We have to show that the numerous and often (to the profane) contradictory Cosmogonies of various nations are all based upon one — the *primitive* Revelation to mankind as taught in the oldest record in the world, now in possession and the safe keeping of the few surviving Initiates in Central Asia.

The Secret Doctrine Würzburg Manuscript

§§

**2. Hermetic and other Books of Antiquity. —
Perfect accord of beliefs and "superstitions" among
various nations. What science proclaims false —
discoveries and facts show true. —
The two *Masters* of Clemens Alexandrinus —**

Hardly in the beginning of the present century, the books called Hermetic, Alchemical and Astrological were in the sight of the profane public what they are yet now in the opinion of the average man of science: simply *a collection of tales, of fraudulent pretences and ridiculous claims.* They ["]never existed before the Christian era["] — it was said, ["]they were all written with the triple object of speculation, deceiving and pious fraud." The XVIIIth century had prepared Europe for the XIXth. In the former, everything that did not emanate from the Royal Academies was false, superstitious, foolish belief in a *false* Hermes, a *false* Orpheus, a *false* Zoroaster, in false Oracles, *false* Sibyls, and a thrice *false* Mesmer and his ridiculous fluids — were tabo[o]ed all along the line. In our own age, all that has its genesis outside the learned and dogmatic precincts of Oxford and the *Salpetriere* of Paris is denounced as ["]unscientific" and *ridiculous*. We think we see the sidereal phantom of the old philosopher and mystic of the Cambridge University, Henry More, moving in the astral light over the antiquated walls of the old town in which he wrote his letter to Glanvil. The "soul" seems restless and indignant as on that day, the 5th May 1678, when he complained so bitterly to the author of *Sadducismus Triumphatus,* of Scot, Adie and Webster. "Our new inspired Saints" . . . the "Soul" murmurs . . . ["]sworn advocates of the witches . . . who against all sense and reason . . . will have no Samuel, but a confederate knave . . . the inblown buffoons puffed up with . . . ignorance vanity and stupid infidelity."

Rest in peace, o restless soul. Lately things are somewhat changed; and since that for ever memorable day when the Academical Committee (Franklin included) investigated Mesmer's phenomena and proclaimed it a clever knavery, every hour brings in some fresh evidence in favour of Mesmerism and phenomena in general. But in the first decades of our century the men of science were blind as bats — as many are still even now — and Hermetic literature was denied, not withstanding the evidence of the most erudite men of all the ages. Father Kircher for one was not even noticed; and his assertions that all the fragments known under the titles of works by Mercury Trismegistus, Berosius, Pherecydes of Scyros, etc. were rolls escaped from the fire that devoured 100,000 volumes of the great Alexandrian Library were simply laughed at. Nevertheless the educated classes of Europe knew then as they do now, that the famous Alexandrian Library — the "marvel of the ages" had been founded and put in order at the desire of Ptolemy Philadelphus by Aristotle, and that most of its MSS. had been carefully copied from hieratic texts and the oldest parchments, Chaldean, Phœnician, Persian etc., which transliterations and copies amounted in their turn to another 100,000 as Josephus and Strabo assert. Moreover there was the additional evidence of Clement Alexandrinus, that ought to be credited to some extent, who testified[17] to the existence of 30,000 volumes of the Books

---

17. The forty-two Sacred Books of the Egyptians mentioned by Clement of Alexandria as having existed in his time, were but a portion of the Books of Hermes. Iamblichus, on the authority of the Egyptian priest Abammon, attributes 1200 of such books to Hermes, and Manetho 36,000. But the testimony of Iamblichus as a Neo-Platonist and theurgist is of course rejected by modern critics. Manetho who is held by Bunsen in the highest consideration as a "purely historical personage" . . . with whom "none of the later native historians can be compared . . . " (see "Egypte," 1, p. 97), suddenly becomes a Pseudo-Manetho, as soon as the ideas propounded by him clash with the scientific prejudices against magic and the occult knowledge claimed by the ancient priests. However none of the archæologists doubt for a moment the almost incredible antiquity of the Hermetic books. Champollion shows the greatest regard for their authenticity and great truthfulness, corroborated as it is by many of the oldest monuments. And Bunsen brings irrefutable proofs of their age. From his researches, for instance, we learn that there was a line of sixty-one kings before the days of Moses, who preceded the Mosaic period by a clearly-traceable civilization of several thousand years. Thus we are warranted in

of Thoth, placed in the library of the Tomb of Osymandius, on the entrance door of which was the inscription "The Cure for the Soul."

Since then — as all know — Champollion found on the most ancient monuments of Egypt the entire texts of that *Pimander* and that *Asclepias* declared by some to this day *apocryphal* and FRAUDULENT. After having devoted their whole lives to the study of the records of the old Egyptian wisdom, both Champollion-Figeac and Champollion Junior, publicly declared, notwithstanding many biased judgments hazarded by certain hasty and unwise critics, that the Books of Hermes "truly contain a mass of Egyptian traditions which are constantly corroborated by the most authentic records and monuments of Egypt of the hoariest antiquity"[18] and that they were ["]the faithful echo and expression of the most ancient verities." Since then also, some of the hymns by the *false* Orpheus and his *apocryphal* verses have been found repeated *word for word* in certain inscriptions of the fourth Dynasty — addressed to certain deities, in hieroglyphics.

Finally Creuzer has rightly pointed out the numerous passages borrowed from the Orphic hymns by Hesiod and Homer, who have hardly understood them correctly, as the great symbologist thinks; and no wonder, as the two Grecian Miltons have anthropomorphized many an abstraction, like the English poet did Satan — thousands of years later. To end, —

---

believing that the works of Hermes Trismegistus were extant many ages before the birth of the Jewish law-giver. "Styli and inkstands were found on monuments of the fourth Dynasty, the oldest in the world," says Bunsen. If the eminent Egyptologist rejects the period of 48,863 years before Alexander, to which Diogenes Laertius carries back the records of the priests, he is evidently more embarrassed with the ten thousand of astronomical observations and remarks that "if they were actual observations, they must have extended over 10,000 years." (p. 14). "We learn however," he adds, "from one of their own old chronological works that the genuine Egyptian traditions concerning the mythological period, treated of *myriads* of years." ("Egypte," 1, p. 15.)

18. *Egypte*, p. 143.

Aeschylus' Prometheus (V. ch. VI §2) shows certainly some prescience in the Sibyls of old.

Thus gradually the ancient claims came to be vindicated. The XIXth century had to submit to evidence, and some of its critics to confess that archaic literature can never be dated *too* far back into the prehistoric ages. Moreover, that the contents of all those ancient books — Henoch included [—] deemed and proclaimed so loudly "apocryphal" are found in the most secret and sacred sanctuaries of Chaldea, India, Phœnicia, Egypt and Central Asia. The merit of Champollion as an Egyptologist none will question. And if he declares that everything demonstrates the accuracy of the writing of the mysterious Hermes Trismegistus, and that his antiquity runs back into the night of time and is corroborated by him in its minutest details.[19] No one could ask for a better proof in favour of the Hermetic philosophy.

Egypt gathered the students of all countries before Alexandria was founded. ["]How comes it,["] asks Ennemoser "that so little has become known of the mysteries? Through so many ages and amongst so many different times and people? The answer is that it is owing to the universally strict silence of the initiated. Another cause may be found in the destruction and total loss of all the written memorials of the secret knowledge of the remotest antiquity." ["]Numa's books described by Livy, consisting of treatises upon natural philosophy and magic were found in his tomb; but they were not allowed to be made known lest they should reveal the most secret mysteries of the state religion. The senate and the tribune of the people determined that the books themselves should be burned, which was done["] in public.[20] Cassien mentions a treatise, well known in the fourth and fifth centuries, which was accredited to Ham, the son of Noah, who in his turn was reputed to have received it from Jared, the fourth generation from Seth, the son of Adam.[21]

---

19. *Egypte*, p. 143.

20. "Hist. of Magic," Vol. I, p. 9.

Herodotus tells us that the Mysteries were brought by Orpheus from India. Orpheus is called the inventor of letters and writing and placed anterior to both Homer and Hesiod. Nevertheless, till very lately Orphic literature and that of the Argonauts were attributed to a contemporary of Pisistratus, Solon and Pythagoras, one named Onomacritus, who is credited with having compiled them in their actual form, toward the middle of the VIth c. B.C., or 800 years after the days of Orpheus. The latest researches, however, lead the Orientalists to believe that this compilation was simply a very late re-edition of the Orphic Hymns, whether, ideographic or pictographic. In their original texts these Hymns are now shown much older than the VIth c. B.C. In *Deser. Graec.* [*Description of Greece*, IX, xxx, 12,] IX, 30 — we are told that in the days of Pausanius there was a sacerdotal family, which like the Brahmins with regard to the Vedas and the Epic poems — had committed to memory those Orphic hymns and that the latter were usually transmitted in that way from one generation to another. As to the poem of the Argonauts, Vivien St. Martin thinks (See Decouvertes geologiques, vol. I, p. 313) "that it really can be traced so far back as the days of Orpheus."

M. Vivien St. Martin is very impartial and fair and no doubt as learned; but there are some who go still further back than that. It is not the writer's province to argue upon the dates of the many poems cited above, but only, by showing their indubitably antediluvian — rather, *prehistoric* origin claim the same for the Occult Sciences. And how these are, aware of the diffidence shown to Asiatic *heathen* chronologists, a Christian philosopher of the early ages may be asked to express our intimate thought as to the date of — say — MAGIC. "If["] — argues Clemens Alexandrinus, the ex-pupil of the Neo-Platonist — "if there is a Science, there must necessarily be a professor of it." And he goes on saying that Cleanthes had Zeno to teach him, Theophrastus — Aristotle, Metrodorus — Epicurus, Plato — Socrates, etc.; and then when he arrived down to Pythagoras, Pherecydes and Thales, he had still to search and enquire who

---

21. Cassien: "Conference," 1, 21. We shall show who or what is *Adam*.

was their master or masters. The same for the Egyptians, the Indians, the Babylonians, and the Magi themselves. He would not cease questioning, to learn who it was they all had for their Masters. And when he, (Clemens) would have forcibly brought down the enquiry to the very cradle of mankind, to the birth of the first man, he should reiterate once more his questioning and ask him [—] Adam no doubt. "Who was *his* professor? Surely it would prove *no man* this once . . . and when we have reached the Angels, we shall have to ask even of them who was *their* Master and doctor of science."[22]

Just so but the secret doctrine need not go to such a trouble. Her professors know well who were the *first* instructors of mankind in the *Occult* Sciences.

The *two* Masters traced out by Clemens, are of course God, and his undying enemy and opponent the Devil, the subject of his enquiry relating to the *dual* aspect of Hermetic Science, as cause and effect. Admitting the moral beauty and virtues preached in every occult book he was acquainted with, Clemens wants to know the cause of the apparent contradiction between doctrine and practice, *good* and *bad* magic and comes to the conclusion, it seems, that magic has two origins — *divine* and *diabolical*. He perceives its *bifurcation* into two channels — hence his deduction and inference. We perceive it too, without necessarily dating such a bifurcation — the *Right* and "*Left* Path" — we call it, to its very beginning. Otherwise judging also by the effects of his (Clemens') own religion, and the walk in life of its professors since the death of his *Master*, the occultists would have a right to come to just the same conclusion, and say that, while Christ, the Master of all *true* Christians was in every way godly, the Master of those who resorted to the horrors of the Inquisition, to the burning and torture of heretic witches and Occultists by Calvin and pupils, etc., must have been evidently the DEVIL — if the Occultists were silly enough to believe in one. Clemens' His testimony however, is valuable as it shows (1) the enormous number of works on Occult Sciences during has epoch; and (2) the extraordinary powers acquired owing to these Sciences by certain men.

---

22. [*Stromateis*, Bk. VI, ch. vii.]

He devotes the whole of his sixth volume of the *Stromates* to this research of the first *two* "Masters" of the *true* and the *false* philosophy respectively, both preserved in the sanctuaries of Egypt. And therewith he apostrophies the Greeks asking why they should not believe in the miracles of Moses when their own philosophers claim the same privileges. "It is Eachus, he says, obtaining through his powers a marvelous rain; it is *Aristeus* who causes the winds to blow, Empedoclus quieting them and forcing them to cease,[23] etc., etc."

The Books of Mercury Trismegistus attracted the most his attention. Their extreme wisdom he remarks, ought to be in every one's mouth — *semper esse in ore* — always. He is high in his praise of Hystaspes (or Gushtasp) and of the Sibylene books.

There has been in all ages use and abuse of magic as there is use and abuse of mesmerism or *hypnotism* in our own. The ancient world had its Apolloniuses and its Pherecydeses, and intellectual people could discriminate then, as they can now. While not one classic or pagan writer has ever found one word of blame for Apollonius of Tyana, not so with regard to Pherecydes. Hesychius of Miletia, Philo of Byblos and Eustathes charge him unstintingly with having built his philosophy and science on *demoniacal* traditions. Cicero declares that Pherecydes is *potens divinus quam medicus*, rather a soothsayer than a physician; and Diogenes Laertius has a vast number of stories relating to his predictions to tell us. One day Pherecydes of Scyros prophesies the shipwreck of a vessel hundreds of miles away from him; another time he predicts the capture of the Lacedemonians by the Arcadians; finally he foresees his own wretched end.[24] But all such accusations prove very little except the truth of *clairvoyance* and prevision in every age. Had it not been for the testimony of his own coreligionists and countrymen, there would not be any proof at all against Pherecydes being guilty of sorcery, for those brought forward by

---

23. Therefore Empedoclus [Empedocles] is called Κωλυσάνεμος the dominator of the wind! See *Strom.*, I, VI. ch. IV.

24. Diogenes I, 1S, 149.

Christian writers are of little value indeed. Baronius for instance and de Mirville find an unanswerable proof in the belief of a philosopher "in the *coeternity* of matter with spirit." Pherecydes postulating in principle the primordiality of Zeus or Ether and then admitting on the same plane another principle coeternal and co-working with the first one — that he calls the fifth element, or *ogenos* — shows, we are told, that he gets his powers from Satan. "*Ogenos* — is Hades["] de Mirville tells his reader and "Hades is our Christian *Hell*" — as we all know, without his going to the trouble to explain.

The *resumé* of the views of the Church — as given out by authors of this character, is, we are told, that the Hermetic Books, their wisdom notwithstanding (admitted even in Rome) — are "the heirloom left by *Cain* to mankind." It is thoroughly proved, says the memorialist of *Satan in History* "that immediately after the Flood, Ham and his descendents had propagated anew the ancient teachings of the accursed *Caïnites* and of the submerged Race." This proves at any rate that Magic, or "Sorcery" as he calls it — is a *prediluvian* art. "The evidence of Berosius [Berosus] is there["] (Antiq. 1, iii). Berosius he says, "shows Ham *identical* with the first Zoroaster; the famous founder of Bactria, and the first author of all the magic arts of Babylonia." "He (Zoroaster) is the *Chemesenna* or '*Ham[*'] (Cham)[25] the *infamous* of the faithful and loyal *Noachians*, and the object of the adoration of the Egyptians, who after receiving from him their country's name *Choemia* (chemistry!) built in his honour a town called *Choemnis* or the 'city of fire.'[26] Ham adored it, it is said — whence the name *Chammaïm* given to the

---

25. The English people who spell the name of Noah's wicked son "Ham" have to be reminded that the right spelling ought to be *Kham* or *Cham*.

26. Choemnis, the prehistoric city, may or may not have been built by Noah's son, but it was not *his* name that was given to the town, but that of the mystery goddess *Choeman* or *Choemnis* (Greek form) that was *created* by the ardent fancy of the neophyte tantalized during his *twelve labours* of probation before final initiation.

pyramids; which in their turn, having become vulgarised — passed on their name to our modern 'chimney'[27] (cheminée)."

The zealous defender of Satan anthropomorphised is wrong, we believe. Egypt was the cradle of chemistry and its birthplace, this is pretty well known. But Henrick shows the root of the word to be *chemi* or *chem*, which is not *Cham* or Ham.

The irrepressible accuser of every pagan wisdom undertakes also to find a Satanic origin to the now innocent *tarot*. "As to the means for the propagation of this magic," he goes on to say — "the *bad, diabolical magic* — tradition points it out to us in certain *runic* characters traced on metallic plates (or leaves *des lames*) which have escaped destruction from the deluge.[28] These might have been regarded as *legendary* had not subsequent discoveries shown it far from being so. Plates were found with other such *Runic* and *Satanic* characters traced upon them, which being exhumed were recognized. (?) They were covered with queer signs undecipherable and of undeniable antiquity to which the *Hamites* of all countries attribute marvelous and terrible powers.["]

We may have to leave the pious Marquis to his orthodox beliefs, as he any rate is sincere in his views, but we shall have to sap his able arguments at their foundation by showing on *mathematical* grounds and the evidence of all the ancient world *who* or rather *what* Cain *really was*. De Mirville is only the faithful Son of his Church interested in Cain's anthropomorphic character and his present place in the Bible. The student of Occultism is interested only in truth. But the age has to follow the natural of evolution. We are at the bottom of a cycle and evidently in a transitory state. Plato divides the intellectual

---

27. This looks like pious philology with a vengeance. It is translated *literally* in view of its novelty. The reader must feel thankful that leading him from Zoroaster to *chimney*, the author has not added to it the picture of the traditional witch flying out of that chimney on a broomstick.

28. How could they "escape" from deluge unless *God willed it so* according to the belief of de Mirville and his coreligionists. Was the Devil once more cleverer than God?

progress of the universe during every cycle into fertile and barren periods. In the sublunary regions, the spheres of the various elements remain eternally in perfect harmony with the divine nature, he says; "but their parts" owing to a too close proximity to earth, and their commingling with the *earthly* (which is matter, and therefore the realm of evil), "are sometimes according, and sometimes contrary to (divine) nature." When those circulations — which Eliphas Levi calls "currents of the astral light" — in the universal ether which contains in itself every element, take place in harmony with the divine spirit our earth and everything pertaining to it enjoys a fertile period. The Occult powers of plants, animals, and minerals magically sympathize with the "superior natures," and the divine soul of man is in perfect intelligence with these "inferior" ones. But during the barren periods, the latter lose their magic sympathy, and the spiritual sight of the majority of mankind is so blinded as to lose every notion of the superior powers of its own divine spirit. We are in a barren period; the eighteenth century, during which the malignant fever of skepticism broke out so irrepressibly, has entailed unbelief as an hereditary disease upon the nineteenth. The divine intellect is veiled in man; his animal brain alone philosophizes.

§II

White and Black Magic — in theory and practice — The Esoteric and Western Kabala and its confessed Esoterism — The "Veil" of Moses — The Taro or the Wheel (Rota) of Enoch — Esoteric reading of the Bible — Numerical value of Jehovah and Elohim Abram — no Brahman.

As already shown — Magic is a dual power; nothing more easy than to turn it into *sorcery*. If anyone would study Occultism he might turn to the *Kabala Denudata*, or the *Zohar*, or again to older works such as the *Sepher Jezirah* and even the *Book of Enoch* called by the Greeks *Enoïchien*, or the "internal eye." But if any of these is approached without the right key to it; if the student is unable to distinguish between the primitive orthodox and the *Left-hand* Magic — let him take our advice and never meddle with such literature. There are numerous works written for the sworn Initiates only, those who have pronounced the for-ever binding oath and who alone can deal with their teachings practically.[29] Well intentioned as such works may be, they can only mislead and guide one imperceptibly to Black Magic — Sorcery.

The mystic characters — alphabets and numerals found in the divisions and subdivisions of the Great Kabala, are perhaps the most dangerous portion for human reason — especially the numerals. Dangerous we say, because they are the most prompt to produce *effects*, and that *with* or *without* the experimenter's will or even knowledge. The point of departure

---

29. There is a curious work in Slavonic sacerdotal language written by the Arch Bishop *Peter Moquila* (the tomb) in the past century. It is a book of *Exorcisms* against the dark powers that trouble the monks and nuns by preference. Some who had the good luck of getting it — for it is severely forbidden and kept secret — tried to read aloud its evocations and counter evocations or exorcisms. Some became lunatics — others died under the *horrors* witnessed. A lady got it by paying 2000 roubles for an incomplete copy. She burnt it a few days after and remained nervous for the rest of her life.

of that special branch of the Occult teaching known as the "science of correspondences" *numerical* and *literal* — has for its epigraph — with the Jewish and Christian Kabalists the two misinterpreted verses from *Ecclesiastes* which say that God made the world by means of *number, measure* and *weight*,[30] .... and he *saw, counted* and *measured* wisdom. The meaning of this can be found out only by the means of a transcendental method of algebra: Jehovah, Adam Kadmon, Adam and Eve, etc., — in the Kabala are themselves more intimately connected with geometrical calculations than the world is prepared to understand, but as a correct interpretation of the number 666 — in that most kabalistic of works — St. John's Revelation may one day show.

But the Eastern Occultists have another epigraph: "ABSOLUTE UNITY, *x*: within number and plurality." Both the Western as the Eastern students of the Hidden Wisdom hold to this axiomatic truth, only the latter perhaps are a little more sincere in their confessions. Instead of putting a mask on their science, they show her face openly, even if they do veil carefully her *heart* and *soul* before the inappreciative public and profane. But even the French Kabalist, Eliphas Levi (the Abbé Louis Constant), says in his *Dogme et Rituel de la Haute Magie*, "Absolute Unity is the supreme and final reason of things. Therefore, this reason can be neither a person nor three persons: it is a *reason* and a *preeminent* reason (par excellence).["]

"GOD GEOMETRIZES" — was said by Plato, because every Cosmogony — from the oldest to the latest from the Vedas down to the Jewish Bible — is based upon, interlinked with, and most closely related to Numerals and geometrical calculations. These, questioned by the Initiates — will yield in numerical value based on the integral value of the CIRCLE — the secret of the *Hidden* deity (as of every other *occult* particular) in connection with cosmogonical architecture, or symbolical glyph of the primitive mysteries — whether anthropological, anthropographical or cosmic. The cosmogonical theory of numerals, which Pythagoras learned in India — from the

---

30. "God geometrizes" — said Plato, who was initiated and knew what he meant.

Egyptian hierophants, is alone able to reconcile the two units — in one, or matter and spirit, and cause each to demonstrate the other mathematically.

The sacred numbers of the universe in their esoteric combination can alone solve the great problem, and explain the theory of radiation and the cycle of the emanations. The lower orders before they develop into higher ones, and when arrived at the turning point, be reabsorbed into the infinite.

Any Kabalist well acquainted with the Pythagorean system of numerals and geometry can demonstrate that the metaphysical views of Plato were based upon the strictest mathematical principles. "True mathematics," says the Magician, "is something with which all higher sciences are connected; common mathematics is but a deceitful phantasmagoria whose much praised infallibility only arises from this — that materials, conditions, and references are made to foundation." And *true* mathematics is the science upon which all the knowledge of Kosmos and its grand mysteries in the possession of our Teachers — rests. Nothing easier for them than to prove that the Biblical in [and?] the Vedic structures are both based upon *God-in-Nature* and *Nature in God*, — as the *radical law*; and that this law, as everything else immutable and fixed in eternity, can find a correct expression only in the purest mathematics referred to by Plato, or *transcendentally* applied geometry. Revealed to man — (we *fear not* and shall not retract the expression) in this geometrical garb, Truth has grown and developed into poetical symbology — otherwise the masses could have never grasped the idea. If later on led by their clergy — crafty and ambitious of power in every age, they have anthropomorphised abstract ideals as well as real and divine Beings, the fault rests with their leaders not with the masses. But the gross conceptions of our forefathers of the present Christian era can satisfy no longer the thoughtful religionist, the scientific and learned mystic, and these have to learn the truth. When it is shown to the world that the *Tres Matres* of Hermes, and the "Three Mothers" of *Sepher Jezirah*, are "Light, Heat and Electricity" revealing themselves in their "coats of skin" to modern science and in their very soul and spirit to ancient and mediæval Alchemists — then the so called learned classes may not spurn them any longer. The Rosicrucian Illuminati shall find followers in the Royal Academies, and the latter shall be more prepared than they are now, to admit the great scientific truths of Archaic natural Philosophy. In Hermetic dialect those "Three Mothers" stand as shown in "Isis Unveiled" as a symbol for the whole of the forces or agents which have a place assigned them in the modern "Force correlation." Synesius mentions books of stone which he found in the temple of Memphis, on which was engraved the following sentence: "One *nature* delights in another, one nature overcomes another, one nature overrules another, and the whole of them are one."

The inherent restlessness of matter is embodied in the saying of Hermes: "Action is the life of Phta"; and Orpheus calls nature πολυμήχανη μήτηρ, "the mother that makes many things," or the ingenious, the contriving, the inventive mother.

The *Books of Hermes*, the Chaldean Kabala or Book of Numbers as well as the *Zohar* — without mentioning the old *plates* made of some unknown pliable and indestructable material in a book called the *Yo-ya-hoo* in the possession of our Teachers — are all a kind of symbolic writing, and a numerical method upon which Moses built his *Genesis*, the first four chapters of which contain the synopsis of all the rest.[31] Some readers wonder at the non demonstrated fact of the Biblical containment of the pyramid structure, "at the use of Biblical names in general and those of Shem, Ham and Japhet especially" as determinative of pyramid measures, in connection with the 600 year period of Noah, and the 500 year period of his sons; or again that "the terms 'Sons of Elohim' and [']daughters of H — Adam,' are for one thing astronomical terms."[32] But all this is only natural. Moses was a priest initiated into all the mysteries of the Egyptian temples. He was as well acquainted therefore with the symbolical and astronomical meaning of that mystery of mysteries — the great Pyramid. And having been so familiar with the geometrical secrets that lay concealed for long æons in

---

31. Now mathematically ascertained.

32. See Key to the Hebrew Egyptian Mystery by J. Ralston Skinner, who shows the Bible "a display of pure and natural mathematics." [p.] 315.

her strong bosom the measurements and proportions of the Cosmos our little earth included — what wonder that he should have made use of his knowledge. The esoterism of Egypt was that of the whole world at one time. During the long ages of the 3rd Race, it had been the heirloom in common of the whole mankind, received from their Instructors "the Sons of Light" — the primeval SEVEN. There was a time when Wisdom Religion was not symbolical, for it had become esoteric only gradually, necessitated by its misuse and the Sorcery of the 4th Atlantean Race. It was *misuse* indeed and not the *use* of power that made the *divine* gift of the Gods, inherent and only *atrophied* in man in our own age, develop into ungodly Sorcery. The *Elect* that escaped from the "Great Flood" preserved and treasured the Divine Science given to their forefathers of the 2nd Race who were incorporeal and pure, as mankind will be once more at the end of its probationary Cycle. Old Plato tells us in his Phaedrus all that man once was, and that which he may yet become again. "Before man's spirit sank into sensuality and was embodied with it through the loss of his wings, he lived among the Gods in the airy (spiritual) world where everything is true and pure." In the Timaeus he says that "there was a time when mankind did not perpetuate itself, but lived as pure spirits," and Plato was an *Initiate*.

Unwilling that his (by him) "chosen people["] should become grossly idolatrous as the profane masses of Egypt, Moses utilized his knowledge of the cosmogonical Mysteries of the Pyramid, to build upon it a Cosmogony more accessible and comprehensive to the hoi polloi than the abstruse truths taught to the educated. He invented nothing, added not one iota. Following the example of older nations he only clothed the truths revealed to him by his Egyptian Hierophant under the most ingenious imagery and national garb calculated to meet the requirements of the Israelites. These were corroborated to him, later on, by his own personal "Initiator" — his divine SELF on Mount Sinai, whither "Moses went up unto God." He understood the great danger of delivering them to the uneducated masses, for he knew the history of the Past. Thus he veiled them from the profanation of public gaze and presented them allegorically. Hence too, the remark in his biography — alleged to have been written by himself — that when he descended from Sinai — "Moses wist not that the skin of his face shone . . . and he put a veil upon his face" (Exod. XXXIV, 29-33). And so did [he] put on a veil — on the face of his *Pentateuch*; and to that extent that (using the orthodox chronology) only 3376 years *after* the event people are beginning to acquire the ultimate conviction that *it is* a "veil" — and a very thick one, — thrown on the archaic Symbols of WISDOM-Religion — and not the face of God that shineth through.

We have the confession of Clement to corroborate the above in *Stromata* (I.V.) he says: "The mysteries of the Hebrews, their rites, their ceremonies . . . etc., are extremely similar (simillima) to the Mysteries of the Egyptians." And so they are, with a very simple reason why. If facts are awkward opponents, mathematical and geometrical axioms are still more so, as will be seen, later on.

1 [2] — *Hermes and the 32 Ways of Wisdom. Confessions.*

Hermes has also a Cosmogony, as veiled but more scientifically so. Says the thrice great Trismegistus:

"In the beginning of time the great invisible one had his holy hands full of celestial matter which he scattered throughout the infinity; and lo behold! It became balls of fire and balls of clay; and they scattered like the moving metal quicksilver into many smaller balls, and began their ceaseless turning; and some of them which were balls of fire became balls of clay; and the balls of clay became balls of fire; and the balls of fire were waiting their time to become balls of clay; and the others envied them and bided their time to become balls of pure divine fire."

Here we have the distribution of matter throughout space; then its concentration into the spherical form; the separation of smaller spheres from the greater ones; axial rotation; the gradual change of orbs from the incandescent to the earthy consistence; and finally, the total loss of heat which marks their entrance into the state of planetary death. The change of the balls of clay into balls of fire would be understood by materialists to indicate some such phenomenon as the sudden ignition of the star in Cassiopeia, A.D. 1572, and the one in Serpentarius, in 1604 which was noted by Kepler. But, do the Chaldeans evince in this expression a profounder philosophy than of our day. Does this change into balls of "pure divine fire" signify a continuous planetary existence, correspondent with the spirit life of man, beyond the awful mystery of death. If worlds have, as the astronomers tell us, their periods of embryo, infancy, adolescence, maturity, decadence, and death, may they not, like man, have their continued existence in a sublimated, ethereal, or spiritual form? The Magians so affirm. They tell us that the fecund Mother Earth is subject to the same laws as every one of her children. At her appointed time she brings forth all created things; in the fullness of her days she is gathered to the tomb of worlds. Her gross material body slowly parts with its atoms under the inexorable law which demands their new arrangement in other combinations. Her own perfect vivifying spirit obeys the eternal attraction which draws it toward that central spiritual sun from which it was originally evolved, and which we vaguely know under the name of God.

"And the heaven was visible *in seven circles*, and the planets appeared with all their signs, in star form, and the stars were divided and *numbered with the rulers that were in them*, and their revolving course was bounded with the air, and borne with a circular course, through the agency of the divine SPIRIT.["][33] Science tells us of a liquid non-permanent shell of uncongealed matter; enclosing a "viscous plastic ocean," within which "there is another interior solid globe rotating.["][34] We, on our part, turn to the *Magia Adamica* of Eugenius Philalethes, published in 1650, and at page 12, we find him quoting from Trismegistus in the following terms: "Hermes affirmeth that in the Beginning the earth was a quackmire or quivering kind of jelly, it being nothing else but water congealed by the incubation and heat of divine spirit; cum adhuc (sayeth he) Terra tremula esset, Lucente sole compacta esto."

In the same work Philalethes, speaking in his quaint, symbolical way, says, "The earth is invisible . . . on my soul it is so, and which is more, the *eye* of *man* never *saw* the earth, nor can it be *seen* without *art*. To make this *element invisible*, is the *greatest secret* in *magic* . . . . as for this *faeculent* gross *body* upon *which we walk*, it is a *compost*, and no earth, *but it hath earth in it*, . . . in a word all the *elements* are *visible* but *one*, namely the *earth*, and when thou hast attained to so much *perfection* as to know why *God* hath placed the earth *in abscondito*, thou hast an excellent figure whereby to know *God Himself*, and how He is visible, how invisible.["][35] *Isis Unveiled*.

Thus while the "revealed word" says to us through the mask of its dead letter: "the world was *created ex nihil*" an

---

33. Hermes, IV. 6. Spirit here denotes the Deity — Pneuma ὁ θεός.

34. Proctor's lectures.

35. "Magia Adamica," p. 11.

Initiate of the *Kabala* in the same sacred volume is made to speak of the "Hand, that made the world of *formless* matter."[36]

All this is contained within the small compass of the *Sepher Jezirah*, in its "32 wonderful Ways of wisdom signed Jah Jehovah Sabaoth." This signature becomes more comprehensible and trustworthy when one learns that with Moses, the "God-names Elohim and Jehovah (were) numerical indices of geometrical relations and stood "(for one meaning) for a *diameter* and a *circumference* value, respectively."[37] Of this however, more anon. Truly says the wise Book, of *Jezirah* . . . "the cup of purity and the cup of sin and *the tongue of doctrine vacillating* between them." (Ch. II, 1, Sect.) And, it disposes of every dead letter doctrine by teaching us that the 30th Way is called "the gathering understanding and is so called because thereby gather the Celestial Adepts' judgements of the stars and celestial signs, and their observations of the *orbits are the perfection of science*"; while the 32nd and last "is called the serving understanding, and is so called because it is a disposer of all those that are *serving in the work of the Seven Planets*, according to their hosts."

The work of the *Seven* Planets is Initiation, during which all the mysteries concerning these, our seven planets are divulged fully. How symbolical and purposely veiled is the Bible may be inferred from these words of the *Zohar* (111, 152; and Franck, 119): "Wo[e] be to the man who says that the Doctrine delivers common stories and daily words! For if this were so, then we also in our time could compose a doctrine in daily words which would deserve far more praise . . . Therefore, we must believe that *every word of the Doctrine contains in it a loftier sense and a higher meaning. The narratives of the Doctrine are its cloak.* The simple look only at the garment . . . the instructed, however, *see not merely the cloak, but what the cloak covers.*" "If we hold to the letters," exclaims Origen, "and must understand what stands written in the law (the Bible) after the manner of the Jews and common people, then *I should blush to confess aloud that it is God who has given these laws*; then the

---

36. "Wisdom of Solomon," xi. 17.

37. "Key to the Hebrew-Egyptian Mystery," p. 67.

laws of men appear more excellent and reasonable." (Origen, Homil. 7 in Levit.) Then again . . . ["]What man is found such an idiot as to suppose that God planted trees in Paradise, in Eden! . . . . Every man *must hold these things for images under which a hidden sense lies concealed.*" (Origen; Venet's *Originiana*, 167; Franck, 121, quoted from Sod. "Genesis," p. 175.)[38]

But the most explicit of all the Church Fathers is certainly Clemens Alexandrinus, who, while in search of the two Masters "for Divine and Satanic Magic,["] seems to repudiate *his own*, for all those who are unable to understand the secret meaning of his words. Says he, in his *Stromata*: "THE MYSTERIES OF THE FAITH are not to BE DIVULGED TO ALL. But since this is not published alone for him who perceives the magnificence of the word; it is requisite, therefore, to hide in a Mystery the wisdom spoken, which the Son of God taught." (12) ["]. . . For we shall find that very many of the dogmas that are held by such sects (of barbarian and Hellenic philosophy) as have not become utterly senseless, and are not cut out *from the order of nature, are held in common with us*, the token of recognition being by CUTTING OFF CHRIST.["] (Strom. 13.)[39]

The greatest of the Kabalistic works of the Hebrews — the *Sohar* [Zohar] זהר — we say in *Isis* was compiled by Rabbi Simeon Ben-Iochai. According to some critics, this was done years before the Christian era; according to others only after the destruction of the temple. However it was completed only by the son of Simeon, Rabbi Eleazar, and his secretary, Rabbi Abba; for the work is so immense and the subjects treated so abstruse that even the whole life of this Rabbi, called the Prince of Kabalists, did not suffice for the task. On account of its being known that

---

38. See *Isis Unveiled*.

39. This sentence "by cutting off of Christ" has reference to an astronomical occult parlance. "The cutting off of the Meshiee" (Messiah) is explained in the "Key to the Hebrew-Egyptian Mystery" and one may well wonder that one *not* initiated, could come so near to the truth.

he was in possession of this knowledge, and of the *Mercaba* which insured the reception of the "Word" his very life was endangered, and he had to fly to the wilderness, where he lived in a cave for twelve years, surrounded by faithful disciples, and finally died there amid signs and wonders.[40]

But voluminous as is the work, and containing as it does the main points of the secret and oral tradition, it still does not embrace it all. It is well known that this venerable Kabalist never imparted the most important points of his doctrine otherwise than orally, and to a very limited number of friends and disciples, including his only son. Therefore without the final initiation into the *Mercaba* the study of the *Kabala* will be ever incomplete, and the Mercaba can be taught only in "darkness, in a deserted place, and after many and terrific trials." Since the death of Simeon Ben-Iochai this hidden doctrine has remained an inviolate secret for the outside world.

In *Die Kabbala* by Franck, the author following its "esoteric ravings," as he expresses it, gives us, in addition to the translations, his commentaries. Speaking of his predecessors, he says that Simeon Ben-Iochai mentions repeatedly what the "companions" have taught in the older works. And the author cites one "Ieba, the *old*, and Hamnuna, the old."[41] But what the two "old" ones mean, or who they were, in fact, he tells us not, for he does not know himself.

---

40. Many are the marvels recorded as having taken place at his death or we should rather say his translation; for he did not die as others do, but having suddenly disappeared, while a dazzling light filled the cavern with glory, his body was again seen upon its subsidence. When this heavenly light gave place to the habitual semi-darkness of the gloomy cave — then only, says Ginsburg "the disciples of Israel perceived that the lamp of Israel was extinguished." His biographers tell us that there were voices heard from Heaven during the preparation for his funeral, and at his interment. When the coffin was lowered down into the deep cave excavated for it, a flame broke out from it, and a voice mighty and majestic pronounced these words in the air: "This is he who causeth the earth to quake, and the kingdoms to shake!"

41. "Die Kabbala," 75; "Sod," vol. II.

Among the venerable sect of the Tanaim or rather the Tananim, the wise men, there were those who taught the secrets practically and initiated some disciples into the grand and final mystery. But the Mishna Hagiga, 2nd Section, say that the table of contents of the *Mercaba* "must only be delivered to wise old ones."[42] The Gemara is still more dogmatic. "The more important secrets of the Mysteries were not even revealed to all priests. Alone the initiates had them divulged." And so we find the same great secrecy prevalent in every ancient religion.

The *Synthetic and Kabalistic Studies* on the Sacred Book of Enoch — the Taro (*Rota*) is before us. It is the MSS copy of a Western Occultist and it is prefaced by these words: "There is but one Law, one Principle, one Agent, one Truth and one WORD — That which is above, is analogically as that which is below. All that which is, is the result of quantities and of Equilibriums."

The axiom of Eliphas Levi and this triple Epigraph show the identity of thought between the East and the West with regard to the Secret Science which, as the same M.S.S. tells us is: — "The KEY of things concealed; the key of the Sanctuary,["] and adds: "This the Sacred Word which gives to the adept the supreme reason of Occultism and its mysteries. It is the quintessence of Philosophies and of Dogmas; it is the Alpha and Omega; it is the Light, Life and Wisdom universal."

The *Taro* of the Sacred Book of Enoch, or *Rota*, is prefaced, moreover, with this explanation: —

"The antiquity of this Book is lost in the night of time. It is of *Indian origin* and goes back to an epoch long before Moses."

"It is written upon detached leaves, which at the first were of fine gold and precious metals . . . It is symbolical, and its combinations adapt themselves to all the wonders of the Spirit. Altered by its passage across the ages, it is nevertheless preserved — thanks to the ignorance of the curious, — in its types and its most important primitive figures."

---

42. "Die Kabbala," 47.

This is the *Rota* of Enoch, now called TARO of Enoch, to which de Mirville alludes as the means used for "*bad* magic," the "metallic plates (or leaves) escaped from destruction during the Deluge" and attributed by him to Cain. They have escaped the Deluge for the simple reason that it was *never* "Universal." And it is said to be "of Indian origin" because its origin is with the Indian Aryans of the first sub-races of the 5th Root-race before the final destruction of the last stronghold of Atlantis. But if it originated with the forefathers of the primitive Hindus, it was not in India that it was first used. Its origin is still older and has to be traced beyond and *into* the Himaleh[43] the snowy range. It was born in that mysterious locality which no one knows where to locate and which is the despair of both geographers and Christian Theologians — the region in which the Brahmin places his *Kailas*, the mount Sumeru, and the *Parbati-Pamer* transformed by the Greeks in Paropamison.

On this locality that still exists, the traditions of the garden of Eden were built. From these, the Greeks obtained their Parnassus[44] and thence proceeded most of the Biblical personages, some of them in their day — men, some demi-gods and heroes, several — though very few myths, the astronomical *doubles* of the former. Abram was one of them. A Chaldean Brahman,[45] says the legend, transformed later, after he had repudiated his Gods and left his Ur (*pur* — town) in Chaldee into A-brahm,[46] (or A-braham), "*no*-brahman["] who emigrated; and thus, his becoming "the father of many nations" — is explained.

---

43. Pococke maybe was not altogether wrong in deriving the German heaven *Himmel*, from Himala or Himalaya; nor can it be denied that it is the Hindu Kailas (Heaven) that is the father of the Greek heaven Koilon and of the Latin *Caelum*.

44. See Pococke's "India in Greece" and his derivation of Mount *Parnassus* from *Parnasa*, the leaf and branch-huts of the Hindu ascetics, half shrine and half habitation.

45. Rawlinson is justly very confident of an Aryan and Vedic influence on the early mythology and history of Babylon and Chaldea.

46. This is a Secret Doctrine affirmation and may or may not be accepted.

The students of occultism have to bear in mind, that invariably every Biblical personage and most of the locality-names are connected at one and the same time, with astronomical, numerical and psychic subjects and qualifications. This is shown not only by the secret teaching but by strictly mathematical methods. They are all related to measures, geometrical figures and time calculations; principal period durations being founded on them.[47] They are connected with Heaven and Earth — truly. For, in the Hindu Pantheon, the oldest, as in the Jewish — the youngest (but one) — their prototypes are the "mind-born" Sons of Light, as they are themselves the "Sin-born" ancestors of our present Humanity. One of such is Abram or Abraham *into whose* bosom every orthodox Jew hopes to be gathered after death[48] — that "bosom" being *localized* heaven, "in the clouds" Abhra (Sanskrit), in Loka Palas.

---

47. This is what C.W. King writes on this subject in "The Gnostics and Their Remains" (p. 13): "This figure of the *man*, Seir Anpin, consists of 243 numbers, the numerical value of the letters in the name *Abram* signifying the different orders in the celestial hierarchy. In fact the *names Abram* and *Brahma are equivalent* in *numerical value*." And, it may seem strange to the reader unacquainted with *esoteric* symbolism that Indra's *elephant* in the Lokapalas — the symbol of wisdom, since it is *this* elephant's head of *Ganesa* (Ganapati) *the god of wisdom*, cut off by Siva — should be named "*Abhra* (matang)" and his wife *Abhramu*. Now when read backward — *Arba* (kirjath) ["]the city of 4." Truly says R. Skinner in his work: "(*Abram* is *Abra* with an appended *m* final, and *Arba* [*Abra*] read backward is *Arba* [. . .)"]!! — Abhra meaning moreover in Sanskrit "*as*, or *of* the clouds["] the whole referring to astronomical and cosmological symbols.

48. Before these speculations — we are willing to call them so — are rejected, the following points ought to be explained: (1) Why after leaving Egypt his name is changed by Jehovah from Abram to Abraham; (2) Why on the same principle (Gen. XVII) Sarai becomes Sarah; (3) Whence the coincidence of names — Brahma and Sara-svati, and Abram and Sarai? (4) Why no such place as "Ur in Chaldee" could be discovered; (5) Is it certain that *ur* is *not pur* — the Aryan name for city; and finally (6) Why Eden and its four rivers should dovetail so strangely with ["]the Sumer, the Kailas and the Pamer of the Hindus."

As Abraham has to be noticed further on in his relation to other universal symbols we need not go out of the way to speak of him here more than necessary. The name itself has a very strong Kabeirian look. The words *Heber*, *Gheber* (applied to Nimrod and the Giants of *Genesis* (VI), and *Kaber* all sound like the mysterious word, for all the Mystery Gods were Kabeir. The Phoenicians were Φοῖνικες or Ph'-Anakes as being of the Anakim, *Kabeirian*, kingly or divine Race, which race was the *Second* Race of our humanity as shown in the *Secret books* in which all the transformations of Brahma throughout the æons of time are given. Brahma was born with the Fourth race; the first — that of unwritten *Rig-Veda* knew him not and he is not even mentioned in this archaic Aryan Bible written in Tibet in the beginning of Tretta [Treta]-Yuga on Lake Manassorovara [Manasarovara]. It is but in the third Race only that the "wheel" of Enoch was invented as a first attempt at symbology, though Enoch No. 1 had naught to do with it.

There are two *taros* — the wheel purely Esoteric, and the Western *tarot* — Kabalistical[ly] remodeled by Shimites, a branch so much younger than the Aryans and even the Hamites. The latter taro (*tarot*) is to be read from right to left like Arabic and Hebrew writing. The former, primitive "Wheel" is in Cuneiform characters and astrological signs. One of the oldest in the world is made on a kind of *tolla* leaves of some chemically prepared and indestructible material which makes them look like burnished metal.

Thus as we see, neither the Sohar nor any other Kabalistic volume contains merely Jewish wisdom. The doctrine itself being the result of whole millenniums of thought, is therefore the joint property of adepts of every nation under the sun. Nevertheless, the Sohar teaches practical Occultism more than any other work on that subject; not as it is translated though, and commented upon by its various critics, but with the secret signs on its margins. These signs contain the hidden instructions, apart from the metaphysical interpretations and apparent absurdities so fully credited by Josephus, who was never initiated, and gave out the *dead letter* as he had received it.

The Secret Doctrine Würzburg Manuscript

§ III

Transcendental-Algebra, and "God-revealed" characters — Occult virtue in mystic names — The Runes and the Kischuph, the magic letters — The Chaldean Targes and the Aryan thunderbolts — Dangers of Magic — Alleged Christian dogmas in the Zohar — The Kabala and the Adepts — Uniformity in Occult teachings — Magic as old as Man — Views upon it by various writers — ancient and modern — Most of its Books destroyed.

I. Mathematics and Geometry — the keys to the Universal Problems

The transcendental Methods of calculation — as well explained in Cornelius Agrippa — are very difficult to practise. Its most perfect exposition, however, is found in the Chaldean *Book of Numbers*[49] and the great Hermetic or Chaldean Kabala cannot be thoroughly understood without becoming an M.A. in this science. Pythagoras was not its inventor as some believe. Thousands of years before his day it was known to the Sages of Aryavarta, whence it was brought by the Samian mystic and philosopher, not as a Speculation but as a demonstrated science. "The numerals of Pythagoras" says Porphyry, "were hieroglyphical symbols, by means whereof he explained *all* ideas concerning the nature of all things." ("De vite Pythag.")

---

49. We are not aware that a copy of this ancient work is embraced in the catalogue of any European library; but it is one of the "Books of Hermes," and it is referred to, and quotations are made from it in the works of a number of ancient and mediæval philosophical authors. Among these authorities are Arnoldo di Villanova's "Rosarium Philosoph;" Francesco Arnolphim's "Lucensis opus de lapide"; Hermes Trismegistus' "Tractatus de transmutatione metallorum," "Tabula smaragdina," and above all in the treatise of Raymond Lulli, "Ab angelis opus divinum de quinta essentia."

The fundamental geometrical figure of the Kabala — that figure which tradition and the esoteric doctrines tell us was given by the Deity itself to Moses on Mount Sinai[50] contains in its grandiose, because simple combination, the key to the universal problem. This figure contains in itself all the others. For those who are able to master it, there is no need to exercise imagination. No earthly microscope can be compared with the keenness of the spiritual perception.

The symbolism of numbers and their mathematical interrelations are also at the foundation of *mental* magic so to say, of divination and correct perception in clairvoyance. Systems differ but the idea is everywhere the same. As Kenneth R. H. MacKenzie IX° says in his *Royal Masonic Cyclopædia*: "One system adopts unity, another trinity, a third, quinquinity; again we have sexagons, heptagons, novems, duodecimals, and so on, until the mind is lost in the survey of the materials alone of a science of numbers. Numbers also are related to proper proportion, and as one scale or the other is adopted in a system, so the proportion varies; and with the devarication we obtain dissimilar forms of architecture.... It is impossible to deny the multiplication table, or to assert that the three angles of any triangle do not comprise the rectangles." Although beings are infinite in numbers, however (as Leibnitz says) it does not follow that their systems should at once receive all the perfection of which they are capable. "For if so," he adds, — "the hypothesis of the rectangle would be demonstrated, for the hypothesis of equal perfection is that of the rectangle."

The Eastern or Oriental Numerical alphabet[51] is like the Chaldean, the Hebrew and the Hermetic alphabets the world

---

50. Exodus, XXV, 40.

51. The so-called "Magic Squares" (the Oriental Square, Zchal), and the *Pythagorean Triangle* are well known. "A magic square is a series of numbers (in two squares) and an equal number of cells constituting a *square* figure, the enumeration of all whose columns, vertically, horizontally, and diagonally will give the same sum ... These magic squares, which almost run to infinity, have attracted the attention of the thoughtful and learned in all ages ... The Oriental Square, named after

over, *plus* — the full and complete significance given of every letter in its relation to spiritual as well as terrestrial things. And, as there are only 22 letters in the Hebrew alphabet and 10 fundamental numbers and in the Sanskrit or Devanagari 35 consonants and 14 vowels, making altogether 49 simple letters (or 7x7) the margins of speculation, or we should say knowledge are vaster in proportion. Every letter has its equivalents in other languages and its equivalent in a figure or figures of the calculation table, as also its numerous significations, the latter depending upon the special idiosyncrasies and characteristics of the person, object or subject to be studied. As the Hindus claim to have received their Devanâger [devanāgarī] characters or alphabet from Sarasvati, the inventress of Sanskrit, "the language of the Devas" or gods[52] — so most of the ancient nations claimed the same privilege for the origin of their letters. The Hebrews called kabalistically theirs the "Alphabet of the Angels" which was communicated by the Angels to the Patriarchs, as the Deva-nagari was by the Devas to the Rishis. The Chaldeans found their letters traced in the heavens by the "yet unsettled stars" and comets — says the Book of *Numbers*; and the Phoenicians, showed a sacred alphabet formed by the twistings of the sacred Serpents. The most ancient is certainly that of the *Secret Doctrine*, in which the oldest work on the Evolution of Cosmos and planets is traced, and the *Netar-Khari* (Hieratic) alphabet and *"Secret Speech"* of the Egyptians.

However it may be, this kind of interpretation of the hidden sense of apocalyptic writings is one of the keys given out in the Zohar and is its most sacred lore. St. Hieronyus assures us that it was known to the school of the Prophets and taught therein which is very likely. Molitor, the learned Hebraist in his

---

the planet Saturn Zohal, the sum of the digits being equal to 45 (1+2+3+4+5+6+7+8+9) being the exact corresponding value of the letters in the word Zohal, in Arabic. The table (a square divided into nine cells) is the Talmud real method, making fifteen each way, being the numerical value of YAH, a form of the Tetragrammaton. Cornelius Agrippa has given all these squares." (*Royal Masonic Cyclopædia.*)

52. The Secret Doctrine teaches otherwise. We shall explain further on. It is one of the few things permitted to be given out.

work on tradition says that "the two and twenty letters of the Hebrew alphabet were regarded as an emanation, or the *visible expression of the divine forces inherent in the ineffable name.*" Those letters find their equivalent in, and are replaced by numbers; for instance: the 12th letter and the 6th of the alphabet yield 18 — in a name; the other letters of that name are added being always exchanged for that figure that corresponds to the alphabetical letter; then all these figures are subjected to an algebraic process that transforms them again into letters; after which the latter yield to the enquirer "the most hidden secrets of divine Permanency (eternity in its immutability) in Futurity (Chaldean *Book of Numbers*)."

2 — The Key of the absolute in Magic — the Hexagon with the Central Point — or the SEVENTH key. The Tantrika Sutras and the Kuku-ma.

Arguing upon the virtue in names or *Baalshem*, Molitor thinks it is impossible to deny that the Kabala, its present abuses notwithstanding, *has some very profound basis to stand upon*. And if it is claimed, he adds "that before the name of Jesus every other *name* must bend, why should not the *Tetragrammaton* have the same power?["][53] This is good sense and logic. For, if Pythagoras viewed the *hexagon* formed of two crossed triangles as the symbol of creation, the Egyptians — as that of the union of fire and water, the Essenes as the Seal of Solomon, the Jews, — the shield of David, the Hindus as the sign of Vishnu to this day, and that even in Russia and Poland the double triangle is viewed as a potent talisman, it only stands to reason that all nations ancient and modern, should have a right to their opinion and truth on *their* side as much as their opponents have.

The great power of the *hexagon*, with its central mystic sign, the T or the *swastica* — a SEPTENARY, is well explained in the 7th key of "Things concealed" for it says: "The seventh key, is the Hieroglyph of the sacred Septenary, of Royalty, of the Priesthood (the Initiate), of triumph and true result by struggle. It is Magic power in all its force, the true 'Holy Kingdom.' In the Hermetic Philosophy it is the *quintessence resulting from the union of the two forces of the greatest* MAGIC AGENT" — Akasa, Astral Light.

"It is equally Jakin and Boaz bound by the Will of the Adept and overcome by his Omnipotence."

The force of this key is absolute in Magic. All Religions *have consecrated this sign in their rites*.

We can only glance hurriedly at present at the long series of antediluvian works in their post-diluvian fragmentary, often disfigured form. Although all of these are the inheritance from the 4th Race — now lying buried in the unfathomed depths of the oceans — still they are not to be rejected. As shown, there was but one science at the dawn of mankind, and it was all

---

53. See Molitor's *Tradition*, Chapt. on NUMBERS.

divine. If when Humanity having reached its adult period has abused of it [abused it?] — especially the last Sub-races of the 4th Root-Race — it was the fault and sin of the practitioners who desecrated the divine Knowledge, not of those who remained true to its pristine dogmas. It is not because the modern Roman Catholic Church, true to her traditional intolerance is now pleased to see in the Occultist and even in the innocent Spiritualist and Mason "the descendants of the *Kischuph*, the *Hamite*, the *Kasdim*, the *Cephene*, the *Ophite* and the *Khartumin*" — all these being "the followers of Satan," that they are such indeed. The state or national Religion of every country has ever disposed easily of rival schools and at all times, by professing to believe they were dangerous *heresies*, the old Roman state-religion as much as the modern one. If Napoleon the Great has one meritorious act to boast of during his career of slaughter — it is that of having abolished the "Holy" Inquisition.

The abolition however, has not made the public any the wiser for that, in the mysteries of the Occult Sciences. In some respects the world is all the better for such ignorance. The secrets of nature are generally double edged weapons and in the hands of the undeserving are more than likely to become murderous. Who knows anything in our modern day of the real significance of and the powers contained in, certain characters and signs, talismans, whether for beneficent or evil purposes? Fragments of the *Runes* and the *Kischuph*, found scattered in old mediæval libraries; copies from the *Ephesian* and the *Milesian* letters or characters; the thrice famous *Book of Thoth*, and the terrible treatises (still preserved) of Targes, the Chaldean, and his disciple Tarchon, the Etruscan — who flourished far before the Trojan war — are so many names and appellations void of sense (though met in classical literature) for the educated modern scholar who believes in the XIXth cent. in art, described in such treatises of Targes of *evoking and directing thunderbolts*. Yet the same is described in the Brahmanical literature and Targes copied his thunderbolts from the *astra*^{54} that terrible engine of destruction known to the Mahabharatan Aryans. Before this art

---

54. This is a kind of magical bow and arrow calculated to destroy in one moment whole armies; it is mentioned in the *Ramayana*, the *Puranas* and everywhere.

if ever understood by the Western, — would pale a whole arsenal of dynamite bombs, for it is from an old *fragment* read and translated to him that Lord Bulwer Lytton got his idea of *vril*. It is a lucky thing, indeed, that in the face of virtues and philanthropy that grace our age — the age of iniquitous wars of anarchist and dynamiters — the secrets contained in the book discovered in Numa's tomb should have been burnt. But the Science of Circe and Medea is not lost. One can discover it in the apparent gibberish of the *Tantrika* Sutras and the *Kuku-ma* of the Bhootanee and the Sikkim *dug-pas* the "Red-caps" of Tibet and even in the sorcery of the Nilgery *Mula Kuroomba*. Very luckily few outside the high practitioners of the *Left* Path — and of the Adepts of the Right one in whose hands the weird secrets of the real meaning are safe — understand the "black" evocations. Otherwise, the Western, as much as the Eastern *dug-pas* might make short work of their enemies. The name of the latter — *is legion*, for, the direct descendants of the antediluvian sorcerers hate all those *who are not with them*, arguing that therefore — they are against them.

As for the "Little Albert" — though even this half-esoteric, small volume has become a literary relic and even the "Great Albert["] or the "Red Dragon" together with the numberless old copies still in existence, the sorry remains of the mythical Mother Shiptons and the Merlins — (we mean the *false* one) — all these are vulgarised imitations of the original works of the same names. Thus the *"Petit Albert"* is the disfigured imitation of the great work written in Latin by Bishop Adalbert — an occultist of the VIIIth century sentenced by the second Roman *Concilium* — a work printed several centuries later and named *Alberti parvi Lucii libellus de Mirabilibus Naturæ arcanis*. The severities of the Roman Church have ever been spasmodic. While one learns of this condemnation, which placed the Church as will be shown in relation to the Seven Archangels — or "Virtues" and "Thrones" of God in the most embarrassing position for long centuries, it remains a wonder indeed, to find that the Jesuits have not destroyed the Archives with all its countless chronicles and annals of the History of France — and those of the Spanish Escurial — along with it. Both History and chronicles of the former speak at length of the priceless talisman received by Charles the Great from a Pope. It was a little volume on magic — true sorcery rather, all full of cabalistic figures, signs, mysterious sentences and *invocations* to the stars and planets. These were talismans *against the enemies* (les ennemis de Charlemagne) [of] the King, which, talismans — the chronicler tells us "proved of great help as *every one of them died a violent death.*" The small volume *Encheridium Lesoris Papœ* — has disappeared and is out of print — very luckily. As to the *Alphabet de Thoth*, it can be dimly traced in the modern *tarot* which can be had at almost every stationary in Paris. As for its being understood or utilized, the many fortune tellers in Paris, who make a professional living of it, are a sad specimen of the failure one is sure to encounter in an attempt to read, let alone correctly interpret Taro's symbology without a preliminary philosophical study of the science. The real *taro*, in its complete symbology, can be found only in the Babylonian cylinders that every one can survey and study in the British Museum and elsewhere. One can *see*, those Chaldean, antediluvian *rhombs* or revolving cylinders covered with weird signs, as for understanding them, the secrets of those divining "wheels" or as de Mirville calls them, "the rotating globes of *Hecate*" have to be left untold for some time to come. Meanwhile there are the "*turning-tables*" of the modern medium — for the babes — and the *Kabala* for the strong. This may afford some consolation.

    The greatest teachers of divinity agree that nearly all ancient books were written symbolically and in a language intelligible only to the initiated. The biographical sketch of Apollonius of Tyana affords an example. As every Kabalist knows, it embraces the whole of the Hermetic philosophy, being a counterpart in many respects of the traditions left us of King Solomon. It reads like a fairy story, but, as in the case of the latter, sometimes facts and historical events are presented to the world under the colours of a fiction. The journey to India represents in its every stage though of course allegorically the trials of a neophyte giving at the same time, a geographical and topographical idea of a certain country as it is even now. The long discourses of Apollonius with the Brahmins, their sage advice, and the dialogues with the Corinthian Menippus would, if interpreted, give the esoteric catechism. His visit to the empire of the wise men, and interview with their King Hiarchus, the oracle of Amphiaraüs, explain symbolically many of the secret dogmas of Hermes — in the generic sense of the name — and of Occultism. Wonderful to relate, and, were not the statement supported by numerous calculations made, and the secret half revealed, the writer would never have dared to say it. Notwithstanding, that the travels of the great Magus are correctly, though allegorically described, that is to say all that is related by Damis under the guidance of Apollonius and translated by Philostratus — it is a marvel indeed. At the conclusion of what remains to be said of the wonderful Adept of Tyana the meaning of this shall be made clear. Suffice to say of the dialogues given that they would disclose if understood, some of the most important secrets of nature. Eliphas Levi points out the great resemblance which exists between King Hiarchus and the fabulous Hiram, of whom Solomon procured the cedars of Lebanon and the gold of Ophir. Only Eliphas Levi according to his invariable habit, mystifies more the reader than he divulges and thus leads him off the right track.

Once the subject broached, it may be as well to exhaust the data about Apollonius; the more so, as his biography and *post mortem* reputation have served as a key-note to his enemies — the Christian clergy, to slander the memory of other Adepts as great and as historical. For there is no use in trying to conceal the truth. Neither the *actual* existence, nor the memory of the wonderful *miracles* produced by Apollonius can be obliterated from History and — preceding him — the life and powers of Simon the Magian. There is more than usual malice displayed by the Church in relation to both — there is *positive fear* for reasons that shall be shown.

As a proof of the existence of a Secret Science, which the Church has vainly tried to discredit, Simon and Apollonius are selected as historical personages of the first century to demonstrate it and the causes *why they are* so anathematized explained.

The Secret Doctrine Würzburg Manuscript

§IV

Apollonius of Tyana — where born and when dead, no one knows — Unanimous evidence of the first centuries of our era that he was no fabled hero — What some critics think of him and what the Latin Church answers — A French Demonologist and an American Mathematician — the opinions of both. The *anguis in herba* of the Roman Church.

1. — *Who was the Adept of Tyana.*

Like most of the historical heroes of hoary antiquity whose lives and "works" strongly differed from those of commonplace mortals, Apollonius is to this day a riddle that, so far, had found no Œdipus. His existence is surrounded with such a veil of mystery that he is often mistaken for a myth. But according to every law of logic and reason it is quite impossible that Apollonius should be ever regarded in such a light. If the Tyana theurgist can be put down as a fabulous character, then history has no right to her Caesars and Alexanders. It is quite true that this sage, who stands unrivalled to this day — on *historically attested evidence* — in his thaumaturgical powers came within, and disappeared from the arena of public life, no one seems to know whence or whither. But the reasons for it are evident. Every means were used — especially during the 4th and 5th centuries of our era — to sweep out from people's minds the remembrance of this great and holy man. The circulation of his biographies — which were many and enthusiastic — was prevented by the Christians and for a very good reason, as we shall see. Damis' *Diary* survived most miraculously and remained alone to tell the tale. Justin Martyr spoke the truth according to his light, and had good cause to wonder and feel bewildered — but not one of the Christian fathers of the first six centuries of our era who have allowed Apollonius to remain unnoticed, have followed his example, but according to Christian custom of charity, as always their pens were dipped in the blackest ink of the *odium theologium.* St. Jerome (or Hieronymous) even gave the narrative of St. John's alleged contest with the Tyana Sage — a competition of *miracles* — in which, of course, the truthful Saint[55] describes in glowing colours the defeat of the latter (See *Preface to St. Matthew's Gospel*, Baronius, vol. I, p. 752); and seeks corroboration in St. John's Apocrypha proclaimed doubtful even by the Church.[56]

Therefore, it is, that nobody can say *where* or *when* Apollonius was born and every one is as ignorant of the date and place where he died. Some think he was 80 or 90, others a 100 and even 117 years old at the time of his death. But, whether he ended his days at Ephesus in the year 96 A.D., as some have it; or whether the event took place at Lindus in the Temple of Pallas-Athene, or whether, again he disappeared from the Temple of Diktymia, or, as others maintain, he did not die at all, but when 100 years old renewed his life by *magic* and went working on for the benefit of humanity — no one can tell. Alone the Secret Records have noted his birth and subsequent career. But then — "who hath believed in *that* report!"

---

55. Jerome is the Father who having found the authentic and original Evangel (the Hebrew text) by Matthew the apostle-publican, in the library of Caesarea, *"written by the hand* of Matthew" (Hieronymus: "De Virus," illust. Cap 3) — as he himself admits it — set it down as heretical and *substituted* his own Greek text for it. And it is also he who perverted the text in the *Book of Job* to enforce belief in *the resurrection in flesh.* (See Isis Unveiled, Vol. II pp. 181 and 182 et seq.)

56. De Mirville gives the following thrilling account of the "contest." John, pressed, as St. Jerome tells us, by all the Churches of Asia to proclaim more solemnly (in the face of the miracles of Apollonius) the divinity of Jesus Christ, after a long prayer with the disciples on the Mount of Patmos and having inebriated himself with divine Spirit, made heard amid thunder and lightning his famous *in principis erat Verbum.* When that sublime extaces [extasy] that caused him to be named the *"Son of Thunder"* — had passed, Apollonius was compelled to retire and disappear. Such was his defeat, less bloody, but as hard as that of Simon — the magician. ("The Magician Theurgist" p. 63, Vol. 6 of *Pneumatologie.*) For our part who have never heard of *extasies producing* thunder and lightning — we are at a loss to understand the meaning.

That which history knows is that Apollonius was an enthusiastic founder of a new school of contemplation. Perhaps less metaphorical and more practical than Jesus, he nevertheless inculcated the same quintessence of Spirituality, the same high moral truths. He is accused of having confined them to the higher classes of society instead of doing what Buddha and Jesus did — to preach them to the poor and the afflicted. Of his reasons for acting in such an exclusive way it is impossible to judge at so late a date. But born, as we are told, among the aristocracy it is very likely that he desired to finish the work undone in this particular direction by his predecessor and sought to offer "peace on earth and good will to *all* men," not alone to the outcaste and the criminal. Therefore, he congregated with the Kings and the mighty ones of the age. Nevertheless the two "miracle workers" exhibited striking similarity of purpose. Still earlier than Apollonius had appeared Simon Magus called "The Great Power of God." His "miracles" are both more wonderful, more varied, and better attested than those either of the apostles or of the Galilean Initiate himself.[57] (Materialism denies the fact in both cases, but HISTORY affirms.) Apollonius followed both; and how great and renowned were his miraculous works in comparison with all others as the Kabalists claim, we have history again and Justin Martyr to corroborate us.

The calumnies set afloat against him were as numerous as they were false. So late as eighteen centuries after his death he was defamed by Bishop Douglas in his work against miracles. In this the Right Reverend bishop crushed himself against historical facts. But it is not in *miracles* but in the identity of doctrines preached that we have to look for a similarity between Buddha, Jesus and Apollonius. If we study the question with a dispassionate mind, we will soon perceive that the ethics of Gautama, Plato, Apollonius, Jesus, Ammonius Sakkas, and his disciples, were all based on the same mystic philosophy. That

---

57. Events change; human nature never does. Therefore knowing by personal experience what fanaticism, and *odium theologium* can do, to what an extent of falsehood and calumny, of malice and invention it can and does go in our modern day, we reject *a priori* the cock and bull story of St. Peter having caused the fall of Simon Magus in their contest for miraculous *flying*. (See *Section* V.)

all worshipped one Deity (God) whom they considered as the "Father" of Humanity, who lives in man as man lives in Him, or as the Incomprehensible Creative Principle; all led God-like lives. Ammonius speaking of his philosophy taught that their school dated from the days of Hermes who brought his wisdom from India. It was the same mystical contemplation throughout as that of the Yogin: the communion of the Brahman with his own luminous Self — the "Atman."

The ground work of the Eclectic School was thus identical with the doctrines of the Yogis, and the Hindu Mystics and proves a common source with the earlier Buddhism of the disciples of Gautama.

The *Ineffable Name*, in the search for which so many Kabalists — unacquainted with any Oriental or even European Adept — vainly consume their knowledge and lives, dwells latent in the heart of every man. This mirific name which according to the most ancient oracles, "rushes into the infinite worlds ἀχοιμήτω σροφάλιγγι," can be obtained in a twofold way: by regular initiation, and through the "small voice" which Elijah heard in the Cave of Horeb, the mount of God. And "when Elijah heard it he wrapped his *face in his mantle* and stood in the entering of the cave. And behold there came the voice.["]

When Apollonius of Tyana desired to hear the "small voice," he used to wrap himself up entirely in a mantle of fine wool, on which he placed both his feet, after having performed certain magnetic passes, and pronounced not the "name" but an invocation well known to every adept. Then he drew the mantle over his head and face, and his translucid or astral spirit was free. On ordinary occasions he wore wool no more than the priests of the temples. The possession of the secret combination of the "name" gave the hierophant supreme power over every being, human or otherwise, inferior to himself in soul strength.

2. — *The Roman Church dreads the publication of the real life of Apollonius.*

Whatever school he belonged to, one fact is evident. Apollonius left *an imperishable name behind him*. Hundreds of works were written upon this wonderful man, historians have seriously discussed him — pretentious fools unable to come to any conclusion about this sage have denied his very existence. As to the Roman Church as said already, *she has ever feared him and dreads his name* to this day. Her policy seems to direct the impression left by Apollonius into another channel — a well known stratagem and a very old one. Indeed, while admitting every one of his "miracles" and calling them by the name, the Jesuits have set afloat a double-current of thought. One party seeks to show Apollonius as *a Medium of Satan*, surrounding his theurgical powers by a most wonderful and dazzing light, while the other pretends to regard the whole as a clever *romance* written with a predetermined object in view.

In his voluminous Memoirs on Satan, the Marquis de Mirville in the course of his pleading for the recognition of the enemy of God in Spiritual phenomena devotes a whole chapter to the great Adept. The following *verbatim* translation of passages in his book unveils the whole plot. The reader is asked to bear in mind that the Marquis wrote every one of his works *under the auspices and authorization of the Holy See of Rome.*

"It would be leaving the first century incomplete and to offer *an insult to the memory of St. John*, to pass in silence the name of one, who had the honour of being his special antagonist, as Simon was that of St. Peter, Elymas that of Paul, etc., etc."

"In the first years of the Christian era, there appeared at Tyana in Capadocia one of those extraordinary men of whom the Pythagorean School was so very lavish. As great a traveler as his [this] master was, initiated in all the secret doctrines of India, Egypt and Chaldea, endowed therefore, with all the theurgic powers of the ancient Magi, he bewildered, each in its turn, all the countries he visited and which, we are obliged to admit it, *seem all to have blessed his memory*. We *could not doubt this fact without repudiating real* historical records. The details of his life are transmitted to us by an historian of the 18th [4th] century, himself the translator (Philostratus) of a diary that *recorded day by day* the life of the philosopher, and was written by Damis a disciple and intimate friend of Apollonius of Tyana."[58]

De Mirville admits the possibility of *some* exaggerations in both recorder and translator; but he does not believe they hold a very wide space in the narrative. "Therefore he regrets to find the Abbé Freppel" in his eloquent Essays,[59] calling the diary of Damis a *romance*. Why? — Because the orator bases his opinion on the perfect similitude, *calculated* as he *imagines* (!!) [of] that *legend* with *the life of the Saviour*. But in studying the subject more profoundly, he (the Abbé Freppel), can convince himself that neither Apollonius or Damis, or again Philostratus, ever pretended to a greater honour than an assimilation to St. John. This programme was in itself sufficiently fascinating and the travesty as sufficiently scandalous; for owing to *magic* arts (*prestiges et de magie*), Apollonius had succeeded in counter balancing in *appearance* (?) several of the miracles at Ephesus (produced by St. John), "etc., etc." (p. 63.)

The *Anguis in herba* has shown its head. It is the perfect, the *wonderful similitude of the life of Apollonius with that of the Saviour* that places the Church between Scylla and Charybdis. To deny the life and the miracles of the former, would be to deny the trustworthiness of the same Apostles and patriotic writers on whose evidence is built the life of Jesus himself. To father the Adept and his beneficent deeds, his resurrections, acts of charity, healing powers, etc., on the "old Enemy" — would be rather dangerous at this time. Hence the stratagem to confuse the ideas of those who rely upon authorities and criticisms. The Church is far more clearsighted than any of our great Historians. The Church *knows* that to deny the existence of that adept would lead her to denying the Emperor Vespasian and his historians, the Emperors Alexander Severus and Aurelianus and *their* historians and finally to deny Jesus and every evidence about him, and thus preparing the way to her flock of denying *herself* finally. It becomes interesting to learn

---

58. *Pneumatologie*, art., Magician Théurge, p. 62.

59. Les Apologistes Chrétiens au second Siècle, p. 106.

The Secret Doctrine Würzburg Manuscript

what she says through her mouth-piece, de Mirville in this emergency.

"What is there so new and so impossible in the (Damis) narrative concerning their voyages to the countries of the Chaldees and the Gymnosophists" he asks. "Try and recall, before denying, what were in those days those countries of marvels *par excellence*, as also the testimony of such men as Pythagoras, Empedocles and Democritus who ought to be allowed to have known what they were writing about. What have we to reproach Apollonius with?["]

"Is it of having made, as the oracles did, a series of prophecies and predictions wonderfully verified? No; because studied better now, the *oracles* are no more for us what they were for every one (in the past century) from Van Dale to Fonteville."[60]

"Is it of having been endowed with *second sight* and having had visions at a distance?[61] — No; for this phenomenon is at the present day *endemical* in half of Europe.["]

["]Is it of having boasted of the knowledge of every existing language without having learned any of them? But who is there that does not know, that such is one of the criteriums [criterions/criteria] of the presence and assistance of a Spirit, *of whatever nature.*"[62]

["]Of having believed in transmigration (reincarnation)[?] It is still believed in (by millions) in our day.["] (No one has any idea of the number of men of science who long for

---

60. Many are they who *do not know*; hence they do not believe in them. (Ed.)

61. Just so; and if Apollonius perceived from Ephesus, during a lecture he was delivering before an audience of many thousands, the murder of the Emperor Domitian in Rome and notified it, *at the very moment it was taking place* to the whole town, then again Swedenborg who saw in the same manner from Gothemburg the great fire at Stockholm and told it to his friends, no telegraph being in use in those days.

62. No *criterium* [criterion] at all. The Hindu Saddhus and Adepts acquire the gift by the holiness of their lives. The *Yog-Vidya* teaches it, and no "Spirits" required for it.

the reestablishment of the Druidical religion and the transformations of Pythagoras.[ )][63]

"Of having exorcised the demons and the plague? — The Egyptians, the Etruscans and all the Roman Pontifs had done it, long before him."

"To have conversed with the Dead? — We do the same today, or *believe* we do so, — which is all the same."

"To have believed in the *Empuses* . . . ? Where is the demonologist that does not know that the Empuse is the *South Demon* signaled in David's *Psalms* and dreaded then as it is feared even now in all northern Europe.["][64]

"To have made himself *invisible at will*." It is one of the achievements of mesmerism.

"To have appeared after his (supposed) death to the Emperor Aurelian above the city walls of Tyana and to have compelled him thereby to raise the siege of that town. Such was the (rolê) mission of every hero *beyond the tomb* and the reason of the worship vowed to the Manes."[65]

"To have descended into the famous den of Trophonius, and to have redeemed from it an old book preserved for years after by the Emperor Adrian in his *Antium* library? — The trustworthy and sober Pausanias [had descended there before him] and came back no less a believer than he had been before going."

"Of having suddenly disappeared? — Yes; like Romulus, like Votan, like Lycurgus, like Pythagoras,[66] that is to

---

63. The Theosophists and their list of *Secret* Members can testify to the truth of it.

64. Psalm XC. — But this is no reason why people should believe in that kind of Spirits. There are better authorities for it.

65. De Mirville's aim is to show that all such apparitions of the Manes or disembodied Spirits are the work of the Devil, Satan's simulacra.

66. He might have added: like the great Sankarâcharya, Tsong Khapa and so many other *real* adepts — even his own Master, Jesus; for this is indeed a criterium [criterion] of true adeptship, though to disappear "one need not fly up in the clouds."

say, always under most mysterious circumstances, ever attended by apparitions and revelations, etc."

["]Let us stop here, and repeat once more: had the life of Apollonius been a simple *romance*, never would that man have obtained such a celebrity during his life time or created such a numerous sect, so true and so enthusiastic, after his death."

And to add to this — never would a Carracala have raised a *heroon* to his memory,[67] or Alexander Severus [68][have placed his bust between those of two Demi-Gods and of the true God, (or an Empress have corresponded with him.) Hardly rested from the hardships of the siege at Jerusalem, Titus would not have hastened to write to Apollonius a letter, asking to meet him at Argos and adding that his father and himself (Titus) owed all to him, the great Apollonius, and that, therefore, his first thought was for their benefactor. Nor would the Emperor Aurelian have built a temple and a shrine to that great Sage, to thank him for his apparition and communication at Tyana. That posthumous conversation, as all knew, saved the city, inasmuch as Aurelian had in consequence raised the siege. Furthermore, had it been a romance, History would not have had Vopiscus,[69]

---

67. *Lampridius* "Adrian" XXIX. 2.
68. [Note: The manuscript here stops. We have added the missing material from *The Secret Doctrine*, Volume III (1897), pp. 136-137. This material can also be found in H.P.B.'s *Collected Writings*, Volume XIV, pp. 135-136.]
69. [The passage runs as follows: "Aurelian had determined to destroy Tyana, and the town owed its salvation only to a miracle of Apollonius; this man so famous and so wise, this great friend of the Gods, long dead since, appeared suddenly before the Emperor, as he was returning to his tent, in his own figure and form, and said to him in the Pannonian language: 'Aurelian, if thou wouldst conquer, abandon these evil designs against my fellow-citizens; if thou wouldst command, abstain from shedding innocent blood; and if thou wouldst live, abstain from injustice.' Aurelian, familiar with the face of Apollonius, whose portraits he had seen in many temples, struck with wonder, immediately vowed to him [Apollonius] statue, portrait and temple, and returned completely to ideas of mercy." And then Vopiscus adds: "If I have believed more and more in the virtues of the majestic Apollonius, it is because, after gathering my information from the most serious

one of the most trustworthy Pagan Historians, to certify to it. Finally, Apollonius would not have been the object of the admiration of such a noble character as Epictetus, and even of several of the Fathers of the Church; Jerome for instance, in his better moments, writing thus of Apollonius:

This travelling philosopher found something to learn wherever he went; and profiting everywhere thus improved with every day.[70]

As to his prodigies, without wishing to fathom them, Jerome most undeniably admits them as such; which he would assuredly never have done, had he not been compelled to do so by facts. To end the subject, had Apollonius been a simple hero of a romance, dramatized in the fourth century, the Ephesians would not, in their enthusiastic gratitude, have raised to him a golden statue for all the benefits he had conferred upon them.[71]]

---

men, I have found all these facts corroborated in the Books of the Ulpian Library." (See Flavius Vopiscus, Divas Aurelianus, XXIV in Scriptores Historiae Augustae). Vopiscus wrote in 250 and consequently preceded Philostratus by a century.] [Cf. de Mirville, Des Esprits . . . Vol. VI, p. 68 fn. — Boris de Zirkoff.]

70. [Ep. ad Paulinam.]
71. [The above is mostly summarized from de Mirville, Op. cit., pp. 66-69.]

The Secret Doctrine Würzburg Manuscript

§V

The Kabeiri, or ["]Mystery Gods" — What the ancients classics said of them, with regard to their Worship, — Christian "Solar" theology. — The seven-branched candlestick and the seven Planets — The "Christ-Sun" and "the Sun — the Second hypostasis of the trinity." — The triple Sun of the Mageans and of the Roman Church. — The explanations of the Kabalists. — Why Socrates and the Emperor Julian died. — The "souls [of] the stars" Universal heliolatry. — A Pope's Bull recommending "Angel-Star" Worship — Kepler — Who is Michael, the Archangel — The trial of the "Sun-Initiates" ["]Visvakarma" and Crucifixion on the lathe. — The Sun and Hiram Abiff

1. *Confession and Property in Common*

. . . . "And the Heaven was visible *in seven circles*, and the planets appeared with all their signs, in star-forms, and the stars were divided and numbered *with the rulers that were in them*, and their revolving course, through the agency of the divine SPIRIT." (["]Hermes" IV. 6)

Here Spirit denotes *Pneuma*, collective Deity, manifested in its "Builders," or as the Church has it "the seven Spirits of the Presence," the *mediantibus* angelis of whom Thomas Aquinas says that "God never works but through them" (Opus, II, ii). These seven "rulers" or *mediating* angels were the Kabeiri Gods of the ancients. This was so evident, that it forced from the Church, together with the admission of the fact an *explanation* and a theory whose clumsiness and evident "make up" for the occasion fail to impress even the Roman Catholics, those who believe in the *infallibility* of the Pope of Rome. (see Section II sub. section 4.) The reader is told, indeed, that while the planetary angels of the Church — to whom the latter has given a Ritual of their own and offers them prayers to this day — are *divine* beings, the genuine *Seraphim*[72] — these very same

---

72. From Saraph שרף "fiery, burning" plural (See Isaiah. VI. 2-6). They are regarded as the personal attendants of the Almighty, his

angels of identical names of planets were, as the Gods of the Ancient "false," no better than pretenders and cunning *copies* produced beforehand and through the craft and power of Lucifer, of the real Angels! Now what are the Kabeiri?

Kabeiri, as a name, is derived from Habir הבר great also Venus, this goddess being called to the present day Kabar, as her star also. The Kabeiri were worshipped at Hebron, the city of *Anakin*, or *anakas* (Kings, princes). They are the highest Planetary Spirits, the "greatest Gods" and "the Powerful." Varron, following in this, Orpheus, calls these Gods θεοὶ εὐδυνατοὶ – "divine Powers." The word Kabirim, when applied to men, and the words Heber, gheber (with reference to Nimrod, or the "giants" of Genesis VI) and Kabir are all derived from the "mysterious word" — ["]the Ineffable and the unpronouncable." Thus it is they who represent tsaba the "host of heaven." The Church however, bowing before the angel Anaël (the regent of Venus)[73] connects the planet Venus with Lucifer, the chief of the rebellion of Satan, apostrophized by the prophet Isaiah, so poetically in Verse 12 of his XIVth chapter. All the Mystery Gods were Kabeiri, as these "seven *lectors*["] relate directly to the Secret Doctrine, their real status is of the greatest importance.

Suidas defines the Kabeiri as the gods who *command* all the others Daïmons (Spirits) "Καβείρους δαίμονας — σημαίνειν." Macrobius introduces them as "those Penates and tutelary deities, *through whom we live, and learn and know*" (Saturn I iii, ch. IV.) The teraphim through which the Hebrews consulted the oracles of the Urim and the Thumim, were the

---

"messengers," angels or metatrons. In Revelations (1st John's) they are the "seven burning lamps" in attendance.

73. Venus with the Chaldees and Egyptians was wife of *Proteus* and is regarded as the mother of the Kabeiri, the sons of Phta or Emepth — the *divine light*, — or the Sun (Aimophtha). The angels answer to the stars in this order. The Sun, the Moon, Mars, Venus, Mercury, Jupiter and Saturn; Michael, Gabriel, Samuel, Anael, Raphael, Zachariel, and Orifiel, — this in religion and Christian Kabalism; astrologically and esoterically — the places of the "Regents["] stand otherwise as also in the Jewish or rather real Chaldean Kabala. How or for what reasons will be shown in the text of this section.

symbolical hieroglyphics of the Kabeiri. Nevertheless, the good Fathers have made of Kabir the synonym of Devil, and of Daimon (spirit) — a demon.

The Mysteries of the Kabeiri at Hebron (pagan and Jewish) were presided over by the seven planetary gods, among the rest by Jupiter and Saturn, under their *mystery names*, and they are referred to as ἀξιόχερσος and ἀξιόχερσα and by Euripides as ἀξιόχρεως ὁ θεός. Creutzer, moreover shows that whether in Phoenicia or Egypt, the Kabeiri were always the seven planets as known in antiquity, who together with their *father* (the Sun) — referred to in otherwise as their "elder brother," composed a powerful ogdoad;[74] the eight superior powers, as πάρεδροι or solar assessors danced around him the sacred circular dance, the symbol of the rotation of the planets around the Sun.[75] Jehovah and Saturn, moreover are one. It is quite natural, therefore, to find a French writer, d'Anselme applying as he does (in the Revue Parïenne, No. 6) the same terms of ἀξιόχερσος and ἀξιόχερσα to Jehovah and Verb, for they are correctly applied. For it the circle dance prescribed by the Amazons for the mysterious being, the "circle-dance" of the planets, and characterized as the motion of the Divine Spirit carried on waves of the ["]great Deep" now be called "infernal" and "lascive" [lascivious] when performed by the pagans, then the same epithet ought to be applied to David's dance, to the dance of the daughters of Shiloh (Judges XXI 2 i et seq.) as much as to the leaping of the prophets of Baal (I Kings XVIII. 26) for they were identical and all pertained to Sabean worship. King David (a "friend of God's") dance, during which he uncovered himself before his maid-servants in a public thouroughfare saying, "I will play (act wantonly) before יהוה and I will be yet more vile than this," etc. was certainly more reprehensible than any circle-dance during the Mysteries, or

---

74. This is one more proof that the ancients knew of seven planets *besides the Sun*, for which is the *eighth* in such a case? The seventh as stated was a "mystery" planet, whether Uranus or any other.

75. [Footnote missing in manuscript.]

even the modern Rasa Mandala in India,[76] which is the same thing. It is David who introduced Jehovistic worship in Judea after sojourning so long among the Tyrians and Philistines where these rites were common. "David knew nothing of Moses; and if he introduced the Jehovah-worship it was not in its monotheistic character, but simply as that one of the many (Kabeirean) gods of the neighbouring nations — a tutelary *deity* of his own, יהוה, to whom he had given the preference and chosen among 'all other (Kabeiri) gods'["] (*Isis Unveiled*, Vol. II, p. 45); and who was one of the "associates" חבר, chabir, of the Sun. The Shakers dance the ["]circle dance" to this day when moving for the Holy Ghost to move them. In India, it is *Nara-yana* who is ["]the mover on the waters"; and Narayana is Vishnu, in his secondary form, Vishnu being Chrishna — his avatar — in whose honour the "circle dance" is enacted now by the Nautches of the temple, he being the SUN (god) and they the Planets symbolized by the *Gopis*.

Let the reader turn to de Mirville's works — a Roman-Catholic writer or to "Monumental Christianity" by Dr. Lundy, a Presbyterian divine, if he wants to appreciate to any degree the subtlety and casuisty of their reasonings. No one *ignorant of the Occult Versions* can fail to be impressed with the proofs brought forward to show how cleverly and perseveringly "Satan has worked for long millenniums to tempt a humanity, *unblessed* with an infallible Church." To compare it the better with our version (that [of] the pagan philosophers), which has already been noticed, it is given here — verbatim: —

"We (Christians)["] he says, ["]are blamed for having plagiarized pagan symbols, planets, Sun and Moon?["] Very well; but St. Peter himself has told us "May the divine Lucifer arise in your hearts";[77] and God says (through Malachi) that the

---

76. This dance, the Rasa-Mandala, enacted by the gopis or shepherdesses of Krishna, the Sun God, is enacted to this day in Rajputana in India and is undeniably the same theo-astronomical and symbolical dance of the planets and the Zodiacal signs that was danced thousand of years before our era.

77. II Epistle II. 19. In the English translation it is said, "until the day-star arise in your heart"; — a little alteration ad libitum. It does not really change the meaning — though Lucifer is the "morning star"

Sun shall arise for those who fear His Name, (IV. 2); and the SUN is Christ . . . "I will send my son FROM the SUN" said the Eternal through the voice of prophetic traditions; and prophecy, having become history (?), the Evangelists respected in their turn: The *sun rising from on high* visited us (Luke I. 78.)[78] (Pneumatologie).

Here it becomes necessary to break the flow of the author's oratory to make a few remarks. What Malachi meant by the "Sun of Righteousness" — no one but the Kabalists know; and what the Greek, and as we believe the Protestant Church also mean, by that "Sun" is Christ, accepting the term and applying it, whether rightly or wrongly, at all events *metaphorically*. As to the above sentence pilfered from a Sibyl and Virgil who repeats it, we really cannot see the right, the Church would have to view this as a prophecy relating to Christ, seeing that both Sibyl and Virgil who repeats after her — "Here comes the Virgin and *Apollo's* reign," are held as pagans, and Apollo or Apollyon is viewed as a form of Satan or the Antichrist. The Latin Church is brave, and had the courage of her opinions at all times. Why does she not try to be as *logical* as she is daring? If the Sibyline promise "He will send *his Son from the sun*" applies to Christ, then either Christ and Apollo are one, then why call the latter a Demon? Or the prophecy had nought to do with the Christian Saviour. In such a case why appropriate it?

But de Mirville goes farther. He shows us St. Denys the Areopagite, affirming that "the Sun is the special signification (?) the sign and the stature [statue] of God" (De Divin. Nom. ch. IV).[79] ["]It is by the Eastern door that the glory of the Lord penetrated into the temples of the Jews and Christians, that

---

before he becomes that of the day — yet the arrangement shocks less pious ears, and there are a number of such in the Bible.

78. In the English text it is mistranslated into "the day-spring from on high." Another little correction of the lapsus calami of an Apostle for whom divine inspiration is claimed.

79. So did the Egyptians and the Sabaeans in the days old, the symbols of whose manifested God or Osiris was the Sun. But they had a higher Deity.

divine glory being sunlight." . . ."We build our churches toward the East" says St. Ambrosius — "for during our mysteries we begin by renouncing *him who is in the West*" (De Trinit.).

"Him who is in the West" is Typhon, the Egyptian — the West having been held by them as the "TYPHONIC GATE OF DEATH." Thus, having *borrowed* from the Egyptians Osiris, the Church Fathers thought as little of helping themselves to his brother. But then again — "The prophet Baruch[80] speaks of the stars that rejoice in their *vessels* and *citadels* (*vasa castrensia*) φυλακη (Chapt. III); and *Ecclesiastes* applies the same terms to the sun, which, is said to be 'the admirable vessel of the most High One,['] and the 'citadel of the Lord' φυλακη too."[81] "For the *sacred* writer (Solomon!)," exclaims de Mirville "there remains no doubt in his heart; it is a Spirit who rules the Sun's course. Hear what he says (in Ecclesiates V. 5.) 'The sun also ariseth,' — and *its spirit* lighting all in its circular-path (*gyrat gyrans*) returneth according to his circuits."[82]

De Mirville seems to quote from texts either rejected by, or unknown to the Protestants, in whose Bible there is no XLIII chap. in *Ecclesiates*; nor is the Sun made to go "in circuits" in the latter, but the wind. (See ch. I. 5. 6). This is a question to be settled between the Roman and the Protestant churches. The point to show is, the strong element of heliolatry in the former — hence Sabeanism to this day.

An Œcumenical Council having put a stop to Christian astrolatry by declaring the absence of any sidereal souls (in Sun or planets) St. Thomas, the angelic doctor, took upon himself to settle every difference by declaring that all such expressions

---

80. Exiled from the Protestant Bible, but put in the Apocrypha, which, according to Art. VI of the Church of England "she doth read them for example of life and instruction of manners" (?) but not to establish any doctrine as the Papists do.

81. Cornelius a Lapide. Vol. V, p. 348.

82. Ecclesiastes XLIII (not found in the English texts). The above quotations belong to de Mirville's chap. "on Christian and Jewish Solar Theology," Pneumatologie, Vol. IV, page 35-40.

meant an intelligence in the Sun and stars, not resident *in* but only an assisting and *directing* intelligence. (See opus cit., X.) Thereupon, de Mirville, comforted, quotes Clement the Alexandrian, and reminds the reader of the opinion of that philosopher, on the interrelation that exists "between the seven branches of the candlestick and the seven stars of the Revelation," and the sun: "The six branches," he says, "fixed to the central candlestick have lamps, for the sun, placed in the midst of the wandering ones (πλανητῶν) pours his beams on them all. But this golden candlestick hides one more mystery still; it is the sign of Christ, not only in shape (non figurâ solâ), but because he sheds his light through the ministry of the seven spirits primarily created and who are the seven eyes of the Lord."

"Therefore," argues de Mirville, "the principal planets are to the seven primeval spirits, according to Clement, that which the candlestick-sun is to Christ himself, namely, their vessels, their φυλακαὶ, etc." (page 39.)

Plain enough, to be sure; and one can make anything he likes with it — *now*. But what we maintain is, that before Christian Scholastics turned their brains upside down to squeeze out of them this meaning (against which the Jews, for one, and their Kabalists too have, and do now, object,) the seven-branched chandelier of the Israelites as well as the "wanderers" of the Greeks, had a far more natural meaning, a purely astrological one, to begin with. Indeed, from Magi and Chaldees, down to the much laughed at Zadkiel, every astrological work will tell its reader that the Sun placed in the midst of the planets, with Saturn, Jupiter and Mars, on one side and Venus, Mercury and the Moon on the other, whose (the planets) line crosses through the whole Earth, has ever meant what Hermes tells us, namely, the thread of destiny, or "whose actions (influence) is called destiny.["][83] But symbols, for symbols, we prefer the Sun to a chandelier. One can understand, how the latter came to represent

---

83. We are told in the Vulgate that it is before the *head of the bed* that Jacob bowed. Is it a mistake, or what, in the R. Catholic interpretation? In the English texts it is also. "And Israel bowed himself upon the bed's head." (XLVII. 31.) What similitude can there possibly be between a *"bed's head"* and a sceptre, a rod? The latter moreover has always a phallic meaning in the Bible.

the Sun and Planets. There is poetry and grandeur in the Sun made to symbolize "the Eye of Ormuzd" or of Osiris, and of being the Vahan (vehicle) of the highest Deity. But one must fail for ever to perceive that any particular glory is rendered to Christ by assigning to Him the *trunk of a candlestick* in a Jewish Synagogue, as a mystical seat of honour!

But let us see how the Marquis disposes of other people's Gods and Saviours.

"Christ then," he says, (pg. 40) ["]is represented by the *trunk* of the candlestick: He is the Vine, the support of all the solar system, and all the planets are merely its branches. St. Clement tells us that it is Christ". . . "It is impossible not to remember at this stage that Jacob on his death bed, *adores the apex of the sceptre* of his son Joseph. Now *Joseph is the prototype of Christ*; hence it is before the latter that the patriarch desired to bow down, by bowing before the apex of Joseph's rod." (Pneumat., page 40. Vol. IV.)[84]

"That there are positively two Suns — one the sun adored and the other the adoring sun" — is proven in the Apocalypse chap. XIX., V. 17 — argues the same author. "We find in it the last angel standing in the sun, inviting all the nations[85] to gather unto the Supper. This once is literally and simply an angel of the sun — who cannot be mistaken for the "Word" (logos), since a distinction is made between him and the "King of Kings" and the "Lord of Lords" etc. The *Verbum* is found in chap. VII. in the angel who ascends from the East, having the seal of the living God . . . in whom [we] have, according to St. Ambrosius and numerous other theologians to recognize Christ personally. He is the *Sun adored*, while the angel *in* the Sun, is the *Sun who adores*. Who may be the latter? . . . And who else could he be but the Morning Star, the guardian

---

84. We have been told that the "morning Star" was Lucifer, the other an infernal. "We admit it is very difficult to recognize between the two" explains the author. "But then we have *the light of the infallible Church* to help us" (page 320).

85. All the *"fowls* flying" not "nations" is said in the text.

angel of the Verbum (?), his ferouer,[86] or *angel of the face*, as the Verbum is the angel of the face (presence) of his father, his principal attribute, and strength, as his name implies. Michael that powerful rector glorified by the church as Rector potens (on Sept. 29th); he — who will fell the Antichrist, that *vice-verb*, in short, *who represents his Master, and makes himself appear one with him.* He is the *suse victor*, etc. (page 43.)

The conqueror of whom? Of Ormuzd, Osiris, Apollo, Mithra, Brahma and of all the solar gods known and unknown. For this is what the author says: —

"Thus the sun-god here is Honover or the Eternal. The prince or *Vice*-Verb (the antichrist, evidently) is Ormuzd, since he is the first of the seven Amshaspands (the demon-copies of the seven originals) *caput angelorum*; the lamb/hamal the Shepherd of the Zodiac (κριός or κύριος) and the antagonist of the snake. But the sun (the eye of Ormuzd) has also his rector — Korshid or mitraton who is the ferouer of the face of Ormuzd, his Ized, or the morning star. The Mazdeans had a triple sun. For us this Korshid-mitraton[87] is the first of the *psychopompean genie*, leading the souls of the dead and the leaders of the Sun. The immolator of the *Bull* whose wounds are licked *by the serpent* in the famous Mithraic monument . . . etc. All these are the aerial *powers* and the *rectors of the World of eternal darkness*. St. Paul said so, he called them cosmocratores, the black potencies of hell, as opposed to the συρστοιχεῖα or the *superior elements*,["] page 81.

---

86. By Ferouer, a word which the author uses freely having taken it from French works on Zoroaster, he means probably the *reverse* aspect of God and Angels, their lining so to say. But if Zoroaster to account for evil imagined a double nature in his Ormezd and Amshespends in whom all that was good and perfect was real and existent, he taught on the other hand that all that was evil was negative imaginary and only a maya. It was *nonexistent*. Therefore de Mirville['s] *ferouers* are a little help to him to prove his case. They are simply a Maya.

87. The spelling is given literally, as de Mirville has it.

"If from the Zend we pass on to the Vedas, we will still find the same ideas there, Indra the god, and Light (?) the first of the seven rulers of the seven (Swargas) spheres, is *found blended to a degree* with Surya the God, who *succeeds* to him and is called in turn *the regent of the Sun* (?) Aditya, and Mithra, or the friend". . . . The reader is asked at the juncture by the pious author, to notice the striking identity between the God Surya and the God Sura, appointed to conduct the souls toward the famous bridge of judgment, named for this reason the *dog of the herds*, whose identity with Sirius-Anubis (dog-star) of the Egyptians has escaped the notice of our orientalists. . . . ["]Yes," goes on the author, — "Yes; all these ideas are common to pagans, to cabalists, gnostics *and Christians*. Nothing then is more puerile than to accuse us of plagiarism. Well, we agree, and do not contest it in the least: *a very large portion of oriental ideas transpires in a great number of our sacred pages, and we blame those defenders of the faith who deny the fact*. We only ask the reader to notice the *wisdom and sobriety* of ORTHODOX gnosticism, (Latin church) as compared with the *folly* of oriental Kabalism and heathenism . . .["] (p. 44)

Nevertheless, it is this "folly," the exuberance of oriental imagery and allegory that is the *ground work* of the modern church. This can be proved on the authority of de Mirville's own statements and the confessions of more than one Roman Catholic. He glories in it and draws with pride the attention of his readers to these facts. And when he says that "the tabernacle of the Sun," and even the *solar ray* serve Christ as a *vehicle* (Vahan) ["]to enter by the door opening to the East" no one can blame us for remarking that *such is precisely* the idea of the uneducated Parsi; and that therefore the educated Zoroastrians may be regarded as far above the Roman Catholic is himself above the Zulu fetish-worshipper in his. Yet the language of the author is as contemptuous as though his church had not helped herself to other nations' property now giving it out as her own. But all that has now to be shown absolutely fallacious and useless. Yes; we all know the Orpheian verse: "It is Zeus, it is Ades, it is the Sun; it is Bacchus," all those names having been synonyms for classic poets and writers. Thus for Democritus "Deity is but a soul in an orbicular fire," and that fire is *the Sun*, for Iamblichus the sun was "the image of Divine intelligence"; for Plato, it was "an immortal and living being." And therefore, the oracle of Claros asked to say who was the יהוה(Jehovah) of the Jews, answered, "it is the Sun." Hence the words in Psalm XIX (v. 4) "In the sun hath he placed a tabernacle for himself"[88] from whence "his going forth from the end of the heaven, and his circuit unto the ends of it; and there is nothing hid from the heat thereof." (v. 6.)

Jehovah, then *is* the Sun, and thence also the Christ of the Roman Church. And now the criticism of Dupuis on that verse becomes comprehensible as also the despair of the Abbé Foucher. "Nothing becomes more favourable to Sabeism than this text of the Vulgate!["] he exclaims (see *Memoires de l'Académie des Inscriptions*, Vol. XXV, p. 2). And however disfigured the words and sense in the English authorized Bible, the *Vulgate* and the Septuagint give both the correct text of the original and translate the latter: "In the Sun he established his abode" τῷ ἡλίῳ ἔθετο ὁ ἔχμα ἀυτοῦ; while the Vulgate applies the "heat" as coming direct from *God* and not from the Sun alone, since it is God who ushers forth from and in the Sun and performs the circuit: *in sole* pursuit . . . et *ipse exultavit*. From these facts will be seen that the Protestants were right in charging St. Justin with saying that "God has permitted us to worship the sun" even though the lame excuse set up that what was really meant was ["]God permitted to worship him *in* or *within* the Sun" (Bergier, art. "Sabeism") proved to be quite correct.[89]

Thus, it stands to reason that whereas the Pagans located in the sun and stars only the Powers and occult forces of nature euhemerized into Apollo, Bacchus, Osiris and other solar gods, at the worst personal Spirits, "Gods," subordinate as a hierarchy to the one ever invisible and unknown Deity — the Christians,

---

88. The English Bible has: ["]In them (the Heavens) hath he set a tabernacle for the sun," which is incorrect and has no sense in view of the verse that follows, for these *are* things "hid from the heat thereof," if the latter word is to be applied to the Sun.

89. See *Memoires del l'Académie des Inscriptions*. Ibid.

in their hatred of philosophy accepted the sidereal localities, limiting to them their anthropomorphic "one living God" — Father, Son and Holy Ghost. Something had to be done in order to dispose of the ancient tenants: they were disgraced into demons. Confessions to solar worship are followed by like avowals of lunar and sidereal symbols being common property of pagans and Christians.

"We have just seen" de Mirville says ["]what the Moon and Crescent were in the ideas of paganism; the Moon goddess 'treading under her feet the Sun whose spouse she becomes, — as Neith, as Hathor, as Isis['] — called Ray [by?] Pharoah Tootmes 'the Mother of God' and the 'Queen of Heaven' (British Museum); as Cybele on a lion with her infant in her arms; as Semele, also [']Queen of Heaven' *at the mention of whose name the demons trembled* as they now tremble *in good earnest* at the name of the *genuine* 'Queen'; as Proserpine, Astarte, Mylitta, Hecate having dominion over the hells and power over the Manes . . . or again, as Maïa, the 'Virgin Mother,' to *whom the month of May was made sacred in Rome*;[90] as Ceres, receiving at Athens, the epithet of the 'Afflicted Mother['][91] Αχάια, and in India that of Devaki, the *immaculate virgin* with God Chrishna in her arms — etc. etc." Does this confessed adoption of the same *names*, titles, qualifications, disturb the writer? Not in the least; for this is what he says, "Well? And how could any of these concordances between these 'Moon goddesses,['] all these MACULATIONS and the really Immaculate Woman of the Apocalypse 'clothed with *the Sun*, and with the Moon *under* her feet' — affect any one? Who can fail to see, that the planet which, in profane antiquity, centered in herself all the goddesses, as the Sun was blended with all the gods, has now to fulfill in the theodicy of old Catholicism, and in the person of the Christian Lucina, quite another mission? That the *true* Queen of Heaven, and the world, *the moon of Justice*, though sharing the same emblem and perchance (?) the same

---

90. Later on that same Rome made the month of May, Maïa, sacred to the Virgin Mary. It is only a question of succession. The Greek Church has nothing of the kind.

91. And at Rome, *Mater Dolorosa*; only a literal translation.

attributes as all others — to wit, those of tabernacle and association fulfills the same mission with regard to the true sun of Justice as the planet which reflects her light (?) fulfills with respect to the Sun?[92] Since then (the Christian era) not a doctor of Divinity, not a hymn, not a faithful son of that Church, or poet, that does not repeat with that Church, 'The *Moon is the type of the Virgin*,' and with St. Bernard: [']Thou clothest thyself with the Sun, and He clothed thee with His beams'; and finally with the Church herself: 'Light that conceived the Sun and daughter of the Sun, thyself, *Aurora quæ solem paris,* et ipsa *solis filia.*[']" (Pneumat. Theologie Christeinne du Soliel 48-49.)

This must suffice. It is thus shown that the only point of difference between the exoterism of the Latin Church and that of the old Astrolators and even the modern Hindus and Parsis — lies in the entirely arbitrary interpretation by the churches of both, the Christians and the pagan systems; — especially by the Catholic, or rather Roman Church. Emblems, symbols, allegories and often even names being shown identical in both, we may proceed to point to a few more parallels in order to explain them in the light of esoterism. The Occultists have no desire to hurt anyone's feelings — the Theosophists least of all. The[y] only claim the same privileges for themselves, that the Christians are monopolizing for nearly two millenniums: common rights for all — mutual respect shown for each other's religions or — an equal liberty of opinion and right of interpretation as their opponents have.

---

92. We had thought that the moon borrowed her light from the sun and not from the Virgin Mary. This is carrying the metaphor a little too far, one should say.

The Secret Doctrine Würzburg Manuscript

2. What the Occultists and Kabalists have to say.

The Zohar — an unfathomable lore of hidden Wisdom and Mystery, indeed — is very often appealed to of late by Roman Catholic writers. A very learned Rabbi, now the Chevalier Drach, having been converted to Roman Catholicism, and being a great Hebraist, found fit to step into the shoes of Picus de Mirandola and John Reuchlin and to assure his new co-religionists that the Zohar contained pretty nearly all the Dogmas of Latinism in it. It is not our province to show here how far he has succeeded, or failed — save to bring one instance of his explanations and preface it with the following: —

The Zohar as already shown *is not a genuine production of the Hebrew mind*. It is the repository and compendium of the oldest doctrines of the East, *transmitted orally* at first, and then written down in independent treatises during the Captivity at Babylon, and finally brought out together by Rabbi Simeon Ben Iochai, towards the beginning of the Christian era. As Mosaic Cosmogony is born under a new form in Mesopotamian countries, so the *Zohar* is a vehicle in which are focused rays from the light of Universal Wisdom. Whatever the similarity found, the editors of the Zohar never had Christ in their minds.

Otherwise there would not be a single *Jew of the Mosaic law left in the world by this time*. This is self-evident. Again, if one wants to accept what the Zohar says *literally*, then any religion under the Sun may find corroboration in its symbols and allegorical sayings; simply because this Work is the echo of the primitive truths, and that every creed is founded on some of these, the Zohar being the veil of the Secret Doctrine. This, is so evident, that we have only to point out to the said ex-Rabbi Drach to prove the fact.

In Part III fol. 87 (col. 346th) the Zohar treats of the Spirit *guiding* the Sun, its "RECTOR," explaining that it is not the sun itself that is meant thereby, but the spirit on, or *under* the Sun. Now having every proof to the contrary, Drach is anxious to show that it was Christ who was meant by that "Sun," or solar spirit in it. In his comment upon that passage which refers to the Solar Spirit as "that stone which the builders rejected" etc. (Psalms CXVIII, 22) he asserts most positively that this "Sun stone (pierre-soleil) is identical with Christ, who *was* that stone" and that therefore, "the SUN is undeniably (sans contredit), the *second* hypostasis of the Deity"[93] or Christ. The latter statement settles the question. If so, then the Vedic and pre-Vedic Aryans, Chaldees and Egyptians as well as all the Occultists past, present and future, Jews included have been Christians from all eternity. Either this, or — the modern Church Christianity is *paganism pure and simple exoterically*, transcendental and practical Magic or occultism — esoterically. Because this "stone" has a manifold significance, and as dual an existence with its graduation as regular progression and retrogration: It is a "Mystery," indeed.

The Occultists are quite ready to agree with St. Chrysostomos, that the infidels (the profane rather) "being blinded by *Sun-light*, thus lose sight of the true Sun in contemplation of the false one." But if that Saint, and along with him now, the Hebraist Drach chose to see in the Zohar and the Kabalistic Sun — "the second hypostasis" this is no reason why all others should be blinded *by them*. The Mystery of the Sun is the grandest, perhaps, of all the innumerable mysteries of Occultism. A Gordian knot, truly, but one that cannot be severed with the double-edged sword of Scholastic casuistry. It is a true *deo dignus vindice nodus* — and can be united only by the *Gods*. The meaning of this is plain and every Kabalist — if really one — will understand it.

Contra solis ne loquaris was not said by Pythagoras with regard to the visible Sun. It was the "Sun of Initiation" that was meant in its triple form — two of which are "Day" and the "Night-Sun." If behind the physical luminary there was no mystery, that people instinctively sensed, why should every nation, from the primitive people down to the Parsis of today have turned during prayer toward the Sun? The Solar *trinity* is not Mazdean, but universal and as old as man. All the temples in antiquity were made invariably to face the Sun, their portals to open to the East. See the old temples of Memphis and Baalbec, the Pyramids of the old and of the New (?) Worlds, the round towers of Ireland and the *Serapeia* of Egypt. The Initiates alone

---

93. Harmonie entre l'Eglise et la Synagogue VII, page 427, by the Chevalier Drach.

can give a philosophical explanation of, and a reason for it, it[s] mysticism notwithstanding, were the world ready to receive it, which, alas — it is not. The last of the *Solar priests* in Europe, was the imperial Initiate — Julian, now called the *Apostate*. He tried to benefit the world by revealing at least a portion of the great mystery of the τριπλάσιος, and — *he* died.⁹⁴ ["]There are

---

94. Julian died for the same crime as Socrates. Both divulged a portion of the *Solar Mystery*: the heliocentric system being only a part of what was given during the Initiation, — one *consciously*, the other *unconsciously*, as the Greek sage had never been initiated. It was not the real Solar System that was preserved in such secrecy, but the mysteries connected with the Sun's constitution. Socrates was sentenced to death by earthly and worldly judges; Julian — died a violent death because the hitherto protecting hand had been withdrawn from him, and no longer shielded by it he was simply left to his destiny or Karma. For the student of Occultism there is a suggestive difference between the two kinds of death. Another memorable instance of *unconscious* divulging of secrets pertaining to mysteries is that of the poet, P. Ovidius Naso, who like Socrates had not been initiated. In his case the Emperor Augustus who was an Initiate, mercifully changed the penalty of death into banishment to Tomos on the Euxine. This sudden change from unbounded royal favour to banishment has been a fruitful theme of speculation to classical Scholars not initiated into the Mysteries. They have quoted Ovid's own lines to show it was some great and heinous immorality of the Emperor of which Ovid had become an unwillingly cognisant. The inexorable law of the death penalty, always following upon the revelation of any portion of the mysteries to the profane, was unknown to them. Instead of seeing the amiable and merciful act of the Emperor in its true light they have made it the occasion of traducing his moral character. The poet's own words can be no evidence, because not being an Initiate, it could not be explained to him in what his offence consisted. There have been comparatively modern instances of poets unconsciously revealing in their verses so much of the hidden knowledge as to make even Adepts think them to be Initiates and talk to them on the subject. This only shows the same poetic temperament is sometimes so far transported beyond the bounds of ordinary sense as to get glimpses into what has been impressed on the "Astral Light." In ["]The Light of Asia" there are two passages that might make an Initiate of the first degree think that Mr. Edwin Arnold had been initiated himself in the Himalayan ashrums, which is not so, however.

three in one," he said of the Sun — the central Sun[95] being a precaution of nature: the first is the universal cause of All — Sovereign Good and perfection; the second Power is paramount Intelligence, having dominion over all reasonable beings, νοεροῖς; the third — the visible Sun . . . the pure energy of Solar intelligence proceeds from the luminous seat occupied by our Sun in the centre of the heavens that pure Energy being the Logos (of our system), — the "Mysterious Word." ["]Spirit produces all through the Sun, and never operates through any other medium," says Mercury Trismegistus. — "For it is *in* the Sun, more than in any other heavenly body that the (unknown) POWER placed the seat of its habitation." "*Quia in sole saltem et non alibi uspiam, sedem habitationis suæ posuit*" (MINERVA MUNDI). Only neither Mercury Trismegistus, nor Julian, an initiated Occultist, nor any other meant by this Unknown Cause — Jehovah, nor Jupiter either — but that Cause that produced all the manifested "Great Gods" or *Demiurgi*, (the Hebrew God included) of our system. Nor was our visible, *material* Sun meant, for the latter was only the manifested symbol. Philolanus, the Pythagorean explains, and completes Trismegistus by saying — "the SUN is a *mirror* of *fire*, the splendour of whose flames by their reflection *in that mirror* (the Sun) is poured upon us, and that splendour we call IMAGE."

It is thus evident that what Philolaus meant by this is the Central SPIRITUAL Sun, whose beams and effulgence are only mirrored by our Central Star the Sun. This is as clear to the Occultists as it was to the Pythagoreans. As for the rabble and the profane of pagan antiquity, it was of course, the physical sun that was ["]the *highest* God" for them, as it seems now to have virtually become for the modern Roman Catholics. If words mean anything then, the statement made by the "Chevalier Drach"[96] to the effect that "this Sun is, *undeniably*, the SECOND HYPOSTASIS of the Deity" — mean what we say: as this sun refers to the Kabalistic Sun, and that "hypostasis" means

---

95. A proof that Julian was acquainted with the helio-centric system.

96. "Harmony between the church and the Synagogue," by Chev. Drach.

substance or subsistence of the Godhead or trinity — *distinctly personal*. As the author, who, being an ex-rabbin thoroughly versed in the Hebrew and the mysteries of the Zohar, ought to know the value of words, and as moreover, in writing this, he was bent upon reconciling "the seeming contradictions" as he puts it, between Judaism and Christianity — the fact becomes quite evident.

But all this pertains to questions and problems which will be solved naturally and in the course of the development of the Doctrine. It is out [not] of worshipping under other names the divine beings worshipped by all nations in Antiquity that the Roman Catholic church stands accused; but of declaring not only the pagans ancient and modern idolatrous but every other Christian nation also, that has freed itself from the Roman yoke, whereas the accusations brought against herself by more than one man of science of worshipping the *Stars* like true Sabaeans of old, stands to this day uncontradicted[. Y]et, no star worshipper has ever addressed his adoration to the *material* stars and planets, as will be shown, before the last page of this work is written even though those philosophers alone who studied astrology and Magic knew that the last word of those sciences was to be sought in and expected from the occult forces emanating [from] those constellations.

The Secret Doctrine Würzburg Manuscript

3. — THE SOULS OF THE STARS.
UNIVERSAL HELIOLATRY.

Thus, in order to show that the ancients have never "mistaken stars for Gods," and God, but have worshipped only the Spirit of ALL and revered the *minor* gods supposed to reside in the Sun and planets — the difference between these two has to be pointed out. Saturn, "the father of Gods" must not be confused with his name-sake — the planet of the same name with its *seven* moons and three rings. The Two — though in one sense as identical as — physical man and his soul, for instance, — must be separated in the question of worship. This has to be done the more carefully in the case of the seven planets and their spirits, as the whole formation of the Universe is attributed to them in the secret teachings. The same difference has to be shown again between the stars of the Great Bear, the Riksha and the *Chitra Sikhandina* "the bright crested" and the Rishis — the mortals and Sages who have appeared on Earth during the *Satya Yuga*. If all of these have been so far closely united in the visions of the Seer of every age — the Bible-Seers included — there must have been a reason for it. Nor need one go back so far into the periods of "superstition" and *unscientific* fancies to find great men in one epoch sharing in them. It is well known that Kepler, the Eminent Astronomer, in common with many other great men who believed the heavenly bodies ruling favorably or adversely the fates of men and nations — fully credited, besides this, the idea that all heavenly bodies — even our own earth — are endowed with living and thinking souls.

Le Couturier's opinion is worthy of notice in this relation. "We are too inclined,["] says that Savant, ["]to criticize unsparing[ly] everything concerning astrology and its ideas. Nevertheless, our criticism, to be one, ought, lest it should be proved aimless to *know at least what are in truth those ideas*? And when among men, that we so criticize there are those who bear the names of and who are known to the world as Regis Montanus, Tycho Brahe, KEPLER, etc. etc., there is some reason *why we should be prudent*. Kepler was an astrologer by profession, who became an astronomer casually, (accessoirement). He was earning his livelihood by genethliacal figures, which indicating the state of the heavens at the moment of birth of individuals, were a means which every one resorted to for horoscopes. That great man was a believer in the principle of astrology without accepting all its foolish results.["][97]

But Astrology is nevertheless proclaimed a sinful science and tabooed together with Occultism by the churches. It is very doubtful, however whether mystic "Star Worship" can be so easily laughed down as people imagine — not at any rate by the Roman Church (see Appendix I to section IV). The hosts of her angels, cherubs and Planetary Archangels are identical with the *minor* gods of the pagans. As to their "Great Gods" if Mars has been shown — on the admission of even the enemies of the pagan astrologer — to have been regarded by the latter simply as the *personified* strength of the one HIGHEST impersonal Deity, Mercury, as its omniscience; Jupiter — its omnipotency and so on, then the superstition of the pagan has indeed become the "religion" of the millions of civilized nations — of the Roman Catholics, for one. For with the latter Jehovah is the synthesis of the seven *Elohim*, the eternal of all attributes and forces, the Alei of the Aleim, and the Adonai of the Adonim. And if with them Mars is now called St. Michael the "*strength* of god," Mercury — has become Gabriel, the "Omniscience and Fortitude of the Lord" and Raphael "the blessing or healing power of God" — this is simply a change of names, the characters behind their masks remaining the same.

Nor are the pagans to be so despised for having adopted the names and numbers of their planets for the days of their week and their appellation (the Arabs calling their week tsaba to this day) — since it is hardly 200 years ago, that the Ausburgian Jesuits clamoured to be permitted to do the same.[98]

---

97. Musée des Sciences, p. 230.

98. This pious and curious attempt was denounced some years since by Camille Flammarion, the French astronomer. He shows two Ausburgian Jesuits, Schiller and Bayer who felt quite anxious to change the names of the whole Sabean host of the starry heavens and worship them again under Christian names! Having anathematized the *idolatrous* sun worshippers for over fifteen centuries, the church now seriously proposed to continue heliolatry — to the letter, this time — as

Only as it was dangerous for their Church owing to reasons given in Appendix A of this chapter, to call them by the names of their "Seven Spirits["] they proposed the plan as given in the footnote below. Yet they believe in these "Seven Spirits" all the same and notwithstanding they are identical gods worshipped by the Sabeans. They regard them as the Powers and *representatives* of God, his attributes, created by him for the purpose of manifesting himself through them. It thus follows that no Astrologer or occultist should be tabooed by His Holiness or any of the Faithful Sons of Rome, since it is admitted by every Roman Catholic that the *"seven spirits of the Presence are represented by an equal number of planets, the living Entities called* ARCH-ANGELS *having a right to being designated as 'Star-Spirits'* (*Esprits-Etoiles*), *Anges des Planetes* and *Anges des astres*["] (Pneumatol. p. 335, *et seq.* Vol. III). The less so since Pope Pius the Vth (a saint) wrote in a Bull addressed to Spain when the *Star Worship* was granted to it, the following: "One could never exalt too much the SEVEN RECTORS of *the worlds, figured* (represented) by the SEVEN PLANETS . . . . It is consoling for this century (XVIth) to see by the grace of God, *the worship* (culte) of *the* SEVEN FLAMING (*Ardoules*) lights

---

their idea was to substitute for pagan myths biblical and (in their ideas) real personages. They would have called the Sun "Christ"; the Moon, "Virgin Mary," *Saturn* "Adam"; *Jupiter*, "Moses!" *Mars* "Joshua"; Venus, "John the Baptist"; and Mercury "Elias." And very proper substitutes too, showing the great familiarity of the Catholic church with ancient Pagan and Kabalistic learning and its readiness perhaps, to at last confess the source whence came their own myths. For is not King Messiah the Sun, the Demiurge of the Sun-worshippers under various names? Is he not the Egyptian Osiris and the Grecian Apollo? And what more appropriate name than Virgin Mary for the pagan Didna Astarte, ["]The Queen of Heaven," against which Jeremiah exhausted a whole vocabulary of imprecations? Such an adoption would have been historically as well as religiously correct. "Two large plates were prepared," says Flammarion (in one of the numbers of *"La Nature"*) ["]and represented the Heavens with popes, saints, martyrs and personages of the Old and New Testament completed this Christian Sabeanism. The disciples of Loyola used every exertion to make this plan succeed."

and their SEVEN STARS (astres) regaining all its lustre in the Christian Republic!"

The above is the textual translation from de Mirville's *Pneumatologie des Espirits* (Vol. II, pp. 357-358) and therefore — *no calumny*.

In that same century — namely in 1561, — a special and privileged temple for the worship of the "Star-Spirits," the church of ["]St. Mary of the Angels," was built at Rome. Paul IV had commissioned Michael Angelo to draw the plan in 1558 *after* a *terrible epidemic* of POSSESSION, that had spread all over the "Holy City," and three years after, the Romans had their *Birs*-Nimrod of the seven planets, whose Regents are known as the "seven Eyes of the Lord, which run to and fro through the whole earth" (Zechar., IV. 10). They are most decidedly — "the seven branches of the candlestick, the seven lamps of the sanctuary that St. Denys the Areopagite represents as placed in the hall of Supersubstantial Trinity, *collo catos vestibule supersubstantialis* TRINITATIS."[99] And as all the mysteries, from Trinity to upholstery, that exists in the Kingdom of heaven must be repeated in the church — "as above, so is it below," says Hermes — "it is to these spirits that Rome dedicates her finest basilicas, and that the sovereign pontifs know by officiating in their temples certain days, surrounded with the seven candlesticks and the seven acolytes *that we find again in all the pagan cults*" — explains de Mirville. (Pneum. V. II. 328.)

The Dalai-Lama's mitre has seven ridges in honour of the seven chief Dhyan-Buddhas. In the *Ritual Funeraire* of the Egyptians,[100] the defunct is made to exclaim, "Salutation to you oh Princes, who stand in the presence of Osiris . . . send me the grace to have my sins destroyed as you have done for the *seven spirits* who follow their Lord . . ."

Brahma's head is ornamented with *seven* rays, and he is followed by the *Seven* Rishis, in the *seven swargas,* etc. China has her *seven pagodas*. The Greeks have their *seven* Cyclopes,

---

99. *De Eivinis Nom*. Chap. V.

100. Chap. VIII and XII of Revelations: "There was war in heaven. Michael and his angels fought against the Dragon." etc. (7) — and the great dragon was cast out (9).

seven Demiurgi and the Mystery gods the Seven Kabeiri, whose chief was Jupiter — Saturn, and with the Jews — Jehovah. Now — the latter deity has become chief of all — the highest and the one God, and his place is taken by *Michael* (Michael). He is the ["]chief of the Host" (tsaba); the *"Archistrategus* of the Lord's Army"; the ["]conquerors of the Devil." — *Victor Diabolis* and the "Archisatrap of the Sacred Militia," he, who slew the ["]great DRAGON." Unfortunately Astrology and Symbology, having no inducement to veil old things with new masks, have preserved the real name of Mikael — "that was Jehovah," Mikael being the angel of the face of the Lord[101] "the guardian of the Planets" and the living image of God, or as well expressed in Hebrew מנאל,— who (is) as God or, who is like unto God — represents the deity in his visits to earth. It is he who cast out the Serpent.[102] "Mikael" — exclaims de Mirville in a fit of pious rapture, ["]Mi-ka-el . . . is the most brilliant star of all the Angelic order . . . the guardian and defender of the CHRIST-SUN so near his Master that several heretics, Calvin among others, have completely confused him with him," (that Master or Christ).[103] At the same time, reviling the God of the Nabatheans, Saturn, [( ]he calls him Le Dieu Mauvais), the "bad," the wicked God or Satan.

Nevertheless, Mikael, being the agent of the planet Saturn is — SATURN. His mystery name is *Sabbathiel*, because he presides over *Sabbath* — the Jewish day, as also over the Astrological Saturday. This accounts for the necessity in Rome, while *reintroducing* Spirit-Worship of having their real Jewish and Kabalistic names rubbed out from their picture, at "St. Marie des Anges" (see app. A). Once identified, the reputation of the Christian conqueror of the Devil is in a still greater danger through the further identifications. Biblical angels are called Malachim, the messengers between God, (or rather gods) and men. In Hebrew מנאל, Malach is also "a King" and Maleck or Meleck was likewise MOLOCK, or again Saturn the Seb of

---

101. Isaiah, LXXIII [LXIII], 9.

102. Translated by Viscount de Rougemont, see des annales des philosophie chritienne, 7th year. 1861.

103. See Pneumatologie des Esprits Vol. II, p. 353.

Egypt to whom *Dies Saturne* or Sabbath was dedicated. The Sabeans separated and distinguished the planet Saturn from its god, far more than the Roman Catholics do their angels from their stars; and the Kabalists make of the Archangel Mikael the patron of the *Seventh* work of Magic. "In theological symbolism Jupiter (the Sun) is the *resurrected* Saviour and Saturn — God the Father: Jehovah" says Eliphas Levi, who *ought* to know, having been *an* Abbé.[104] Jehovah and the Saviour *Saturn* and *Jupiter* being thus one and Mikael called the ["]*living image of God*" it does seem dangerous for the Church to call Saturn — SATAN — le dieu Mauvais.

However, Rome is strong in casuistry and will get out of this as she gets out of every other *identification,* with glory to herself and to *her own* full satisfaction. But all her dogmas and rituals do seem like pages torn out from the history of Occultism.

And if, we are told, that "Star" or angel-worship in Rome happened in days of old, in the XVIth century and was abolished by the church — we say not at all and have the means of proving what we assert. We point to the year 1862, hardly twenty years ago. Most energetic efforts were made in those days by the whole Roman Catholic world, as at Rome, for the restoration of "Star and Angel worship." The numerous and imposing associations formed in Italy, Bavaria and throughout all Germany for the reestablishment in Roman Catholic Europe of religious services in honour of our (Kabeirian and Kabalistic) seven spirit-planets — are well known to all, and need no corroboration.

But what is less known, is the extremely thin partition that separates the Kabalistic and Chaldean theosophy from Roman Catholic angelology and theodicy and which is now confessed to by the latter. One can hardly believe one's eyes in reading the following. The reader will please notice the underlined passages: —

"One of the most characteristic features of our holy Scriptures is, *the calculated discretion used in the enumeration of mysteries the less directly useful to our Salvation* . . . Thus,

---

104. *Dogma et Ritual,* Vol. II. 116.

beyond those 'myriads of myriads' of Angelic creatures just noticed, beyond the nine choirs (of Archangels and Angels)[105] and all these divisions prudently elementary, there are, certainly many others, whose very names have not yet reached us:[106] For, as says very excellently St. Chrysostomus, 'There are doubtless *sine dubio*, many other orders of Virtues (celestial beings) whose denominations, we are far from knowing . . .The nine orders are not by a great deal the only populations in heaven, where, on the contrary, *are to be found* numberless tribes, inhabitants infinitely varied, and of which, it would be impossible *to give the slightest idea* through human tongue . . . Paul, who *had learned their names*, reveals to us their existence. . .'["] etc. etc. (De Incomprehensibili naturâ *Dei*, 1. IV).

["]It would thus amount *to a gross mistake to see merely errors* in the angelology of the Kabalists and Gnostics, so severely treated by the Apostle of Nations" explains the Marquis de Mirville now coquetting with those whom he generally designates "as demon-worshippers." — ["]For his (Paul's) imposing censure reached *only their exaggerations, vicious interpretations*, and what is more, the *application of those handsome (beaux)* titles, *to the miserable personnel* of DEMONIACAL USURPATORS.[107] Often, nothing so resembled each other as the *language of the Judges and that of the convicts* (of Saints and Occultists). One has to penetrate deeply into this *dual comparative* study (of creed and profession) and what is still better, *to trust blindly* for it, *to the* TRIBUNAL (the Church of Rome, of course) to make oneself to seize precisely the difference that constitutes the error . . . . The Gnosis

---

105. If enumerated, they will be found the Hindu "divisions["] and choirs of devas and the Dhyan Chohans of Esoteric Buddhism.

106. But this fact has not prevented the Roman Church from adopting them all the same, accepting them from ignorant though perchance sincere church fathers, who, had borrowed them from Kabalist Jews and Pagans.

107. To call "USURPATORS" those who *preceded* the Christian Beings for whose benefit these same titles were *borrowed* is carrying *paradoxical anachronism* a little too far.

condemned by St. Paul remains nevertheless, for him as for Plato, 'the Supreme Knowledge['] of all truths and of THE BEING, par excellence, ὁ ὄντως ὤν (Repub. I. VI). The Ideas, *types,* ἀρχαί of the greek philosopher, the Intelligences of Pythagoras, the *æons* or *emanations* the occasion of so much reproach to the first heretics, the *Demiurge,* the architect of the world under his father's direction (of the pagan), the Λογος or *Verbum,* chief of those Intelligences, the σοφια or Wisdom, the *unknown* God, the EnSoph, or the It of *the Infinite* (of the Kabalists), the angelical periods —¹⁰⁸ the *seven* spirits, the depths of Ahriman, the World's Rectors, the Archontes of the air, the *God of this world,* the *pleroma* of the intelligence, and down to *Metraton* the angels of the Jews, *all this is found word for word, as so many truths,* in *the works of our greatest doctors of divinity* and IN ST. PAUL."¹⁰⁹

If an Occultist eager to charge the church with a *numberless series* of *plagiarisms* were to write the above could he have written more strongly? And have we, or have we not the right after such a complete confession to reverse the tables and say of the Roman Catholics and others, what is said of the Gnostics and Occultists. "They used our expressions and rejected our doctrines." For it is not the "promoters of the *false gnostics"* who had all these expressions from their archaic ancestors, who helped themselves to our (your) expressions, but verily the "fathers["] and *your* theologians, who helped themselves to *our* nest and have tried ever since to soil it.

All this is of a piece with the regular tactics of the Jesuits, who are, in fact, the Roman Catholic church, and not the Pope and Cardinals as is commonly supposed. We say the Jesuits are the Roman church in the sense that a parasite twining itself round a tree and living a vampire life upon it may be said to be the tree itself. This militant or Military Ecclesiasticism fastened itself upon Popery, because in its Subtle wisdom, it perceived in it the likeliest tool to enable it to carry out its vast designs of

---

108. Or the *divine ages,* the "days and years of Brahma."

109. Pneumat.: Vol. II, pa. 326.

Universal dominion, in which its predecessors, the Knights Templars, so signally failed.

Avoiding their mistakes, they have had a great, though not [un]alloyed success.[110] The attempt that is detailed above of substituting the material worship of the starry and Planetary Host is a mere subtle device to bring the popular mind back to that state of ignorance and abject dependence upon priestly craft and domination which prevailed when the true Kabeiric and Spiritual worship was perverted, corrupted and made gross, sensual and materialistic, in place of the Ancient Wisdom.

We need make no excuse to our readers for bringing in what may appear, at first sight, an apparent digression from the Secret Doctrine, which is now, to some extent being declared *coram populo*. The history of the Jesuits is intimately bound up with that of Occultism. It is that Protean and all pervading organisation which has, for its own purposes kept back the great truths of Occultism, making its name synonymous with charlatanism, fraud and demon worship. To this purpose was the Inquisition organised. Every imaginable device has been unscrupulously put in operation to keep the more secret laws of Nature entirely to themselves and the rest of the world in servile submission and fear. To use this knowledge and great power for such a purpose is necessarily a perversion of the laws of Nature and becomes what is known as BLACK MAGIC. When once the human mind has descended to this desecration of holy things and mental degradation there is no crime too great or too black for it to commit. It can then contemplate the greatest human misery, individual or Natural, caused by its machinations with the utmost *sang-froid* and complacency as they would upon a stepping stone to their advancement. The history of Jesuitism is the history of assassinations and poisonings, underhand dark plottings against Kings, Princes, Churches, States and Solitary

---

110. A proof of this has just come, as we were writing this statement. In the Daily News of March 29th, 1886, we find that "The General of the Jesuits has published the statistics of the Order, showing that it counts 2,500 missionaries, and that it can boast of having had 248 saints, 1,500 martyrs, 13 popes, 60 cardinals, 4,000 archbishops and bishops and 6,000 authors." Evidently the Jesuits like to boast of these results.

individuals who consciously or unconsciously cross their path. Many a maniac in a mad house owes the calamities which drove him there to their contriving. Their horrifying Principles are described at length in Chap. VIII. Vol. II. of *Isis Unveiled*. With the Jesuits murder, adultery, perjury — are condoned. To gain his aim, a Jesuit may become an idolator, has a right to kill the husband of the wife, by him seduced, and a son to kill his father (see p. 363. *Isis*, Vol. II), or even whom he (the Jesuit) regards as his calumniator.

We pretend not to give proofs of this as being inconsistent with the plan of this work. The reader who would want fresh instances is asked to turn to the "Appendix" of this INTRODUCTION and read *"On Jesuits and their Policy."* Besides which, this military and despotic Ecclesiasticism has brought the art of secret crime to such perfection, that it is next to impossible to give the proofs necessary to satisfy the rigorous demands of either Legal or Mathematical Logic. It is a vulgar error to suppose that "murder will out" always. The average and ignorant criminal is, as a rule, found out and brought to justice. The more knowing instigators and therefore the more guilty, mostly escape. If our readers will look into the history of the Jesuits as connected with that of Europe for the last 300 years and more, with an impartial mind, they will every where find the evidence leading up to the inference of what we assert. There is abundance to satisfy the Court of Equity residing in a well balanced and pure human mind.

It is to the Jesuits, unmistakably that the millions of pagan-populations, the modern Gentiles owe the volumes of the Marquis de Mirville, who, under the inspiration of his superiors makes short work of the Wisdom of the Ancients. But, we have said enough and shown sufficiently for our purposes that we, Occultists, could be hardly blamed for claiming our own property and showing our rights to it.

After de Mirville's confession no Christian will have any right to cast it into our teeth charges of blasphemy. They explain, the hitherto inexplicable, and give a reason for the strange rites of early Christendom in which so late as the fifth and sixth centuries A.D. such words as "Our Lord, *the Sun*" were embodied in the Liturgy, altered later on, into Our Lord, the God!

The early Christians painted on the walls of their subterranean *necropolis* Christ, as a shepherd in the guise of, and invested with all the attributes of Apollo, driving away the wolf Fenris, who seeks to devour the "Sun and his Satellites."

Verily those who will understand the real mystic signification of the figures of the old Indian and Egyptian *Zodiacs*[111] will have a key to every religion including the creed of the so called "*Superior, civilized* nations." It is neither "chance or prophecy" which marked with the asterisk *a* the figure of the Bull, *Aleph* or the first, many millenniums before the birth of him who is now called the Alpha; nor is it chance or prophecy again that placed that bull's head on the throne in certain spheres, pointing to a *dragon*, his horns decorated with the *ansated* or JAINA cross, the tau and swastica. Because the constellation of Taurus was never the "lamb," and that is sacred in India as well as in Zoroastrian Cosmogony, but has nothing to do with the Mosaic. The Secret meaning, among several others, of this constellation was, indeed "the divine City," the "Mother of Revelation," and also the "Interpreter of the voice of God," as the sacred bull Apis had always delivered oracles. But when other grotry [Grotry?] and his coreligionists want people to believe that the Bull *Apis pacis* of Heliopolis proferred [proffered] prophecies relating to the birth of Christ, we say it was not so. Our Solar system may gravitate toward the constellation of Taurus without necessarily Landing [standing?] for it in the "city of God" in John's Revelation. There is another prophecy concerning "a city of the Gods" that is in store for the humanity of the Seventh Race in the Seventh Round. The Occultist and the theosophists must understand the meaning of it.

---

111. Except those, who like our Orientalists deny that the people of India have ever had a Zodiac, before it was introduced to them by the Greeks of Alexander.

4: THE MYSTERY "SUN OF INITIATION." THE TWO GODS, IAO AND JA-VA.

The Antiquity of the Secret Doctrine may be better realized when it is shown at what point of History its Mysteries had already been desecrated, by being made subservient to the personal ambition of despot-ruler and crafty priest. These profoundly philosophical and scientifically composed religious dramas during which were enacted the grandest truths of the Occult, or Spiritual Universe, and the hidden lore of learning had become subject to persecution, long before the days of Plato and even Pythagoras flourished. Withal, primal revelations given to Mankind have not died with the Mysteries: they are still preserved, as heirlooms for the future and more spiritual generations.

It has been said already in *Isis Unveiled* (Vol. I. p. 15) that so far back as in the days of Aristotle, the great Mysteries had already fallen off from their primitive grandeur and solemnity. Their rites had fallen into desuetude, having to a great degree degenerated into mere priestly speculations and become religious shams. It is useless to state *when* they have first appeared in Europe and Greece when History hardly begins with Aristotle every thing beyond, appearing in an inextricable chronological confusion. Suffice to say for the present that in Egypt they had been known before the days of Menes, and that the Greeks adopted them only since Orpheus had introduced them. In an article "Was Writing Known before Panini"[112] it is stated that the Pandus had acquired universal dominion and *taught the "Sacrificial"* MYSTERIES *to other races* ("Mahabharata," book XIV) as far back as 3300 B.C. Indeed when Orpheus the son of Apollo or *Helios* received from his father the phorminx — the seven stringed lyre, symbolical of the seven-fold mystery of Initiation — these Mysteries were already

---

112. ["]Five Years of Theosophy" pa. 415. Reeves and Turner. London. A curious question to start, and *to deny*, when it is well known even to the Orientalists that in one case, at least there's Yaska who was a predecessor of Panini; that his work still exists and that there are seventeen writers of *Nirukta* (glossary) known to have preceded Yaska.

hoary with age in Asia and India. According to Herodotus it was Orpheus who brought them from India and he is far anterior to Homer and Hesiod. Thus in the days of Aristotle few were the true adepts left in Europe and even in Egypt. The heirs of those who had been dispersed by the conquering swords of various invaders of Old Egypt, were dispersed in their turn, as 8 or 9,000 years earlier the stream of *Knowledge* had been slowly running down from the table land of Central Asia into India and toward Europe and Northern Africa, so now, about 500 y. B.C. it had begun to flow backward to its old home and birthplace. During the two thousand subsequent years the knowledge of the existence of great adepts had nearly died out in Europe. Nevertheless in some places the MYSTERIES were still enacted in all their primitive purity. The "Sun of Righteousness" was still blazing high *in the midnight sky,* while darkness was upon the face of the Earth, there was eternal light in the Adyta on the nights of the Initiations. The *true* mysteries were never public. *Eleusinia* and *Agrae* for the multitude — the God Εὐβουλη of the good counsel the Orphic great deity for the neophyte.

This mystery God — that our symbologists mistake for the *Sun,* who was it? Every one who has any idea of the ancient Egyptian *Exoteric* faith is quite aware that for the multitudes — Osiris was the Sun in Heaven, "the heavenly King" *Ro-imphab*; that by the Greeks the sun was called the "Eye of Jupiter." As for the modern orthodox Parsee, he is the "eye of Ormuzd." That the Sun, moreover, was addressed as the "all seeing God" πολυόφθαλμος, "The God Saviour" and the "saving God["] αἴτιον τῆς σωτηρίας. See the papyrus of Tapheroremes [Papheronmes] at Berlin, already mentioned and the *stéle* in the rendering by Mariette Bey,[113] what do they say? "Glory to thee, oh Sun, *divine child*! Thy rays carry life to the pure and *those ready* . . . The Gods, (the 'Sons of God') who approach thee tremble with delight and awe . . . Thou art *the first born*, the *Sun of God*, the *Word*"[114] — says another inscription at Berlin. The

---

113. *La mère d'Apis.* "The mother of Apis," p. 47.

114. One just initiated is called the "first born" and in India he becomes *dwija* "twice born["] only after his final and Supreme initiation. Every adept is a "Son of God" and a "Son of Light" after receiving the

Church has now seized upon such terms and sees in those expressions of the initiatory rites, and prophetic utterances of the pagan oracles — *presentments of the Coming Christ*. They are not; for they applied to every *worthy Initiate*.

If the same expressions — as are used in hieratic writings and glyphs thousand[s] of years before the year I. of our era — are now found in hymns and laudatory prayers of Christian Churches — it is simply because they have been unblushingly appropriated by the Latin Christians; in the full hope, moreover, of never being detected by posterity, as every thing that could be, had been done, to destroy the original pagan Manuscripts. No doubt, but Christianity had her great Seers and prophets like any other nation; yet, every one of them, it seems, *has failed to foresee* a Champollion.

Listen to Plato: "know then Glaucus, that when I speak of the protection of good, it is the *Sun* I mean.["] "The Son has a perfect analogy with his father" (Epinomis). Iamblichus calls the Sun, "the image of divine intelligence" or Wisdom. "It is Zeus, it is Ades, it is the Sun, it is Bacchus," says the orphic hymn. Even Democritus characterized the deity by saying "Deity is a soul in an orbicular fire, and that fire is the sun." There was the central spiritual sun, the Sun Paradigm or the type. Socrates saluted the rising Sun as a true Parsi, or Zoroastrian does in our day; and Homer and Euripides mention several times, as Plato did after them, the Jupiter-Logos, the "Word" or the Sun. But, because the oracle of Claros consulted on the God *Iao*, answered: — "it is the Sun,"[115] — therefore, "the Jehovah of the Jews was well known to the Pagans and Greeks";[116] and "that *Iao* is our Jehovah." — exclaims the Christian. The first part of the proposition has nothing, it seems, to do with the second part and least of all could it stand as a conclusion. But, if the Christians are so anxious to prove the identity, the Occultists have nothing against it. Only, in such case, Jehovah is Bacchus.

"Word" when he becomes the "Word" himself after receiving the seven divine attributes or "the lyre of Apollo," "the phorminx."

115. *Diodorus,* "Hist." XX, Vol. III.

116. Pneumatologie p. 15. Vol. III.

It is very strange that the people civilized Christendom should hold on until now, and so desperately, to the skirts of the idolatrous and Sun-worshipping Jews; and that they fail to see that the later Jehovah has naught to do with יהוה, the YA-VA, or the Iao of the Phoenicians. *Ya-Va* was one of the secret names of a "Mystery God," a Kabeirid [Kabeiri], himself one of the many. He was the highest in *semi*-esoterisms for one nation, but in those Mysteries — he was a simple *planetary Spirit*, no God. And "the *Angel of the Lord*["] said unto him (Manoah) "Why asketh after my name, seeing it is SECRET.["][117]

However it may be, the identity of the Jehovah at Mount Sinai, with the God Bacchus is hardly disputable and he is surely — as is already shown in *Isis* — Dionysos. Wherever Bacchus was worshiped there was a tradition of *Nysa*[118] and a cave where he was reared. Outside of Greece Bacchus was the all powerful "Zagreus, the highest of Gods" in whose service was Orpheus, the founder of the Mysteries.[119] Now, unless it is

---

117. *Judges* XIII. 18. Samson, Manoah's son was an *initiate* of *that* "mystery" Lord — Ja-va, consecrated before his birth to become a "Nazarite," a *chela*, an adept. His sin with Dalila [Delilah] and the cropping of his long hair that "no razor was to touch" shows how well he kept his sacred vow. The allegory of Samson proves the esoterism of the Bible as also the character of the "Mystery Gods" of the Jews. Movers gives a definition of the Phoenician idea of the ideal sun light as a spiritual influence issuing from the highest God, Iao, "the light conceivable only by intellect — the physical and spiritual Principle of all things; out of which the soul emanates." It was the male Essence, or Wisdom, while the primitive matter or *Chaos* was the female. Thus the two first principles — co-eternal and infinite were already with the primitive Phoenician spirit and matter. But that IAO was not "Ya-Va."

118. See *Isis Unveiled*, Vol II. pp. 165 and 526.

119. Beth-San or Scythopolis in Palestine had that designation; so had a spot on Mount Parnassus. But Diodurus declares that Nysa was between Phoenicia and Egypt; Euripides states that Dionysos came to Greece from India; and Diodurus adds his testimony: "Osiris was brought up in Nysa in Arabia the Happy; he was the son of Zeus and was named from his father (nominative Zeus, genitive Dios) and the place Dio-Nysos" — the Zeus or Jove of Nysa. This identity of name

conceded that Moses was an *initiated* priest, an adept, whose actions are all narrated allegorically — then it must be admitted that he, together with his hosts of Israelites *worshipped Bacchus personally*. "And Moses built an altar; and called the name of it *Jehovah*-NISSI," or, *Iao-nisi*, or again *Dionisi*. (Exod. XVII. 15.) To strengthen the statement, one has to remember that the place where Osiris, the Egyptian Zagreus or Bacchus, was born, was Mount Sinai, which is called by the Egyptians Mount *Nissa*. The brazen serpent was a *nis* נהש and the month of the Jewish Passover is *Risan* [Nisan].

---

or title is very significant. In Greece Dionysos was second only to Zeus and Pindar says: "So Father Zeus governs all things, and Bacchus he governs also."

The Secret Doctrine Würzburg Manuscript

5. THE TRIAL OF THE SUN-INITIATES.

We will begin with the oldest mysteries of all — those of the primitive Ayrians [Aryans], whose mental and intellectual state Prof. Max Müller has described with such a masterly hand, yet left so incomplete withal. "We have it (in the Rig Veda),["] he says, ["]a period of the intellectual life of man to which there is no parallel in any other part of the world. In the hymns of the 'Veda' we see man left to himself to solve the riddle of the world. He invokes the gods around him, he praises, he worships them. But still with all these gods . . . beneath him, and above him, the early poet seems ill at rest with himself. There, too, in his own breast, he has discovered a power that is never mute, when he prays, never absent when he fears and trembles. It seems to inspire his prayers, and yet to listen to them; it seems to live in him and yet to support him and all around him. The only name he finds for the mysterious power is 'Brahman'; for *brahman* meant originally force, will, wish and the propulsive power of creation. But this impersonal brahman, too, as soon as it is named, grows into something strange and divine. It ends by being one of many gods, one of the great triad, worshipped to the present day. And still the thought within him has no real name; that power which is nothing but itself, which supports the Gods, the heavens and every living being, floats before his mind, conceived but not expressed. At last he calls it 'Âtman' for Âtman, originally breath or Spirit, comes to mean Self, and self alone, *Self*, whether divine or human; Self whether creating or *suffering*, Self — whether one or all; but self always, independent and free. 'Who has seen the first-born' says the poet, 'When he who had no bones (form) bore him that had bones? Where was the life, the blood, the Self of the world? Who went to ask this from any one who knew it?' (*Rig Veda* 1.164.4). This idea of a divine self over [once] expressed every thing else must acknowledge its supremacy: *Self* is the Lord of all things; it is the King of all things; and as all the spokes of the Wheel are contained in the nave and circumference all things are contained in the self; all selves are contained in this SELF.["] (Ibid, p. 478, ["]Khandogya Upanishad" VIII. 3.3.4.)

This SELF the highest, the One and the Universal was symbolized by the Sun, its life giving effulgence being in its turn the emblem of the *Soul* — killing terrestrial passions which have ever been an impediment to the reunion of the unit *Self* (the Spirit) with the ALL-SELF. Hence the Allegorical mystery, the broad features of which may only be given here. It was enacted by the Sons of the "Fire-Mist" and of "Light." The *second* Sun (the *second Hypostasis* of Rabbi Drach) appeared on his trial, "Visva-Karma" (the Hierophant) cutting off seven of his beams, and replacing them with a crown of brambles, when the "Sun" became VIKKARTANA (shorn of his beams or rays). After that, the Sun (enacted by a neophyte ready to be initiated) was made to descend into "Patal" (the nether regions) *on a trial of Tantalus*[. C]oming out of it triumphant, he emerged from this region of lust and iniquity, to rebecome KARMA SAKSHI (witness of the *Karma* of men) and arose once more triumphant in all the glory of his regeneration, as the GRAHA RAJAH "King of the Constellation," and was addressed as GABHASTIMAN "repossessed of his rays."

Now, the "fable" in the popular pantheon of India, founded upon, and born out of the poetical mysticism of Rig-Veda whose sayings mostly of all were dramatized during the religious Mysteries — grew in the course of exoteric evolution into the following allegory. It may be found now in several of the *Puranas* and other Scriptures. In the Rig-Veda and in its Hymns, Visva-Karma, a *Mystery-God* is the Logos, the Demiurge, one of the greatest Gods and in two of the hymns the *highest*. He is the "Omnificent" (Visva-Karma), called the great Architect of the Universe "the all-seeing God . . . the *father*, the *Generator,* the disposer, who gives the Gods their names and is *beyond the comprehension of Mortals*" as every mystery-god. *Esoterically* he is the personification of the Creative manifested Power, and mystically the seventh principle in man, *in its collectivity.* For he is the Son of BHUVANA — the Self-created luminous Essence and of the chaste and virtuous, "the lovely YOGA SIDDHA["]; the virgin Goddess, whose name speaks for itself since it personified *Yoga* power, "the chaste Mother" that creates the Adepts.

The Secret Doctrine Würzburg Manuscript

In the Rig-Vedic Hymns, Visvakarma performs the "Great Sacrifice" *i.e.* sacrifices himself for the World; or as the *Nirukta* is made to say translated by the Orientalists: ["]Visvakarma first of all offers up all worlds in a sacrifice and then ends by *sacrificing himself.*" (See Hindu Classical Dic.) In the Purana his story varies, and he is shown [words illegible: with his daughter?] *Sanjna* (consciousness, spiritual perception) who marries the Sun. And he is "the *Carpenter* of the Gods" their artificer, a kind of Vulcan in the timber line. Perceiving his daughter greatly disturbed by the Sun, her husband, whose effulgence and ardent embraces she can endure no longer, Visvakarma places the culprit upon his *lathe* and cuts off (seven) of his hottest beams. In the mystical representations of his character, Visvakarma is often called Wittoba and pictured as the "Victim" the "man-god" or *avatar* crucified in space (see Moor's Pantheon). But of this further on. We will say a few words of the programme of the "Mystery" enacted upon this theme.

In the secret work upon the Mysteries and rites of Initiation, in which very rough but correct prints are given of the sacramental postures and trials to which the postulant was subjected — together with the test, the following details are found. (1) The neophyte representing the Sun as "Sahasrakirana" ["]he of the thousand rays" — is shown kneeling before the ["]Hierophant." The latter is in the act of cutting off *seven locks* of the Neophyte's long hair,[120] and in the following (2) — illustration, the postulant's bright crown of golden beams is thrown off, and replaced by a wreath of sharp ligneous spines, symbolizing the loss.[121] This was enacted in India. In trans-Himalayan regions it was the same.

---

120. See Judges chap. XVI where Samson, also symbolical personification of the Sun, as Hercules speaks of seven locks of his hair which if cut off, will deprive him of his strength, of ["]seven green withes," etc.

121. No need of explaining that Sanjna, pure spiritual *conscience* is the *inner* perception of the Neophyte (or chela) and Initiate; the scorching of it by the too ardent beams of the Sun being symbolical of the terrestrial passions. Hence the *seven* locks symbolical of the seven cardinal sins. As to the seven cardinal virtues — in order to be

In order to become a "Perfect one" the Sakridāgāmin ("he who will receive new birth" lit.) had, among other trials to descend into *Patal*, the "nether world," after which process only, he could hope to become an "Anāgāmin" — ["]one who will be *reborn* no more." The full Initiate had the option of either entering this (second) Path by appearing at will in the world of men under a human form, or he could choose to first rest *in the World of Gods* (the Devachan of the Initiates), and then only be reborn in this our earth. Thus, the next stage shows the Postulant preparing for this journey. — (3) Every kind of temptation — (we have no right to enumerate these or speak of them) were being placed in his way. If he came out victorious of these, then further Initiation was proceeded with; if he fell — *it was delayed* and often entirely lost for him. These rules [rites] lasted *seven* days. During the first three, as said he was tried and examined as to his proficiency in Occult learning. On the fourth day — (4) — he was tied, extended, full length and with his arms stretched out on a *wooden lathe*, symbolical, of purification, his impurities having to be smoothed off, like a piece of rough, unfashioned wood. After this he was left alone, in a subterranean crypt, in utter darkness, for two days and two nights. In Egypt, the neophyte was placed in an empty sarcophagus, in the Pyramids where the initiatory rites took place. In India and Central Asia he was left tied on his lathe; and when his body had become like that of one dead (entranced) he was carried into the crypt. Then, the Hierophant kept watch over him, "Guiding the apparitional soul (astral body) from this world of Samsāra, (or delusion) to the *nether* kingdoms, from which, if successful he had the right of releasing *seven suffering souls*" (Elementaries). Clothed with his *Sambhogakāya* body of bliss — the *Sakridagamin* remained there where we have no right to follow him, and upon returning received the WORD, with, or *without* the heart's blood of the latter.[122] Only in India, the Hierophant was never killed; the

---

regained by the Sakridāgāmin (the candidate ["]for new birth") they could be attained by him only through seven trials and suffering.

122. In *"Isis Unveiled,"* Vol. II. p. 41-42, a portion of this dreadful rite is referred to. Speaking of the Dogma of atonement, it is traced to ancient "Heathendom" again we say: This cornerstone of a church

which had believed herself built on a firm rock for long centuries, is now excavated by Science and proved to come from the Gnostic. Prof. Draper shows it as hardly known in the days of Tertullian, and as having ["]*originated* among the Gnostic heretics." (See Conflict between Religion and Science, p. 224.) But there are sufficient proofs to show that it *originated* among them no more than their "anointed" Christos and Sophia. The former they modelled on the original of the "King Messiah," the male principle of wisdom, and the the latter on the third Sephiroth, from the Chaldean *Kabala* (See "Sohar"; "Kab. Den."; "The Book of Mystery," the oldest book of the Kabalist; and Milman: "History of Christianity," pp. 212, 213-215.) and even from the Hindu Brahma and Sara-âsvati (Milman: "History of Christianity," p 280. The *Kurios* and *Kora* are mentioned repeatedly in "Justin Martyr["]. See p. 97.) and the Pagan Dionysus and Demeter. And here we are on firm ground, if it were only because it is now proved that the *New Testament* never appeared in its complete form, such as we find it now, till three hundred years after the period of Apostles, (See Olhausen [Olshausen]: ["]Biblischer Commentar über sammtliche Schriften des Neuen Testaments." ii.) and the Sohar and other kabalistic books are found to belong to the first century before our era, if not to be far older still.

The Gnostics entertained many of the Essenian ideas; and the Essenes had their "greater" and "minor" Mysteries at least two centuries before our era. They were the *Isarim* or *Initiates*, the descendents of the Egyptian hierophants, in whose country they had settled for several centuries before they were converted to Buddhistic monasticism by the missionaries of King Asoka, and amalgamated later with the earliest Christians; and they existed probably, before the old Egyptian temples were desecrated and ruined in the incessant invasions of Persians, Greeks and other conquering hordes. The hierophants had their *atonement* enacted in the Mystery of Initiation ages before the Gnostics, or even the Essenes, had appeared. It was known among hierophants as the *Baptism of Blood*, and was considered not as an atonement for the "fall of man" in Eden, but simply as an expiation for the past, present, and future sins of ignorant but nevertheless polluted mankind. The hierophant had the option either of offering his pure and sinless life as a sacrifice for his race to the gods whom he hoped to rejoin, or an animal victim. The former depended entirely upon their own will. At the last moment of the solemn "new birth" the initiator passed "the Word" to the initiated, and immediately after that the latter had a weapon placed in his right hand, and was ordered to *strike*. This is the true origin of murder being simply feigned — unless the Initiator had chosen the Initiate for his successor and had decided to pass to him the last and Supreme WORD, after which *he had to die*; no more than one man in a nation having the right to know the Word. Many are those grand Initiates who have thus passed out of the world's sight, disappearing as mysteriously as Moses has, from the top of Mount Pisgah (*Nebo*, oracular Wisdom) after he had *laid his hand* upon Joshua who thus became "full of the Spirit of Wisdom."

This initiatory mystery, spoken of in *Isis Unv.* (Vol. II. p. 42) we find corroborated by Ballanche: "Destruction is the great God of this world." (which would justify the philosophical Mythos of the Hindu Siva). ["]According to this immutable and sacred law, the initiate *was compelled to kill the Initiator*; otherwise, initiation remained [in]complete. (Cruel emblem!) It is Death that generates Life!" (Orpheus, Book iii.)

All these Hierophants and Initiates were types of the Sun and the creative Principle (*Spiritual potency*) as VisvaKarma and VikKartana were, from the origin of the mysteries. Ragon, the famous Mason, gives curious details and explanations with regard to the *Sun* rites. He shows the biblical Hiram, the great hero of Masonry (the "widow's sun") a type taken from Osiris — the sun-god, the inventor of arts, and the "architect" meaning the *elevated* as high as the Sun.

---

the Christian dogma of atonement. As Ballanche says: (fol. II to 11 or page 80 bis). [See H. P. Blavatsky, *Collected Writings*, Vol. XIV, p. 263 fn., where the footnote continues as follows: "As Ballanche says, quoted by Ragon: 'Destruction is the great God of the World,' justifying therefore the philosophical conception of the Hindu Śiva. According to this immutable and sacred law, the Initiate was compelled to kill the Initiator: otherwise initiation remained incomplete. . . . It is death that generates life.' *Orthodoxie maçonnique*, p. 104. All that, however, was emblematic and exoteric. Weapon and killing must be understood in their allegorical sense." But most of the material just quoted from Vol. XIV is found two paragraphs later in the main text of the Würzburg manuscript that we are transcribing.]

Every Occultist knows how closely related are the narratives in Kings concerning Solomon, his Temple and its construction with Osiris and the Pyramid. Also the whole of the Masonic rite of Initiation is based upon the Biblical Allegory of the construction of that Temple, Masons conveniently forgetting, or ignoring perhaps that the latter narrative is remodeled from Egyptian and still earlier symbolism. Ragon explains it by showing the three companions of Hiram, the "three *murderers*," as the typifying [as typifying] the three last months of the year; and Hiram the Sun — from its summer solstice downwards, when it begins decreasing — the whole rite being an astronomical Allegory. During the summer solstice, all nature rejoices and sings; hence Hiram can give to whomsoever has the right to it — the WORD. When the Sun is in the inferior signs all nature becomes mute — and Hiram can give no longer *the Word* to his companions, the three inert months of the year. Then, the *first* companion strikes Hiram with a rule 24 inches long — symbol of the 24 hours. It is the first slight blow, to the existence of the luminary. The *second* companion strikes him with an *iron* square [—] symbol of the last season figured in the intercessions of two right lines, which would divide into four equal parts the Zodiacal circle, whose centre symbolizes Hiram's heart, where touches the point of the four squares representing the four seasons: — second distribution of time, which, in that period, strikes a heavier blow to the Sun.

The *third* companion deals him now a *mortal* blow with his mallet, whose cylindrical form symbolises the year, the *ring*, or *circle*: third distribution of the time of the year, the accomplishment of which deals the last blow to the existence of the *expiring* Sun.

"From the interpretation, it was inferred that *Hiram* a *founder* of metals, became the hero of the new legend with the title of *Architect*, is *Osiris* (the Sun) of modern initiation; that *Isis* his widow, is the *Lodge* the emblem of the Earth (*loka* in Sanskrit, the WORLD) and that *Horus*, son of Osiris (or of *light* and the "Widow's Son") is the *free-Mason*, *i.e.*, the Initiate who inhabits the terrestrial lodge (the child of the *Widow* (Isis) and of *Light*, the Sun): *Free Masonry, or Modern Initiation*. And here again our friends the Jesuits have to be mentioned, for the above rite is of their making. To give one instance of their success in throwing dust into the eyes of ordinary individuals and prevent their seeing the truths of Occultism, we will point out what they did in what is now called Freemasonry.

This Brotherhood does possess a considerable portion of the Symbolism, formula and Ritual of Occultism handed down from time immemorial, of the Primeval Initiations. To render the Brotherhood a mere harmless negation to themselves, the Jesuits themselves sent some of their most able emissaries into the Order who first made the simple brethren believe that the true secret was lost with Hiram Abiff; and then induced them to put this belief into their formularies. They invented specious but spurious higher degrees, pretending to give further light upon this lost secret, to lead the candidate on and amuse him, the forms borrowed from the real thing, but containing no substance, and all artfully contrived to lead the aspiring Neophyte to nowhere. (See Ragon's *Orthodoxie Maçonnique*.) And yet men of good sense and abilities in other respects, will meet at intervals, and with solemn face, zeal and earnestness go through all the Mockery of revealing "substituted Secrets" in stead of the real thing, whilst the Jesuits laugh in their sleeve, at the facile credulity of human nature.

If the reader turns to a very remarkable and still more useful work called "The Royal Masonic Cyclopedia," art. *Rosicrucianism,* he will find its author, a high and learned Mason showing what the Jesuits have done to destroy.

Speaking of the period when the existence of this mysterious Brotherhood, of which many pretend to know "something" if not a good deal and know in fact nothing — was first made known, he says, ["]There was a dread among the great masses of Society in byegone days of the unseen — a dread, as recent events and phenomena show very clearly, not yet overcome into its entirety. Hence students of nature and mind were forced into obscurity. The Kabalistic reveries of a Johann Reuchlin led to the fiery action of a Luther, and the patient labours of Trittenheim produced the modern system of diplomatic cipher writing . . . . . It is worthy of remark, that one particular century, and that in which the Rosicrucians first showed themselves is distinguished in history as the era in which most of these efforts at throwing off the trammels of the past, (Popery and Ecclesiasticism) occurred. Hence, the opposition of the losing party, and their virulence against anything mysterious or unknown. They freely organised *frauds*, Rosicrucians and Masonic Societies in return; and these Societies were instructed to irregularly entrap the weaker brethren of the TRUE and INVISIBLE Order, and then triumphantly betray anything they might be so inconsiderate as to communicate to the superiors of the transitory and unmeaning associations. *Every wile was adopted* by the authorities fighting in self-defense against the progress of truth, to engage, by persuasion, interest, or terror, such as might be cajoled into receiving the Pope as Master — when gained, as many converts to that faith knew, but dare not own, they are treated with neglect, and left to fight the battle of life as best they may, not ever being admitted to the knowledge of such miserable aporrheta as the Romish faith considers itself entitled to withhold. . . ."

It would be well perhaps, if the Jesuits contented themselves with making dupes of Freemasons, and converting that order into a mere convivial Benefit Club, which allures members by the prospect of refined Banquets in the Societies of Princes, statesmen and eloquent orators in speech and song. Their lethal plottings, however, have a much wider scope, and embrace a minuteness of detail and care of which the world in general has no idea. Everything must be done by them to bring the mass of mankind again to the state of passive ignorance and superstition. Which, they well know is the only one which can help them to the consummation of their purpose of universal Despotism. Little the Protestant Missionaries know that they have been made more than once to serve their hereditary enemy the Roman Catholic Padris as the "cat's paw" to draw the chestnuts for them out of the fire, especially in India and China. The proofs of it are at hand and they are carefully preserved to be made public, when the day of squaring the accounts between the Occultists and their Roman Catholic and Protestant detractors, their mortal enemies — arrives at last.

The greatest statesman in Europe, the illustrious Prince Bismark knows accurately all their secret plottings, and that it has ever been the aim of the Jesuit priestcraft to stir up disaffection and rebellion in all countries with the view to the advancement of its own interest. That greatest and most far-seeing of men in addressing the German Parliament on the 5th Dec. 1874, stated that in a conversation which passed between the Wurtemberg Envoy and the Nuncio, the latter insolently and arrogantly said, "The Roman Church had to look to revolutions as the sole means of securing her rightful position." (Times, Dec. 7th 1874.) Several historians of the so called "Indian Mutiny" have accused the Protestant missionaries of having been the direct and indirect means of breeding discontent and leading to the outburst of national feeling. We do not write political history. Therefore, it will suffice to say that in this case as in many others the reformed church and its members had been made a stepping stone and a convenient because unconscious agent. There never was an Occult Society, however opened [open] and sincere that has not felt the hand of the Jesuit trying to pull it down by every secret means. If the reader interested in the question takes the trouble of recapitulating such Societies, in England alone, and thinks of their fate he will recognize the truth of the assertion. Protestantism is losing ground among the richest and the most illustrious of the land. A few years more, and the greatest of Protestant nations will stand face to face with WHITE and BLACK MAGIC. Which will the English choose?

But all efforts and the greatest craft are doomed to failure on the day they are discovered. If Masonry was spoiled by the Jesuits they are unable to crush the *real, invisible* Rosicrucians and the Eastern Initiate. The symbolism of VisvaKarma and Surya Vikkartana has survived, where Hiram Abiff was indeed murdered, and we will now return to it. It is not simply an astronomical, but the most solemn rite, an inheritance from the Archaic mysteries that has crossed the ages and is used to this day. It typifies a whole drama of the CYCLE of LIFE of progressive incarnations and psychic as well as of physiological secrets of which neither the Church or Science know anything, though it is this rite, that has led the former to the great test of its Christian mysteries. The *newest* Initiate, the proud Rome of the Catacombs, has given *the death-blow* to her HIEROPHANT-INITIATOR, indeed — but only in Europe. Only, she has done it so *too hastily*; the Hierophant died, before he had been given the time to pass his *would-be* Successor the WORD. The sacrifice has thus proved useless and the initiation but too "incomplete." The Hierophant of the *Sapta Sindhava* (seven rivers) and of the SAPTARSHI (the seven great Rishis) is not killed and may have something to say to the modern Initiate of the "Seven Hills." It is only a question of time and patience, more details will be found in Section V.

The Secret Doctrine Würzburg Manuscript

Appendix I.
THE STAR-ANGEL WORSHIP IN THE ROMAN CHURCH, ITS REESTABLISHMENT, GROWTH AND HISTORY.

The following is compiled from several sources, — documents in the Archives of the Vatican, and other independent works. Another version of this narrative may be found in the made up history of it, by the Marquis de Mirville (in his *Pneumatologie des Esprits*. Vol. II. pp. 350 and seq.) who seeks to justify thereby the star-worship of his church. At any rate no Roman Catholic would venture to deny or even contradict any of the given facts.

In the middle of the VIIIth Cent. A.D. the Archbishop Adalbert of Magdeburg, famous in the annals of Magic, was charged with and convicted by the 2nd Council of Rome presided over by the Pope Zacharia — of using during his performances of ceremonial magic the names of the "seven spirits," — among others that of URIEL, by the power of which he had succeeded to produce his greatest phenomena. As already stated the church is *not against Magic proper*, but only against those Magicians who fail to conform to her methods and rules of evolution [evocation?]. As the wonders wrought by the holy Sorcerer were not of that character that would permit of their classification among "miracles by the grace of and to the glory of God" — they were declared *unholy*. The Archangel URIEL (*lux et ignis*) having been compromised by such exhibitions his name had to be discredited. The explanation resorted to was crafty, nevertheless unsatisfactory: de Mirville assures his reader that "this" Uriel was not the one mentioned by Esdras and so revered by the "Fathers of the Church,"[123] but quite another sidereal being. The Bishop Adalbert was sentenced and suspended. But, he had a formidable party behind him, in Germany, that thoroughly supported him. The famous Father Gastaldi moreover the Dominican monk and Inquisitor having proven in his great work "On the Angels" that the worship of the "Seven Spirits" by the church *was legal*, the name of Uriel appears to

---

123. [Footnote text not found.]

have been left, at that time merely under a strong suspicion. According to her invariable policy the church declared that "Uriel the blessed Archangel" had nought to do with Uriel, the demonical power used by and ever ready to serve the Kabalist.

To make the whole thing clear to the students of occultism, the hierarchy of the primal heavenly Powers as taught by the Occult Doctrine has to be recalled. The World of Being begins with the Seven "Sons of Light" the *Dhyan-Chohans*, who are the Hindu Rishis, as will be shown. They are called "Double" on account of their belonging to, and leading, so to say, a dual life on heaven and on Earth.[124] It is our Dhyan-Chohans then, who became the sidereal gods of the Sabians, later on, who have also become the Archangels of the Church, under their *Jewish Kabalistical names*. These are — MIKAEL — the *quis ut Deus*, or "like unto God"; GABRIEL — the "Strength or Power of God"; RAPHAEL, or "divine Virtue"; URIEL — God's light and fire"; SAALTIEL — "Divine Prayer"; JEHUDIEL "the praise of God" and — BARACHIEL "the blessing of God." These *"seven"* are *absolutely canonical*. But this does not alter the fact of their being in name and even in the occult attributes attached to their designations identical with the (*a*) Aryan Devatas and Rishis, our Dhyan Chohans, the Chaldean, Sabian Gods and the Seven Powers of the Kabalists invoqued [invoked] by these during ceremonial magic. The Kabalistic "Virtues" and the "Seven Seats" in the invisible regions of the Astral World, have thus become with the Roman Catholics and their church Hierarchy — the "seven Virtues" and the seven Thrones, "the Eyes of the Lord" and such other names.

This much explained, — their story may be continued. Until about the XVth c. and after the misadventures of Bishop Adalbert, only the first three names of the seven archangels were in odour of sanctity in the Church. But in 1460, there appeared in Rome a great "Saint," a Portuguese Monk by the name of

---

124. Any one acquainted even superficially with the Brahmanical narratives in the Puranas and other Scriptures about the Rishis, who are first Gods and then men and then again *Stars* etc.; who are sometimes Seven, then 10 and even 21 — will see esoteric meaning underlying their story.

Amadeus.[125] He soon became famous for his prophecies and beatific visions, during one of which, he had a revelation. The "Seven" appeared to the Saint and revealed to him their real *primeval* names, adding that the Chaldean ones were only *substitutes* though indeed as correct. Now these, having been used and dragged about too publicly by the Kabalists, the Church very naturally shrinked from using them in the Church Service — except the first three. "They were names of DEMONS" — *i.e.* of pagan Gods — explains Baronius. But then, asks very pertinently de Mirville, — "if these seven names are those of demons, why are they given to Roman Catholics and other Christians at baptism?"

Any how, at the same hour of Amadeus' vision at Rome, at Palermo, "a miraculously *painted* picture of the Seven Spirits, was as miraculously exhumed from under the ruins of an old chapel, on which paintings moreover, were found inscribed the same seven *mystery-names* that had been revealed to the Saint." Each name was found traced under one of the angels. Pope Sixtus IV who believed in Amadeus implicitly was greatly impressed with the coincidence. Therefore, when also on that very same day an old prophecy in Archaic Latin referring to the find and revelation was discovered at Pisa — these revelations produced the greatest commotion among the faithful. The prophecy foretold also *the revival of the* "Planetary-Angels" worship for that very period, and that, under the reign of Pope VIIth the convent of St. François de Paul would be raised on the emplacement of the little ruined chapel — which event occurred as predicted.

But it was only in XVIth century that the church deemed it her duty to comply with the requests of the heavenly visitors in its completeness. If at that time, there was hardly a church or chapel in all Italy that had not a copy of the *miraculous* picture either in painting or mosaic, and that actually, in 1576, a splendid "temple to the Seven spirits" had been raised and finished near the ruined chapel at Palermo — the Angels failed to be satisfied. In the words of their Chronicler — "the blessed Spirits were not contented with Sicily alone. They wanted a

---

125. He died in Rome 1482.

world-wide worship and the Whole Catholic world to recognize them."

Heavenly denizens themselves, it seems, are not free from ambition and vanity on quite a material plane!

Antonio Duca, another "Seer" (otherwise a MEDIUM of the Church of Rome) had been named the Rector of the above named "temple of the Seven Spirits" and began about that period to have the same beatific visions. The "Archangels" would not cease pressing him to have the Popes recognize them and to establish a regular worship in their names. As Duca submitted his visions and the messages he was entrusted with to the approval of the Church, the revelations made to him, were of course, accepted as authentic and declared divine.

There has [have] been a good many "Seers" of that sort — priests and laymen — during the early centuries of Christianity, and the middle ages. Occasionally there are such even in our own days of materialism and unbelief. The question of authenticity of those phenomenal occurrences and the trustworthiness of the *agents* chosen by the invisible visitors, rests on the methods adopted and the concern taken in them by the Church.

Thus the "Spirits" went on clamoring through Antonio Duca, demanding a wider recognition and a more solemn worship than they hitherto had received. They insisted upon having a special temple *built for them alone* on the emplacement of the famous Thermæ of Diocletian, on which according to tradition 40,000 Christians and 10,000 Martyrs were put to death. In a bull of Pope Pius IV the place [was] referred to as " a den of profanity used for demonical (magic) practices."

But there was still the difficulty which the reader is asked to bear in mind. The *"Mystery-names" of the seven Angels could not be given*: when the old and "miraculous" picture had been found, the seven names inscribed on it had been freely used in the church services, and — had provoked remarks. At the period of the *Renaissance*, however Pope Clement XI had ordered a report to be made to him on the picture and especially the names on it, with which delicate mission a famous astronomer of that day, one named Joseph Biancini, a Jesuit — was entrusted. The result to which the astronomer's inquest led to was as unexpected as it seemed fatal to the worshippers of the Seven Sabian Gods: the Pope, while commanding that the picture should be preserved, ordered the Seven Angelic names *carefully rubbed out* — "though these names are traditional and that they have naught to do with, and were even very different from the names used by Adalbert." (the Bishop-Magician of Magdeburg — cunningly adds and explains the Marquis de Mirville (p. 357).

Thus for nearly a period of thirty four years, Duca had to work in vain, before a church appeared on the spot that had been selected by the Seven Angels; and then it was only called "church of *St. Mary*,["] the "Holy" ones. A war soon broke out during which that Church was completely destroyed. But revelations — the *written* as well as the *verbal* messages — from the "Angels" never ceased, meanwhile. They still clamoured through Duca, as loudly as ever for a special "Temple of the Seven Spirits" on the Thermæ.

Thus the affairs went on from 1527 till 1561; the Rector trying to satisfy the orders of the *Seven Spirits* — the church fearing to adopt the Chaldean Substitutes for the ["]mystery names" as they had been so desecrated by magical practices. We are not told, however, why *the Mystery names should not be given* in such emergency — the "Seven" had never prohibited their use.

But the reason is self-evident; they were used as the true Chaldean forms of the Jewish *exoteric* names, now known to all, by the greatest Kabalists and were absolutely *magical*. Some of them are still to be found in old Roman missals, printed in 1563. There is one, perhaps, there are two, in the Barberini library *with the mass*-service in them and the forbidden, truly Sabian names of the "Seven *great* Gods" flashing out hither and thither.

Finally, "in consequence of a terrible epidemic of *obsession and possession* in 1553, when nearly all Rome saw itself possessed by the devil" — says the Chronicler (without explaining whether the clergy were included) — Duca's wish was realized. His Seven Inspirers were invoked and the epidemic ceased as by enchantment; the *blessed ones* "proving by their miraculous power that they had nothing in common *with the demons of the same name*" used by the Kabalist.[126]

"Then Michael Angelo was summoned in all haste by Paul IV to the Vatican." His magnificent plan was accepted and the building of the famous Church begun. Its construction lasted three years. In the archives of this now celebrated monument one can read that: "The narrative of the miracles that occurred during that period could not be undertaken, as it was *one incessant miracle of three years duration.*"

In the presence of all his cardinals, Pope Paul IV ordered that the seven names as originally written on the picture, should be restored and inscribed around the large copy from it that surmounts to this day the high Altar.

The admirable temple was consecrated to the Seven Angels in 1561. The object of the Spirits was reached; three years later, nearly simultaneously Michael Angelo and Antonio Duca both died. They were no longer needed.

But what became of the names, the *"mystery names"*? First of all, came the substitution of the name EUDIEL, for one of the seven well known Kabalistic names; — then, just one hundred years later, by order of the Cardinal Albitius all the seven names disappeared again one fine day. A little while after that, the mass and Vesper Services of the Seven Angels were eliminated from the Missals used, though the "Seven" we are still informed by de Mirville "are quite distinct from those other names" (read Kabalstic names). But in 1825 a Spanish grandee supported by the Archbishop of Palermo made an attempt before Leo XII for the simultaneous restablishment *of the Service and names*. The Pope granted the church service but refused the old adoption of the seven names.[127]

In 1832 the same demand in the petition to spread the worship of the "Seven Spirits of God," was reiterated, endorsed this time by *eighty-seven bishops* and thousand[s] of officials

---

126. But they had proved their *power* earlier by sending the war, the destruction of the church and finally the epidemic, and this does not look very *angelic* — to an Occultist.

127. Considering that the Popes are claiming to be *infallible*, such difference in their respective opinions does seem rather startling!

with high sounding names in the Church of Rome. Again, in 1858 Cardinal Patrizzi and King Ferdinand II, in the name of all *the people of Italy* reiterated their petition. And finally — 1882. Thus the Church-Services in honour of the Seven "Spirit-Stars" have never been abrogated since 1825. To this day they are in full vigour in Palermo, in Spain and even in Rome at "St. Mary of the Angels" and the "*Jésu*," though entirely suppressed every where else; all this "because of Adalbert's heresy" Mirville is pleased to think; and we say — on account of the Chaldean rabble and Jewish Kabalists using those "Angel-names" and of something more that will be explained further on.

The Marquis de Mirville is in despair; and, as he dares not blame his church he vents his wrath upon the old Alchemists, the Rosicrucians and the innocent modern mediums. With the courage of the true believer, he denies nothing, and proudly confesses to the *worship of Stars*, thrown into his teeth by the French Academicians.

"We are accused" — he writes "of having always mistaken *stars* for angels.[128] The accusation is acquiring such a wide notoriety that we are forced to answer it very seriously. It is impossible that we should try to dissimulate it without failing in frankness and courage, since this *pretended mistake* is repeated incessantly in the Scriptures as in our theology. We shall examine . . . this opinion hitherto so accredited, to say, discredited, and which attributes rightly to our SEVEN PRINCIPAL SPIRITS the rulership, not of the seven known planets, with which we are reproached, but of the seven PRINCIPAL planets which is quite a different thing."[129]

And the author hastens to cite the authority of Babinet, the astronomer, who sought to prove in an able article of the *Revue des Deux Mondes* (May 1855) that in reality, besides the earth we had only SEVEN big planets.

---

128. Pneumatologic des Esprits. Vol II. p. 359 et seq.

129. No one can see the slightest difference in it — except himself. The "principal planets" are not one particle holier than any other — for the Earth is included among the seven *principal* dominions or abodes of the Seven Chaldean Spirits and has also its ["]mystery god," which name *is in the Missal*.

This belief all along its line is Occultism and a dogma of the Secret Doctrine — pure and simple. Only as taught and practiced in the Church *Rituals* — it is ASTROLOGY as pure and simple. To avoid the accusation and rather embarrassing charges in view of the utter impossibility of denial, the Roman Church would have to resort to the philosophy and the explanations given of the sacredness of number *Seven* and the mystic connection between the Planetary Spirits (Dhyan Chohans) and their stars — by the Eastern Occultists; and this she will never consent to. Therefore, since after borrowing, Rome will neither acknowledge the origin of her "Angels["] nor desist in her anathema and public denunciation of Magic, Sabianism and finally Occultism, it is but natural that in their turn the Student of the Sacred Science should tell the truth to her face.

[VOLUME II
Evolution of Cosmos]

The Secret Doctrine Würzburg Manuscript

THE SECRET DOCTRINE

PART I
(ARCHAIC PERIOD)
CHAPTER I

A GLIMPSE INTO ETERNITY
COSMIC EVOLUTION IN SEVEN STAGES

§I

PAGES FROM A PREHISTORIC PERIOD

An archaic manuscript; a collection of palm-leaves made impermeable to water, fire and air, by some specific unknown process — is before the eye of the writer. On the first page is a circle with a point in the centre. This, the disciple knows, represents Kosmos in Eternity before the Emanation of the WORD — which is the manifested universe, — the periodical, "Only-born Son" — the ever present and the "One with the Father." The former is the Point, the MUNDANE EGG, or the germ, within the latter — the Universal and absolute ALL, the circle or boundless Kosmos, while the germ is latent and active periodically and by turn. The *one* circle is divine Unity from which all proceeds, whither all returns, its circumference — a forcibly limited symbol in view of the limitation of human mind — indicating the abstract ever invisible PRESENCE, and its plane the Universal Soul — though the two are one. Only the face of the sphere being white and the ground all around black, shows clearly that its plane is the only knowledge, dim and hazy though it still is — that is attainable by man. It is on this plane that the Manvantaric Manifestations begin; for it is in this SOUL that slumbers during the Pralaya DIVINE THOUGHT — wherein lies concealed the plan of every future cosmogony and Theogony. (See Appendix No. 1, "Is the Key Really Revealed?").

It is the ONE LIFE, eternal, invisible, yet omnipresent; without beginning or end, yet periodical in its regular manifestations between which reigns the dark mystery of Non-Being; *unconscious*, yet absolute Consciousness; *unrealizable* — yet the One self-existing Reality; truly "a chaos to the sense, a Kosmos to the reason." Its one absolute attribute, which is ITSELF — eternal, ceaseless motion, called in Esoteric parlance the Great Breath,[125] which is the perpetual motion of the Universe, in the sense of limitless ever present space. That which is motionless cannot be divine. But then, there is nothing in fact and reality absolutely motionless within the Universal Soul. (Almost five centuries B.C. Leucippus, the instructor of Democritus, maintained that space was filled *eternally* with atoms *actuated by ceaseless motion*, the latter generating in due course of time, when those atoms aggregated — *rotary* motion through mutual collisions producing lateral movements. Epicurus and Lucretius taught the same, only adding to lateral motion of the atoms affinity — an occult teaching.)

From the beginning of man's inheritance from its architects of the Globe he lives in, the unrevealed Deity was recognized by and considered since under its only philosophical aspect — Universal MOTION, the thrill of divine Breath in Nature. Occultism sums [up the "One Existence" thus: "Deity is an arcane, living (or moving)] FIRE and the eternal witnesses to this unseen Presence are — Light, Heat, Moisture" — this trinity including, and being the cause of every phenomenon in Nature. Cosmic Motion is ceaseless, intra-cosmic motion (the visible or that which is subject to perception,) is periodical. As an eternal abstraction it is the EVER PRESENT; as a manifestation — it is finite, in both the coming direction and its opposite, the two being the Alpha and the Omega of successive *reconstructions*. Kosmos — the ONE Reality — has naught to do with causal relations of the phenomenal World. It is only with reference to the Cosmic Soul, the *ideal* Kosmos in the immutable *Divine*

---

125. Plato proves himself an Initiate, versed in the lore communicated during the Mysteries, when saying in *Cratylus* that *Theos* – "God" is derived from the verb *the'cin* "to move," to "run," after observing the motion of the heavenly bodies. (See App. II. "The Mysticism of the Circle"). Later the word produced *aletheia* the ["]breath of God."

Thought that we may say — "it never had a beginning, nor will it ever have an end." With regard to its body, or Cosmic organization, though it cannot be said that it had a *first*, or will ever have a *last* construction, at each New Manvantara, its organization may be regarded as *the first* — and the *last of its kind*, as it evolutes every time on a higher plane . . . . A few years ago only the following was stated:

The esoteric doctrine teaches, like Buddhism and Brahminism, and even the *Kabala*, that the one infinite and unknown Essence exists from all eternity, and in regular and harmonious successions is either passive or active. In the poetical phraseology of Manu these conditions are called the "day" and the "night" of Brahma. The latter is either "awake" or "asleep." The Svâbhâvikas, or philosophers of the oldest school of Buddhism (which still exists in Nepaul), speculate but upon the active condition of this "Essence," which they call Svabhâvât [svabhâva], and deem it foolish to theorize upon the abstract and "unknowable" power in its passive condition. Hence they are called atheists by both Christian theology and modern scientists; for neither of the two are able to understand the profound logic of their philosophy. The former will allow of no other God than the personified *secondary* powers which have worked out the visible universe and which became with them the anthropomorphic God of the Christians — the male Jehovah, roaring amid thunder and lightning. In its turn, rationalistic science greets the Buddhists and the Svâbhâvikas as the "positivists" of the archaic ages. If we take a one-sided view of the philosophy of the latter, our materialists may be right in their own way. The Buddhists maintained that there is *no* Creator, but an infinitude of *creative powers,* which collectively form the one eternal substance, the *essence* of which is inscrutable — hence not a subject for speculation for any true philosopher. Socrates invariably refused to argue upon the mystery of universal being, yet no one would ever have thought of charging him with atheism, except those who were bent upon his destruction. Upon inaugurating an active period, says the *Secret Doctrine*, an expansion of this Divine essence without inwardly and *from within* outwardly occurs in obedience to eternal and immutable law, and the phenomenal or visible universe is the ultimate result of the long chain of cosmical forces thus progressively set in motion. In like manner, when the passive condition is resumed, a contraction of the Divine essence takes place, and the previous work of creation is gradually and progressively undone. The visible universe becomes disintegrated, its material dispersed; and "darkness," solitary and alone, broods once more over the face of the "deep." To use a metaphor —

from the Secret Books *which will convey the idea* still more clearly, an outbreathing of the "unknown essence" produces the world; and an inhalation causes it to disappear. *This process has been going on from all eternity, and our present universe is but one of an infinite series which had no beginning and will have no end.* (See *Isis* [volume II, pp. 264-265] and App. "The Days and Nights of Brahma [brahmâ]").

This passage will be explained as far as it can be done in the present work. Though; as it now stands, it contains nothing new to the Orientalist, its esoteric interpretation may contain a good deal that was hitherto, entirely unknown to Western students. And then, the supposed atheism of the Buddhist and Advaitee, may perhaps be better understood.

The second illustration in the Archaic Mss. symbolizes the primitive religion of *divine* mankind also by a circle known as the astronomical cross ⊕; the purely abstract generative and procreative powers in nature — androgynous rather than male and female, the two cross-lines being supposed to embrace infinitude. The cross became the symbol (also the Egyptian *Tau*) — and sign of the *origin of human life*, or the phallic form, far later, namely, after the physiological change of the separation of the sexes had taken place with mankind. It has this sexual meaning only when separated from the circle; when it is inscribed within a circle, it loses entirely its phallic character. The ⊕ was the pure Pantheism of the first Races.

The next illustration represents a circle with a diameter line across its face thus ⊖,[126] and the third one, with a tau

---

126. We are told by Western mathematicians and some American Kabalists that in the Kabala also "the value of the Jehovah name is that of the diameter of a circle." Add to this the fact that Jehovah is the *third* Sephiroth *Binah*, a feminine word and you have the key to the mystery. By certain Kabalistic transformations this name, *androgynous* in the first chapters of Genesis, becomes in its transmutations entirely masculine and finally phallic. The fact of a deity among the pagan gods and of making it a special *national* God to call upon it as the "One living God," the ["]God of Gods" and thus proclaim this worship monotheistic, does not change it into the ONE Principle whose "Unity

inscribed within ⊕, and also with a *Svastica* — the "Jaina Cross,["] or "Thor's hammer" so called thus — ⊕. By the glyph of the first one — the circle separated in two by the horizontal line in the diameter — the first manifested creative Nature was meant: The first shadowy deity in the perception of man was the feminine goddess Nature, the Spirit-Principle that fructified it being concealed. By adding to it the *tau* or perpendicular line, it became the glyph of the last race, of the 3rd Root-race, typifying its FALL or the separation of sexes. Then comes the Svastica separated from its circle, thus becoming purely phallic. The symbol of *Kali yuga* — is the five pointed star *reversed* the pentacle of Sorcery, thus ⛤ with its two points turned heavenward, in which position every Occultist will see and recognize in it the pentacle of the left hand science used in ceremonial magic.

It is hoped that during the perusal of this work the erroneous ideas of the public in general with regard to Pantheism will be modified. It is wrong and unjust to regard the Buddhists and Advaitee Occultists as Atheists. If not all of them philosophers, they are at any rate all logicians, their objections and arguments being based on strict reasoning. Indeed if the Parabrahman of the Hindus may be taken as a representative of the hidden and nameless deities of other nations, this absolute Principle will be found to be the prototype from which all the others were copied. Parabrahm is *not* "God, because he is not *a* God." "He is *he* who is Supreme and not Supreme" (parâvara) explains *Mundakopanishad* (2.2.8). He is "Supreme" — as CAUSE, not Supreme as *effect*. Parabrahm is simply, as a "Secondless reality" – the *all inclusive Kosmos* — in the highest spiritual sense, of course. Brahma (neuter) being the unchanging, pure, free, undecaying "Supreme Root," ["]the ONE true Existence pâramarthika" and the absolute *chit* and *Chaitanya* (intelligence, consciousness), cannot be a *cognizer*,

---

admits not of multiplication, change or form" — especially a Priapic one, as now demonstrated by the Symbologists.

["]for THAT can have no subject of cognition." Can the flame be called the Essence of Fire? This Essence is "the LIFE and Light of the Universe, the visible fire and flame are Destruction, Death, and Evil.["] "Fire and Flame destroy the body of an Arhat, their Essence makes him immortal" (*Bod[h]i-Mur*, Book II). "The knowledge of the absolute Spirit, like the effulgency of the Sun, or like heat in fire, is naught else than the absolute Essence itself" says Sankarâchârya. He is "the Spirit of the Fire," not fire itself; therefore, ["]the attributes of the latter, heat or flame, are not the attributes of the Spirit, but of that, of which that Spirit is the unconscious cause." Is not the above sentence the true key-note of later Rosicrucian philosophy? Parabrahm is, in short, the collective aggregate of Kosmos in its infinity and eternity; the "That" and "This" to which distributive aggregates cannot be applied. "In the beginning THIS was the Self, one only" (*Aitareya Upanishad*); and the great Sankarâchârya explains that "THIS" referred to the Universe (jagat) the sense of the words "in the beginning" meaning before the production of the phenomenal Universe (*pragutpattah*) [prâg-utpattih].

Therefore, when the *Advaita* [*Advaitees*] say after their Upanishads, and that the latter repeat, as in the Secret Doctrine, that "This" cannot *create*, they do not deny a Creator or rather a *collective aggregate* of creators, but only refuse very logically to attribute "creation" or *formation* rather something finite, to an Infinite Principle. With them, Parabrahman is a *passive* because an ABSOLUTE cause, the unconditioned *Mukta*. It is only *manifested* Omniscience and Omnipotence that the latter is refused because these — *sarvajñatva* and *sarvaśaktitva* [—] are still attributes (as reflected in man's perceptions); and that Parabrahm being the "Supreme ALL," the ever invisible spirit and soul of Nature, changeless and eternal, can have no attributes, absoluteness precluding very naturally any idea of the finite or conditioned connected with it. And if the Vedantin postulates attributes simply to its emanations, calling it "Isvara *plus* Maya," — and *Avidya* (*agnosticism* and nescience rather than ignorance), it is difficult to find any atheism in this. Since there can be neither two INFINITES nor two ABSOLUTES in a Universe supposed to be Boundless, this so long as it lasts, to wit, for one Mahamanvantara; nor from applying Akasa, the radiation of Mulaprakriti[127] to practical purposes, connected as the World Soul is, with all natural phenomena known and unknown to Science.

The two oldest religions of the world — exoterically, for the esoteric root or foundation is one — are the Indian and the Egyptian. Then come the Chaldean, the outcome of these two — entirely lost to the world now except its disfigured Sabeanism as at present rendered by the archeologists; then passing over a number of religions that will be mentioned later comes the Jewish, esoterically, as in the *Kabala* following in the line of Babylonia, Magism; exoterically as in Genesis and the Pentateuch, a collection of allegorical legends. Read by the light of the *Zohar* the initial four chapters of Genesis are the fragments of a highly philosophical page in the World's Cosmogony. Left in their symbolical disguise, they are a nursery tale, an ugly thorn in the side of Science and logic, an evident effect of Karma. To have made this serve as a *Prologue* to Christianity, was a cruel revenge of the Rabbis, who knew better what their Pentateuch meant. It was a silent protest against their spoliation, and the Jews were certainly now the better of their traditional persecutors. The above named exoteric creed will be explained in the light of the Universal doctrine as we proceed with it.

Asks the catechism of the beginners in Occultism: ["]What is it that ever *is*? — SPACE, the eternal *Anupadaka*.[128] What is it that ever *was*? — The germ in the Root. — What is it

---

127. In contradistinction to the manifested Universe of matter, the term "Mulaprakriti" (from *Mula* "root" and prakriti "material nature") — or the *unmanifested primordial matter* (called by the Western Alchemists — Adam's Earth) is applied by the Vedantists to Parabrahman. Matter is *dual* in religious metaphysics, and septenary like all the rest in the *esoteric* teachings. In the former case in its undifferentiated and unmanifested state, it is Avyakta — the non manifested Root "or Mulaprakriti"; it becomes *Vyakta* in its manifested, hence differentiated condition — according to *Svetasvatara Upanishad* 1.8 and *Devi Bhagavat.*

128. See explanation further on in commentary I. It means the "parentless."

that is ever coming and going? — 'The Great Breath.' — Then, there are four eternals? — No; the four are one. That which ever is — is one; that which ever *was* is — one; that which is ever being and becoming — is also one.

["]'Explain, oh Lanoo (disciple).' — The ONE is an unbroken circle (ring) with no circumference, for it is nowhere and everywhere; the one is the boundless plane of the Circle, manifesting a diameter only during the Manvantara periods; the One is the invisible Point found nowhere, perceived everywhere during those periods; it is the Vertical and the Horizontal, the Father and the Mother; the Summit and base of the Father, the two extremities of the Mother, reaching in reality nowhere, for the One is the Ring as also the rings that are within that Ring. Light in Darkness and Darkness in Light; the 'Breath which is eternal.['] It proceeds from *without inwardly* — when it is everywhere, and from *within* outwardly when it is nowhere, *i.e.* a maya,[129] one of the centres.[130] It expands and contracts,

---

129. Esoteric philosophy, regarding as *Maya* (or illusion of ignorance) every finite thing, must necessarily view in the same light every intra-cosmic planet and body, as being something organized, hence *finite*. The expression therefore, "it proceeds from *without* inwardly etc." refers in the first portion of the sentence to the dawn of the Mahamanvantaric period, or the great re-evolution after one of the complete periodical dissolutions of every compound form in nature (from planet to molecule) — into its ultimate essence or element; and, in its second portion, to the partial or *local* manvantaras, which may be a solar or even a planetary one.

130. By "centre," a centre of energy or a cosmic *focus* is meant; when the so-called "creation," or formation of a planet, is accomplished by that force which is designated by the Occultists LIFE, and by Science — *energy*, then the process takes place from *within* outwardly, every atom being said to contain in itself creative energy or the *divine* breath. Hence, whereas after an *absolute* pralaya when the pre-existing material consists but of *one* Element, and BREATH "is everywhere" the latter acts from *without inwardly*; after a minor *pralaya*, everything having remained in *Statu quo,* in a refrigerated state, so to say, like the moon — at the first flutter of manvantara, the planet or planets begin their resurrection to life from *within* outwardly.

(exhalation and inhalation). When it expands —— the MOTHER diffuses and scatters; when it contracts —— the Mother draws back and ingathers; and this is what we call the periods of Manvantara and Pralaya (of evolution and dissolution).[131] The GERM is invisible and fiery, the ROOT (the plane of the circle) is cool and during Manvantara her *garment* is radiant.[132] Hot Breath is the Father that devours his progeny of the many faces (heterogeneous) leaving only those that are uniform (homogeneous). Cool Breath is the Mother who forms them and receives them back into her bosom, as units when dissipated at the hour of pralaya, to *reform* them at Manvantara, or 'the Day of Brahma.'["]

---

131. It is curious to notice how in the evolutionary cycles of ideas, ancient thought seems to be reflected in modern thought. Has Mr. Herbert Spencer read and studied ancient Hindu philosophers when he wrote a certain passage in his "First Principles" (p. 482), or is it an independent flash of inner perception that made him say half correctly, half incorrectly, "Motion as well as matter, being fixed in quantity (?) it would seem that the change in the distribution of Matter, which Motion effects, coming to a limit in whichever direction it is carried (?) the indestructible Motion thereupon necessitates a reverse distribution. Apparently, the universally coexistent forces of attraction and repulsion which as we have seen, necessitates rhythm in all minor changes throughout the Universe, also necessitates rhythm in the totality of its changes — produce now in an immeasurable period during which the attractive forces predominating cause universal concentration, and then an immeasurable period during which the repulsive forces predominating cause universal diffusion — alternate eras of Evolution and Dissolution."

132. Whatever the views of physical science upon the subject, Occult Science has been teaching for ages that *Akasa* — in its grossest form Ether — the *fifth* Universal or Cosmic principle is a radiant, cool diathermanous and plastic matter, *creative* in its physical nature, correlative in its lower aspect, and immutable in its higher principle. In the former condition it is called the *sub-root*, and in conjunction with radiant heat "calls dead worlds to life." In its higher aspect it is the "Soul of the World" during Manvantara and when Pralaya comes "it merges back into the MOTHER."

For the clear understanding of the general reader it must be stated that Occult Science recognizes seven cosmical elements, four entirely physical, one (Ether) —— semi-arcane, that will become as visible and tangible towards the end of our fourth Round and reign Supreme over the others during the whole of the Fifth; the remaining two are as yet absolutely occult. These will be known in the Sixth and Seventh Rounds, respectively. All these Seven elements, with their numberless *sub*-Elements (of which there are far more than the sixty-odd constituents of Science) are simply *conditional* modifications and aspects of one and the only Elements [Element], which is not Ether —— "the subtle ethereal Medium," nor even *Akasa*. This fifth Element, believed in by Sir Isaac Newton, is now advocated quite freely, initiated as it was by Professor W. R. Grove, in 1842; and the hope of discovering *that all* the elements are resolvable into one Element is entertained by many. For, as remarked by Newton, "Nature is a perpetual circulatory worker, generating fluids out of solids, fixed things out of volatile, and volatile out of fixed; subtle out of gross, and gross out of subtle. . . . Thus, perhaps may all things be originated from Ether" (*Hypoth.* 1675).

The reader has to bear in mind that the Stanzas given treat only of the Cosmogony of our own planetary system after a Solar Pralaya.

The Secret teachings with regard to the Evolution of the universe at [universal] Kosmos cannot be given, since they could not be understood by the highest minds in this age, and there seem to be a very few Initiates, even among the greatest, who are allowed to speculate upon this subject. Moreover, the Masters say openly that not even the highest Dhyani-Chohans have ever penetrated *all* the mysteries beyond those boundaries that separate the milliards of solar systems from the "Central Sun," as it is called. Therefore, that which is given relates only to our *visible* Kosmos, after a "night of Brahma."

The *Stanzas* that form the thesis of every Section are given everywhere in their modern translated versions, as it would be worse than useless to make the subject still more difficult by introducing the Archaic phraseology of the original with its puzzling style and words.[133] The glossaries and comments upon each Stanza, translated into Sanskrit, Chinese and Tibetan have been *retranslated* now for the first time into a European language. It is almost useless to add that *only portions* of the seven stanzas are here given. Were the whole to be written it would be incomprehensible save to the few higher chelas. Nor is there any need to assure the reader that the writer, no more than the profane, understands those prohibited passages. To facilitate therefore the reading, and avoid referring the student too often to the footnotes — it was thought best to blend together text and glossary, using in preference Sanskrit and Tibetan proper names (whenever these cannot be avoided) to those given in the original and made use of only among the Masters and chelas. These names are all accepted synonyms.

In view of the abundant comments and explanations required, the asterisks for references in the foot notes will be given in the usual way. While the sentences to be glossed upon in the *Commentaries* that are appended to every stanza, marked with figures, corresponding to the order they are given in them — thus (1) (2) (3) etc. Additional glossaries in Appendices complete the rest, and they are the most important.

---

133. Were one to translate *literally* into English, using only the substantives and technical terms as given in one of the Tibetan and Senzar translations, Verse I would read as follows: — "*Tho-ag* in *Zhi-gyü* slept seven Khorlo. *Zodmanas zhiba*. - All Nyug bosom. *Konchhog* not; *Thyan-Kam* - not; Lha-Chohan - not; *Tenbrel Chugnyi* - not; *Dharmakaya* ceased. *Tgen-chang* not become; Barnang and Ssa - in Ngovonyid. Alone *Thô-og Yin-Sin* in night of *Sun-chan* and Yong-*grub* (*Parinishpanna*), etc. etc. As this work is written for the students of occultism, and not for philologists, we may well avoid such foreign terms wherever it will be possible to do so.

The Secret Doctrine Würzburg Manuscript

Stanza I.

The Eternal Mother (space) wrapped in her ever invisible robes (cosmic prenebular matter) had slumbered for seven Eternities (1). Time was not, for it lay asleep in the infinite bosom of Duration. Universal Mind was not, for there were no Dhyan Chohans to contain (hence to manifest) it. The seven Ways to Bliss (Moksha, or Nirvana) — were not.[134] The great causes of Misery (Nidana[135] (2) and Maya) — were not, for there was no one to produce and get ensnared by them. DARKNESS alone filled the boundless ALL, for Father, Mother and Son were once more *one*[136] and the Son had not awakened yet for the new wheel[137] (3). The seven sublime Truths, and the seven Srutis (4) — had ceased to be, and the Universe, the son of necessity, was plunged in *Paranishpanna* (absolute perfection, Paranirvana, which is *Yong-grüb*) — to be outbreathed by that which is, and yet is not (5). Naught was. The causes of existence having been done away with, the visible that *was* and the invisible that *is*, rested in eternal Non-Being, — the ONE BEING. Alone, the one Form of Existence (6) stretched boundless, infinite, causeless, in dreamless Sleep; and life pulsated unconscious in Universal Space, throughout that ALL PRESENCE which is sensed by the "opened Eye"[138] of the

---

134. *Nippang,* in China; *Neibban,* in Burmah; or Moksha, in India.

135. The "12" *Nidanas* (in Tibetan *Ten-brel chug-nyi*) the chief cause of existence, effects generated by a concatenation of causes produced. (See *comment*: (21))

136. Male and Female principles in nature, and the Universe, (the Son) as the resultant. They are "once more ONE" when in the "Night of Brahma" during Pralaya, when all in the objective Universe has returned to its one primal and eternal cause, to reappear at the following Dawn — which it does periodically.

137. The "Great Wheel" is the whole duration of our Cycle of being, or *Maha Kalpa* i.e., the whole revolution of our special chain of seven spheres or planets from beginning to end, the "Small Wheels" meaning the *Rounds* of which there are Seven also.

Dangma.[139] But where was the Dangma when the ALAYA of the Universe (absolute Soul) was in PARAMARTHA (absolute being) (7) [and] the Great Wheel was Anupadaka? ("Great Wheel" is our planetary chain, "Anupadaka" ["]parentless") (8).

---

138. Called in India "The Eye of Siva," the inner, spiritual eye of the Seer.

139. Dangma is a "purified soul," the highest adepts.

COMMENTARY ON STANZA I.

(In order not to break the Stanzas by making the comments too long, the reader is referred for additional explanations to the general glossary which follows every chapter in the appendix attached.)

The Secret Doctrine postulates three fundamental propositions.

(a) An omnipresent, Eternal, Boundless and Immutable Principle, on which every speculation is forbidden, since it transcends the power of human conception, and could only be dwarfed by an[y] human expression or similitude. It is beyond the range and reach of thought — in the words of *Mandukya* "unthinkable and unpronounceable."

(b) The Eternity of the Universe *in toto* as a boundless plane, "the playground of numberless universes incessantly manifesting and disappearing" called — "shooting stars" and the ["]sparks of Eternity." "The Eternity of the Pilgrim"[140] is like a wink of the Eye of "Self-Existence" (Book of Dzyan). "The appearance and disappearance of Worlds, is like a regular tidal ebb of flux and reflux["] (See App. III ["]Nights and Days of Brahma["]; and App. ["]Plurality of Worlds").

(c) The Homogeneity and Unity of all Souls with the Universal OVER SOUL, the latter being itself an aspect of the unknown ROOT; and the obligatory *pilgrimage* for every soul

---

140. Pilgrim is the appellation given to our seventh principle during its cycle of incarnations. It is the only immortal and eternal principle in us, being an indivisible part of the integral whole — the universal Spirit, from which it emanates and into which it is absorbed at the end of the cycle. When it is said to *emanate* from the one spirit, an awkward and incorrect expression has to be used for lack of appropriate words in English. The Vedantin calls it Sûtratmâ (Thread Soul) but his explanation too differs somewhat from those of the Occultists (See App. IV "The Pilgrim").

— a spark of the former — through the Cycle of Incarnation (or "Necessity"), in accordance with Cyclic and Karmic Law, during the whole term. In other words, no purely spiritual Buddhi (divine Soul) can have an independent (conscious) existence before the spark issued from the pure Essence of the Universal Sixth Principle, or the OVER SOUL — has passed (a) through every elemental form of the phenomenal world of *that* Manvantara, and (b) acquired individually, first by natural impulse, and then by self-induced and self devised efforts, checked by its Karma. All the degrees of intelligence, from the lowest to the highest *Manas*, from mineral and plant up to the holiest archangel (Dhyan-Buddha). The dogma of the Esoteric Doctrine admits no privileges or special gifts in man, save those won by its own *Ego* through personal effort and merit through a long series of metempsychosis and reincarnations. This is why Hindus say that the Universe is Brahma, for Brahma is in every atom of the Universe, the sixth [six] principles in nature being all the outcome and various gradations of this *Seventh* and *ONE,* the only Reality in the Universe whether Cosmical or Microcosmical; and also why the permutations (psychic, spiritual and physical on the plane of manifestation and form) of the Seventh are viewed by metaphysical Antiphrasis — as illusive and mayic. For although the root of every atom individually and of every form — collectively, is, that *seventh* principle or the one reality, still in its manifested and *temporary* appearance it is no better than an evanescent illusion of the senses. (See for clearer definition App. IV "The Pilgrim Soul").

In its absoluteness, the One Principle under its two appellations (Parabrahman and Mulaprakriti) is sexless, unconditioned and eternal. Its periodical (manvantaric) emanation — or primal radiation — is also One, Androgynous and *phenomenally,* finite. When the radiation radiates in its turn all its radiation[s] are also androgynous to become male and female principles in their lower aspects. After Pralaya — whether the great or the minor pralaya (the latter leaving the world *statu quo*[141]) the first that resurrects to *active* life, is the

---

141. It is not the physical organisms that remain *statu-quo*, least of all their psychical principles, during the great cosmic or even solar pralayas, but only their Akasic or Astral photographs. But during the

plastic Akasa, Father-Mother Ether, or *the plane on the surface of the Circle*. Space is called the "Mother" before its Cosmic Activity, and Father-Mother at the first stage of reawakening (See comment No 2). In the *Kabala* it is also Father-Mother-Son. But whereas in the Eastern Doctrine these are the Seventh Principle of the *manifested* Universe or its "Atma-Buddhi[-]Manas" (Spirit, Soul, Intelligence) branching off and bifurcating later on, into the seven cosmical and the seven human principles; in the Western Kabala of the Christian Mystics, it is the *Triad* or trinity and with their Occultists, the male-female Jehovah, Jah-Havah. In this lies the whole difference between the pagan and the *Christian* trinities. The Mystics and the Philosophers, Eastern and Western Kabalists synthesize *pregenetic* triad in the pure divine abstraction. With them it is Father-Mother Nature, giving birth to the first Ray — the Son, — this triad emanating from and being so to say the manifesting resultant of the ever hidden deific Principle, — thus forming the first perfect CUBE — the Quaternary (or the Esoteric Tetractis); whereas the orthodox religionist, Pagan and Christian, Monotheists or Polytheists, personify and anthropomorphize it. The Appendices explain the idea clearly. It is impossible to treat of it here with sufficient clearness. (See Appendix V. "On the Identity of *Gupta-Vidya and the Zohar*.) En-Soph the infinite and concealed All, exists only for the true Kabalist and Occultist. The profane dispense with the Spiritual abstraction altogether. (See App. VI "On Creation in the Zohar" and also ["]Brahmâ-Vach,["] App. XIV.)

At this stage of the reawakening of the Universe the sacred symbolism represents it as a perfect circle with the (root) point in the centre. This sign or figure was adopted by all the ancient nations. Therefore we find it also in the Chaldean Kabala (the original *Book of Numbers*). The Western Kabala however, now in the hands of Christian Mystics, ignores it altogether though it is plainly shown in the texts of the *Zohar*. They begin with the circle and the cross thus ⊕ calling it, "the

---

minor pralayas, once overreached by the "Night" the planets remain intact, though dead, like a huge animal caught between polar ices remains the same for ages.

union of the Rose and Cross" the great mystery of Occult generation from whence the name *Rosicrucians*[142] (Rose-Cross).

As may be judged, however, by the most important, as the best known of the Rosicrucian symbols, *one moreover that has never been hitherto understand even by modern mystics* — that of a "Pelican" tearing open its breast to feed its *seven* little ones — the real creed of the Brothers of the Rosie-Cross was a *direct outcome* from the Eastern Secret Doctrine. Brahma (neuter) is called *Kalahansa,* the Eternal *Swan* or *goose.* (See STANZA III and No. 7 commen.) and so is Brahmâ the creator. A great mistake is brought under notice; it is Brahma (neut.) who ought to be referred to as *Hansa-vahana* (He who uses the Swan as his Vehicle) and not Brahmâ, the *creator* who is the real Kalahansa, as we explain in the commentary.

(1) By "Eternities" *aeons,* or periods are meant. The word "Eternity" as understood in christian theology has no meaning to the asiatic ear, except in its application to the ONE existence; nor is the term *sempiternity* or Eternal only in futurity anything better than a misnomer. Such words do not, and cannot exist in philosophical metaphysics and were unknown till Christianity. "The Seven Eternities" meant, are the seven periods, or a period answering in its duration to the seven periods of a Manvantara, and extending throughout a *Maha Kalpa* or the "great age" (100 years of Brahma), making a total of 311,040,000,000,000 of years; each year being composed of 360 "Days" and of the same number of "Nights" of Brahma (reckoning by the Chandrayana or lunar year[ )]; and a "Day of Brahma" consisting of 4,320,000,000 of mortal years. These "Eternities" belonging to the most secret calculations; in which, in order — say — to arrive at the *true* total every figure must be 7^x, 7 to the power of x; x, varying, according to the nature of the cycle, in the subjective or the *real* world; and every figure or number relating to, or representing all the different cycles from the greatest to the smallest — in the objective or *unreal* world —

---

142. Which symbol, meaning the male and female Elements in abstract or spiritual nature is still more degraded in our day by certain writers who would like to father upon the Rosicrucians a mystical phallic worship of the most revolting character. See "Phallicism["] by H. Jennings.

must be necessarily multiples of 7. The key to this cannot be given, for herein lies the Mystery of esoteric calculations, and for purposes of ordinary calculus — it has no sense. "The number *seven*,["] says the Kabala, ["]is the great number of the divine Mysteries["]; number *ten* is that of all human knowledge (Pythagorean Decade); 1000 is the number 10 to the third power and therefore number 7000 is also symbolical. In the Secret Doctrine the figure and number 4 are the male symbol and the 3, the female the upright and the horizontal *in the fourth stage* of symbolism, when symbols became the glyphs of the generative powers on the physical plane.

(2) The 12 Nidanas, or causes of Being. Each is an effect relatively to the preceding one and a *cause* to the following effect; the sum total of the Nidanas being based on the 4 truths. They belong to the theory of the causal connections, or concatenations of the causes of being, that produce merit and demerit and finally moved — KARMA.

(3) ["]Father-Mother-Son," are in esoteric parlance Spirit, Soul, and Body, each a degree of the emanation of *Divine Breath*, in its cyclic graduation — retrogressive and progressive. In the Cosmic physical sense — the Universe, our planetary Chain, and the Earth; in the purely spiritual, the Unknown Deity, Planetary Spirit and Man — the Son of the two, the creature of Spirit and Matter and a manifestation of them in his periodical appearances on Earth during the "Wheels" — or the Manvantaras (See "Days and Nights" of Brahma app. to this chapter).

(4) Out of the seven Truths and *Srutis* ("revelations["]) *four* only have been handed to us, as we are still in the 4th Round. So far "there are only Four *truths* and Four *Vedas* — say the Hindus and the Buddhists; and the Europeans might add perhaps — and only four gospels. But, as every new Root race, at the head of a round must have its revelation, the next Round will bring the 5th, the following the 6th, and so on.

(5) "That which is, and yet is not." The three periods — the present, the past and the future are in esoteric philosophy, a compound time, as the three are a composite number only in relation to finite things; but, in infinity, correlative to each other. "The past time is the present time, as also the future, which

though it has not come into existence, *still* is" as states a precept in the Prasanga Madhyamika teaching whose dogmas are known ever since it has broken away from the purely esoteric schools.[143]

(6) The "one form of Existence," the "One Reality," the "Secondless" are all names given to Brahma (neuter), or the Parabrahman. It is evident that the philosophical Buddhist (of both the Northern and Southern Churches, as of the Esoteric Schools) who give[s] no name to "God" and does not recognize a personal deity, has to regard that abstract, yet omnipresent *root* of all, Svâbhâvat, which is a self-existent plastic essence and the supposed cause of all-being, in the same dual light as the Vedantin views his Parabrahm and Mula-Prakriti — the one under two aspects. It seems rather incredible to find great scholars speculating on the possibility of the Vedanta, and the Uttara-Mimansa, especially having been "evoked by the teachings of the Buddhists," whereas, it is on the contrary Buddhism that was "evoked" and entirely built on the tenets of the Secret Doctrine on which also the Upanishads are made to rest. The above after the teaching of Sri Sankarachârya,[144] is undeniable.

(7) "Alaya" has a double meaning in the esoteric teaching. In the Yogachârya system of the contemplative Mahayâna School, Alaya is both the Universal Soul (anima Mundi) and the SELF in the case of the progressed Adept. "He who is strong in the *Yoga* can introduce at his own will his Alaya by means of meditation *into the true nature* of existence." The "Alaya has an absolute eternal existence" says Aryâsanga, the great rival of Nagarjuna.[145]

---

143. See Dsungarian *Mani Kumbum* (the Book of the 100,000 Precepts), also Wassileff's "*Der Buddhismus*["] pp. 327 and 357 et *seq.*

144. It is even argued that all the six Darsanas (schools of philosophy) *show traces of Buddhist influence* (!) being either taken from Buddhism, or due to Greek teaching. (See Weber, Max Müller, etc.) We laboured under the impression that Colebrooke, "the *highest* Authority" in such matters, had long ago settled the question by showing that "the Hindus were in this instance *the teachers not the learners.*"

It is a mistake of those who know nothing of the universality of the Occult doctrines from the very cradle of the human race, and especially of those scholars who reject the very idea of a "primordial Revelation" — to teach that the *anima Mundi*, the one Life or ["]Universal Soul" was made known, only by, or during the age of, Anaxagoras. This philosopher has brought the teaching forward simply to oppose the too materialistic conceptions on Cosmogony of Democritus, with his theory of blindly working atoms. Anaxagoras of Clazomenae was not its inventor but only its propagator, as was Plato. That is what he called Mundane Intelligence. The Nous (νοῦς), the principle that according to his views is absolutely separated and free from matter and acts on design,[146] was called MOTION, the one LIFE, or *Jivatma* — ages before the year 500 B.C. in India. Only the Aryan philosophers never endowed the principle which with them is infinite, with the *finite* attribute of thinking. The matter-moving *Nous*, the animating soul immanent in every atom from Man to the germ of lichen on the stone — has different degrees of power, and this pantheistic idea of a general Spirit-Soul pervading all nature, is the oldest of all the philosophical notions. Nor was the *Archaeus* a discovery of Paracelsus or of his pupil Van Helmont; for it is again the same Archaeus, or Father-Ether, the *Manifested* root and mover of the innumerable phenomena of life — localised. The whole series of the numberless philosophical speculations of this kind are but variations on the theme, the keynote of which was struck in an primeval Revelation. (See app. VII "Primordial Substance.")

(8) The term Anupadaka "parentless" or without progenitors, is a mystical designation having several meanings in the philosophy. By this name celestial beings the Dhyân-Chohans or Dhyâni-Buddhas are generally meant. But as these correspond mystically to the human Buddha and *Bodhisatwas*,

---

145. Aryasanga is a pre-Christian Adept and founder of a Buddhist esoteric school though Csoma de Koros places him for reasons of his own in the 7th Century A.D.

146. See Schwegler's ["]Hand book of the History of Philosophy" in Sterling's translation page 28.

known as the Mânushi (or human) Buddhas, the latter are also designated "Anupadaka," once that their whole personality is merged in their compound sixth and seventh principles — or Atma-Buddhi, and that they have become the "diamond-souled" *Vajrasattvas*[147] the *full* Mahatmas. The ["]concealed Lord" (*Sangbai Dag-po*) can have no parents, since he is *self*-existent, and one with the Universal Spirit *Svayambhu* — the Svabhâvat in the highest aspect. The mystery in the hierarchy of these Anupadaka is great, its apex being the Universal Spirit-Soul, and the lower rung, the Manushi-Buddha; and even every soul-endowed man; is an Anupadaka in a *latent state*. Hence, when speaking of the Universe in its formless, eternal or *absolute* condition before it was *fashioned* by the Builders — the expression "the Universe was Anupadaka." (See Glossary Ap. VIII, ["]Divine Thought.")

---

147. *Vajra* — diamond-holder. In Tibetan *Dorjesempa*, sempa meaning the Soul, its adamantine quality referring to its indestructibility in the hereafter. The explanations with regard to the "Anupadaka" given in the *Kala Chakra*, the first in the Gyu(t) division of the *Kanjur* is half Esoteric. It has misled the Orientalists into erroneous speculations with respect to the Dhyani Buddhas and their earthly correspondencies — the Manushi Buddhas. The real tenet is hinted at in one of the Appendices — "The Mystery about Buddha" and will be more fully explained in its proper place.

Stanza II.

Where were the BUILDERS (1), the luminous Sons of Manvantaric Dawn? In the UNKNOWN DARKNESS, in their Dhyan-Chohanic (Dhyâni Buddhic) *Parinishpan[n]a* (2). The producers of Form (rupa) from no-Form (arupa); the Root of the World — the *Deva-Matri*[148], and Svabhâvat, rested in the bliss of non-Being.[149] Where was Silence? Where were the ears to sense it? No; there was neither Silence, nor sound. Nought, save ceaseless, eternal Breath (motion) which knows itself not[150] (3). The hour had not yet struck; the RAY had not yet flashed into the GERM; the Matri-Padma (Mother Lotus) had not yet swollen[151] (4); her heart had not yet opened for the ray to enter, thence to fall into the lap of Maya (5). The seven (Sons) were

---

148. "Mother of the Gods." Aditi, or Cosmic Space. In the *Zohar*, she is called Sephira the Mother of the Sephiroths and Shekinah in her primordial form, in abscondito.

149. The *non-being* is — ABSOLUTE Being in esoteric philosophy. In the tenets of the latter even *Adi-Budhi* (First or *primeval* Wisdom) is while manifested, in one sense an illusion, *Maya*, since all the gods, including Brahmâ, have to die at the end of the "age of Brahma," — the abstraction called Parabrahm alone — and, whether we call it En-Soph, or Herbert Spencer's *unknowable* — being the one Absolute Reality, the one secondless Existence being ADWAITA "without a second,["] and all the rest is — Maya.

150. To *know* itself or oneself, necessitates consciousness and perception, both limited faculties in relation to any subject (excepting Parabrahman) to be cognized. Hence the "eternal Breath which knows itself not." Infinity cannot comprehend Finiteness. The Boundless can have no relation to the bounded and the conditioned. In the occult teachings, the unknown and unknowable MOVER of the Self-existing is the Absolute Divine Essence, and thus being *absolute* Consciousness, and *Absolute* Motion — to the limited senses of those who describe this indescribable, it is *unconsciousness* and *immoveableness*.

151. An unpoetical term, still very graphic. (See footnote to Stanza III.)

not yet born from the web of light. Darkness alone was Father-Mother, Svabhâvat,[152] and Svabhavât was in DARKNESS. These two are the germ, and germ is — ONE. The Universe was still concealed in the divine Thought and the divine bosom (6).

---

152. Svabhâvat, the "plastic essence" that fills the Universe, is the *root of all things*. Svabhâvat is, so to say, the concrete aspect of the abstraction called *Mulaprâkriti* — the body of the soul, and that which Ether would be to *Akasa*, the latter being its informing principle. Chinese Mystics have made of it the synonym of "being." In the *Ekasloka-Shastra* of Nagarjuna (the *Lung-shu* of China) called by the Chinese the *Yih-shu-lu-kia-lun*, it is said that the original word of *Yeu* is "being" or *Subhava* "the substance giving substance to itself," also explained by him as meaning "without action and with action," and the nature which has no nature of its "own." Subhava, from which *Svabhâvat*, is composed of two words Su "fair" "handsome" — good (Sva or Swa — "Self") bhava — "being," or ["]states of being."

COMMENTARY

(1) The "Builders," the ["]Sons of Manvantaric Dawn," are the real *creators* of the Universe, and in this doctrine which is wholly confined to our Planetary System, they, as the architects of the latter, are also called the "Watchers" of the Seven Spheres which exoterically are the seven planets, and *esoterically* the seven earths or spheres (planets) of our chain. (See app. IX, "Who the Creators.")

(2) Parinishpanna is the *Summum bonum*, the absolute, hence the same as Paranirvana. Besides being the final state it is that condition of mind which has no relation to anything but the one *absolute* truth (*Paramarthasatya*[ )];[153] it is that which leads one to appreciate correctly the full meaning of NON-BEING, which is [as] explained, is ABSOLUTE Being. Sooner or later, all that now *seemingly* is, will be, in reality and actually in the state of Parinishpanna. But there is a great difference between *conscious* and *unconscious* "being." The condition of Parinishpanna; without Paramartha the self-analyzing consciousness (Svasamvedana) is no bliss but simply *extinction* for seven Eternities. Thus an iron ball placed under the scorching rays of the Sun will get heated through, but will not feel or appreciate the warmth, while a man will. It is only ["]with a mind clear and undarkened by personality, and an assimilation of the merit of manifold existences devoted to *being* in its collectivity (the whole living and *sentient* Universe)" that one gets rid of personal existence, merging into, becoming one with, the absolute, and continuing in the full possession of Paramartha.

---

153. "Paramartha" is self-consciouness, in Sanskrit *Svasamvedana*, or the "Self-analyzing reflection" — from two words *parama* "above every thing" and *artha* — "comprehension." *Satya* meaning — absolute true being or Esse. In Tibetan "Paramarthasatya["] is *Dondampai denpa*. The opposite of this absolute reality or *actuality* is *Samvritisatya* — the relative truth only (Samvriti meaning "false conception" and being the origin of illusion *Maya*) in Tibetan *Kundzabchi denpa*, illusion creating appearance.

(3) The "Breath" of the One Existence, is used in its application only to the spiritual aspect of cosmogony in Buddhist esoter[ic]ism; otherwise, it is replaced by its equivalent in the material plane — MOTION — is SPACE, dimensionless in every sense; coexistent with which are: endless *duration*, primordial (hence indestructible) matter, and motion — absolute "perpetual motion" which is the "breath" of the "ONE["] Element. This breath, as seen, can never cease, not even during the Pralayic eternities. (See app. X "Theos, Chaos, Cosmos.["])

(4) One of the symbolical figures for the Dual creative power in nature (matter and Force on the material plane), is *Padma*, the lotus flower, the water lily of India. The lotus is the product of heat (fire) and water (Vapour or Ether), fire, standing in every philosophical and religious system as a representation of the Spirit of Deity[154] the active male, generative principle; and *Ether*, or the Soul of Matter, the light of the Fire — the passive, female principle from which every thing in this Universe emanated. Hence, Ether or Water is the Mother, and Fire is the Father. Sir W. Jones (and before him Archaic botany) showed that the seeds of the lotus contain even before they germinate, perfectly formed leaves, the miniature shape of what one day, as perfect plants, they will become: "nature thus giving us a specimen of the preformation of its production, the seed of all *phaenogamous* plants bearing *proper* flowers, containing *an embryo plantlet* ready formed.["][155] (See App. "The Lotus Flower, as an Universal Symbol.") This explains the sentence "the Mother had not yet swollen" — the form being usually sacrificed to the inner, or root idea in Archaic Symbology.

(5) The Secret Doctrine occupying itself chiefly with our solar system, and especially with our planetary chain in it, the "seven Sons" are the creators of it, and the teaching is fully explained in the glossary. (See App. VI "Who are the Creators?["])

---

154. Even in Christianity. (See app. VIII *Divine Thought* and Primordial Substance.)

155. [Gross, "The Heathen Religion," p. 195.]

(6) "The universe was still concealed in the Divine Thought and the Divine Bosom." The *Divine Thought* does not imply the idea of a divine *Thinker*. The Universe, not only past present and future [—] which is a human and finite idea expressed by finite thought — but in its *totality* and the SAT (an untranslatable term) the absolute BEING, with the Past and Future crystallized in an eternal PRESENT is that Thought itself, reflected in a secondary or manifest cause. Brahma (neuter) as the MYSTERIUM MAGNUM of Paracelsus is an absolute mystery to the human mind. Brahmâ the male, its emanation and anthropomorphic reflection, is conceivable to the perceptions of blind faith, though rejected by human intellect when it becomes a reasoning power. (See Ap. ["]Divine Thought.["])

The Secret Doctrine Würzburg Manuscript

Stanza III

The last vibration of the Seventh Eternity thrilled through Infinitude. The Mother swelled expanding from *within without* like the bud of the lotus. The vibration swept along touching with its swift wing simultaneously the whole universe, and the germ that dwelleth in Darkness,[156] the Darkness that breathes (moves) over the slumbering waters of Life.[157] Darkness radiated Light, and light dropped one solitary Ray into the Waters of Mother Space. The ray fructified (recalled to life) the "Eternal virgin Egg."[158](1) . . . . The radiant essence within the *Hiranya garbha* (golden Egg) curdled and spread throughout the depths (2) in milk white curds[159] throughout the depths of the Mother, the Root which grows in the Ocean of Life. The root remained; the light remained, the curds remained; and still the three were one, for the root of life was in every drop of the Ocean (of Amrita)[160] and the drop was in the root, and the whole floated in the radiant light which was Fire and Heat and was

---

156. The Pythagorean MONAD also dwells in solitude and Darkness.

157. "The Waters of Life" are the chaos — the female principle in its symbolism, or the *vacuum*, in which lie latent Spirit and matter, which made Democritus assert after his instructor Leucippus that the primordial principles of all were atoms and a *vacuum* — in the sense of space but not *empty* Space, as nature abhors a *vacuum* according to the Peripatetics.

158. Called the *Egg* because the Occult Sciences teach that the primordial form of everything manifested, from globe to atom and angel to man, is spheroidal.

159. Cosmic matter, which according to the revelation received from the primeval Dhyan Buddhas — is, during the periodical sleep of the Universe of the ultimate tenuity conceivable to the Eye of the perfect Bodhisâtva, *radiant* and cool becomes at the first reawakening of *cosmic motion* scattered through space when seen from the earth in clusters and lumps like curds in thin milk. These are the seeds of the future worlds, the star-stuff. (Comment[ary] Sansk[rit])

160. *Amrita* — "immortality."

motion. "Darkness" retired and was .... no more:[161] it vanished in its own Essence, the essence of Fire and Water, of Father and Mother[162].......... Behold, oh Lanoo the radiant Son of the two, the unparalleled refulgent glory emerging from the depths of the Waters .... It is x x x when [whom] thou knowest now as Kwai[n]–Shai–Yin,[163] (4) who shines forth like the blazing "divine Dragon of Wisdom,["] (5) EKA — (one) and in whom are the seven, and in the seven the multitudes. Behold him at his work in the solitudes of the sidereal Ocean, transforming Space into a shoreless sea of Fire (6) and the one manifested (Element) into the great Waters. — Where was the germ, and where was now DARKNESS[?] Where's the Spirit of the flame that burns in thy lamp, oh Lanoo?[164] The germ is *that*, and *that* is Light, the white brilliant Son of the dark, hidden Father, who uses *Kala-hansa* (black Swan or goose). Light is flame and flame is Fire, and the fire produces heat, which yields water, the water of Life in the great Mother (Chaos). Father-Mother spin a web[165] whose upper end is fastened to Spirit (Purusha) the light of the great Darkness and the lower one to matter (Prakriti), and this web is the Universe, spun out of the two substances made in one, which is Svabhâvât. It expands when the breath of fire is upon

---

161. See No I in commentary to the stanza.

162. Chaos, from this union with spirit, obtaining sense shone with pleasure and thus was produced the *Protogonos*, (the first born light) says a fragment of Hermias. Damascius calls it *Dis* in "Theogony" — the disposer of all things (See Cory's ["]Ancient Fragments" p. 314.)

163. See App XI ["]Kwan–Shin–Yin.["] The real name in the stanzas cannot be given.

164. *Lanoo* — is a student, a chela who studies practical Esoterism.

165. In the *Mundaka Upanishad* it is written "as a spider throws out and retracts its web, as herbs spring up in the ground .... so is the Universe derived from the undecaying one" (i, 1.7) Brahmâ "as the germ of unknown darkness" is the material from which all evolves and developes ... "as the web from the spider, as foam from the water," etc.

it, its sons (the elements) dissociate, scatter and return into their mother's bosom to rebecome one with her;[166] when it cools, and rebecomes radiant, its sons expand and contract through their own selves and hearts . . . . for embracing infinitude Svabhâvat sends out *Fohat* and hardens the atom[s]. Each is a part of the web (Universe). Reflecting the "Self-existent Lord" (primeval light) — like a mirror, each becomes in turn, a World,[167] . . . . (See App. XII "On the Plurality of the Worlds.")

---

166. "Great heat breaks up the compound elements and resolves the heavenly bodies into their primeval one element" explains the commentary. Once disintegrated, into its primal constituent by getting within the attraction and reach of a focus, or centre of heat (energy) of which many are carried about to and fro in space, the body, whether alive or dead will be vaporized and held in the bosom of the Mother until *Fohat*, gathering a few of the clusters of cosmic matter (nebula) will by giving it an impulse, set it on motion anew, develop required heat, and then let it to follow its own new growth.

167. This is said in the sense that the flame from a fire is endless and that the lights of the whole Universe could be lit at one simple rush-light without diminishing its flame. *Brahmâ* (not the absolute but the "creator" so called) —— is as a term derived from the root *Brih* to increase or *expand*: Brahma "expands" and becomes the Universe weaved out of his own substance.

COMMENTARY.

(1) The "Mundane Egg" is, perhaps, one of the most universally adopted symbols, highly suggestive as it is, both in the spiritual, physiological and cosmological sense. Therefore it is found in every world-theogony, where it is largely associated with the serpent symbol, the latter being everywhere — in philosophy as in religious symbolism an emblem of eternity, infinitude, regeneration and rejuvenation as well as of wisdom, and is, moreover oviparous in its generation. The mystery of apparent self-generation and evolution through its own creative power, repeating in miniature the process of cosmic evolution in the egg, both being due to heat and moisture under the efflux of the unseen creative spirit — justified fully the selection of this graphic symbol. The "Virgin Egg" is the microcosmical symbol of the Macrocosmical prototype — the "Virgin Mother" Chaos or the Primeval Deep. The male Brahma[â] (under whatever name) springs forth from the Virgin female the immaculate Root fructified by the Ray. Who versed in astronomy and natural sciences can fail to see its suggestiveness? Kosmos as receptive nature is an Egg fructified — yet left *immaculate*; once regarded as boundless it could have no other representation than a spheroid. Thus the "mundane Egg" came soon to play a part in every cosmogony as will be seen from the instances given fully in the glossary. (See App. VIII "On the Mundane Egg.")

(2) "The Radiant essence, curdled and spread throughout the depths" of space. From an astronomical point of view this is easy of explanation: it is the "milky way," the world stuff or primordial matter in its first form. It is more difficult, however, to explain it in a few words or even lines from the stand-point of occult science and symbolism as it is the most complicated of all. Herein are connected more than a dozen symbols; to begin with, the whole pantheon of the mysterious objects,[168] every one of these connected with occult *practical* meaning, extracted from the allegorical "churning of the Ocean" by the Hindu Gods.

---

168. The "fourteen precious things." The narrative or allegory is found in the *Satapatha Brahmana* and others. (See App. IX. "On the Cow as Nature's Symbol.")

Besides *Amrita*, the water of life, or immortality "Surabhi" the "cow of plenty" called the "fountain of milk and curds" was extracted from this "sea of milk." Hence, the universal adoration of the cow and bull (See App. IX ["]The Cow and Bull as Nature Symbols["]), one the production, the other the generative powers in nature, these symbols being found connected with both the Solar and the Cosmic deities. The specific properties, for occult purposes of the ["]fourteen precious things," being explained only at the fourth initiation — cannot be given here; but the following may be remarked. In the "Satapatha Brahmana" it is stated that the churning of the "Ocean of milk" took place in the *Satya Yug*, the first age and directly after the "deluge." As however neither the Rig Veda or Manu both preceding Vaivasvata's "deluge" — that of the bulk of the 4th Race, it is evident then, that it is not the great deluge, that which carried away the Atlantis (save one small island mentioned by Plato) that is meant here. That which is really meant by the "Churning of the Ocean" will be explained farther on. It relates to a period before the earth's foundation and is in direct connection with that other universal legend, the various and contradictory versions of which, culminated in the Christian dogma of the "War in Heaven" and the Fall of the angels (see *Revelation* Ch. XII). It will be given in the Appendices of another chapter. The *Brahmanas* reproached by the Orientalists with their versions on the same subjects, often clashing with each other are *preeminently occult works* hence used purposely as *blinds*. They were allowed to survive for public use and property, only because they were and are absolutely unintelligible to the masses. Otherwise they would have disappeared from circulation as long ago as the days of Akbar.

(3) According to the Rosicrucian tenets — as handled and explained by the profane for once partially correctly [—"]Light and Darkness are identical in themselves, being only divisible in the human mind;" and ... according to Robert Fludd, ["]Darkness adopted illumination in order to make itself visible." (*Phallicism*). According to the tenets of Esoteric Occultism, DARKNESS is the one true actuality, the basis and the root of light, without which the latter could never manifest Itself nor even exist. Light is matter and *Darkness* pure Spirit. Darkness

in its radical metaphysical basis is *subjective* and absolute light; while the latter in all its seeming effulgency and glory is merely a mass of shadows. As it can never be eternal it is simply — an illusion or *maya*. Even in the mind-baffling, and science-harassing *Genesis*, light is created out of Darkness ("and darkness was upon the face of the deep" ch I v 2) — and not *vice versa*. "In him (in 'Darkness') was life, and the life *was the light of men*" (John 1.4). A day may come when the eyes of men may be opened; and then they may comprehend better than they do now that verse in the Gospel of John that says "and the light shineth in darkness, and the darkness comprehendeth it not." They will see then that the word "darkness" does not apply to man's spiritual cecity [blindness], but indeed to "Darkness" the absolute, that comprehendeth not (cannot cognize) transient light, however transcendent to human eye. *Daemon est Deus inversus*; and the Devil is now called Darkness by the Church whereas in the Bible he is called the "son of God" (See *Job*) the bright star of the early morning Lucifer (See Isaiah.) There is a whole philosophy of dogmatic craft in the reason why the first Archangel who sprung from the depths of chaos and was called *Lux* — (Lucifer), the "Luminous son of the morning," or manvantaric Dawn. He was transformed by the church into Lucifer or Satan, because he is higher and older than Jehovah and had to be sacrificed to the new dogma.

(4) Kwan-shi-yin, is identical with and an equivalent of the Sanskrit Avalokiteshwara; and as such he is an androgynous deity, as all the *logoi* of antiquity. It is only by some sects in China that he is anthropomorphized and represented with female attributes.[169] Under his female aspect he becomes Kwan-Yin, the "goddess of mercy" and the "divine voice." The latter is the

---

169. No religious Symbol can escape profanation and even derision in our days of Politics and Science. In Southern India, the writer has seen a converted native making *puja* with offerings before a little statue of Jesus clad in women's clothes and a ring in his nose. When asked the meaning of this masquerade we were answered that it was *Jesu-Maria* blended in *One*, and that it was done by the permission of the *Padri*, as the zealous convert had no money to purchase two statues or idols as they, very properly, were called by a witness — another but a *non converted* Hindu.

patron deity of Tibet and of the island of Pu-to, in China where they both have a number of monasteries. (See App. in Prel. Sect., "Kwan Yin and Kwan-Shi-Yin.").

(5) The "Dragon of Wisdom" or the ONE, the "Eka" (Sansk.). It is curious that Jehovah's name in Hebrew is also One, *Echod*. "His name is *Echod*" say the Rabbins. The Philologists ought to decide which of the two is derived from the other — linguistically and symbolically: Surely not the Sanskrit. "The One" and the Dragon are expressions used by the ancients in connection with their respective *Logoi*. Jehovah — esoterically (as Elohim) is also the Serpent or Dragon that tempted Eve, and the Dragon is an old glyph for astral Light (primordial principle) "which is the wisdom of chaos." Archaic philosophy recognizing neither Good nor Evil as a fundamental or independent power, but starting from the *Absolute* all, (universal perfection originally) traced both, through the course of natural evolution to pure light concreting gradually into form, hence becoming matter or Evil. It was left with the early and ignorant Christian fathers to degrade the philosophical and highly scientific idea of this emblem (the Dragon) into the absurd superstition called Devil. They took it from the Zoroastrian Chaldees who saw in the Hindu Devas — devils, and the word *Evil* thus became by a double transmutation D'EVIL in every tongue (*Diabolis, Diable, Diavol, Teufel*). But the Pagans have always shown a philosophical discrimination in their symbols. The primitive symbol of the Serpent designated *divine Wisdom* and Perfection, and had always stood for *psychical regeneration* and Immortality. Hence Hermes, calling the Serpent the most spiritual of all beings, and the gnostic's serpent with the seven vowels over its head — the emblem of the seven Hierarchies of the Septenary, and Planetary Creators. Hence, also, the Hindu Serpent *Sesha*, or Ananta "the Infinite," a name of Vishnu, whose first Vahan or vehicle on the primordial Waters is this Serpent. Yet they all made a difference between the *Good* and the *Bad* Serpent (astral light), the former, the embodiment of divine Wisdom in the region of the spiritual, the latter — or Evil — on the plane of matter. Jesus accepted and taught the Serpent as a synonym of wisdom, "Be ye wise as the Serpent," he says. "In the beginning, before Mother became

Father-Mother, the fiery Dragon moved in the infinitudes alone." (Book of *Sarpa Râjni*). The *Aytareya [Aitareya] Brahmana* calls the earth *Sarpa Râjni*, "the serpent Queen["] and "the mother of all that moves." ["]Before our globe became egg-shaped" (and the Universe also) "a long trail of Cosmic dust (or fire mist) moved and writhed like a serpent in space.["] "The Spirit of God moving on the chaos" was symbolized by every nation in the shape of a fiery serpent breathing fire and light upon the primordial waters, until it had incubated Cosmic matter and made it assume the annular shape of a serpent with its tail in its mouth — which symbolized not only Eternity and infinitude but also the globular shape of all the bodies formed within the Universe from the fiery mist. The Universe as well as the Earth and man, cast off periodically, serpent-like their old skins, to assume after a time of rest new ones. The Serpent is, surely not less graceful or more unpoetical an image than the caterpillar and chrysalis from whence springs the butterfly, the Greek emblem of *Psyche*, the human soul. The "Dragon" was also the symbol of the Logos, with the Egyptians as with the Gnostics. For the "Book of Hermes," Pimander, the oldest and the most spiritual of the Logoi of the western continent appears to Hermes in the shape of a fiery Dragon, of Light, Fire and Flame. Pimander, the "Thought Divine" personified, says: — ["]The Light is one, I am the *Nous* (the Mind), I am thy God, and I am far older than the human principle which escapes from the shadow ('DARKNESS' or the concealed Deity). I am the germ of thought, the resplendent WORD, the *Son* of God . . . . All that thus sees and hears in thee, is the verbum of the Master, it is the thought which is God, the Father.[170] . . . The celestial ocean, the Æther . . . is the BREATH of the Father, the life giving Principle the MOTHER the Holy Spirit . . . for these are not separated and their union is Life."

Here we find the unmistakable Echo of the Archaic secret Doctrine, as now expounded.

(6) The "Sea of Fire" is then the astral light, the first radiation of the ROOT or *Mulaprakriti*. It is also called the

---

170. By "God the Father" the 7th principle in man is here unmistakably meant.

Fiery Serpent as above described. If the student bears in mind that there is but ONE universal, infinite, unborn and undying Element, and that all the rest — as in the world of manifestations are but so many various and numberless aspects and transformations (*correlations* they now call it) of the One, from cosmical down to microcosmical, human and other beings, objects, forms and effects, then, the first difficulty in the occult cosmology will be mastered.[171] All the Kabalists and Occultists, Eastern as Western recognize (*a*) the identity of Father-Mother in Æther or the astral Light, and (*b*) its homogeneity before it evoluted its *seven* principles. It is the fathomless and eternal source of all good and all Bad. "There exists one universal agent *unique* of all forms and of life that is called *Od*,[172] *Ob* and *Aour*, which is active, positive and negative, like day and night: it is the first light in creation" (El. Levi).

All the ancients represented it by a Serpent. The Hebrew Kabala figures it with the letter Teth ט whose symbol is the serpent, (playing a great part in the Egyptian and Chaldean mysteries) and by the numerical value 9. It is the ninth letter of the Hebrew Alphabet and is called the 9th door of the 50 portals or gateways that lead to the concealed mysteries of Being. It is the magical agent par *excellence* and designates in hermetic philosophy "primordial matter," which is the essence that composes all things and the spirit that determines their form. But there are two hermetic operations — one spiritual, the other material correlative and for ever united. "Thou shalt separate the

---

171. In the Egyptian as in the Indian theogony there was a *concealed* deity, the ONE of the creative. Thus *Shoo* is the god of creation and Osiris is in its original, primary form the "God whose name is unknown." (See Mariette's *Abydos* II pl. 63 and vol III. (pp. 413, 414, no 1122).

172. *Od* is the pure life-giving light or magnetic fluid, *ob* the messenger of death used by the sorcerers, the nefarious, bad fluid[, and] *aur* is the synthesis of the two, astral light proper. Can the Philologists tell why *Od*, a term used by Reichenbach to denominate the vital fluid — is also a Tibetan word meaning light, brightness radiancy? It equally means "sky" in an occult sense. Whence the root of the word?

earth from the fire, the subtile from the solid . . . that which ascends from earth to heaven and descends again from heaven to earth. It (the astral light), is the strong force of every force, for it conquers every subtile thing and penetrates into every solid. Thus was the world formed" (Hermes).

It was not Zeno, the founder of the Stoics alone who taught that the universe evolutes, when its primary substance is transformed from the state of fire into that of air, then water etc. Heraclitus of Ephesus maintained that the one Principle that underlies all phenomena in nature was fire. The intelligence that moves the universe is fire and the latter is intelligence. And while Anaximenes said the same of air, and Thales of Miletus (600 years B.C.) of water, the Esoteric doctrine reconciled all these philosophers by showing that though each was right, the system of none was complete.

(7) In the Sanskrit commentary of this *Stanza*, the terms used for the concealed and the *unrevealed* Principle are many. Among such appellations as the "unfathomable Darkness," the "whirlwind" etc. it is also called the "He of the Kalahansa or *Kali Hamsa*.["] Here the *m*, and the *n* are convertible and both sound like the nasal French *an* or *am*, or again *en*, or em (*e*nnui, *e*mbarras etc).

As in the Hebrew Bible many a mysterious and sacred name in Sanskrit conveys to the profane ear no more than some ordinary, and often vulgar word, because it is concealed anagrammatically and otherwise. This word of *"hamsa"* is just such a case. *Hamsa* is equal to (*a*)*ham sa*, three words meaning, *I am he* (in English[ )], while divided in still another way it will read — "*So-ham*" — ["]He (is) I," — Soham being equal to *Sah* "he" and *aham* — to ["]I," or "I am." In this alone is contained the universal mystery, the doctrine of the identity of man's essence with God-essence. It is useless to explain the whole mystery. All that can be now given is, that in both cases the (*hansa*) (whether *goose* or *swan*) is an important symbol that of Divine Wisdom for one, Wisdom in darkness beyond the reach.

To all exoteric purposes *Hamsa* as every Hindu knows, is a fabulous bird, which, when given milk mixed with water for its food, separated the two, drinking the milk and leaving the water, thus showing inherent wisdom, milk standing here for spirit, and water for matter. That the allegory is very ancient and is connected with the earliest archaic period is shown by the mention (in Bhâgavata Purana) of a certain caste named "*Hansa* or *Hamsa*,["] which was the "ONE caste" when in days of old there was only among the Hindus "one Veda, one Deity and one Caste." There is also a range in the Himalaya, described in the old scriptures as being situated north of *Mount Meru*, called Hansa, and connected with episodes pertaining to the History of religious Mysteries and Initiations.

As to the name of *Kala Hansa* being the supposed vehicle of Brahma–Prajapati in the exoteric texts and the translations of the Orientalists — it is quite wrong. Brahma the neuter, is called by them *Kala hansa* and Brahmâ, the male *Hansa-Vahana* because "his vehicle" or *Vahan* is a swan or goose says the "Hindu Classical Dictionary." This is a purely exoterical gloss. Esoterically and logically, if Brahma the infinite is all that it is described by the Orientalists, namely, agreeably with the Vedantic texts an abstract Deity with none of the humanly conceived attributes in him or in it, and it is still maintained that he or it, "is called Kalahansa" then how can it ever become the *vahan* of Brahmâ, the manifested male god? It is quite the reverse. The "swan or goose" (hansa) is the latter, as he, the emanation of the primordial Ray, is made to serve as a *vahan* or vehicle for that divine Ray, which, otherwise could not manifest itself in the Universe being *antiphrastically* itself, an emanation of "DARKNESS" — for human intellect, at any rate. It is Brahma then who is the *Kala-hansa* and the Ray — the *Hansa Vahan*. There is a great difference moreover between *Kali hansa* and *Kala Hansa.* The first means *black* swan (or goose) and the second the "Swan in the eternity," *Kala* meaning infinite time or duration. As to the strange symbol chosen, it is as suggestive. The true mystic significance being the idea of a universal matrix, figured by the primordial waters of the Deep, opening, so to say, for the reception and then the issue of that one ray (the *Logos*) which contains in itself the other seven procreative *rays* or Powers (the Builders), hence the choice of the aquatic fowl — whether goose, swan or pelican[173] — with seven goslings. Subsequently the symbol was modified and adapted to the religion of every country. *En-Soph* is called the "fiery soul of the pelican" in the book of Numbers.[174] (See App. X ["]The Hidden Gods and Symbols.["])

Appearing with every Manvantara as Narayan, or Swayambhuva (the self existent) and penetrating into the Mundane Egg, it emerges from it, at the end of the divine incubation as Brahmâ or Prajâpati, the progenitor of the future Universe into which he *expands*. He is Purusha (spirit), but he is also *Prakriti* (matter). Therefore it is only after separating himself into two halves, Brahma-Vâch (the female) and Brahma-Virâj (the male) that Prajâpati becomes the male Brahma. (See App. "Adam-Adami" in Sect I Introductory Chap.).

---

173. Whether the genus of the bird be *cygnus*, *anser* or *pelecanus* is all one, it is an aquatic bird floating or moving on the waters like the spirit, and thus issuing from those waters to give birth to other beings. The true significance of the symbol of the eighteenth Degree of the Rose-Croix is precisely this one though poetised later on into the motherly feeling of the pelican rending its bosom to feed its seven little ones with its blood.

174. The reason why Moses forbids eating the pelican and swan holding the two among the *unclean* fowls and permits eating "bald locusts, *beetles* and grasshopper after his kind" (Leviticus XI and Deut. XIV) is a purely physiological one and has naught to do with mystic symbolics.

The Secret Doctrine Würzburg Manuscript

Stanza IV

Listen, ye sons of the Earth, to your instructors the sons of the Fire. (1) Learn there is neither first nor last, for all is ONE number issued from NO-NUMBER. Learn what we, who descend from the primordial SEVEN (2) that are born from the primordial Flame — have learned from our Fathers. From the effulgency of Light — the Ray of the EVER-DARKNESS — sprung in Space (3) the reawakened Energies (Dhyani-chohans) the *One* from the Egg, the *six* and the *five*; then the ONE the THREE, the FIVE and the twice SEVEN the Sum Total (4). And these are: the Essences, the Flames, the Elements, the Builders, the Numbers, the Arupa (Formless) the Rupa (*with bodies*) and the FORCE or Divine man — the sum Total (5). And from the Divine Man emanated the FORMS, the SPARKS, the sacred Animals, (6) and the messengers of the sacred Pitris within the holy FOUR.[175] This was the army of the Voice (7) — the divine Septenary. The Sparks of the seven are subject to, and the servants of the First, Second, Third, Fourth, Fifth, Sixth and the Seventh of the Seven. These "Sparks" are called Spheres, Triangles, Cubes, Lines (8) and Modellers; for thus stands the eternal Nidana — the OI-HA-HOU.[176] (Adi-Nidana Svabhavat)

⊙ [( )for X, unknown quantity) — "Darkness," the boundless, or "The NO NUMBER" (See foot-note to N° III of this Enumeration).

I The Adi-Sanat (9)[177] the Number, for he is *one*.

---

175. The Tetractes, the Sacred or Perfect Square represented in the occult Numerals by 4.

176. The literal signification of the word is among the Eastern Occultists of the North a *circular wind*, whirlwind; but in this instance it is a term to denote the ceaseless and eternal Cosmic motion or rather the Force that moves it which Force is tacitly accepted as the Deity, but never named.

II The VOICE of the Word, Svabhâvat (10) the Numbers for he is ONE and NINE.

III The "Formless Square" (Arupa).

And these three enclosed within the ◯ (Boundless Circle) are the sacred FOUR, and the TEN are the Arupa (Subjective Formless) Universe (11). Then come the "Sons," the Seven Fighters, the One the Eighth rejected, (12) their Breath (13) which is the Light-maker (Bhâskara); then the *Second* SEVEN, who are the *Lipika* (14) produced by the THREE (Word, Voice and Spirit[ )] (15). The Rejected (Sun is One, the Sun-Suns, who are countless).

---

177. "Adi-Sanat" lit. — is the first Ancient. See No 8 comments. Brahma is sometimes called Sanat, "the Ancient." It is the name of Sephira also.

COMMENTARY to St. IV

(1) "Sons of Fire" — because they are the first Beings (in the S. Doctrine they are called "minds") evoluted from Primordial Fire. "The Lord is a consuming Fire." (Deut. 4-24). "The Lord Jesus shall be revealed with his mighty angels in *flaming fire*." (2nd Thessal. I 7.8.). The Holy Ghost descended on the Apostles like "eleven tongues of fire." (Acts II-3). Vishnu will return on Kalki, the white Horse as the last Avatar amid fire and flames; and *Sosiosh* will be brought down, equally on a white Horse "in a tornado of fire." "And I saw heaven opened and behold a *white horse* and he that sat upon him . . . is called the Word of God" (Rev. XIX v. 13) amid flaming Fire. Fire is Æther in its purest form hence is not regarded as *matter* but is the unity of Æther — the *second* or manifested Deity, it is universality. But there are two "Fires" and a distinction is made between them in the occult teachings. The first or the purely *Formless* and *invisible* Fire concealed in the *Spiritual Central Sun* is spoken of as "triple" while the Fire of the manifested Kosmos is Septenary, both throughout the Universe and our Solar System.

(2) The distinction between the "primordial," and the subsequent seven "Builders" is clearly pointed out in the Hindu Scriptures though misunderstood by the Orientalists who find in them great contradictions, "the number and names of the Rishis and Prajâpatis varying in different authorities.["] This is not so and results simply from the European scholar's inability to understand the division since he will allow no such thing as esotericism in the Hindu Pantheon. (See App. VI "The Theogony of the Seven["] and IX "Who are the Creators?")

(3) "According to Manu, Hiranya-garbha was Brahmâ the *first male*, formed by the undiscernible eternal First Cause in a golden egg resplendent as the Sun," states the *Classic Hindu Dict.* "Hiranya-garbha["] means the *golden* or rather the "Effulgent *Womb*" or Egg. The meaning tallies awkwardly with the epithet of "male." Surely the esoteric meaning of the sentence is clear enough. In the Rig-Veda it is said that "the one Lord of all beings . . . the one animating principle of Gods and

men arose in the beginning *in* the golden womb *Hiranya garbha*["] which is the Mundane Egg or Sphere of our Universe.

(4) "The *one* from the Egg, the six and the five," give the number 1065, the value of the *first-born* — Brahma Prajâpâti who answers to the numbers 7 and 14, and 21 respectively. The Prajâpâti are, as the Sephiroth, only seven including their synthetic Sephira from which they sprang. Thus, from Hiranya garbha or Prajâpâti, the *triune* (primeval Vedic trimurti — Agni, Vayu and Sûrya) the six other emanate, or *ten*, if separating the first three, which exist in one and one in three, all, moreover, being comprehended within that one "Supreme" *Parama*, called Guhya or "secret" and SARVÂTMA — the "Super Soul." "The Seven lords of Being lie concealed in Sarvatma like thoughts in one brain." So are the *Sephiroth*. It is either *seven* when counting from KETHER or ten *exoterically*. In the Mahabhârata the Prajâpâti are 21 in number or 10, 6, and 5 (1065) thrice seven.[178]

"The One, the three, the five and the twice seven" represent 13514, the numerical hierarchy of the Dhyani Chohans of various orders and of the *inner* or circumscribed world.[179] When placed on the boundary of the great circle of "Pass Not" (See Stanza V) called also *Dhyani pasa*, (the rope of the angels) the "rope" that hedges off the manifested from the unmanifested

---

178. In the Kabala the same numbers are a value of Jehovah viz., 1065, since the numerical values of the three letters which compose his name, namely *Jod, Vau* and twice *he* are respectively 10 (י), 6 (ו) and 5 (ה); or again thrice seven, 21. "Ten is the Mother of the Soul, for *Life* and *Light* are therein united" says Hermes. "For number *one* is born from the spirit and the number *ten* from matter (*chaos*, fem.); the Unity has made the *ten*, the ten the Unity." (*Book of the Keys*). By the means of the *Themura* (the anagrammatical method of the Kabala) and the knowledge of 1065 (21) a universal science may be obtained regarding Kosmos and its mysteries (Rabbi Yogel). The Rabbis regard the numbers 10, 6, 5 — as the most sacred of all.

179. The reader has seen in the Introductory volume that Mr. Ralston Skinner of Cincinnati, has now found out the same number for the Elohim. It came to the Jews from Chaldea.

Kosmos (not visible to our mortal eye) this number enlarges by permutation and expansion to 31415 — anagrammatically and kabalistically, being both the number of the circle and the mystic *Svastica*, the "twice seven" once more; for whatever way the two sets of figures are counted when additioned separately, one figure after the other, whether cross ways, from right or from left they will always yield 14. Mathematically, they represent the well known calculation, namely that the ratio of the diameter to the circumference of a circle is, as 1, to 3.1415 or "the value of the π" (pi) as this ratio is called — the symbol π being always used, in Europe in mathematical formulae to express it. Whether the value of the π, or the figure that is used for it, was the same in ancient India — is very doubtful for, in esoteric calculation another symbol and figures are used. Yet the European set of figures used for it must have some meaning since they are worked out to express the various ages and days of Brahmâ, as 311,040,000,000,000 — with fractions, yielding the same 31415. But we are not at present concerned with this. Yet it may be interesting to show the reader that the Hebrew word Alhim (Elohim) reads in the same way, in number values (by omitting as said the ciphers) 13514: since א (*a*) is 1; ל (*l*) is 3 (or 30); ה (*h*) is 5; י (i) 1 (or 10); and ם (m) is 4 (40).

Thus, while in the metaphysical world, the circle with the one central Point in it has no numbers and is called *Anupadaka* (parentless and numberless) viz. it can fall under no calculation; in the manifested world the mundane Egg or Circle is circumscribed within the groups called the Line, the Triangle, the Pentacle, the second Line and the Cube (or 13514); and when the Point having *generated a line* thus becoming a diameter which stands for the androgynous *Logos*, then the figures become 31415 or a triangle, a line, a cube, the second line and a pentacle. "When the son separates from the Mother he becomes the Father," the diameter standing for nature or the feminine principle. Therefore it is said: "In the world of Being, the one Point fructifies the Line — the Virgin Matrix of Kosmos (the egg shaped zero) and the immaculate Mother gives birth to the Form that contains all forms." Prajâpati is called the first procreating male and "his Mother's husband."[180] This gives the key note to all the later divine sons from immaculate mothers. This is greatly corroborated by the significant fact that *Anna* (the name of the mother of the Virgin Mary) now represented by the R.C. church as having given birth to her daughter in an immaculate way, ("Mary conceived without sin") is derived from the Chaldean *Ana*, heaven, or Astral light *Anima Mundi*; whence Anaitis, Devi-Durga, the wife of Siva is also called *Anna*-purna, and *Kanya* the Virgin, "Umâ-Kanya" being her esoteric name and meaning the ["]Virgin of light" or Akasa in one of her multitudinous aspects.

(5) The Devas, Pitris, Rishis; the *Suras* and the *asuras* the Daityas and Adityas, the Danavas and gand[h]arvas etc. etc. have all their synonyms in the Kabala and Hebrew angelology. Every one of them may be found now, even in the Christian hierarchy of divine and celestial powers. All those Thrones and Dominions, Virtues and Principalities, Cherubs, Seraphs and Demons, the various denizens of the Sidereal World, are all modern copies from the archaic prototypes. The very symbolism in their names transliterated and arranged in Greek and Latin are sufficient to show it as will be proven in several cases. (See App. XVII, and also for the "sum total.")

(6) The "sacred animals["] are found in the Bible as in the Kabala, and they have their meaning and a very profound one too on the page of the Origin of Life. In the *Sepher Jezirah* it is stated that "God engraved in the *Holy Four* the throne of his glory, the *Ophanim* (wheels or the worlds, spheres) the Seraphim,[181] the sacred animals, and the ministering angels and

---

180. We find the same expression in Egypt. The word *mout* signifies the Mother and shows the character assigned to her in the triad of that country. "She was no less the mother than the wife of Ammon, one of the principle titles of this god being the husband of his mother. The goddess Mout, therefore, is addressed as 'our Lady,' the 'Queen of Heaven and of the Earth,' thus sharing these titles with the other mother goddesses, Isis, Hathor." etc. (Maspero).

181. This is the literal translation from the IXth and Xth Sections: "Ten numbers without what? ONE: the spirit of the living God . . . who liveth in eternities! *Voice* and *Spirit* and *Word* and this is the Holy

from these three (the *air, water* and *fire* or æther) he formed his habitation. Thus was the world made "through three Seraphim [should be Sepharim] — *Sepher, Saphar* and *Sipur*" or through NUMBER, NUMBERS and *Numbered.* (See the same App. XVII.)

(7). The "army of the Voice," then, is the prototype of the ["]Host of the Logos," or the "Word" of the Sepher Jezirah, called in the Secret Doctrine, "the ONE Number issued from NO NUMBER" — the one eternal principle. The esoteric theogony begins with the ONE manifested, therefore — *not eternal in its* presence and being — the number of the numbers and numbered, — the latter proceeding from the VOICE the feminine Vach "of the hundred forms" SATARUPA or Nature. It is from this Number 10 or creative nature, the mother (the occult *cipher*, "naught" by itself ever procreating and multiplying with the Union of I (One) or spirit of life) that the whole Universe proceeded.

(8). Cosmic matter scattering and forming itself into elements; grouped into the mystic *four* within the fifth Element — Ether, the *Anima Mundi* or mother of Kosmos. "Dots, lines, triangles, cubes, circles["] and finally spheres — why or how? Because says the Commentary such is the first law of nature, and that nature *geometrizes* undeniably in all her manifestations. There is, [not] only in the primordial, but in our *manifested* matter, a law by which she correlates her geometrical forms as her compound elements later on — in which accident and

---

Spirit. TWO: Spirit out of Spirit. He designed and hewed there with twenty two letters of foundation, three mothers and *seven* double and *twelve* single, and *one spirit out of them*. THREE: Water out of Spirit; he designed and hewed with them the barren and void, mud and earth. He designed them as a flower bed, hewed them as a wall, covered them as a paving. FOUR: fire out of water; He designed and hewed therewith the throne of glory and the wheels and the seraphim and the *holy animals* and the ministering Angels and of the three he founded His dwelling, as it is said. He makes His angels spirits and His servants fiery flames." Which words "founded His dwelling" show clearly that in the Kabala the Deity was considered as in India — the Universe and was not in the origin the extra *Cosmic God* he is now.

chance have no room.¹⁸² *There is no rest or cessation of motion in nature. That* WHICH SEEMS REST IS *only the change of one form into another; the change of substance going hand in hand with that of form* — we are taught in Occult physics which thus seem to have anticipated the discovery of "correlation of matter" by a considerable time. Says the ancient commentary to Stanza IV:¹⁸³ "The mother is the fiery Fish of Life. She scatters her spawn and the Breath (motion) heats and quickens it. The grains (of spawn) are soon attracted to each other and form the Curds in the Ocean (of space). The larger lumps coalesce and receive new spawn — in fiery dots, triangles and cubes, which ripen when the time comes, some of the lumps detach themselves and assume a spheroidal form, which they can perform only when not interfered with by the others. After which law No ˣˣˣ comes into operation. Motion (the breath) becomes the whirlwind and sets them into rotation.¹⁸⁴

(9) "Adi Sanat" translated literally is the *First* or "Primeval ancient," which name identifies the Kabalistic "ancient of days" and the "Holy Aged" (Sephira and Adam

---

182. It is the knowledge of this law that permits and helps the Adept to perform his various phenomena, such as disintegration of matter, and the apport from one place into another.

183. There are ancient Commentaries attached to the Stanzas and modern glossaries, as the former in their symbolical language are usually as difficult to understand as the Stanzas themselves.

184. In a so called scientific work, The *Modern Genesis*, the author Rev. W. B. Slaughter criticizing the position assumed by the astronomer asks: "It is to be regretted that the advocates of this (nebular) theory have not entered more largely into the discussion of it (the beginning of rotation). No one condescends to give us the rationale of it. How does the process of cooling and contracting the mass impart to it a rotary motion?" (p 48). The occult Doctrine answers by showing motion eternal and the existence of a law when this motion owing to one of its modifications — heat, caused by the motion of particles — becomes "whirlwind." A drop of liquid assumes a spheroidal form owing to its atoms *moving round themselves* in their ultimate unresolvable essence. Unresolvable for western science at any rate.

Kadmon) with Brahmâ, the creator called also *Sanat* among his other names and titles.

(10) Svabhâvat is the mystic Essence, (or plastic Ether) of nature — "numbers" when manifesting the *number* in its unity of substance. The name is Buddhistic and a synonym for *Anima mundi*, the Kabalistic Astral light from whence proceed the scintilla or sparks — the various worlds. The worlds are all subject to *rulers* or Regents — Rishis and Pitris with the Hindus — Angels with the Jews and Christians — gods with the ancients in general.

(11) This means that the ["]boundless circle," (Zero) becomes a figure or number only when one of the 9 figures precedes it and thus manifests its value and potency, the *Word* or Logos, in union with Voice and Spirit (or understanding) standing for the nine figures and thus forming with the Cipher the *Decade* which contains in itself all the Universe. The triad forms within the Circle the *Tetraktis* or sacred Four, the square within the circle being the most potent of all the magical figures.

(12) The "One rejected" is the Sun of our system. The exoteric version may be found in the Hindu Sanskrit versions. In the Rig-Veda *Aditi*, the "boundless" or infinite space, translated by Mr. Max Müller "the visible infinite, visible by the naked eye (?); the endless expanse beyond the earth, beyond the clouds, beyond the sky["] is the equivalent of "Mother Space["] coeval with "Darkness." She is called very properly "the Mother of the Gods" DEVA-MATRI, as it is from her cosmic bosom that all the heavenly bodies of our system were born — planets and sun. Thus she is described this wise, "Eight sons were born from the body of Aditi; she approached the gods with seven, but cast away the eighth, Mârttânda" — our Sun. The seven sons called the Aditya are cosmically or astronomically — the seven planets and the Sun being excluded from their number shows plainly that the Hindus *knew* of a seventh planet without knowing Uranus.[185]

---

185. The Secret Doctrine teaches that the Sun is a central *star* not a planet. Yet the ancients knew of and worshipped seven great gods excluding the Sun and Earth. Which was that "mystery god" they set apart? Of course not *Uranus* discovered only in 1781 by Hershell. But could it not be known by another name? Says the author of

But esoterically and theologically, so to say, the Adityas are, in their primitive most ancient meanings the eight, and the twelve great Gods of the Hindu Pantheon. "The seven allow the mortals to see their dwellings, but show themselves only to the Arhats" says an old proverb — "their dwellings["] standing here for planets. The commentary, (the ancient) gives an allegory and explains it — "Eight houses were built by Mother. Eight houses for her eight divine Sons, four large and four small ones. Eight brilliant suns, according to their age and merits. Mârttânda was not satisfied though his (house) was the largest. He began (to work) as the huge elephants do. He breathed (drew in) into his stomach, the vital airs of his brothers. He sought to devour them. The larger (four) were far away; far on the margin of their kingdom.[186] They were not robbed (affected), and laughed. Do your worst, Sir, you cannot reach us — they said. But the smaller wept. They complained to the Mother. She exiled Mârttânda to the centre of her kingdom, from whence he could not move. Since then he only watches and threatens. He pursues them turning slowly around himself, always following from afar the direction in which his brothers move on the path that encircles their houses.[187] From that day he fed on the sweat of Mother's body. He filled himself with her breath and refuse. Therefore, she rejected him."

"Maconnerie Occulte": — ["]Occult sciences having discovered through astronomical calculations that the number of the planets must be seven, the ancients were led to introduce the sun into the scale of the celestial harmonies and make him occupy the vacant place. Thus, every time they perceived an influence that pertained to none of the six planets known they attributed it to the Sun. The error only *seems* important but was not so in practical results, if the ancient astrologers replaced Uranus by the Sun which is a central star relatively motionless turning only on its axis and regulating time and measure and which cannot be turned aside from its true functions.["] The nomenclature of the days of the week is thus faulty. ["]The Sun-day ought to be Uranus day (*Urani dies*, Urandi)["] adds Ragon.

186. Planetary system.

187. "The Sun rotates on his axis in the same direction always that the Planets revolve in their respective orbits" — astronomy teaches us.

The meaning of the allegory is plain, for we have both Djan Commentary and modern science to explain it, though the two differ in more than one particular. The occult Doctrine rejects the hypothesis born out of the nebular theory that the seven great planets have evoluted from the Sun[']s central mass. The eight "Great Gods" are born simultaneously at the first manvantaric stage, formed from the eternal substance, which having become visible is now called cometary matter,[188] "world stuff" and so on, and which is known as the *sixth* principle of kosmos, the universal soul in occultism. There is a whole poem, on the, so to say, *pregenetic* battles fought between the planets before the final formation of Kosmos, thus accounting for the seemingly disturbed position of the systems of several planets, the plane of the satellites of some (those of Neptune and Uranus for one) being tilted over, giving them an appearance of retrograde motion. These planets called the seven Fighters and the Architects, are accepted even by Christians as the leaders of the "Heavenly Host" thus showing the same traditions as a basis and starting point. Having evolved from Cosmic Space and before the final formation of the primaries and the annulation of the planetary nebula, the Sun we are taught, drew into the depths of its mass all the "cosmic vitality" he could, threatening to engulph his weaker "brothers" before the law of attraction and repulsion was finally adjusted; after which he *feeds* on "Mother's refuse and sweat" — in other words on those portions of Ether (the "breath of the universal *soul*") of which, science as yet knows nothing. A theory of this kind having been propounded by W. R. Grove (See *Correlation of the Physical Forces* 1843, p. 81; and address at the British Association, 1866.) who thought that the systems "are gradually changing by atmospheric additions or subtractions, or by accretions or diminutions arising

---

188. This essence of cometary matter — the occult science teaches is *totally different from any of the chemical — or physical characteristics* with which modern *science is acquainted.* It is homogeneous in its primitive form beyond the solar system and differentiates entirely once it crosses the boundaries of our Earth's regions vitiated by the atmospheres of the planets and the already compound matter of the interplanetary stuff, heterogeneous only in *our* manifested world.

from nebulous substances" . . . and again that "the Sun may condense gaseous matter as it travels in space, and so heat may be produced" — the archaic teaching seems scientific enough even in this age.[189] Mr. W. Mattieu Williams "suggested that this diffused matter or ether which is the recipient of the heat radiations of the Universe, is thereby drawn into the depths of the solar mass. Expelling thence the previously condensed and thermally exhausted ether, it becomes compressed and gives up its heat, to be in turn itself driven out in a rarefied and cooled state and to absorb a fresh supply of heat which he supposes to be in this way taken up by the ether and again concentrated and redistributed by the Suns of the Universe (chap. V)."[190]

This is about as close an approximation to the occult teachings as can be and explains "the dead breath" given back by Mârttânda and his feeding on "Mother space[']s sweat and refuse." What could affect Neptune, Saturn and Jupiter but little, would have killed such comparatively small "houses," as Mercury, Venus, and Mars. As Uranus was not known, before the end of the eighteenth century, the name of the Fourth planet mentioned in the Allegory must remain to us a mystery.

(13) The "breath" of all the "seven" is said to be *Bhâskara* (light making) because they (the planets) were all comets and *suns* in their origin. Started into Manvantaric life from primeval Chaos (*irresolvable nebula* now), by aggregation and accumulation of eternal material, according to the beautiful expression in the Commentary, — "the sons of Light clothed themselves in the stuff of darkness." They are called allegorically "the Heavenly snails" on account of their (to us) formless Intelligences inhabiting their starry and planetary homes and so to say carrying them along in their revolutions and rotation. That they all belong to one family and have a common origin was taught of the heavenly bodies and planets by the

---

189. Every [Very] similar ideas are to be found in W. M. Williams, "*The Fuel of the Sun*, in Dr. C. W. Siemens' ["]On the Conservation of Solar Energy["] (*Nature* xxv, 440-4, March 9, 1882); and also in Dr. P. Martin Duncan's "Address of the President of the Geological Society.["] London, May 1877.

190. *Comparative Geology*, by Alex. Winchell L.L.D. (p. 56).

Archaic Occultists before Kepler, Newton, Leibnitz, Kant, Herschell, and Laplace. Heat (the breath), attraction and repulsion the three great factors of motion are the conditions under which all the members of this primitive family are born, developed and die to be reborn after a "night of Brahma," during which eternal matter rebecomes every time once more *conditionless*. The most attenuated gases can give no idea of its nature to the modern physicist. (See *Summary* at the end of Chap. I). Centres of Forces at first, the invisible sparks of primordial atoms grow into molecules and become *Suns* — growing gradually into objectivity — gaseous, radiant, cosmic, finally the One "whirlwind" (or Motion) giving the impulse to the *form* and regulating its initial motion by the never ceasing Breath.

(14) The *Lipika*, from the word *lipi* "writing" means literally the "scribes." Mystically, these divine Beings are connected with *Karma*, the law of retribution, for they are the Recorders or Annalists, who impress on the to us invisible tablets of Astral Light — "the great picture gallery of Eternity" — a faithful record of every act and even thought of man, — of all that was, is or ever will be, in the phenomenal Universe. As said in *Isis* — this divine and unseen canvas is the BOOK OF LIFE. As it is the *Lipika* who transmit from the passive universal mind the ideal plan of the universe upon which the "Builders" reconstruct the Kosmos after every Pralaya, it is they who stand parallel to the "Seven Angels of the Presence" whom the Christians recognize in the seven "Planetary" or the "spirits of the stars" for thus it is they who are the direct amanuenses of the Eternal Ideation — or, as called by Plato the "Divine Thought." The Eternal Record is no fantastic dream, for we see the same records in the world of gross matter. "A shadow never falls upon a wall without leaving there upon a permanent trace which might be made visible by resorting to proper processes" . . . says Dr. Draper . . . ["]The portraits of our friends, or landscape views, may be hidden on the sensitive surface, from the eye, but they are ready to make their appearance, as soon as proper developers are resorted to. A spectre is concealed on a silver or glassy surface, until by our necromancy, we make it come forth into the visible world. Upon the walls of our most

private apartments, where we think the eye of intrusion is altogether shut out, and our retirement can never be profaned, there exist the vestiges of all our acts, silhouettes of whatever we have done.["] (["]Conflict,["] pp. 132-133). Drs. Jevon and Babbage believe that every thought, displacing the particles of the brain and setting them in motion, scatters them throughout the Universe and think that each particle of the existing matter must be a register of all that has happened (*Principles of Science* Vol II p. 455). Thus the ancient doctrine has begun to acquire rights of citizenship in the speculations of the scientific world.

(15) The "rejected" Son, as [is] our SUN as shown above; and the Son-Suns are not only our planets but heavenly bodies in general. Himself the *reflection* of the "central, spiritual Sun," Surya is the prototype of all those bodies that came after him. In the Vedas he is called *Loka-Chakshuh* "the eye of the world" (our world) and he is one of the three chief deities. He is at times called the Son of *Dyaus* and sometimes of *Aditi* because no distinction or room is allowed for the esoteric meaning. He is often shown in symbolism, drawn in a chariot by seven horses — the *seven planets*, and often by one horse with seven heads, showing their common cosmic origin from one element.

Stanza V

The Primordial seven, the first Seven Breaths of the Dragon of Wisdom produce in their turn from their holy circumgyrating Breaths the Fiery whirlwind. (1) They make of him the messenger of their Will. (2) The *Dgyn* [Dzyu in the 1888 edition] becomes FOHAT. (3) The swift Son of the divine Sons and the *Lipika*[191] (4) runs circular errands under the impulse of their guiding Thought. He passes like lightning through the Fiery clouds (cosmic mists); takes three and five and seven strides through the seven regions above and the seven below (the wor[l]ds to be). (5) He lifts his voice and calls the innumerable sparks (atoms) and joins them. He is their guiding spirit and leader. When he commences work, he separates the sparks of the lower kingdom (mineral atoms) that float and thrill with joy in their radiant dwellings (gaseous clouds), and forms therewith the germs of wheels. (6) He places them in the six directions of space and one in the middle — the central wheel. (7)[192] Fohat traces spiral lines to unite the six: an army of the Sons of Light stands at each angle and the Lipika — in the middle wheel. When they (the Lipika) have said — ["]This is good["] — the first *divine* World is ready (See ["]Seals of the 7 Worlds["] in App. XVII.), the first being the second. (8) Then the "*divine* Arupa" (the formless world) reflects itself in the Intellectual Rupa Loka (the eternal world of Form), the first garment of the Divine (9) the Manava-loka of the Mind-born sons. Fohat takes five strides (having performed the first three) and builds 4 winged wheels at each corner of the square, for the four Holy ones (10) and their armies (hosts). The *Lipika* circumscribe the Triangle, the first Line the Cube; the second Line and the Pentacle within the Egg (circle). It is the ring called "Pass Not"

---

191. The difference between the "Builders," Planetary Spirits and the Lipika must not be lost sight of. (See number 9 of this commentary.)

192. The "Double Triangle" is here meant, the junction and blending together of pure spirit and matter, of the *Arupa* and the *Rupa*, of which the triangle is a symbol. This double triangle is the sign of Vishnu as it is Solomon's seal and the *Sri Antara* of the Brahmins.

(11) for those who *descend and ascend* as also for those, who during the Kalpa are progressing toward the great Day "*Be with us.*" (12) Thus were formed the Arupa and the Rupa (the Formless world and the world of Forms): from One LIGHT seven Lights; from each of the seven, seven times seven lights. The wheels "watch the RING."

(The Stanza proceeds with a minute classification of the orders of Angelic Hierarchy. From the group of seven, emanates the "mind born group of Ten of Twelve of Twenty one, etc. all these divided again into sub-groups of septenary, novems, duo decimals and so on until the mind is lost in this endless enumeration of celestial hosts and Beings, each having its distinct task in the ruling of the visible Kosmos during its duration.)

The Secret Doctrine Würzburg Manuscript

Commentary

This is, perhaps, the most difficult of all the Stanzas, to explain. Its language is comprehensible only to him who is thoroughly versed in Eastern allegory and its purposely obscure phraseology. The question will be surely asked — "Do the Occultists believe in all these "Builders," "Lipika" and "Sons of Light" as Entities, or are they simply imageries? To this the answer is given as plainly: After due allowance to the imagery of personified Powers; we must believe in these Entities, if we would not reject the existence of spiritual humanity within physical mankind. For the hosts of those Sons of Light and "mind-born Sons" of the first manifested Ray of the *Unknown all* — are the very root of that spiritual Humanity, unless man has to believe the unphilosophical dogma of a specially created soul for each human birth and a fresh supply of them pouring in daily, since Adam. The occult doctrine teach[es] that to become an angel or god — aye even of the highest, that Entity must first pass through human shape, must have won for himself the right to become *divine*. The Kabalists say: the stone becomes a plant, the plant an animal, the animal a man, and the man a spirit — and the latter — a God. The "Mind-born Sons" and the "Builders" here spoken of, were men in preceding worlds and manvantaras. More reasons for it are given else where. Let us see what the meaning of this *Stanza* may be.

This sentence reminds strongly of a like one in the Kabala and the King Psalmist (civ) both speaking of God making the wind his messenger and "his ministers a flaming fire." But in the Esoteric Doctrine it is used figuratively. The "fiery wind" is the incandescent Cosmic Dust following the thought of the Creative Powers.

(1[,]2) "The *Dygn* [so spelled in ms.] becomes FOHAT" the expression shows it. Dygn is the one real (Occult or magic) knowledge — Wisdom; one which dealing with eternal truths and *primal* causes, becomes omnipotence when applied in the right direction. Its antithesis is Dygn in dealing only with illusions and false appearances as our exoteric sciences. In this case *Dgyn* [so ms.] is the expression of the collective wisdom of the Dhyani-Buddhas.

(3) Fohat is the personified power that acts as a living force generated by the strong desire of the magnetizer; and on the Cosmic plane, the building or constructive power that carries out in the formation of things, from planetary system down to the simple daisy, the plan in the mind of nature or in the Divine thought, in the development and growth of that special thing. He is the messenger of the Cosmic and human ideations; the active force in Universal life; in his *secondary* aspect. Fohat is the Solar Energy, the electric, vital fluid and the preserving *fourth* principle, the animal soul of nature, so to say. In India, Fohat is connected with Vishnu and Surya as in the early character of that God; for Vishnu is not a high God in the Rig Veda. The name of Vishnu is from the root *vish* "to pervade" and Fohat is called the "Pervader." In the exoteric Hindu Pantheon Vishnu is "a manifestation of the Solar Energy" and he is described as striding through the seven regions of the Universe in three steps, and . . . "he has little in common with Vishnu of later times." (See Dowson's *Hindu Class. Dict.*)

(4) The forty "assessors" who stand in the region of Amenti as the accusers of the Soul before Osiris belong to the same class of deities as the Lipika and might stand parallel, were not the Egyptian gods, so little understood in their esoteric meaning. The Hindu Chitra-gupta who reads out the account of every soul's life from his register, called *Agra sandhani*; the "Assessors" who read theirs from the heart of the defunct which becomes an open book before, (whether) Yama, Minos, Osiris or Karma — are all so many copies from the Lipika, and their astral records. Nevertheless, the *Lipi-ka* are not deities connected with Death, but with Life Eternal. (See Nos 10 and 11, below.)

(5) The "three and seven" strides refer to the "Seven Spheres" inhabited in turn by man — (of the esoteric Doctrine) as well as to the seven regions of the Earth. Notwithstanding the frequent objections made by would be Orientalists the seven worlds or spheres of our planetary chain are distinctly referred to in the exoteric Hindu Scriptures. That these accounts are *blinds*, is shown by their contradicting each other, a different construction, being found in almost every Purana and Epic Poem. Read all esoterically — they will all yield the same meaning. Thus one account enumerates seven, exclusive of the

nether worlds also seven in number — these fourteen upper and nether worlds having nothing to do with the classification of the septenary chain and belonging to the purely ethereal, invisible worlds. These will be noticed elsewhere. Suffice for the present to show that they are purposely referred to as though they belonged to the chain. "Another enumeration calls the seven worlds earth, sky, heaven, middle region, place of birth, mansion of the blest and abode of truth; placing the 'sons of Brahmâ' in the sixth division, and stating the fifth or Jana Loka to be that where animals destroyed in the general conflagration are born again." (See Hindu Class. Dict. Dowson's). The real esoteric teaching is given in the Appendices. He who is prepared for it, will understand the esotericism.

(6) "Wheels" as already explained, are the centres of force, around which, primordial cosmic matter expands and passing through all the six stages of consolidation becomes spheroidal and ends by being transformed into globes or spheres. It is one of the fundamental dogmas of esoteric cosmogony, that during the Kalpas (or æons) of life, *motion*, which, during the periods of Rest "pulsates and thrills through, every slumbering atom"[193] (Commentary on *Djan*) assumes an ever growing tendency from the first awakening of Kosmos to a new "Day" to a circular movement. The ["]Deity becomes a *whirlwind*." They are also called *Rotæ* — the moving wheels of the celestial orbs participating in the World's creation (See *Kabala Denud.*, "De Anima," p. 113) when the meaning refers to the animating principle of the stars and planets; for, in the Kabala they are

---

193. It may be asked — and the writer has not failed to do so — who is there to ascertain the difference in that motion since all nature is reduced to its primal essence and there can be no one — not even a Dhyani Chohan (who are all in *Nirvana*) to see it. The answer to this is "Every thing in nature has to be judged on analogy. Though the highest Deities (Archangels or Dhyani Buddha) are unable to penetrate the mysteries too far beyond our planetary system and the visible kosmos, yet there were great seers and prophets in olden times who were permitted to perceive the mystery of motion and breath in Spaces, wherein systems of worlds were at rest and plunged in their periodical sleep."

represented by the *Ophanim*, the Angels of the Spheres and stars of which they are the informing Souls.

This law of vortical movement in primordial matter, is one of the oldest conceptions of Greek philosophy whose first historical Sages were nearly all Initiates of the mysteries. The Greeks had it from the Egyptians and the latter from the Chaldees who had been the pupils of Brahmans of the esoteric school. Leucippus and Democritus of Abdera — the pupil of the Magi, taught that this gyratory movement of the atoms and spheres existed from the eternity.[194] *Hicetas, Heraclides, Ecphantus, Pythagoras* and all his pupils taught the rotation of the Earth; and Aryabhata of India, Aristarchus, Seleucus and Archimedes calculated its revolution as scientifically as the astronomers do now; while the theory of the Elemental Vortices was known to Anaxagoras and maintained by him 500 years B.C. or nearly 2000 before it was taken up by Galileo, Descartes and Swedenborg and finally with slight modifications by Sir W. Thompson (See his *Vertical Atoms*). All such knowledge is, if justice be only done to it — *an echo* of the archaic Doctrine, an attempt to explain which is now being made. How men of the few last centuries have come to the same ideas and conclusions that were taught as axiomatic truths in the secrecy of the *Adyta* dozens of millenniums ago, is a question that is treated

---

194. "The Doctrine of the rotation of the earth about an axis was taught by the Pythagorean Hicetas, probably as early as 500 B.C. It was also taught by his pupil Cephantus, and by Heraclides, a pupil of Plato. The immobility of the Sun and the orbital rotation of the earth were shown by Aristarchus of Samos as early as 281 B.C., to be suppositions accordant with facts of observation. The heliocentric theory was taught about 150 B. C. (It was taught 500 B.C. by Pythagoras. H.P.B.) by Seleucus of Seleucia on the Tigris. It is said also that Archimedes in a work entitled *Psammites* inculcated the heliocentric theory. The sphericity of the Earth was distinctly taught by Aristotle, who appealed for proof to the figure of the earth's shadow on the moon in eclipses (Arist. *De Coelo*, lib. ii, cap. XIV). The same idea was defended by Pliny (*Nat. Hist.* ii 65). These views seem to have been lost from knowledge for more than a thousand years . . ." (*Comp. Geology*, Part IV, Prekantian Specul. p 551, by Al. Winchell, L.L.D. Profes. of Geology and Paleontology at the University of Michigan.)

separately. Some were led to it by the natural progress in physical sciences and personal observations; others — such as Copernicus, Swedenborg and a few more owe their knowledge far more to *innate*, than to acquired ideas developed naturally by a course of study — their great learning notwithstanding. (See "A Mystery about Buddha" — App. to Sect. VI).[195]

(7) The "army" at each angle, is the host of angelic Beings (Dhyani Chohans) appointed to guide and watch over each respective region from the beginning to the end of Manvantara. They are the "mystic Watchers" of the Christian Kabalists, and Alchemists, and relate symbolically as Cosmogonically to the numerical system of the Universe. The numbers with which these Celestial Beings are connected are extremely difficult to study as each number refers to several groups of distinct ideas according to what particular group of "Angels" it is made to represent. Herein lies the nodus in the study of symbology, that, unable to untie by disentangling it, so many scholars have preferred dealing with, as Alexander dealt

---

195. That Swedenborg who could not have possibly known anything of the Esoteric ideas of Budhism, came independently very near the Occult teaching in his general conceptions — is shown by his Essay on the Vortical Theory. In Clissold's translation of it quoted by Professor Winchell, we find the following *resumé*. "The first Cause is the infinite or unlimited. *This gives existence to the first finite or limited.*" (The *logos* in his manifestation and the Universe.) "That which produces a limit is analogous to motion. (See the 1st Stanza above.) The limit produced is a point, the Essence of which is motion; but being without parts, this Essence is not actual motion but only a conatus to it." (In our doctrine it is not a "conatus" but a change from eternal vibration in the unmanifested to vortical motion in the phenomenal or manifested world.) . . . "From this first proceed extension, space, figure and succession or time. As in geometry a point generates a line, a line a surface, and a surface a solid, so here the Universe is contained *in ovo* in the first natural point . . . The motion toward which the conatus tends, is *circular*, since the circle is the most perfect of all figures["] . . . "The most perfect figure of the motion . . . must be the perpetually circular; that is to say, it must proceed from the centre to the periphery and from the periphery to the centre." This is occultism pure and simple. (Quoted from *Princip. Rerum Naturalia*.)

with the Gordian knot; and hence the erroneous conceptions and teachings as a direct result.

(8) The *"first* is the second," because the "first" cannot really be numbered or regarded as the first, as it is the REAL *World*, in its primary manifestation, the World of Truth, or SAT, being the direct energy that radiates from the ONE REALITY, the nameless Deity. Here again the untranslatable term Sat (*be-ness*) is likely to lead into an erroneous conception, as that which is manifested cannot be *Sat* but only temporary, not everlasting, not even *sempeternal*, in truth. It is coeval and coexistent with the one Life "Secondless," but as a manifestation it is still a Maya — like the rest. This "world of Truth" can be described only in the words of the Commentary "a bright star dropped from the heart of Eternity; the beacon of hope on whose seven rays hang the seven worlds of Being." Truly so, since those are the seven lights whose *reflections* are the human immortal monads — the *Atma* or spirit-soul of every mortal creature of the mankind family. First this septenary light, then —

(9) The "Divine World," — the countless lights lit at the primeval lights — the Buddhic or formless divine souls, of the last *Arupa* (formless) World the "Sum Total" in the mysterious language of the old Stanza. In the *Catechism*, the Master is made to ask the pupil.[:]

"Lift thy head, oh Lanoo; dost thou see one, or countless lights above thee, burning in the dark midnight sky?"

"I *sense* one Flame, Oh Gurujee; I see countless undetached sparks shining *in* it."

"Thou sayest well — And now look around, and into thy self. That light which burns inside thee, dost thou feel it different in any wise from the light that shines in thy brother men?" —

"It is in no way different, though the prisoner is held in bondage by Karma and that its outer garments delude the ignorant into saying — thy soul and *my* soul."

The radical unity of the ultimate essence of each constituent part of compounds in nature — from star to mineral atom, from the highest Dhyan-Chohan to the smallest infusoria in the fullest acceptation of the term, and whether applied to the spiritual, intellectual or physical world — is the one fundamental law in the occult sciences. "The Deity is boundless and infinite expansion," says an axiom of Occult sciences. And hence, as remarked, the name of Brahma, from the word *brih* to expand or grow.[196] There is a deep philosophy underlying the earliest worship in the world, that of the Sun and of Fire. Of all the Elements known to physical Science *fire* is the one that has ever eluded definite analysis. We proudly proclaim air as a compound fluid containing oxygen gas and nytrogen; we view complacently the Earth as matter composed of particles that form the globe, we speak of the *primitive ten earths* endowing each with a Greek or Latin name; water is chemically another compound of oxygen and hydrogen; but what is FIRE[?] It is the effect of combustion — we are gravely answered. It is heat and light and motion, and a correlation of physical and chemical forces in general this scientific definition being philosophically supplemented by the theological one in Webster's Dictionary, explaining fire as "the instrument of punishment, or the punishment of the impenitent in another state" — the "state" supposed to be *spiritual* but the fire remaining it seems as *material* as ever. What do the Occult Sciences say. "Fire," they teach, "is the most perfect and unadulterated reflection up in the heavens as on earth, of the ONE Deity. It is life and death, the origin and the end of every material thing. It is, in short, *divine matter*." Thus, not only the fire-worshipping Parsi, but even the wandering primitive and savage tribes of America who proclaim themselves as "born of fire" show far more true philosophy and truth in their "superstitions" than all the speculations of modern scholars of physics and metaphysics put together. The Rosicrucians were the only Kabalists who defined Fire in the right and correct way. Procure a six penny lamp, and keep it only supplied with oil and you will be able to light at its flame

---

196. In the *Rig-Veda* we find the names *Brahman*aspati and *Brih*aspati alternating and an equivalent to each other. See also "Brihad. Upanishad["] and Brihaspati is a Deity and called "the father of the Gods."

the lamps, candles and fires of the whole globe without diminishing that flame. If the Deity, the *radical* ONE, is eternal and an infinite substance — "The Lord thy God is a consuming fire" truly (Deut. 4-24) — and never consumed, then it does not stand to reason why the occult teaching should be held as unphilosophical, when saying, "Thus were the Arupa and Rupa worlds formed. From ONE Light the seven lights, from each of the seven seven times seven" etc.

(10) There are the "four Maharajahs" or great Kings of the Dhyan Chohans, the Devas who preside, each over one of the four cardinal points. They are the Regents or Angels who rule over the cosmical Forces of North, South, East and West, forces having each a distinct occult property. These Beings are also connected with karma as the latter needs physical and material agents to carry out her decrees such as the four kinds of winds for instance professedly admitted by science to have their respective evil and beneficent influences upon the health of mankind and every living thing. The[re] is occult philosophy in that Roman Catholic doctrine that traces the various public calamities, such as epidemics and disease and wars and so on, to the invisible "messengers" from North and West. "The glory of God comes from the way of the East" says Ezekiel, while Jeremiah, Isaiah and the Psalmist assure their readers that all the evil under the Sun comes from the North and the West — which, proposition when applied to the Jewish nation sounds like an undeniable prophecy to themselves. And this accounts also for St. Ambroise (*On Amos* ch. iv) declaring that it is precisely for that reason that ["]we curse the North-Wind, and that during the ceremony of baptism we begin by turning toward the West (sidereal), to renounce the better, *him* who inhabits it; after which we turn to the East."

Belief in the "Four Maharajahs" the Regents of the Four cardinal points — was universal and is now that of Christians,[197]

---

197. Says the scholarly Vossius, in his *Theol.* Cir. I. VII: "Though St. Augustine has said that every visible thing of this world had an angelic virtue as an overseer near it, it is not *individual* but *entire species* of things, that must be understood, each such species, having indeed its *particular angel to watch it.* He is at one in this, with all the

who call them after St. Augustine, "Angelic Virtues" and spirits when enumerated by themselves and devils when named by Pagans. But where is the difference between the Pagans and Christians in this case? Following Plato, Aristotle explained that by the term στοιχεῖα they understood only the *incorporeal* principles placed at each of the four great divisions of our cosmical world to supervise them. Thus, no more than the Christians did they *adore* and *worship* the Elements and the cardinal (imaginary) points, but the "Gods" that ruled these respectively. For the Church there are two kinds of Sidereal beings, the Angels and the Devils. For the Kabalist and Occultist there is but one; and he makes no difference between "the Rector of Light" and the *Cosmocratores,* or ["]*Rectores tenebrarum harum*" that the Roman church imagines in the same Being as soon as he is called by another name than that which she addresses him by. It is not the "Rector" or "Maharajah" who punishes or rewards, with or without, God's permission or order, but man himself, his deeds, or karma — that attract individually and collectively, as whole nations sometimes do, every kind of evil and calamity. We produce Causes and these awaken the corresponding powers in the sidereal world, which powers are very magnetically and irresistibly attracted to those who produced them — whether the latter are practically the evil-doers or simply *Thinkers* who only brood mischief. *Thought is matter* . . . we are taught by modern science; and *"every particle of the existing matter must be a register of all that has happened"* as the "Principles of Science" by Messrs Jevons and Babbage tell the profane. Modern Science is drawn into the Maelstrom of Occultism unconsciously, no doubt, still very sensibly. Anyhow, if the Egyptian temples — according to Clemens Alexandrinus had an immense curtain separating the tabernacle from the place for the congregation — so had the

---

philosophers . . . For as these angels are *spirits* separated from the objects . . . whereas for the philosophers (pagan) they were *Gods.*" Considering the Ritual established by the R. C. church for "spirits of the Stars" — the latter look suspiciously like "Gods" and were no more honoured and prayed to by the ancient and modern pagan rabbi [rabble] than they are now at Rome by the highly cultured Catholics and Christians.

Jews. Both were drawn over *five* pillars (the pentacle) symbolizing our five senses and five root-races, esoterically while the four colours of the curtain represented the four cardinal points and the four elements (the terrestrial). The whole was an allegorical symbol: it is through the four high Rulers over the four points and Elements that our five senses may become cognizant of the hidden truths of nature; and not at all as Clemens would have it that it is the elements *per se* that furnished Pagans with divine knowledge or — the knowledge of God,[198] while the Egyptian emblem was *spiritual*, that of the Jews was purely materialistic, and honoured the blind elements and the imaginary "Points," indeed. For what was the meaning of the *square* tabernacle raised by Moses in the wilderness if it had not the same cosmical significance? "Thou shalt make a hanging . . . of blue purple and scarlet" and "five pillars of shittim wood for the hanging" . . . four brazen rings in the four corners thereof . . . boards of fine wood for the four sides north, south, west and east . . . the tabernacle . . . "with *cherubims* of cunning work." — (Exodus ch. XXVI, XXVII.) The tabernacle and the square courtyard, cherubim and all was precisely the same, as in the Egyptian temples. The *square* form of the tabernacle meant just the same thing as it still means now, to this day, in the exoteric worship of the Chinese Tibetans — the four cardinal points signifying that, which the four sides of the pyramids, obelisks and other such square buildings mean. Josephus takes care to explain the whole thing. He declares that the Tabernacle pillars are the same as those *raised at Tyre to the four Elements*; that were placed on pedestals whose four angles faced the four cardinal points; adding that "the angles of the pedestals had equally the four *figures of the Zodiac*" on them, which represented the same orientation. (*Ant.* I, VIII ch. xxii).

The same idea is found in the Zoroastrian caves, in the rock cut temples of India, as in all the sacred *square* buildings of antiquity that have survived to this day. This is shown definitely

---

198. Thus the sentence "Nature elementorum obtinet revelatronem Dei" in Clemens' *Strom.* I, V §6. — is applicable both ends or — neither. Consult the Zends vol. II p. 228 and Plutarch *de Iside* as compared by Layard, *Acad. des Inscrip.* 1854, Vol. XV.

by Layard, who finds the four cardinal points and the four primitive elements, in the religion of every country, under the shape of square obelisks, the four sides of the pyramids etc. etc. Of these elements and their points the 4 *Maharajahs* were the regents and also directors.

If the student would know more of them, he has but to compare the vision of Ezekiel (chap. 1.) with what is known of Chinese Buddhism even in its exoteric teachings; and examine the *outward* shape of these "great Things." In the words of Rev. Joseph Edkins, they are "the Devas who preside each over one of the four continents into which the Hindus divide the world.["][199] Each leads an army of spiritual beings to protect mankind and Buddhism. With the exception of the last specification the 4 celestial Beings are precisely that. They are the *protectors* of mankind, as also the agent of karma on Earth, whereas the Lipika are concerned with the Humanity's hereafter. At the same time, they are the *four* living creatures "who had the likeness of a man["] of Ezekiel's visions, called by the translators of the Bible "Cherubs," by the Occult sciences the "winged fiery wheels," and in the Hindu Pantheon by a number of names gandharvas, the "sweet voiced," the golden winged Garudas, the Kinnaras — "horses with *horned* heads" and especially the former with his white face, red wings, the beak of an eagle, with a luster so brilliant that he is mistaken for Agni — (fire) — are multiplications and exoteric fancies upon the descriptions of the "Four Maharajahs" called the "Avengers" and "the winged wheels." Their mission and character being explained, let us see what the Christian Bible interpreters say of the Cherubs: "The word signifies in Hebrew fullness of knowledge; these angels are so called from their exquisite knowledge and were therefore *used for the punishment of men* who affected divine knowledge." (Interpreted by Cruden in his *Concordance* from Gen. 3-25) very well; and vague as the

---

199. The Hindus happen to divide the world into seven continents, exoterically as esoterically; and their four cosmic devas preside over the four cardinal points, and not the continents. But this is a trifling mistake to make even in a presumably scientific and scholarly work, since after all Hindus and Chinese are only Pagans. The author commits many more mistakes. (See *Chin. Buddhism* p. 216.)

information is, it shows that the cherub placed at the gate of the garden of Eden after Adam's and Eve's "fall" suggested to the venerable interpreters the idea of punishment connected with forbidden science or *divine* knowledge as they knew nothing of karma, or the occult meaning of the allegory either. But in Ezekiel the four cosmical angels are plainly[200] described. "I looked, and, behold, a whirlwind came out of the north, a great cloud and a fire in folding it . . . also out of the midst thereof came the likeness of four living creatures, and this was their appearance, they had the likeness of a man, and every one had four faces . . . and four wings . . . The four had the face of a man, and the face of a lion and the face of an ox, and the face of an eagle . . . Now as I beheld the living creatures *behold one wheel upon the Earth with his four faces* . . . as it were a wheel in the middle of a wheel . . . for the spirit of the living creature was in the wheel . . . their appearance was like burning coals of fire . . ." etc. etc. (chap. I. Ezekiel.)

There are three chief groups of *Builders* and as many of the *Planetary Spirits* and the *Lipika*, each group being again subdivided into seven sub-groups. It is impossible even in such a vast work as this one to enter into a minute examination of even these three principal groups, as it would demand an extra volume. The "Builders" are the representations of the first "mind-born" Spiritual Entities, (therefore the primeval Rishi Prajapati, the seven great gods of Egypt of which "Osiris" is the chief, the seven Amshaspends of the Zoroastrians, with Ormuzd at the head, the seven "spirits of the Face," the seven Sep[h]iroth separated from the first Triad etc. etc). They build (or rebuild, rather) every "System" after its night. The second group is the

---

200. The Jews (save the Kabalists) having no names for East, West, South and North, expressed the idea by words signifying, before, behind, right and left, confounded very often the terms, exoterically, thus making the blinds in the Bible still more confused and difficult to interpret. Add to this the fact that out of the forty seven translators of King James I, of Englands's Bible "*only three* understood Hebrew, and of these two died *before the Psalms* were translated." (Royal Masonic Cyclopedia) and one may understand well what reliance can be placed on the English translation of the Hebrew Bible and its correctness. In this work the Roman Catholic version is generally followed.

architect of our planetary chain exclusively; and the third, the progenitors of our Humanity — the Macrocosmic prototype of the microcosm. The planetary spirits are the informing spirits of the stars, in general, and of the Planets especially, those who rule the destiny of men, born all under one of their constellations; the second and the third groups pertaining to other systems in the same functions, and all ruling various departments in nature. In the Hindu exoteric Pantheon they are the guardian deities who preside over the eight points of the compass — the four cardinal and the four intermediate points of the compass and are called *Loka-Palas,* "Supporters or guardians of the world["] (in our *visible* kosmos) — of which Indra (East), Yama (South), Varuna (West) and Kuvera (north) are the chief; their elephants and their spouses pertaining of course to fancy and afterthought, though some have an occult significance. The Lipika, a description of which is given in the Commentary for Stanza IV (See No. 14). They are the Spirits of the Universe, whereas the Builders are only our own planetary deities. They belong to the most occult portion of Kosmogenesis — that which cannot be given here. Whether the Adepts (the highest) know this Angelic order in the completeness of its triple degree or only of the lower one connected with the records of *our* world — is something which the writer is unprepared to say — rather the latter; as of its highest order one thing is only taught: the Lipika are connected with karma being its direct Recorders.[201]

(11) The "Ring PASS NOT" that the *Lipikas* circumscribe around the triangle, the 1st Line, the Cube, the 2nd Line and the Pentacle, is the Circle of 31415, again, the geometrical figures standing here for numerical figures. According to the Occult teaching this Ring is beyond the region

---

201. The four faces of the Lion, the Ox, the Eagle and man mentioned in *Ezekiel* and that represent the *Lipika* in their aspect of the Four *Maharajahs* have been adopted by the Christians for the Four Evangelists when their pictures precede their respective gospels. A face of [here in the manuscript there is a blank space] of the four accompanies generally the Apostle. Thus Matthew is represented with an ox by his side, St. John with an eagle and so on. Such was the idea, we believe, of Sir W. Hershell [Herschel] and Laplace, [word(s) illegible; as has?] ever been an axiom with the Occultists.

of what is called nebulae — in astronomy, and in occultism — the 1008 worlds of the Deva-loka; worlds and firmaments at such incalculable distances, that the light of the nearest of them, that has just reached our modern Chaldees, had left its luminary before the day in which the words "Let there be light" were pronounced — if one accepts genetic [Genesis?] chronology. No spirit except the "Recorders" (lipika) has ever crossed its forbidden line and will not unto the day of the next *Pralaya*. It is the boundary that separates the finite — however infinite in man's sight — from the truly INFINITE. The spirits referred to, who "ascend and descend" are the "hosts" of what we loosely call "celestial beings" though they are nothing of the kind, in fact, being Entities of the higher worlds in the hierarchy of Being, so immeasurably higher, that, to us, they must appear as Gods and collectively — GOD. But so we, mortal men, must appear to the ant, which reasons on the scale of its special capacities. The ant may also, for all we know, see the avenging hand of a personal God in the act of the urchin, who, under the impulse of mischief destroys its nest — the labour of many weeks, long years in the chronology of the insect — in one moment. The ant feeling it acutely, may too, attributing the undeserved calamity, to its Providence and sins, see in it the result of the *sin* of *its* first parent, also who knows, and who can affirm, or deny? The refusal to admit in the whole solar system of any other reasonable and intellectual being, on the human plane except ourselves, is the greatest conceit of our age. All that science has a right to affirm is, that there are no generally invisible men and women living *in the same* conditions and under the *same* laws as we do. It cannot *deny point-blank* the possibility of their [there] being *worlds within worlds* under totally different conditions to those that constitute the nature of our World; nor, that there may be a certain limited communication between some of those worlds and our own. To the highest, we are taught, belong the seven orders of the purely *divine* Spirits; to the six lower ones, — hierarchies that can occasionally be seen and heard by men; and who do communicate with their progeny of the Earth, which progeny is indissolubly linked with them, each principle in man *having its direct source in the nature* of those great Beings, who furnish us with the respective invisible elements in us.

(12) Physical science is welcome to speculate upon the objective organisms of living beings and to continue her fruitless efforts in trying to connect our feelings, our sensations, mental and spiritual, with the various parts of that organism. Nevertheless, all that will ever be accomplished in this direction has already been done, and science will go no further, she is before a dead wall, on the face of which she traces, great physiological and psychic discoveries as she imagines, but every one of which will be shown later on, no better than the cobwebs of her scientific fancies and speculations. The outward tissues of our *objective* bodies alone are subservient to the analysis and researches of physical sciences. The six higher principles in them will evade for ever the hand that is led by a spirit which purposely ignores and rejects the Occult Sciences.

(12) The "great Day of BE WITH US" is an expression the only merit of which is in its *literal* translation. Its significance is not so easily described to a public unacquainted with the mystic dogmas of Occultism or rather of Esoteric *Bhudism* [*sic*]. It is an expression peculiar to the latter and as hazy for the profane as that of the Egyptians who called the same "the day of 'COME TO US'["][202] which is identical with the former, though the verb "be," in this sense, might be still better replaced with either of the two words "Remain" or "Rest-with-us," as it refers to that long period of REST which is called *Paranirvana*. As in the exoteric interpretation of the Egyptian rites, every defunct's soul — from the Hierophant down to the sacred bull Apis — became an Osiris, — was *osirified* though the secret doctrine had always taught, that the real *osirification* was the lot of every monad only after 3,000 cycles of existences; so in the present case. The "monad," born of the nature, and the very *Essence* of the "*Seven*" (its highest principle becoming immediately inshrined in the seventh Cosmic element), it has to perform its septenary gyration throughout the cycle of Being and

---

202. See for an explanation the *Funerary Ritual of the Egyptians*, by Viscount de Rougé. The prayer of the newly translated "Osiris to the 7 Spirits of Osiris.["]

forms, from the highest to the lowest and then again, from man to god, when at the threshold of Paranirvana it reassumes its primeval essence and becomes the Absolute once more.

Stanza VI.

By the power of Kwan-Yin,[203] the bright Mother of Mercy and knowledge, the "triple"[204] of Kwan-Shi-Yin residing in Kwan-yin-tien, [205] Fohat the Breath of their progeny, the "Son of the Sun" calls forth from the *lower* Chaos the illusive form of *Sien-tchen* (one [our] universe) out of the seven Elements: first, *one* manifested, six concealed; then *two* manifested, — five concealed, again *three* manifested *four* concealed; four manifested three hidden; *four and one half* manifested — *two and one half* concealed; *six* to be manifested — one laid aside (1). Lastly seven wheels revolving emanating one from the other[206] (2). He builds them in the likeness of the older wheels (worlds). How does he build them[?] Fohat collects the dust. He makes balls of fire with it and sets them in motion, some one way, others in the opposite direction. They are cold, he makes them hot. They are dry, he makes them moist. They shine, he fans and makes them cool putting out their lustre. Thus acts Fohat from the dawn of the DAY till the twylight of NIGHT during the seven Eternities[207] (3). ....

---

203. This stanza is translated from the Chinese text, and the names, as the equivalents of the original terms are preserved. The real nomenclature cannot be given.

204. Triple because in her cosmic correlations she is the ["]Mother, the wife and the daughter," and in the astronomical the ["]Father, Son, and Energy" or divine spirit.

205. The "melodious Heaven of Sound" — the abode of Kwan-yin, or *Divine Voice* literally.

206. *Fohat* has several meanings. (See No. 2 Comm.) He is called the "Builder of the Builders" the Force that he personifies having found[ed] our Septenary chain.

207. A period of 311,040,000,000,000 years according to Brahmanical calculations.

At the beginning of the first, the "Sons" are told to create their images. The *one third* refuse. The two (thirds) obey. The curse is pronounced. They will be born on the Fourth (globe) suffer and cause suffering . . . This is the first war . . . . . .

The older wheels had rotated downward and upward for one, and one half of an eternity. The Mother's spawn filled the whole (kosmos). There had been battles fought between the creators and the rebels, and battles fought for space, the seed appearing and reappearing continuously (4) since the first impulse had been given to our wheels . . . . . . Make thy calculations, Lamas [Lanoo], if thou wouldst learn the correct age of thy small wheel (5). Its fourth spoke is our mother (Earth). Reach the *fourth* "fruit" of the Fourth Path of knowledge, that leads to Nirvana and thou shalt comprehend for thou shalt see. (6) . . . . . .

The Secret Doctrine Würzburg Manuscript

COMMENTARY

(1) This sentence, as any student of Occultism may see, refers to the evolution and final formation of the primitive four Elements now fully manifested, and of the fifth — Ether — only partially, as we are hardly in the second half of the Fourth Round, and that the fifth Element will manifest fully only in the fifth Round. The worlds including our own were, of course as germs, primarily emanated from the one Element in its *second* stage ("Father, Mother," World's *Soul*) whether we call it with modern science cosmic dust and fire-mist or, with Occultism — Akasa, Jivatma, Astral Light or the "Soul of the World." But this first stage of evolution was swiftly followed by the next one. No world or heavenly body could be constructed on the objective plane, had not the Elements been sufficiently differentiated already from their primary — Cosmic Fire [—] to allow of such growth and evolution. Nevertheless — and here lies the great mistake of our modern physicists — differentiated as they were in the beginning, *they were not the Elements known to science as they are now,* to wit, neither Water, Air, Earth (or Matter) were the *compound* elements they are at present; for all these are the production of the globes already formed, aye, *even to fire.* Now that the conditions and laws ruling our solar system are fully developed; and that the atmosphere of our earth, as of each other globe, has become, so to say, a crucible of its own, correlating with space, and exchanging elements and forces with our planet, the elements known to science are our own special elements, differing widely from those of other planets, let alone the kosmic elements present beyond our solar system, cannot be made the standard for comparison with the same in other worlds. Lying enshrined in their virgin state within the bosom of the eternal mother, Space — the Ether of Occultism, each breath of the latter differentiates every element by sending out forth unto the plane of manifestations; and as soon as those waves of the ever breathing, boundless Ocean cross the boundary of any planetary atmosphere, the influx changes their character, they partake of the specific nature of the respective planet, so long as they work within the boundaries, to be thrown out exhausted with the outflux, and get once more purified once that they get back in

this cyclic journey into their birthplace. Thus breath during Manvantara, the infinite and the boundless, as the finite and the bounded; and it is only during their stay in the regions of the manifested that the elements become many and various: at the end of every manifestation they merge again into *One*. "The breath of the FATHER-MOTHER issues cold and radiant, and gets hot and dim to return and cool once more in the eternal bosom" says the commentary. Thus man absorbs cold pure air and throws it out impure and hot.

(2) This process takes place in the sixth region counting from above, or in the second, if we enumerate them from below — of the manifested kosmos, on the plane of the most material world. These seven wheels are our planetary chain. (See No. 54-75 com. [1888 ed. has "see Commentary Nos. 5 and 6"]). By "wheels" the various spheres and centres of force are generally meant, but in this case our chain and planet are referred to.

(3) Fohat, or the constructive Force that builds the worlds by means of magnetic attraction and repulsion, acts during the whole period of the Manvantara, or the *æon* of Life. *Fohat* builds them "in the likeness of the older worlds" and out of the same inexhaustible to us *subjective* material. The primordial atom cannot be multiplied, neither in its pregenetic state, its primogenity, or its after growth into full objectivity. Therefore it is called "the sum total" although this "sum total" is boundless. That which is the abyss of nothingness to the physicist who knows but the world of visible causes and effects — is the boundless space of the divine *plenum* to the Occultists. Among many objections to the doctrine of an endless evolution and reinvolution (or reabsorbtion) of the kosmos, a process which, according to the esoteric and Brahmanical doctrine is without a beginning or an end, the Occultist is told that it cannot be, as, "by all the admissions of modern scientific philosophy, it is a necessity of nature to run down." To this the reply is, that it is only a portion of the laws ruling the cycles that has fallen under the direct observation and perception of modern philosophy. That out of all the manifested elements, Science busies itself with and knows only matter, or the world elements in their most material manifestations. For what is matter? And above all what is our *scientific* philosophy so politely defined by

Kant as "the science of the *limits* to our knowledge." Whither have a number of attempts made by science to bind, to connect with, and define *all* the phenomena of organic life by mere physical and chemical manifestations — brought it to[?] To mere soap-bubbles — speculations generally, that burst one after the other before the men of science were permitted to discover *real* facts. All that would have been avoided and the progress of knowledge would have proceeded at gigantic steps had Science and its philosophy abstained from accepting hypothesis on the mere one sided knowledge of matter.[208]

If no physical intellect is capable of counting the grains of sand covering a few miles of sea-shore; or, fathom the ultimate essence and nature of that grain, palpable and visible on the palm of the naturalist, how can anyone limit the laws changing the conditions and being of the atoms in primordial chaos, or know anything certain about the capabilities and potency of their molecules before and after their formation into worlds? These changeless and eternal molecules — far thicker in space than the grains of sand on the ocean sea shore — may

---

208. The instance of Uranus and Neptune whose four and one satellites it was first thought revolve in their orbits from East to West, whereas all the other satellites rotate from West to East, is a very good one, as showing how unreliable are all *a priori speculations* even when based on the strictest mathematical analysis. The famous hypothesis of the formation of our solar system out of the nebulous rings, by Laplace and Kant also, was chiefly based on the above fact of the revolution of all the planets in the *same direction*. It is on this *mathematically demonstrated fact* during the time of Laplace, that this great astronomer, calculating on the theory of probabilities offered a bet of *three milliards against one* that the next planet that would be discovered, would have in its system the same peculiarity of motion *eastward*. The *immutable laws* of scientific mathematics got "worsted by further experiments and observations," it was said. This idea of Laplace's *mistake* prevail[s] generally to this day; but some astronomers have finally succeeded in demonstrating that the mistake had been in accepting Laplace's assertion *for a mistake*, and steps to correcting it without attracting general attention to the bevue are now being taken. Many are such unpleasant surprises in store for hypotheses of even a pure *physical* character. What may not be further disillusions then in questions of a transcendental *occult* nature[?]

differ in their constitution as the soul-substance differs from its vehicle, the body on one end of the line, before they reach the lower end. Each atom has seven planes of being or existence we are taught; and each plane is governed by its specific laws of evolution and absorption. Ignorant of any, even approximate, chronological datum to start with for the age of our planet or the origin of the solar system, astronomers, geologists and physicists are drifting with each new hypothesis farther and farther away from the shores of *fact* into the fathomless depths of scientific speculation. The law of analogy in the plan of structure between the trans-solar systems and the intra solar planets, does not necessarily bear upon the finite conditions to which every visible body is subject to, on this our plane of being. In occult Science, this law is the first and one key to this [these] world problems, but it has to be studied in its minutest details and — "to be turned seven times" before one comes to understand it. *Occult philosophy* is the only science that can teach it. How then can any one hang the truth or the untruth of the Occultist's proposition that ["]the kosmos is eternal in its unconditioned collectivity and finite but in its conditioned manifestations" on this one sided philosophical enunciation that "it is a necessity of nature to run down?" (See SUMMARY after Stanza VII .)

(4) ["]The seed appears and disappears continuously." The seed refers here to the world-germs now called by science material particles in a highly attenuated condition. "In the beginning the Central Sun (not the sun of our system) causes Fohat to collect primordial dust to form of it balls, and to impel them to move in converging lines and to finally approach each other and aggregate." (Book of *Djan*) . . . . ["]Being scattered in space, without order or system the world-germs come into frequent collisions until final aggregation, after which they become wanderers (comets). Then the battles and struggle begin. The older (bodies) attract the younger, while others repel them. Many perish devoured by their stronger companions. Those that escape become worlds.["]

The secret books distinctly teach, as will be seen, an astronomy that would not be rejected even by modern speculation. Save such "heresies" that every world, planet or heavenly body within and beyond the solar system, every star known and unknown in short was at first a comet, something that will be rejected by science, ancient physical and mathematical sciences, knew it seems all that our modern science knows and — a vast deal more. A "struggle for life" as a ["]survival of the fittest" in the worlds above as in our planet below is distinctly taught. Born in the unfathomable depths of space out of the homogeneous Element called the World-Soul, every nucleus of cosmic matter launched on its heavenly tour, begins life under the most trying circumstances. Through a series of countless ages, it has to conquer for itself a place in the infinitudes. It circles round and round between denser and already fixed bodies, moving by jerks and pulling toward some given point or centre that attracts it and trying to avoid, like a ship between a dense forest of submarine rocks, other bodies that draw and repel it in turn. Many perish, their mass disintegrating within stronger masses, and when born in our system, chiefly within the insatiable stomach of Mârttânder [Mârtanda] (the *Sun*. See No. 12. Comm. to Stanza IV.) Those which move slower, propelled into an elliptic course are doomed to annihilation sooner or later. Others moving in parabolic curves escape generally destruction owing to their velocity. "When the head loses its luminosity and the tail is disintegrated comes the last stage of the Wanderer" — says the Commentary. "It ends by either adding to the body of the star (or planet) that devours it, or, it becomes an independent sphere, matter thrown off from its body (the tail?) often forming its satellites." (Ibid.)

This will no doubt appear very unscientific in the light of modern researches. Occultism, however holds to this doctrine and maintains it. The time will come when it will be demonstrated. The sentence however, "Fohat sets (the primitive germs of the worlds or the aggregations of cosmic matter) in motion, *some one way, others in* the opposite direction" looks scientific enough. There is at all events one recognized scientific fact in support of this position. The meteoroidal showers (periodical in November and August) belong to a system moving in an elliptical orbit around the Sun. The aphelion of this ring is 1,732 millions of miles beyond the orbit of Neptune, its plane is inclined to the earth's orbit at an angle of 64° 3′, and the direction of the meteoroidal swarm moves around this orbit is contrary to that of the Earth's revolution. This fact recognized only in 1833, shows it to be the modern rediscovery of what was very anciently known — Fohat, turning with his two hands in contrary directions the "seed" and the "curds" or Cosmic matter, "particles in an highly attenuated condition" and nebulae. The occult doctrine explains it by the dual force residing in the Sun: one attracting, the other repelling, the future direction of the rotating agent being determined by the degree under which the "seed," germ or nucleus is first set in motion in our planetary system. "The rejected Son, Mârttânda (the Sun) blows hot and cold" says the Commentary. "The hot breath (the positive) moves and propels the brothers onward; the cold breath (the negative) fails to affect the *seed* and it pursues its own (contrary) way." This applies only to our solar system. Outside its boundaries it is other Suns and especially the "Central Sun" — the "abode of the invisible Deity" that determines the motion of the bodies and their direction; that motion, serving also to differentiate the homogeneous Element (matter) they are composed of, into such or other sub-elements, regarded by modern science as distinct individual elements whereas they are merely temporary appearances, or as the occult books call them "Manvantaric masks." The Secret Doctrine, as well known to the Occultists, teaches as an incontrovertible axiom that which modern science has named "the homogeneity of the primal elements of matter," as also the *continuity of the states of matter*.[209]

(5) The "small wheel" is our Earth, the fourth sphere in the septenary number of our chain. It is one of those on which "hot (positive) breath" of the Sun has a direct effect. To calculate its age, however, is rather difficult, since we are not

---

209. The seven fundamental transformations of the globes or heavenly spheres, or rather of their constituent particles of matter is described as follows (1) the *homogeneous*; (2) the Aeriform and radiant (gaseous); (3) Curd-like (nebulous); (4) atomic, Ethereal (beginning of motion, hence of differentiation); (5) germinal fiery (to wit, differentiated but composed of the germs only of the Elements, in their earliest states, they having seven states when completely developed on our earth); (6) Four-fold vapoury (even future *Earth);* (7) Cold and depending (on the Sun for life and Light).

permitted to give the real figures. "The older wheels rotated for one Eternity, and one half of an Eternity" it says. We know, that by "Eternity" the seventh part of 311,040,000,000,000 years, is meant or "an age of Brahma," hence, it must be approximately 66,651,428,571,428 4/7 of years. But what of that? We also know, that to begin with, if we take for our basis the above figures, that we have first of all to eliminate from the 100 years of Brahma (or 311,040,000,000,000) two *years* taken up by the Sandhyas (twilights) which leaves 98, as we have to bring it to 14 x 7 = . But we have no knowledge at what time precisely the evolution and formation of our little earth began. Therefore it is impossible to calculate its age unless the time of its birth is given — which the TEACHERS refuse to do, so far. In Book the IId, however some chronological hints will be found. We must remember moreover that the law of analogy stands good for the worlds as it does for man; and that as "the ONE (Deity) becomes TWO (Deva or Angel), and *Two* becomes *Three* or man" etc. etc. so, we are taught that the CURDS (*nebulae*) become Wanderers (Comets), these become stars and the stars (the centres of vortices) *our Sun and planets* — to put it briefly.[210]

(6) There are four grades of chelaship, which are known respectively in Sanskrit as "Srôtapanna" [Srotaâpanna], "Sagardagan" [Sakridâgâmin], "Anaganim" [Anâgâmin], and "Arhan" [Arhat] the four paths to Nirvana, in this our Round bearing the same appellations. The Arhan is not yet the highest Initiate, though he can see the Past, the Present and the Future.

---

210. This cannot be so very *unscientific*, since Descartes thought also that "the planets rotate on their axis because they were once lucid stars, the centre of vortices."

The Secret Doctrine Würzburg Manuscript

The Secret Doctrine Würzburg Manuscript

Stanza VII.

....

  Behold the beginning of sentient, formless Life. First the Spiritual, from the ONE, the "Atman" (Spirit); then — "Atma-Buddhi" (Spirit-Soul) — this, the three, the five and the seven (1); then, the Three-fold, the Four-fold and downward; the mind-born Sons of the FIRST-LORD (Prajapati) the shining Seven (Builders). It is they who are thou, me, him (2), Oh Lanoo; They, who watch over thee and thy mother Bhumi (the Earth). The one Ray multiplies the smaller rays (3). Life, precedes Form, and life survives the last atom of *St[h]ula Sarira* (external body) (4). Through the countless rays proceeds the life-ray, the One, like a thread through many pearls. When the one becomes two — the "Three-fold" appears (5). The three are (linked into) one; and it is our thread, oh Lanoo, the heart of the Man-Plant called Suptasarma (6). It is the root that never dies, the three-tongued flame of the four Wicks (7). The wicks are the sparks, and use, the three-tongued flame (8) shot out by the Seven; *their* flame; the beams and sparks of one moon reflected in the running waves of all the rivers of Bhumi (Earth) (9). The spark hangs from the flame by the finest thread of Fohat. It journies through the seven and seven worlds of *Maya*. It stops in the first (kingdom) and behold — a planet [plant]; seven changes more and it becomes an animal. From the combined attributes of these — Manu (man) the thinker, is formed. Who forms him[?] "The One Life"; who forms his body? the many lives (10) . . . . .
....
  From the first-born (primitive or the first man) the thread between the Silent Watcher and his Shadow becomes more strong and radiant with every change (reincarnation) (11). The morning sun-light has changed into noon-day glory. . . . .
....
  This is thy present wheel — said the Flame to the Spark. Thou art myself, my image and my shadow. I have clothed myself in thee, and thou art my Vahan to the Day "Be with us," when thou shalt rebecome myself and others, thyself and me (12). . . . Then the Builders having donned their first clothing

descend on the cooled earth and reign over MEN (13) who are themselves (14) ....

Commentary ———

(1) The Hierarchy of the Spiritual Beings is divided into seven chief orders, subdivided in their turn into numberless groups and orders. The former are thus described:

(I) The first *formless* sentient conscious[211] group is composed of pure spirit. They are the direct rays of the absolute and ONE Spirit, and may be called entities only for convenience of clearer understanding, since they are what we would term pure essences. They are the parent fountain, the Flame at which are lit the six other descending lights. They are not directly concerned with either the inhabited spheres or their humanities, but remain during Manvantara, the beating heart of Kosmos, so to say, its life and being.

III [*sic*, II] The second group; the "Atma-Buddhi" are still formless, but more substantial, as they have a vehicle the divine Soul and are composed of the two higher principles. They are the spiritual compound monads, as the first ones are the primitive monads. They are directly concerned with only the divine Beings of the three higher worlds. They represent the three degrees of the highest spiritual consciousness unrelated to our perceptions but through the agency of the group that emanates from them.

(III) The "Three-fold Entities.["] These Dhyan Chohans (angels) are compounds of Spirit-Soul and Intelligence *Atma-Buddhi-manas*, therefore called the Three-fold, or the Triads. This order is the *nursery of the human souls*. The "Shining Seven" are —

(2) "Thou, me, him" — a reference to *Hamsa*; or "a-ham sa["] and So ham (*Sah a ham*) "I am thou (or he)["]; and "Thou art (or he is) *I*.["] (The definition of "Kalahamsa."[ )] In this reference, must be studied the mysterious doctrine of the projections of Divine Essence (Spirit and Soul) into the world of *Maya* including its faculty of living throughout Eternities — divided — yet indivisible[,] countless in numbers — yet ONE.

---

211. Their consciousness has no relation to our human consciousness; it is, if not absolute, at any rate unconditioned consciousness.

Moreover, there is another and as great a mystery contained in this dogma, with regard to the "Seven" which is rather difficult to explain. While the Souls of Humanity in their triple aspect of Atman Buddhi and Manas (or Spirit, the *Divine* and the *human* Souls) proceed directly from, and are in fact part and parcel of the essence of those "Seven[,]"[212] the latter being themselves part of the Supreme and One Essence or LIFE; and that everything living on Earth is an emanation of this fourth remove from the DEITY, nevertheless these "Mind-born" Sons of Heaven have withal an independent existence. Gods as they may be in comparison with mortal men, they have to progress, if they would rise, in the hierarchy of the superior worlds. They are subject to Karma which they have to work out, and which lies in wait for them since the preceding manvantara, and which they accumulated in their previous existences. For the Doctrine teaches that there are no such privileged beings in the Universe, whether in ours, or in the *inner*, superior ones[213] (superior in quality and essence not by virtue of its location as the angels preached by the exoteric religions). A Dhyan Chohan *has to become one*. He cannot be born or suddenly appear on the plane of life and being created as a full blown angel. The hierarchy of the present Manvantara, will find itself transferred in the next cycle of life into higher, superior worlds and will make room for a new hierarchy, composed of the Elect ones of our Mankind. Being is an endless cycle within the one absolute Eternity, wherein move numberless inner cycles finite and conditioned. Gods *created* as such would have no personal merit in being Gods; and such a class of Beings, who would be perfect, only by virtue of a special immaculate nature inherent to them and in the face of suffering and struggling humanity, and even of the lower creation, would be the symbol of eternal divine *injustice*, a living and eternal crime. It is an anomaly and an impossibility in nature. Therefore, the Seven have to incarnate, as well as those

---

212. The number *seven* does not imply that there are only Seven Entities but seven *hosts* as explained before.

213. Paracelsus calls them the *Flagæ*, the Christians the "Guardian Angels." They are Dhyan Chohans with six principles in them — and are men *minus* the external bodies.

lower in grade than they are themselves — the "four fold" the five and the six fold, beings, the latter being those directly above us. When asked how can that be? How can the "Gods" or angels, be at the same time their own emanations and their *personal* Selves? Is it in the same sense as in the material world, the Son is, in one way his father being his blood, the bone of his bone and the flesh of his flesh[?] To this the Teachers answer in the negative. How then, can this be explained? By resorting to a similar, to a graphic instance, though necessarily imperfect and conditioned as every thing must be here.

(3) Fancy to yourselves lightning detached from a boundless sheet of electricity falling — say, on a country as densely covered with buildings as mankind covers Europe. Let the latter represent the inhabited globe and the buildings — distinct individuals, or men in short. If, forgetting for a moment that lightning destroys by combustion, we regard it as the animating principle or soul, and imagine, that it sets on fire, (animates) every atom as every building, which will therefore live so long as its material will last, then the Simile will become clear. Lightning, or the emanation from the Electric Ocean has animated indistinctly, every atom it had come in contact with. But at the same time, distinct balls of the same electric fire, these balls representing the Angelic Entities, may, each, entering one of the buildings (men) become for the time being, until its final consummation that building or tabernacle; when one is consumed the same ball may enter another, a higher, or a lower one according to the causes produced in this world of results; and thus act indefinitely. This is then precisely what happens. The bulk of our present Humanity is now animated only by the emanations of the angelic host. But during its childhood, in the first Race, sinless mankind was composed wholly of that Host, which had to incarnate in the (then) monstrous tabernacles of clay built by and composed *(as they are now, also), of countless myriads of lives.* The latter sentence will be explained in No. 10 of this Commentary. The "tabernacles" have improved in texture and symmetry of form, hand in hand in this, with the outward appearance and texture of our globe — their home; but the physical improvements took place at the expense of the *inner man*, the three principles between the external body and Manas

becoming with every race more physical and gross, and the human Soul itself,²¹⁴ intelligence, losing its spirituality as it gained in physical brain-strength and purely human intellectuality. Hence, instead of a mankind *en masse*, being direct incarnations (Avatars) of the ["]Three-fold" Dhyan Chohans, the latter form in our age an exception being a small minority. Nevertheless even now it is no *very* rare instance, especially in the East, to find persons who are evidently animated by no simple "emanations" but truly by the Dhyan Chohanic Entities themselves on their Earthly cycle of probations and incarnations.

(4) But even all these units of the Celestial Hosts who for one reason or the other are free from terrestrial incarnations, are considered *multiples*, so to say, or ubiquitous to a degree. "The one ray multiplies the smaller rays." The angelic Entity may be bodily present on Earth without for all that abandoning its status and post in the heavenly regions. This needs explanation although there are very few persons now who have not heard of the same possibility even among living beings. As certain men and women, whether by virtue of a peculiar organization (mediumship), or through the power of mystic knowledge acquired, can be seen in their "double" in one place, while their body is miles and miles away; the same in the case of superior Beings. This fact is corroborated by the evidence of nearly every age including our own. The only difference between a Dhyan Chohan and man resting in the following: the former can live in a terrestrial form bodily and in his spiritual entity in the inner regions,²¹⁵ while his astral semi-material form

---

214. Outward man evolutes progresses and gets more perfect as the inner spiritual man does. There is a great difference between the same ethereal giant forms of primitive mankind and our own pigmy race, now already degenerating.

215. Occultism does not admit in the boundless, or at any rate *to us* limitless extension of space, of a world *above* our heads where Heaven and the celestial regions are generally located by the pious. There is no *above* or *below* for us, for one if no other good reason — that the Earth is ever rotating and we revolve with it. It is therefore mere nonsense to speak of a God, or angels or a heaven "above us." The good law

may be in a third place, thus leading three distinct *conscious* existences permanently, whereas man can produce an appearance only, as it were spasmodically; his body being in one place and his astral body projected a few minutes elsewhere; or if an adept this double life may last for days. Such was the belief of and a dogma with the antediluvian races, and it is fast becoming that of modern intellectual Society, besides the hoi polloi. At any rate it is one with the Roman Catholics notwithstanding that they have distorted it for theological purposes; and it was part and parcel also of the Religion of the Zoroastrians, who regarded their *Amshaspends* as dual entities (ferouers) applying this duality — in their esoteric interpretations, at any rate to all the spiritual and usually invisible denizens of the numberless worlds in the space visible to our eye. In a note of Damasc[i]us, on the *Chaldean Oracles*, we have a triple evidence of the Universality of this doctrine; for he says: "In these *Oracles*, the Seven COSMOCRATORES of the world ('the World Pillars' mentioned likewise by St. Paul in the Greek texts) — are *double*; one set being commissioned to rule the superior worlds the spiritual and the sidereal and the other to guide and watch over the worlds of matter.["] Such is also the opinion of Jamblichus who makes an evident distinction between the *Archangels* and the ["]*Archontees*." (See De *Mysteriis*, Sect II. chap iii.) The above may be applied, of course to the distinction made between the degrees or orders of Spiritual Beings; and it is in this sense that the R. Catholic Church tries to interpret and teach the difference, for while the Archangels are, in her teaching *divine* and holy, their doubles are denounced by her as details [devils].[216] But the word *ferouer* is not to be understood in this

---

teaches the existence of worlds within and without our planetary system, as within and without our very globe and its atmosphere. They are invisible to us because they are entirely outside of all our terrestrial conditions and laws but their seers and denizens know of us, as our Seers and Elect Adepts know of them. (See No. 10 of the present Comm.)

216. This identity between the Spirit and his *material* "Double" [( ]in man, it is the reverse) explains still better the confusion, alluded to already in this work, made in the names and individualities as well as

sense, for it means, simply the reverse or the opposite side of some attribute or quality. Thus when the Occultist says that the "Demon is the lining of God" (Evil, the opposite side of the medal, or good), he does not mean two personalities but one and the same individuality in its two opposite aspects. Now the best man on Earth would appear by comparison with an Archangel (as described in theology) — a *fiend*. Hence a certain reason to depreciate a lower "double" immersed far deeper in matter than its original. But there is still no reason to regard him as a devil and this is what the R. Catholics maintain against all reason and logic.

(5) "When the One becomes two, the threefold appears," to viz —, when the One Eternal life drop[s] its one reflection into the world of manifestation that reflection or Ray differentiates; the Water, or Chaos becomes male-female and the three-fold Being composed of Spirit in its dual vehicle (the divine and human soul) issues as its first-born (Brahmâ, Viraj, Osiris, etc. etc.) who emanates in its turn after differentiating, or separating into male and female its first septenary group.

(6) The "man-plant, Saptasarma" that never dies is the immortal spiritual triad, the *Atma-Buddhi-Manas* and the "four wicks" — the four lower principles including our physical body.

[Note (7) is missing in the Wurzburg manuscript.]

(8) It means and refers to the same.

(9) As the milliards of bright sparks, lit simultaneously on all the waters above which the one same moon is shining, so our evanescent personalities — the illusive envelopes of the immortal MONAD-EGO — twinkle and dance on the waves of

---

the numbers of the Rishis and the Prâjapâtes [Prajâpatis]; especially between those of the Satya *Yuga* and the Mahab[h]aratian period. It also throws additional light on what the Secret Doctrine teaches with regard to the *Root* and the *Seed* Manus. (See Chapter II "On the Primitive Manus of Humanity.") Not only those progenitors of our mankind but every human being, we are taught, has its prototype in the spiritual spheres which prototype is the highest Essence of his seventh Principle. Thus, the Seven Manus become 14, the root Manu being the *Prime Cause* and the "Seed-Manu" its effect; and when the latter reach from *Satya Yuga* (the 1st age) the Heroic period, these Manus or Rishis become 21 in number.

Maya. They last and appear, as the thousands of sparks produced by the moon beams, only as long as the Queen of the night radiates her lustre on the running waters of life: the period of a *Manvantara*; and then they disappear, the beams — symbols of our eternal Spiritual *Egos* — alone surviving re-emerged as they are in the Mother-Source.

(10) "Who forms Manu (the man), and who forms his body? The LIFE and the LIVES.["] Here *Manu* stands for the spiritual heavenly man, real and non dying EGO in us, which is the direct emanation of the "One Life" or the absolute Deity. As to our outward physical bodies, the house or tabernacle of the Soul, the Doctrine teaches a strange lesson; so strange that unless thoroughly explained and as rightly comprehended, it is only the *exact sciences of the future* that are destined to vindicate the theory fully.

It has been stated before now, that Occultism does not accept anything *inorganic* in kosmos. That which Science regards as *inorganic* substance means simply that life in its organism does not assert itself to our senses. ALL IS LIFE and every atom of even mineral dust is *a life*, though beyond our comprehension and perception because outside of the range of the laws known to those who reject the Occult Sciences. "The worlds to the profane" says a Commentary "are built up of the known elements. To the spiritual perception of the true Arhan these elements are themselves collectively — a *divine* life, distributively, in the plane of manifestations — numberless and countless crores of lives.[217] Fire alone is ONE on the plane of

---

217. Pasteur is taking unconsciously the first step toward Occult Science in saying that if he dare express his full idea upon this subject he would say that the organic cells are endowed *with a vital potency* that does not cease its activity with the cessation of a current of oxygen towards them, nor does it break for it, its relations with life itself which is supported by the influence of that gas. "I would add["] — goes on Pasteur — ["]that the evolution of the germ is accomplished by means of complicated phenomena among which we must class the processes of fermentation," and *life* according to Claude Bernard and the great Pasteur *is nothing* less than a process of fermentation. That there exists in nature beings or lives that can live and thrive without air, even on our globe was demonstrated by the same men of Science. Pasteur

the one Reality; on that of manifested, hence *illusive* being, its particles are fiery lives which live and have their being at the expense of every other life that they consume. Therefore, they are named the 'DEVOURERS.' 'Every visible thing in this Universe was built by such lives, from conscious and primordial man down to the unconscious agents that construct matter' . . . [']From the one LIFE formless and Uncreate proceeds the Universe of lives. First was manifested from the Deep Chaos cold luminous fire (gaseous light?) which formed the Curds in Space.' (irresolvable nebulae, perhaps?) . . . . These *went to war* and a great heat was developed by the encountering and collision, which produced rotation. Then came the first manifested *material* Fire, the hot flames, the wanderers in Heaven (comets); heat generates moist vapour; *that* — forms solid water (?); then *dry* mist, then *liquid* mist, watery that puts

---

found that many of the lower lives such as vibrions and some microbes and bacteria could exist without air, which on the contrary killed them. They derive the oxygen necessary for their multiplication from the various substances that surround them. He calls them *aerobes* living on the tissues of our matter when the latter has ceased forming a part of an integral and living whole (and called very *unscientifically* by science *dead* matter) and *anaerobes*. The one kind binds oxygen and contributes vastly to the destruction of animal life and vegetable tissues, furnishing to the atmosphere materials, which enter later on, into the constitution of other organisms; the other destroys or rather annihilates finally the so-called *organic* substance, ultimate decay being inadmissible without their participation. Certain germ cells, as those of yeast develop and multiply in air, but when deprived of it, they will adapt themselves to life without air and become ferments absorbing oxygen from substances coming in contact with them and thereby ruining the substances. The cells in the fruit when lacking free oxygen act as ferments and stimulate fermentation. "Therefore, the vegetable cell manifests in this case its life as an *anaerobic* being. Why should then an organic cell form in this an exception[?"] asks Prof. Bagolobof [Bogoluboff]. Pasteur shows that in the substance of our tissues and organs the cell, upon not finding sufficient oxygen for itself, stimulates fermentation in the same way as the fruit cell. And Claude Bernard thought that Pasteur's idea of the formation of ferments found its application and corroboration in the fact that urea increases in the blood during strangulation. LIFE therefore, is everywhere in the Universe as Occultism teaches us.

out the luminous brightness of the pilgrims (wanderers, comets?) and forms solid watery wheels (globes). Bhumi (the Earth) appears with six sisters. These produce by their continuous motion the *inferior* fire, heat and an aqueous mist, which yields the third world element — WATER; and from the breath of all atmospheric AIR is born. These four are the *four lives* of *the first four periods* (Rounds) of Manvantara. The three last will follow."

Which means that every new Round develops one of the Elements as now known to Science, which rejects the primitive nomenclature preferring to subdivise [subdivide] them into their constituents. If NATURE is the "Ever becoming" on the manifested plane, then those Elements are to be regarded in the same light: they have to evolute, progress and increase to the manvantaric end. Thus, the 1st Round we are taught, developed but one Element, and a nature and humanity in what may be called one *aspect of Nature* — called by some very unscientifically though it may be so *de facto*, "one dimensional Space." The second Round brought forth and developed two Elements — fire and Earth — and its humanity adapted to this condition of nature, if we can give that name to beings, living under conditions now unknown to man, was — to use again a familiar phrase in a strictly figurative sense (the only way in which it can be used correctly) — "a two dimensional" species. The processes of natural development we are now considering will at once elucidate and discredit the fashion of speculating on the attributes of the *two*, *three*, and *four* or more "dimensional space"; but in passing, it is worth while to point out the real significance of the sound but incomplete intuition that has prompted — among Spiritualists and Theosophists and several great men of Science for the matter of that[218] [—] the use of the modern expression — "the *fourth* dimension of space." To begin with, of course, the superficial absurdity of assuming that space itself is measureable in any direction is of little consequence. The familiar phrase can only be an abbreviation of

---

218. Dr. Zollner's theory has been more than welcomed by several men of Science who are Spiritualists — Professor Butleroff and Wagner of St. Petersburg — for one.

the fuller form — the fourth dimension of MATTER *in* space. But it is an unhappy phrase even thus expanded, because, while it is perfectly true that the progress of evolution may be destined to introduce us to new characteristics of matter, those with which we are already familiar, are really more numerous than the three dimensions. The faculties or what is perhaps the best available term the *characteristics* of matter must clearly bear a direct relation always to the senses of man. Matter has extension, colour, motion (molecular motion), taste and smell, corresponding to the existing senses of man, and by the time that it fully develops the next characteristic, — let us call, for the moment, *permeability*, — that will correspond to the next sense of man — let us call it *clairvoyance*. Thus when some bold thinkers have been thirsting for a fourth dimension to explain the passage of matter through matter, and the production of knots on an endless cord, what they were really in want of, was a sixth characteristic of matter. The three dimensions belong really but to one attribute or characteristic of matter — *extension*; and popular common sense justly rebels against the idea that under any condition of things there can be *more than three* of such dimensions as length, breadth and thickness. These terms, and the term "dimension" itself, all belong to one plane of thought, to one stage of evolution, to one characteristic of matter. So long as there are foot-rules, within the resources of the Kosmos, to apply to matter, so long will they be able to measure it three ways and no more; and from as far back as the idea of measurement occupied a place in the human understanding it has been possible to apply measurement in three directions and no fewer. But these considerations do not militate in any way against the certainty that in the progress of time, — as the faculties of humanity are multiplied, so will the characteristics of matter be multiplied also.

We now return to the consideration of material evolution through the Rounds. Matter in the second Round, it has been stated[,] may be figuratively referred to as two dimensional. But here another *caveat must be entered*. That loose and figurative expression may be regarded, — in one plane of thought, as we have just seen, — as equivalent to the second characteristic of matter corresponding to the second perceptive faculty or sense of man. But these two linked scales of evolution are concerned with processes going on within the limits of a single Round. The succession of primary aspects of Nature with which the succession of the Rounds is concerned has to do, as already indicated, with the development of the "elements" (in the occult sense) — Fire, Earth, Water, Air. We are only in the fourth Round, and our catalogue so far stops short. The centres of consciousness (destined to develop into humanity as we know it) of the third Round, arrived at a perception of the third Element [a line or lines are apparently missing here in the manuscript; see *The Secret Doctrine*, vol. 1, pp. 252-253] *akasa* (Ether) will become a familiar fact of Nature to all men, as air is familiar now to us. And only during that Round will those higher senses, the development of which akasa subserves, be susceptible of their complete expansion. As already indicated a *partial* familiarity with the characteristic of matter permeability — which should be developed concurrently with the *sixth* sense, may be expected to develop at the proper period in this Round. But with the next element added to our resources in the next Round, *permeability* will become so manifest a characteristic of matter that the densest forms of this will seem to man[']s perceptions as obstructive to him as a thick fog and no more.

Returning to the *lives* however, and without entering at length upon the description given of the higher "*Lives*" we must turn our attention at present simply to the earthly beings and Earth herself. This, we are taught is built up for the 1st Round by the "Devourers," that disintegrate and differentiate the germs of other lives in the Elements pretty much, it must be supposed, as in the present state of the world, the *aerobes* do, when undermining and loosening the chemical structure in an organism they transform the animal matter and generate substances that vary in their constitutions. These germs produce lives of another kind and living under other conditions, which *lives* work on the structure of our globe in the 2nd Round and so on. It is only in the 4th our present Round or over 20,000,000 of years ago[219] that the Earth has assumed its definite material shape its outward shape of course varying greatly with every period. And from its beginnings countless myriads of *kinds* and *species*, have been working on its construction, its rocks and crust, adding to its bulk and changing the face of our Earth every decimillennium in its chief features.

The same with regard to man. While his higher principles — Spirit and soul, emanate from, and are of the divine Essence, and that of the 3rd Principle Manas (the human soul), only the purely spiritual attributes survive, by blending themselves with the higher monad, being as it is (*Manas*) the handiwork of the collective Intelligence (the Dhyan Chohans); and that again, the 4th, 5th and 6th principles are the production of the various Elements — the human body is the work, from its very conception of "lives," self-generated, or rather *self-evolved* since every atom is a living germ. The human tabernacle is built by, and *is in its essence and nature* as the mother Earth, whence the lives composing it were first evolved — a *living* building of ever changing beings, themselves the tabernacles and the worlds of other still smaller beings and this *ad [in]finitum*. Is it because the microscope fails to detect the latter that we shall reject the doctrine?

Science teaches us that the living as well as the dead organism of both man and animal are swarming with bacteria of a hundred various kinds; that from without, we are threatened with the invasion of microbes with every breath we draw and from within with *leicomains* [leucomaines], *aerobes* and *anaerobes* and what not. But science never went yet so far as to assert with the occult Doctrine that our bodies as well as those of animals plants and stones are themselves built of such beings which except the few larger ones no microscope can detect, and that to the eye of the naturalist armed with the most powerful glasses known, appear simple molecules or *inorganic* atoms so far, as regards the purely animal and material portion of man, Science is on its way to discoveries that will go far towards

---

219. According to the Secret Doctrine, our present humanity (not mankind, since the outward form has greatly changed) — has appeared in the Round just 18,613,727 years ago.

corroborating this theory. Chemistry and physiology are the two great magicians of the future, who are destined to open the eyes of mankind to the great *physical* truths. With every day, the identity between the animal and the physical man, between the plant and man and even between the reptile and its nest — the rock and man is more and more shown. The physical or chemical constituents of all, being found to be identical, chemical science may well say that there is no difference between the matter that composes an ox and that of man. But the Occult Doctrine is far more explicit. It says: Not only the chemical compounds are the same, but the same infinitesimal *invisible lives* compose the atoms of the bodies of the mountain and the daisy, of man and the ant, of the elephant [and] of the tree which shelters him from the Sun. Each particle — whether you call it organic or inorganic — *is a life*. Every atom or molecule in the Universe is both *life-giving and death-giving* to that form, inasmuch as it builds by aggregation Universes and the ephemerous [ephemeral] vehicles ready to receive the transmigrating spirit, and is as eternally destroying and changing *forms*, forcing out the spirit from its temporary abodes. It creates and kills; it is self-generating and self-destroying; it brings into being and annihilates that mystery of mysteries — the *living body* of man, animal or plant, every second in time and space; and, it generates equally life and death, beauty and ugliness, good and bad and even the agreeable and disagreeable, the beneficent and maleficent sensations. It is that mysterious LIFE represented collectively by countless myriads of lives that follows in its own sporadic way the hitherto incomprehensible law of atavism; that copies family resemblances as well as those it finds impressed in the aura of the generators of every future human being, a mystery, in short, that will receive fuller attention elsewhere. For the present one instance may be used in illustration. Modern Science begins to find out that the *ptomain[e]* (the alcoholate [alkaloid] poison generated by decaying matter and corpses, a *life* also) extracted with the help of volatile ether, yields a smell as strong and equal to that of the freshest orange blossoms; but that free from oxygen, these alcoloides [alkaloids] yield either a most sickening disgusting smell, or the most agreeable aroma recalling that of the most delicately-scented flowers. And, it is *suspected* that such blossoms owe their agreeable smell to the poisonous *ptomaina* [ptomaine]; the venomous essence of certain mushrooms (fungi), being nearly identical with the venom of the *Cobra* of India, the most deadly of serpents.[220] Thus having discovered the *effects* Science has to find out their *primary* causes, and this it can never do without the help of the Occult Sciences. The latter assert that every physiological change besides diseases — nay life itself — is due to what is called *microbes* in a loose, general way. The knowledge of these primary causes and of the ultimate essence of every element — of its *lives*, their functions, properties and conditions of change — constitutes the basis of MAGIC. Paracelsus was perhaps, the only Occultist in Europe, during the last centuries since the Christian era, who was versed in this mystery. Had not a criminal hand put an end to his life, years before the time allotted him by nature, *physiological* magic would have fewer secrets for the civilized world than it now has.

(11) This is another mystery and entirely psychical and spiritual: "The thread between the silent *watcher* and his *shadow* becomes stronger" with every reincarnation. He and his *shadows* in the many successive reincarnations are — one. The Watcher or divine *prototype*, is at the upper rung of being, his

---

220. The French *Savants* Armand [Arnaud,] Gautier and Villiers have found in the saliva of living man the same venomous alkaloid as in those of the toad and the salamander, and of the Cobra and the *trigonocephalus* of Portugal. It is proven that venom of the deadliest kind, whether called *ptomaine* or *leckomaine* [leucomaine], as alcoholate [alkaloid] — is generated by living men, animals and plants. The same Gautier discovered alcoholate in the fresh meat on an ox and in its brains, and a venom that he calls *xantho creatinine* similar to the substance extracted from the poisonous saliva of reptiles. It is the muscular tissues as being the most active organ in the animal economy, that are suspected of being the generators or factors of venoms, having the same importance as carbonic acid and urea in the functions of life, and which venoms are the ultimate products of inner combustion. And though it is yet not fully determined whether poisons can be generated by the animal system of *living* beings without the participation and interference of microbes, it is ascertained that the animal does produce venomous substances in its physiological or living states.

shadow at the lower. Nevertheless, the *monad* of every human being (spirit and divine soul) is a Dhyan Chohan, individual and distinct from all other Dhyan Chohans — a kind of spiritual *personality* during the Manvantaras, whose primary — (Atman or pure spirit) is unconditioned and one with the universal spirit, and Vehicle (*Vahan* which is the *Bhuddi* [Buddhi] or divine soul) of the highest Dhyan Chohanic Essense, viz — , of a substance though radically the same as the former, yet differentiated already and adapted to an existence on the planes of manifestations.

(12) (The day when the Spark) man will rebecome the Flame (the informing Dhyan Chohan) "myself and others, thyself and me" as the Stanza gives it — means this: In Paranirvana, when *Pralaya* will have reduced not only material and psychical bodies but even the spiritual Egos to their original principle, the past and present and even future humanities, like all other things, will be one and the same. Every thing will have re-entered the GREAT BREATH; in other words will find itself "merged in Brahma," the divine Unity. Is it annihilation as some think? Or atheism, as some worshippers of a personal deity, believers in an unphilosophical paradise, are inclined to suppose? Neither! It is worse than useless to return to the question of implied atheism in that which is a theism of a most refined nature. As to the charge of preaching final annihilation and loss of personality and individuality, in this doctrine of the ultimate reabsorption into the Deity — as well say of a man plunged in a sound, dreamless sleep that he is "annihilated." The latter simile answers to only one side of the question — the most material; since reabsorption is by no means such a "dreamless" sleep, but on the contrary — *absolute existence*, an absolute and unconditioned UNITY in a state, to describe which there are no words in any of the terrestrial languages. An approach to anything like a comprehensive idea of it, can be attempted only in the soul panorama, through the thought and conception of the divine monad. Nor is the individuality of the EGO reabsorbed, therefore, lost. For however prolonged and endless, from a human standpoint, this paranirvanic state, it has yet a limit. Once ended, the same monad emerges therefrom as a still higher Dhyan Chohan, on a far higher plane, to recommence its cycle of

activity. Human thought in its present stage of development cannot go beyond this nor even so far. It trembles here on the threshold of incomprehensible Eternity . . .

(13) The Watchers reign over Man[221] during the whole period of *Satya-Yuga*, the First age, at the end or close of which appear the first Ethereal Humanity over the evolution of which the "Builders["] have watched. It is the dynasty of the Pitris our "lunar" ancestors. (See App. XI "The Pitris.") The second Dynasty, that will reign over men is the divine Dynasty, recorded in the Egyptian and other annals and viewed in our age as the Mythoposic [Mythopoeic] period, by our symbologists. To the latter, it is of course, only as fairy tales. But since traditions and even Chronicles of such dynasties of *divine* Kings — of gods reigning over men followed by dynasties of Heroes or Giants — exist in the annals of every nation, it is difficult to understand how every people under the Sun, some of whom are separated by vast Oceans and belong to different hemispheres, such as the Ancient Peruvians and Mexicans as well as the Chaldeans, could have worked out the same "fairy tales" and in the same order of events. However, as the Secret Doctrine teaches *history*, the Occultists are as entitled to their beliefs as the religionists are to theirs, most of which are founded on blind faith. And that Doctrine says that while the lower groups of the divine Beings called by us Dhyan Chohans, and by the Hindus, the Rishis and Prajâpâtis [Prajâpatis] and by the Christians Archangels and Angels — incarnated in the men of our Round (with which we are solely concerned at present) the higher group, namely the "Watchers" or the "Builders" furnished the various and many races with Kings and leaders. It is the latter who taught Humanity their arts and sciences, and the former who revealed to the incarnated monads evolved out of the lower kingdoms and who had, therefore, lost every recollection of their divine origin,

---

221. The word *Manu* (or man) is from the root *man* "to think" (Sansk.) Manas, or the human soul, the seat of thought and intellect is the thinking principle whose vehicle is the human physical brain. It is from the Sanskrit *man* that the Latin mens is derived; and from *mens* that the name of Menes (Egypt) and *monas* the first intellect or Wisdom spoken of by the Pythagoreans have sprung; MANU (or man, the Thinker) being the product of the Universal Mind — the Dhyani-Chohans.

— the great spiritual truths of the transcendental worlds. Thus — (See ["]Divine Dynasties" App. XII.)

(14) As expressed in the Stanza — the ["]Watchers" descended on Earth and reigned over men — "*who are themselves.*" The reigning Kings had finished their Cycle on Earth and other worlds in the preceding Rounds. In the future Manvantaras they will have risen to higher systems than our planetary world; and it is the Elect of our Humanity, the Pioneers on the hard and difficult path of Progress, who will take the places of their predecessors. The *fifth* (our next) Round will witness *men* of the present one as the instructors and guides of a mankind whose monads may now be yet imprisoned, semi-conscious, in the most intellectual of the animal kingdom, while their lower principles are animating the highest specimens of the vegetable world. Thus proceed the cycles of the septenary evolution in septenary nature: the spiritual, psychical, intellectual, passionate, instinctive semi-ethereal and purely material or physical nature or the formless, the intangible and the objective, subservient to, and depending on, our present five senses. Thus also, is the Universe periodically manifesting itself for purposes of personal and collective progress of countless lives, the outbreathings of the ONE LIFE; in order that through the EVER-BECOMING, every atom in Kosmos, passing from the material and through the semi-ethereal, instinctive, passionate, intellectual, psychical and spiritual natures, may reach by its individual efforts, that plane where it will rebecome the one Unconditioned, absolute ALL. Having descended immaculate from the region of absolute purity into the spheres of being; identified itself on its cyclic pilgrim's journey with every atom in manifested space, struggled through and suffered in every form of life, till it reaches the glorious stage of collective Humanity in its own manifested image — the Deity is now only at the bottom of the cycle of the Valley of matter. In order to progress homeward, the "God" has now to ascend the weary up-hill path of Golgotha — the martyrdom of fully conscious life. *He has to sacrifice Himself to Himself* in order to redeem all creatures, and to resurrect from the many into the One Life. There, he ascends into Heaven indeed; where, plunged in the incomprehensible, absolute Being and the Bliss of Paranirvana,

He reigns unconditionally; and whence he will redescend again at the next COMING, which, one portion of Humanity expects under the allegorical term of the "Second Advent," the other under that of the last AVATAR. (See App. ["]*Sapta Surya,* The Seven Sins [Suns"].)

A very imperfect, and superficial explanation of the esoteric meaning of the first seven stanzas in the 1st Book of *Dzyan* has now been given. The Appendices help to explain the more hazy points: they withhold still more, which has to be worked out by individual exertions or — left incomplete. The Occult Doctrine teaches, as is now seen, the *Universality* of God, not an extra cosmic Deity; a boundless Kosmos interpenetrated by countless other worlds, all as boundless and as infinite in their *inner* natures and as finite and limited as our own — on the plane of objectivity. The whole philosophy rests upon this one point, the unity of all. This in a Christian sense, limited to our manifested Universe of matter, is — we are told — also the dream of modern science; namely "that all the recognized chemical elements will one day be found but modifications of a single material element."[222] The Occultist who goes further, who

---

222. "World life" — *Comparative Geology*, p. 48. The author Professor Winchell says: "It is generally admitted that at excessively high temperature, matter exists in a state of dissociation — that is, no chemical combinations can exist," and would appeal to prove the Unity of matter to the spectrum, which, in every case of homogeneity will show a *bright* line, whereas in the case of several molecular arrangements existing — in the nebulae say, or a star — "The spectrum should consist of two or three bright lines[."]! This would be no proof either way to the physicist Occultist, who maintains that beyond a certain limit of *visible* matter no spectrum, no telescope, as no microscope are of any use. The Unity of matter, of that which is real cosmic matter to the Alchemist or "Adam's Earth" as the Kabalists call it — can hardly be proved or disproved, by neither the French savant Dumas, who suggests "the composite nature of the 'Elements' on certain relations of atomic weights," or Dr. Crooke's "radiant matter" his experiments seeming to be best understood on the hypothesis of the homogeneity of the elements of matter. For all this does not go beyond *material* matter, so to say, even in what is shown by the *spectrum*, that modern "Eye of Siva" of physical experiments. It is of this matter only that Dr. Ste. Claire Deville could say that "when bodies deemed to be

resolves that "single *material* element" into one absolute *irresolvable* Element — Spirit or *Root-matter*, thus placing the latter at once outside the reach and province of physical philosophy — has of course but little in common with the orthodox man of science. He maintains that Spirit and Matter are homogeneous in their radical Unity, their apparent differentiations or aspects depending (*a*) on the various planes of evolution occupied by them; and (*b*) on the planes of consciousness of man himself. This is *metaphysics* and has very little to do with *physics* — however great in its own terrestrial limitation that physical *philosophy* may now be.

Nevertheless, once that science admits, if not the actual existence, at any rate the possibility of the existence "of a Universe with its numberless forms, conditions and aspects built out of a 'single Substance,'["]"[223] it has to go further. Unless it admits of the possibility also of the One Element, or the ONE LIFE of the Occultists, the "Mulaprakriti" of the Vedantin — it will have to hang that "single substance" especially if limited to only the solar nebulae like the coffin of Mahomet only minus the attractive magnet that holds it in mid air. Fortunately for the physical speculators, if unable to state with any degree of precision what the nebular theory *does* imply, thanks to Professor Winchell we are now able to know what *it does not* imply. As we are told by that erudite author, that the Planetary theory —

(1) "*Is not a theory of the Evolution of the Universe* but only and primarily a genetic explanation of the phenomena of the solar system and accessorily a coordination of the principal phenomena in the stellar and nebular firmament *as far as human vision has been able to penetrate.*" That —

---

simple combine with one another, they vanish, they are *individually annihilated*,["] simply because he could not follow those bodies in their further transformation in the world of spiritual cosmic matter. Verily modern science will never be able to dig deep enough into the cosmological formations to find the *roots* of the world stuff, or matter unless she works on the same lines of thought as the mediaeval alchemists did.

223. "World Life," Ibid.

(2) ["]It does not regard the Comets as involved in that *particular evolution which has produced the solar system"* — and that the Esoteric doctrine does: precisely because it *too* "recognizes the comets as forms of cosmic existence *coordinated with earlier stages of nebular evolution*" and actually assigns to them, chiefly the formation of all the worlds; that —

(3) "*It does not deny an antecedent history of the luminous fire mist.*" — [( ]The *secondary* stage of evolution in the Secret Doctrine) . . . "and makes no claim to having reached an absolute beginning.["] And that even, it allows that this "fire mist may have previously existed in a cold, non luminous and *invisible* condition["] . . . and that finally: —

(4) ["]It does not profess to discover the ORIGIN of things, but *only a stadium* in *material history*" . . . . leaving "the philosopher and theologian as free as they ever were to seek the origin of the modes of being" . . .[224] Considering all this, the Occultists believe they have a right to present their philosophy — however misunderstood and ostracised it may be, at first.[225] But this is not all: While admiring the modest impulse that caused one of the great philosophers of the day, Mr. Herbert Spencer, to confess that (*a*) "the problem of existence is not resolved" . . . ; (*b*) the nebular hypothesis ["]throws no light upon the origin of diffused matter["]; and that (*c*) ["]The nebular hypothesis implies a *First* Cause" (*Western [Westminster] Review*, IXX [LXX], [p.] 127 July 1858) — the Eastern Occultists would object even to the last term — as being unphilosophical, too materialistic, and as unsatisfactory in its incompleteness as the said hypothesis itself. A "*First* Cause" implies a time when there was *no* Cause, or its progenetic state; and therefore an *Eastern* Occultist or philosopher, would say a

---

224. "World Life" p. 196.

225. Unfortunately for us, Prof. A. Winchell the author of that instructive clear and most liberal work "The World Life" is one of the very few who thus recognizes the rights of independent speculation upon the origin of things. The majority of the physicists deny it to outsiders and especially to the "philosophers" and metaphysicians.

"*Causeless*" or an *Eternal* Cause, — if he would avoid creating anthropomorphic conceptions.

Now, if Science only admits the existence of one infinite absolute Principle in a boundless Universe of which our visible Universe is but an atom; and does not *object* at any rate to an Eternal and causeless Cause of ALL, the *root* of both Spirit and Matter which as it expands into manifestation passes through, and merges into, every degree of material form as of spiritual state, why should not our doctrine properly expounded and amplified become one day — the axiomatic Science of the future ages? Helped only by the discoveries of physical science, the world risks to come back to the original knowledge of the 4th Race mankind — to the most sublime (paradoxically speaking) state of sorcery compared to the evil of which traditional Satan will appear a wretched tyro. The world-evolution proceeds in cycles; and we are already approaching the APEX of European materiality. We are in *Libra* and the left side plate of the scales is dragging our race downwards. We are decreasing in physical strength and beauty; and unless we equilibrize our nature and avail ourselves of the light of Enoch — it is into the tail of the serpent that we will fall, instead of progressing onward. (See *Isis Unv.* Vol. II. p. 462. *Ezekiel's wheel*.)

From Deity to man, from world to atom, from star to a rush light, from the Sun to the vital heat of the meanest organic being, the world of Form and Existence is an immense chain, whose links are all connected together. The law of analogy is the first key to the world problems and these have to be studied coordinately in their occult relations to each other. He who has understood this verity will see how Langel, the author of *la Philosophie de la Chimie* — was right in his views. The more one studies Science and its metaphysics, — he said — the more one acquires the conviction that the former has nothing of irreconcilable [*sic*] whatever with the most idealistic philosophy. What is there indeed, that need dig an abyss between the two? Science analyzes the relationship of things. It measures, it weighs, and it thus discovers the laws which rule the phenomenal world on its lower and most material scale. But where is that simplest, that smallest phenomenon that does not place the exact sciences face to face with two problems, on which the experimental methods have no hold? First of all it is encountered by the ultimate *essence* of the substance modified by natural phenomena; secondly — by the *Force* which gives matter the impulse that results in such modifications. The men of science can neither know, nor see anything outside external appearance; the true fundamental reality, the substantial nature and its cause escape every investigation. It is *no more then worthy* of the highest philosophy to consider all those particular forces, the effects of which are analyzed by science, *as emanating from a first and one Force* — eternal, indispensable, the source of all motion, the centre of every action and energy. Having reached a certain stage, science *has either to blind [blend] itself with metaphysics* or to remain empirical and become very soon stationary. For, as expressed by a philosopher, if the former shows us that phenomena are only *realised ideas*, metaphysics gives us the assurance that the only reality of facts is to be sought for and found in the *absoluteness* of divine THOUGHT.

When, therefore, the Secret Doctrine postulating that conditioned or limited space (location) has no real being except in this world of illusion, or, in other words in our perceptive faculties[,] teaches that every one of the higher as of the lower worlds is interblended with our own objective world; that millions of things and beings are, in point of localization around and *in* us as we are around, with, and in them, it is no metaphysical figure of speech but a sober fact in nature, however incomprehensible to our senses.

The Doctrine refuses to use the words "above" and "below" — "higher" and "lower" in reference to *invisible* spheres as having no sense. Even the terms "East" and "West" are merely conventional, necessary only to aid our human perceptions. For, though the Earth has its two fixed points in the poles, North and South, yet, both East and West are variable relatively to our own position on the Earth's surface, and in consequence of its rotation from West to East. Hence, when we speak of ["]*other* worlds" — whether better or worse, more spiritual or still more material, though both invisible, the Occultist does not locate *these spheres* either *outside* or *inside* our Earth — as the theologian and poet do, for their location is nowhere in the Space *known to*, and conceived by us. They are, as it were, blended with our world — interpenetrating it and interpenetrated by it. There are millions and millions of worlds and firmaments visible to us; there are still greater numbers beyond those visible to the telescopes, and, as many of the latter kind that do not belong to our *objective* sphere of existences. Although as invisible as though they were a million of miles beyond our solar system, they are yet with us, near us, *within* our own world, as objective and material to their respective inhabitants as ours is to us. But, again, the relation of these worlds to ours is not that of a series of egg-shaped boxes enclosed one within the other, as the toys called Chinese nests; each is entirely under its own special laws and conditions, having no direct relation to our sphere. The inhabitants of these, as already said, may be for all we know or feel, passing *through* and *around* us as through empty space, their very habitations and countries being interblended with ours, though not disturbing our vision, because we have not yet the faculties necessary for discerning them, with our *physical* sense. As to the spiritual sight of the adepts and even of some seers and sensitives they are always able to discern, whether in a greater or smaller degree, the presence and close proximity to us of Beings pertaining to other spheres of life. Those of the (spiritually) higher worlds communicate with only those terrestrial mortals who ascend to them through individual efforts, on the high plane they are occupying.

"The Sons of *Bhumi* (Earth) regard the Sons of *Deva-lokas* (angel-spheres) as their gods; and the sons of lower Kingdoms look up to men of *Bhumi* as to their *devas* (gods)[;] men, remaining unaware of it, in their blindness . . . They, (men) tremble before them while using them (for magical purposes) . . . . The first Race of men were the '*mind-born*' *sons* of the former. They (the *pitris* and *devas*) are our progenitors." . . . (Book II of Comm. on *Dzyan*).

"Educated people" so called, deride the idea of Sylphs, Salamanders, Undines and Gnomes; the men of science regard as an insult any mention of such superstitions; and with a contempt of logic and common good sense that is often the prerogative of accepted "authority," they allow those whom it is their duty to instruct, to labour under the absurd impression that in the whole Kosmos or at any rate not in our own atmosphere, there are no other conscious intelligent beings save ourselves.[226] Any other humanity (i.e. composed of distinct, *human* beings) than a mankind with two legs, two arms and a head with man's features on it, would not be called human; though the etymology of the word, would seem to have little to do with the general appearance of a creature. Thus, while Science sternly rejects even the possibility of there being such (to us generally) invisible creatures, society is made to deride the idea and hails merrily works à la *Comte de Gabalis*, because it fails to understand the real meaning of such works and sees in them — a satire only.

Nevertheless; of such invisible worlds inhabited as thickly as our own, there are an immense number; some far more material than our own, others gradually etherializing until they become formless and are — as *Breaths*.

If, we find, even in the natural world with which we are acquainted, matter affording a partial analogy in the difficult conception of such *invisible* worlds — there seems little difficulty in allowing the possibility of such a presence. The tail of a comet, which though attracting our attention by virtue of its luminosity, yet does not disturb or impede our vision of objects, which we perceive through and beyond it, affords the first stepping stone towards a proof of the same. The tail of a comet passes rapidly across our horizon, and we should neither feel it nor be cognizant of its passage but for the brilliant coruscation perceived often only by a few interested in the phenomenon, while every one else remains ignorant of its presence and passage *through* or across, a portion of our globe. This tail may or may not, be an integral portion of the being of the Comet, but its tenacity serves us a purpose for our illustration. Indeed it is no question of superstition, but simply a recall of transcendental science, and of logic still more, to allow the existence of worlds formed of such and far more attenuated matter than the tail of a

---

226. Even the question of the plurality of worlds inhabited by sentient creatures is rejected or approached with the greatest caution! And yet see what the great astronomer Camille Flammarion says in his *Pluralite des Mondes*.

comet. By denying such a possibility, science has played for the last century into the hands of neither philosophy or true religion, but simply into those of theology. To be able to dispute the better the plurality of even material worlds, a belief as thought by many Church men incompatible with the teachings and doctrines of the Bible,[227] Maxwell had to calumniate the memory of Newton and try to convince his public that the principles contained in the Newtonian philosophy are those "which lie at the foundation of all atheistical systems." (*"Plurality of Worlds."*) "Dr. Whewell disputed the plurality of worlds by appeal to scientific evidence" writes Professor Winchell.[228] And, if even the habitability of physical worlds, of planets and distant stars which shine in myriads over our heads are so disputed, there is little chance for the acceptation of invisible worlds within our regions.

    Thus, if we can conceive of a world composed (for *our* senses) of matter still more attenuated than the tail of a comet, hence of inhabitants in it, who are as ethereal in proportion to *their* globe as we are, in comparison with *our* rocky, hard-crusted earth — no wonder if we do not perceive them, or even sense their presence or even existence. Only, in what is the idea contrary to science? Cannot men and animals, plants and rocks be supposed endowed with quite a different set of senses than we are? Cannot their structure and organisms be born, developed and exist under other laws of being than those that rule our little world? Is it absolutely necessary that every corporeal being should be clothed in "coats of skin" like those that Adam and Eve were provided with in the legend of Genesis? Corporeality, we are told by more than one man of science may exist under very divergent conditions.[229] Do not we know through the

---

227. Nevertheless, it will be shown on the testimony of the Bible itself and of such good Christian theologian[s] as Cardinal Wiseman was, that this plurality is taught in both the Ancient and the *new* Testaments.

228. See App. III on "The Plurality of the Worlds" wherein the list of all the men of science who wrote to prove the theory, is given.

229. Professor A. Winchell a distinguished geologist in America — arguing upon the plurality of worlds indulges in the following remarks.

discoveries of that very all denying science that we are

"It is not at all improbable that substances of a refractory nature might be so mixed with other substances, known or unknown to us, as to be capable of enduring vastly greater vicissitudes of heat and cold than it is possible with terrestrial organisms. The tissues of terrestrial animals are simply suited to terrestrial conditions. Yet even here we find different types and species of animals adapted to the trials of extremely dissimilar situations . . . . That an animal should be a quadruped or a biped is something not depending on the necessities of organization, or instinct, or intelligence, that an animal should possess just five senses is not a necessity of percipient existence. There may be animals on the earth with neither smell nor taste. There may be beings on other worlds and *even on this*, who possess more numerous senses than we. The possibility of this is apparent when we consider the high probability that other properties and other modes of existence lie among the resourses of the kosmos and even of terrestrial matter. There are animals which subsist where rational man would perish — in the soil, in the river and the sea.["] . . . . (and why not *human* beings of different organizations, in such case) . . . . "Nor is incorporated rational existence conditioned on warm blood, nor on any temperature which does not change the forms of matter of which the organism may be composed. *There may be intelligences corporealized* after some concept not involving the processes of injection, assimilation and reproduction. Such bodies would not require daily food and warmth. They might be lost in the abysses of the ocean, or laid up on a stormy cliff through the tempests of an artic winter, or plunged in a volcano for a hundred years, and yet retain consciousness and thought. It is conceivable. Why might not psychic natures be enshrined in indestructible flint and platinum. These substances are no further from the nature of intelligence than carbon, hydrogen, oxygen and lime. But, not to carry the thought to *such an extreme*, (?) might not high intelligences be embodied in frames as indifferent to external conditions as the sage of the western plains, or the lichens of Labrador, the rotifers that remain dried for years or the bacteria which pass living through boiling water . . . These suggestions are made simply to remind the reader how little can be argued respecting the necessary conditions of intelligent organized existence from the standard of corporeal existence found upon the earth. Intelligence is, from its nature, as universal and as uniform as the laws of the Universe. Bodies are merely the local fitting of intelligence to particular modifications of Universal matter and Force." (World Life or Comparative Geology p. 496-498 et seq.)

surrounded by myriads of invisible lives? If these microbes, bacteria and the *tutti quanti* of the [in]finitesimal[l]y small are unseen to us by virtue of their size, cannot there be, at the other pole of it, beings as invisible owing to the quality of their texture or matter to its tenuity? Conversely, as to the effects of cometary matter, have we not another example of a half visible form of life and matter? The ray of sun-light entering our apartment and revealing in its passage myriads of tiny beings "living their little life" and "ceasing to be" independent and heedless of whether they are perceived or not by our grosser materiality. And so again of the microbes and bacteria and such like unseen beings in other elements. We passed them by during those long centuries of dreary ignorance, after the lamp of knowledge in the heathen and highly philosophical systems had ceased to throw its bright light on the ages of intolerance and bigotry during early Christianity; and we would fain pass them as well now.

And yet these lives have surrounded us then, as they do now; they worked on, as obedient to their own laws, and it is only as they were gradually revealed by science that we have begun to take cognizance of the effects produced by them.

How long has it taken the world, as it is now, to become what it is at present? If it can be said of cosmical dust that some of it comes to the present day *"which had never belonged to the earth before"* (*"World-life"* Winchell) how much more logical to believe that through the countless ages and millions of years that have rolled away since that dust has aggregated and formed on the globe we live on, many humanities differing from our present mankind, as that which will evolve millions of years hence will differ from us — have appeared but to disappear from the face of the Earth, as our own will. Those primitive humanities may have not left tangible relics of themselves because, as we are taught, the bodies of those beings had no such material, lasting skeletons as ours are built upon; their organisms needed no warm blood or feeding. The author of the "World-Life" is right indeed. And it is no *such* great "extreme" as he seems to think, to believe that as there may be on scientific hypothesis "psychic natures enshrined in indestructible flint and platinum" to this day, so there were objective beings — the real forefathers of our humanity — clothed in ethereal bodies of the texture of which the modern chemist and physicist may have no idea.

    This work gives all that is lawful to give out of the *Secret* Books of the East; and may prove to a degree, even useful as an occasional suggestion, to the unprejudiced Unbeliever. Book II will now treat of that age of the Earth and Humanities from the aspect of physical as well as of Spiritual or Esoteric Science — .

The Secret Doctrine Würzburg Manuscript

**[VOLUME III
Evolution of Man]**

The Secret Doctrine Würzburg Manuscript

The Secret Doctrine Würzburg Manuscript

Book II
Archaic Chronology, Cycles, Anthropology

Facies, totins [totius] Universe [Universi], quamois [quamvis] infinitis modis variet, manet tamen semper endem [eadem]. SPINOSA [SPINOZA].

Stanza

This (wheel) rolled on for one half of an Eternity generating progeny; first mineral — soft stones that hardened; then vegetal — hard plants that softened; then tiny *visibles* from *invisibles* (insects and animals) which grew and expanded, each in its way and of its kind. When they became too huge and numerous she (the Earth) shook them off her back — once, twice, many a time . . . . Then the MIND-BORN, the boneless rupa (Forms of Beings) gave life to the first mind-born manu with softest bones. . . . How was the manu born?[230] First, the SELF-EXISTENT; then the Self-born — the sons of *Will and Yoga*; then the SWEAT-BORN[231] who were still one (androgynous) when they said — Let us make sons and daughters in our image but in solid form (*Manushya*) . . . Then, the *one became two*. (Book III Comm. "*Books of Dzyan*.["])

---

230. From the root *man*, to think (Sansk.); Manas or the human soul is the thinking principle. It is from the Sanskrit *Man* that sprung the Latin *Mens* and from "Mens" that were formed the words and the names of *Menes* the Egyptian, Monas, the first and one Intellect or "Wisdom" of Pythagoras etc. Manu or man, the thinker is thus the product of "Universal Mind" man — in Sanskrit is *Manushya*; add also — [*sic*]

231. Sweat born means as will be seen, a race of Humanity born not as present men are, but through the pores of its skin like perspiration. Spiritualists and clairvoyants are ???? [word illegible] to remember the way *materialized* forms ooze out of the medium's body, and then they, at any rate, will understand the process and the suggestive name given to the mankind of the SECOND Root-race. To this day in India, yogis are credited with a mysterious power of creating human beings through their WILL.

The first sentence "one half of an Eternity" would seem to allow a glimpse into some definite yet only an approximate age of the world and its Humanity. The rest has a direct reference to the four Root races which preceded ours. That Humanity evolved gradually into its present form from one almost ethereal, having of the physical in it but its objective appearance was ever a *universal* tradition. Plato mentions in *Phaedrus* a winged race of men; Aristophanes (Plato's *Banquet*) mentions another race androgynous and "with round bodies"[232] in the ancient Quichi manuscript, published by Brassier de Bourbourg — the *Popol Vuh* — the first men are mentioned as a race whose sight was unlimited and who knew all things at once — thus showing divine Omniscience of gods, not of mortals. As to the Secret Doctrine it teaches all this *as a fact*. As already mentioned in Book I, Humanities developed parallel and coordinately with the four root Elements, every race being physiologically adapted to first one, then two, three and four elements our fifth Race running rapidly toward the fifth, ???? [word illegible, still?] unrecognised Element, *Ether*, since it is of almost a spiritual nature. We can live in every climate whereas the first peoples had no climate, so to say[,] even the traditions of *Eden* at the end of the third Race — being based upon that of an eternal spring that reigned once over the whole globe. The few sorry remnants of the third race, met in the tribes of Australian savages have gradually been transformed and adapted to other lives.[233]

What say the *exoteric* Hindu Scriptures of the age of the world, and its earliest Humanities. As will be shown now the same as the *esoteric* teaching. No nation's scriptural records can

---

232. See App. II ["]Divine *Hermaphrodite*["] Sect. V *Prelimin.* Vol[ume.]

233. It would be erroneous to view those Savages as *they are now* as the descendants of the IIId Race. When a race has accomplished its cycle completely, its remnants begin to degenerate rapidly, falling back and being drawn more and more physically and intellectually toward the Kingdom that precedes the human — i.e. the *animal* one. Once they become stationary they rapidly die out — such is the la[w].

ever be accepted in their dead-letter only surface deep, meaning. Therefore the few lines from the Old Book will now be divided into three principal groups and commented upon, both in the light of ancient and modern sciences.

I The ages of the World, our globe and that of man; (*a*) from the hypothesis of modern science (*b*) the teachings of exoteric Hinduism and (c) those of the Secret Doctrine.

II The primeval "Manus of Humanity" or *Races*, under their various differentiations — from Devas (gods or angels) to mortal men. — Divisions of Cycles and periodical occurrences, both on the physical and the spiritual or moral planes.

III The first men of the Fourth Root-race and the Fifth, of present mankind: *i.e.* from the last *seventh* sub race of the Third Root-race — which *fell into generation,* down to the first sub-races of the 5th great Aryan Race of which we are one of the last offshoots.

The Secret Doctrine Würzburg Manuscript

§ I

(*a*) Calculation and Hypothesis of Geology and Anthropology; conclusions and modern theories.

So far, no trustworthy numerical estimate of the ages of the world and man could be made, it seems[,] by modern geologists and anthropologists. The best efforts to arrive even to an approximate agreement have signally failed. Hence, with every generation Science becomes more cautious and less explicit upon the subject. This is to be regretted though no one could be blamed for it. Indeed in the Cimmerian darkness of those silent prehistoric ages, the explorers are lost like in a labyrinth whose great corridors would be doorless and thus allow no visible issue into the Archaic Past. Moreover, among that mass of conflicting theories and rejecting as they always do the evidence of Sanskrit works without any clue or certainty to guide it — Archaeology has to pick up *nolens volens* the slender thread of Ariadne where it first perceives it, — and — can do no more. Thus we learn that — "the farthest date to which documentary record extends is now generally regarded by anthropology as but the earliest distinctly visible point of the historic period."

At the same time, it is confessed that — "beyond that period stretches back a vast indefinite series of *prehistoric* ages." (Encyclopedia Britannica.)

It is with those specified "ages" that we shall begin. They are "prehistoric" to the naked eye of matter, only. To the spiritual eagle eye of the Seer and the prophet of every race, as under every sky, Ariadne's thread stretches beyond that "historic period" without break or flow, surely and steadily into the very night of Time: and the hand that holds it is too mighty to let it break or even drop. Records exist although they may be rejected as fanciful; and many among them are tacitly accepted by more than one man of learning though refused invariably by the collective bodies of science.

But the reader's memory must be first refreshed with the teachings and figures — the various hypotheses of our men of exact science — with regard to the ages of our globe and its Humanity. We may take the figures from Professor Winchell's work on Comparative Geology — the World-Life. Here we find — concerning sidereal and cosmical phenomena — based on their respective relations to terrestrial duration, an opponent of the nebular theory, showing a most serious and suggestive difference in scientific opinions, that the author admits, though trying to account for it on very reasonable grounds. Thus — "Sir William Thomson, on the basis of the observed principles of cooling, concludes that not more than *ten million* years can have elapsed since the temperature of the earth was sufficiently reduced to sustain vegetable life;[234] . . . Helmholz calculates that *twenty* million years would suffice for the original nebula to condense to the present dimensions of the sun. Professor S. Newcomb requires only ten million years to attain a temperature of 212° Fahr.[235] . . . . Croll estimates seventy million years[236] for the difference of the heat which would be produced by the collision of two such nebulae as would constitute the primitive nebula postulated by the theory. But meantime Bischof calculates that *350 million* years would be required for the earth to cool from a temperature of 2,000° to 200° centigrade. (!) Reade basing his estimate on observed rates of denudation, demands 500 million of years since sedimentation began in Europe.[237] Lyell ventured a rough guess of 240 million years; Darwin thought 300 million years demanded by the organic transformations which his theory contemplates; and Huxley is disposed to demand a 1000 millions." (!!)

To this Professor Winchell answers with the admission that there are "some biologists" who seem to close their eyes tight and leap at one bound into the abyss of millions of years, of which they have no more adequate estimate than of infinity," (p. 180) and proceeds to suggest what he thinks to be more

---

234. Thomson and Tait *Natural Phil.* App. D. *Trans. Roy. Soc. Edin.*

235. *Popular Astronomy* [p.] 509.

236. Climate and Time [p.] 335.

237. Reade. Address *Liverpool Geol. Soc.* 1876.

correct geological figures. A few will do. Thus it may be assumed according to Sir W. Thomson that — "the whole incrusted age of the world is — 80,000,000 years"; and, agreeably with Professor Haughton's calculations of a minor limit for the time since the elevation of Europe and Asia: three hypotheses for three possible and different modes of upheaval are given from the modest period of 640,730 years, again 4,170,000 years, and up to the tremendous figures of 27 million, 491,000 years! Further calculations which the reader can find in Prof. Winchell's ["]World Life" (pp. 367-8) bring Revd. S. Haughton to an approximation of the sedimentary age of the world — 11,700,000 years. These figures are forthwith shown by Prof. Winchell "too small" a period and are increased to 37,000,000 years. Again according to Professor Croll ("Climate and Time") 2,500,000 years represents the time since the *beginning* of the Tertiary age; therefore, the whole incrusted age of the world must be 131 million 600,000 years. As the last glacial period extended from 240,000 to 80,000 years ago (Prof. Croll's view), therefore, man must have appeared on earth from 100 to 120,000 years ago. But, as says Prof. Winchell with reference to the antiquity of the Mediterranean race "it is generally believed to have made its appearance during the later decline of the continental glaciers." Yet, he adds, — this "does not concern, however, the antiquity of the Black and *Brown races*, since *there are numerous evidences of their existence in more southern regions, in times remotely* pre-glacial." (p. 379).

    This remarkable divergence of opinions, as much among geologists as between biologists, and physicists who allow themselves such calculations incidentally — gives one the key to the unwillingness of our modern scientists, or rather, the absolute impossibility in this case — to come even to any approximation of either the age of the world or that of man. At this rate the calculators ought to follow the wise example of the Masons. As chronology cannot, they think;[,] measure the era of the creation, therefore their "ancient and Primitive Rite" uses 000,000,000 as the nearest approach to reality.

    Leaving individual private opinions — however learned — aside, we will now take for the base of our comparison and as the mean accepted by science the figures found in that ["]circle of Sciences" — The *Encyclopaedia Britannica*. For, therein, though modern geology refuses to assign any definite chronological dates — even to such, comparatively speaking late epochs as the Neolithic era — it has, nevertheless, established ages for the beginnings of certain geological periods: at any rate to such few, the duration of which could hardly be shortened any more, without an immediate conflict with facts.

Thus it is surmised in the great Encyclopaedia (vol. X art. *Geology* p. 227) that 100 million years have passed . . . since the solidification of our Earth, when the earliest form of life appeared upon it.[238]

The argument from Geological evidence being thus in favour of one hundred million years, we need say no more; for that number of years is as "simply sufficient" for our purposes. Geology knows but of one earth or globe; the Secret Doctrine teaches us that there are *seven* (See Esoteric Buddhism). And, if the years given from the beginning of Cosmic Evolution (which relates in truth, to the 1st Round, *i.e.* to the beginning of activity of the first globe A, on our planetary chain — up to the year of grace 1885, and its corresponding (the then) current Hindu year *Tarana* amount to the enormous figure of 1,955,884,685 years — this calculation concerns our Earth, *only in the general calculations* that includes its six *unknown* companions[239] as all the Brahma and other lokas of the Hindu Scripture.

But, if it can be easily shown that in point of geological conclusions there is a remarkable agreement between Archaic and the modern sciences, not so in regard to the antiquity of

---

238. "1,000,000,000 [*sic*] of years is probably amply sufficient for all the requirements of geology" says the text. In France some *savants* do not find it nearly "sufficient." Le Couturier claims for the same 350 million years; Buffon was satisfied with 34 millions — but there are in the more modern schools who will not be content under 500 million years.

239. The figures 1,955,884,685 relate to the very beginning of the Cosmic Evolution of *our chain*, if not of COSMOS, and do not refer to the *last* geological *transformation* of our little globe standing forth in the chain, and which has passed, ????? [word illegible] through three *obscurations*, or three *minor pralayas* already.

man; for in this the teachings of the two clash enormously. The "probable" figures given by Anthropology in respect to the date of the first appearance of Humanity upon our globe, are more than hesitating and vague: — they amount in fact to a confession of total ignorance. As an "exact" and strictly *experimental* science Anthropology has to be cautious in her conclusions and therefore on this important point it refuses to premise anything, though it refutes, a priori, as little with the majority of the Anthropologists, it may be called — "a policy of expectations." Committing themselves to no definite statement — as indeed they hardly could — they leave thus enormous latitude to bolder speculators. As an illustration, while the majority of the Anthropologists "carry back the existence of man into the period of the post-glacial drift in what is now called the Quaternary period"; and that as many of them trace mankind to the Pleostecine [Pleistocene? or Pliocene?] age in the Tertiary period, Mr. Boyd Dawkins, — if we mistake not in a paper read by him some years since before the Royal association of science, seeks to prove that the human period, so called, dates — if we remember correctly — so far back as 27,000,000 of years.

These figures may not reach the calculations in the *Book of Manu* which says that the time from the *first* evolution of Humanity on our *"Planetary chain"* — equals, 1,664,500,986 years up to present date — for our *Planetary chain* does not mean — our globe. But, it falls in very well otherwise with the number of years given by both orthodox Brahmins and the *Secret Doctrine*. Then calculating since the beginning of the "Vaivasvata Manvantara," or the *human* period in which we are now[,] speak [sic] only of the present humanity on our earth since it received its new "human tide-wave" after its last "Obscuration." And that number of years is: — 18,618,727. Therefore, while we have nothing to say against the theory of 27,000,000 of years — we must reject entirely that other one given by the *Encyclopaedia Britannica* as *the last word of Science*.[240] Indeed, the antiquity for man is allowed to stretch only over "tens of thousands of years." For it is evident that

---

240. See art. *Geology* in *Encyclopaedia Britannica*.

such figures as those may be made to fluctuate between 50,000 and 500,000 of years and therefore mean little, if anything. The figures are calculated to puzzle and throw still more darkness upon the question. For what matters it that Science places the birth of man in the *pre* or the "post-glacial drift," if we are told at the same time that the so called *Ice age* is a long succession of ages which "shaded without abrupt change of any kind into what is termed the Human or Recent Period . . . . the overlapping of geological periods having been the rule from the beginning of time." The latter "rule" only results in the still more puzzling, even if strictly *scientific* and correct information, that — "even today man is contemporary with the Ice age in the Alpine Valleys and in the Finmark."[241]

Thus, had it not been for the lessons taught by the *Secret Doctrine*, we would be left to this day to float in perplexed uncertainty between the 27,000,000 of one school of science, the "tens of thousands of years" of the other, and the 6,000 years of the Bible interpreters. This is one of the several reasons why with all the respect due to the conclusions of the men of learning of our modern day, in all such questions of prehistoric antiquity we are forced to ignore them, giving our reasons for it: We believe in ancient Wisdom and prefer even its "vague traditions."

---

241. *Ibid.* This allows a chance even to the Biblical "Adam chronology" of 6,000 years.

Appendices

by Daniel H. Caldwell

The Secret Doctrine Würzburg Manuscript

The Secret Doctrine Würzburg Manuscript

THE WRITING OF
THE SECRET DOCTRINE
A Chronology

Compiled by Daniel H. Caldwell
http://hpb.cc

[**Note:** In compiling this "Chronology," I have used material provided by Boris de Zirkoff in his book *Rebirth of the Occult Tradition* and some of his other writings, as well as material provided me by Henk J. Spierenburg plus material I have gathered over the years through my own study and research.—D.H.C.]

1884

January 1884—H. P. Blavatsky at the Theosophical Society headquarters at Adyar, Madras, India writes to A.P. Sinnett in London:

> ". . . I, crippled down and half dead, am to sit up nights again and rewrite the whole of *Isis Unveiled*, calling it *The Secret Doctrine* and making three if not four volumes out of the original two, Subba Row helping me and writing most of the commentaries and explanations."

(Source: *The Letters of H. P. Blavatsky to A.P. Sinnett*, p. 64.)

January 1884—In the Supplement to *The Theosophist* for this month, a Publisher's Notice with the title **THE SECRET DOCTRINE: A New Version of "Isis Unveiled"** is printed:

> "Numerous and urgent requests have come from all parts of India, to adopt some plan for bringing the matter contained in *Isis Unveiled*, within the reach of those who

could not afford to purchase so expensive a work at one time. On the other hand, many, finding the outlines of the [Esoteric] doctrine given too hazy, clamoured for 'more light,' and necessarily misunderstanding the teaching, have erroneously supposed it to be contradictory to later revelations, which in not a few cases, have been entirely misconceived. The author [H. P. Blavatsky], therefore, under the advice of friends, proposes to issue the work in a better and clearer form, in monthly parts. All, that is important in *Isis* for a thorough comprehension of the occult and other philosophical subjects treated of, will be retained, but with such a rearrangement of the text as to group together as closely as possible the materials relating to any given subject. Thus will be avoided needless repetitions, and the scattering of materials of a cognate character throughout the two volumes."

"Much additional information upon occult subjects, which it was not desirable to put before the public at the first appearance of the work, but for which the way has been prepared by the intervening eight years, and especially by the publication of [A.P. Sinnett's two books] *The Occult World* and *Esoteric Buddhism* and other Theosophical works, will now be given. Hints will also be found throwing light on many of the hitherto misunderstood teachings found in the said works. A complete Index and a Table of Contents will be compiled. It is intended that each Part shall comprise seventy-seven pages in Royal 8vo. . . . to be printed on good paper and in clear type, and be completed in about two years. . . . the first Part will be issued March 15th."

February 20, 1884—Leaving on their European tour of France, England and Germany, H.P.B. and Colonel Henry Olcott sail from Bombay, India for Marseilles, France.

(Source: *The Theosophist*, March 1884, p. 154.)

The Secret Doctrine Würzburg Manuscript

April 25, 1884—H.P.B. in Paris, France writes to Mr. Sinnett:

"I thank you *for the intention* you had of writing the Preface for *Secret Doctrine*—I did not ask you to do it but the Mahatmas and Mohini here, and Subba Row *there* [at Adyar T.S. headquarters] are quite sufficient for the task of helping me. If you *do not* think that 'the scheme is feasible as announced' [in *The Theosophist*] I am sorry for you and your intuition. Since the Guru thinks it otherwise I will take my chance of following rather his order and advice than yours. This, in sincere friendship, but in as great a determination. To say that I 'would do *wisely* to direct the repayment of subscriptions and withdraw the announcement' is to talk sheer flapdoodle. I did not undertake to rewrite and bother myself with that infernal book for my own sweet pleasure. Could I annihilate it by hurling the accursed work into the 8th sphere I would. But my own predilictions or wishes have naught to do with my duty. MASTER orders and wills it be rewritten and rewrite it I *will*; so much the better for those who will help me on the tedious task, and *so much the worse for those* who do not and will not. Who knows but with God's blessing and help the thing may turn out 'a splendid piece of work' anyhow. Nor will I ever, with your permission and begging your pardon, of course, agree with you that 'it is madness to try and write such a book for monthly parts' *once that the Guru so ordains it.* For, notwithstanding the remarkable respect I feel for your western wisdom and business like talents, I would never say of anything my Master (in particular) and *the* Masters (in general) tell me to do—that it is sheer *madness* to do their bidding.

"One chapter at any rate, 'on the Gods, Pitris, the Devas and Daimonia, Elementaries and Elementals, and other like spooks' is finished. I have found and followed a very easy method given me, and chapter after chapter and part after part will be rewritten very easily. Your suggestion that it must not 'look like a mere reprint of Isis' is nowhere in the face of the announcement (which please see in *The Theosophist* last page). Since it promises only 'to bring the matter contained in Isis' within the reach of all; and to explain and show that the 'later revelations,' i.e. *Esot[eric] Buddhism* for one, and other things in the *Theosophist* are not contradictory to the outlines of the doctrine given — however *hazy* the latter is in that *Isis*, and to give in the *Secret Doctrine* all that is important in 'Isis' grouping together the materials relating to any given subject instead of leaving them scattered throughout the 2 vol[umes] as they are now — then it follows that I am bound to give *whole pages* from 'Isis' only amplifying and giving additional information. And unless I do give numerous reprints from *Isis*, it will become *Osiris* or *Horus* — never what it was originally promised in the 'Publisher's Notice' which — please read."

(Source: *Letters of H. P. Blavatsky to A.P. Sinnett*, p. 88-89.)

[This chapter by H.P.B., "on the Gods, Pitris, the Devas and Daimonia, Elementaries and Elementals, and other like spooks" was finally published after H.P.B.'s death in *Lucifer*, August, September, and October, 1893 issues. In this chapter, H.P.B., writing about Lunar Devas and Rounds, says: "Let the student consult *The Secret Doctrine* on this matter, and he will there find full explanation." —D.H.C.]

May, 1884—William Q. Judge writes:

". . . At Enghien [France] especially, H.P.B. wanted me to go carefully through the pages of her copy of *Isis Unveiled* for the purpose of noting on the margins what subjects were treated, and for the work she furnished me with what she called a special blue and red pencil. I went all through both volumes and made the notes required, and of those she afterwards wrote me that they were of the greatest use to her. . . ."

(Source: Constance Wachtmeister, *Reminiscences of H. P. Blavatsky*, 1893, p. 102.)

June 1884—In *The Theosophist* (p. 232) a notice is published about *The Secret Doctrine*:

> "We regret to announce that, owing to unavoidable causes, the publication of the *Secret Doctrine* has to be delayed for two months more. The first Number will therefore be out on the 15th of August, instead of 15th of June as originally announced."

September 1884—In *The Theosophist* (p. 304) another notice is published:

> "The delay in the issue of Part I of the *Secret Doctrine* was due to the MSS. not having reached this office in time, from London from Madame Blavatsky, who, besides being in bad health, has a good deal of Society business to do in connection with the European tour. The MSS. have, however, now come and been put in the printer's hand. The first number is expected to be out by the middle of this month...."

October 1884—In *The Theosophist* (p. 143) the reader is informed that:

> ". . . As, in consequence of recent events, Madame Blavatsky's early return to India is expected, it has been decided to postpone the issue of the first part of the *Secret Doctrine*, so as to insure an uninterrupted succession of numbers after her arrival. . . ."

November 15, 1884—Colonel Olcott arrives in Madras, India, back from his European tour. H.P.B. is coming back to India later.

November 27, 1884—Colonel Olcott writes:

> ". . . The delays in the appearance of the work [*The Secret Doctrine*] have been mainly due to two causes — Mme. Blavatsky's almost constant ill-health since her departure [from India] for Europe, in February last; and the interference with her literary labours by her travels and official engagements. The paper for the entire edition was purchased several months ago and is at Adyar; the Introduction and First Chapter are in type; and the two volumes of Isis Unveiled have been carefully read and annotated for use in the new book. . . . As Mme. Blavatsky is expected at Adyar during the present month, it is hoped and expected that the work will soon appear, and the monthly parts follow each other uninterruptedly."

(Source: *The Theosophist*, December 1884, p. 74.)

December 21, 1884—Mme. Blavatsky arrives (from Europe via Egypt) back at the Theosophical Society, Adyar, Madras, India.

December (late), 1884—Master K.H. writes to A.P. Sinnett about Sinnett's *Esoteric Buddhism*:

> ". . . no one, so far, has noticed the real vital errors in [your] *Esoteric Buddhism* . . . nor are they likely to. We can give no further information on the subject already approached by you and have to leave the facts already communicated to be woven into a consistent and systematic philosophy by the chelas at the Headquarters. The *Secret Doctrine* will explain many things, set to right more than one perplexed student."

(Source: *The Mahatma Letters to A. P. Sinnett*, chronological edition, Letter 128, p. 428.)

1885

Jan. 9, 1885—H.P.B. receives from Master M. a new plan for her *Secret Doctrine*. Colonel Henry S. Olcott writes about this as follows:

> "...as my Diary entry states — 'H.P.B. got from her Teacher the plan for her *Secret Doctrine,* and it is excellent. Oakley and I tried our hands at it yesterday, but this is much better.' Meanwhile, the accumulation of materials for the book had long been going on. It will be news to some that this was not originally intended to be a new book, but only a recasting and amplification of *Isis Unveiled,* with the late T. Subba Row, B.A., B.L., as co-editor with H.P.B. As first advertised in the *Theosophist,* it was to have been issued in monthly parts of 77 pages each, and to have run to about twenty parts. This new scheme, given her by her Teacher, changed this programme, and the gradual building up of the present grand work [as published in 1888] was the result."
>
> (Source: Henry S. Olcott, *Old Diary Leaves*, Volume III, pp. 199-200.)

March 31, 1885—In poor health, H.P.B. leaves the Theosophical Society at Adyar, Madras, India, and sails for Naples, Italy, accompanied by Miss Mary Flynn, Bawaji (Dharbagiri Nath), and Franz Hartmann. She will never return to India.

> (Sources: Henry S. Olcott, *Old Diary Leaves*, Volume III, p. 222; Henry Olcott's Diaries; *Theosophist*, Volume VI, Supplement, May, 1885, p. 195; letter of H. S. Olcott to Francesca Arundale, April 1, 1885, in *Theosophist*, October, 1932; H.P.B.'s letter to Henry Olcott, April 11, 1885.)

April, 1885—While on the voyage to Naples, H.P.B. frequently gets many pages of MSS. for her *Secret Doctrine* in an occult manner. Franz Hartmann writes:

> "...in April, 1885, when I accompanied H. P. Blavatsky from Madras to Europe, while on board the *SS. Tibre* and on the open sea, she very frequently received in some occult manner many pages of manuscript referring to *The Secret Doctrine*, the material of which she was collecting at the time...."

> (Source: Letter of Franz Hartmann to Mrs. Vera Johnston, June 2, 1893, in Countess Constance Wachtmeister, *Reminiscences of H. P. Blavatsky*, 1893, p. 109.)

April 11, 1885—H.P.B. on board ship writes to Colonel Olcott back in India:

> "...When preparing to go on the steamer, Subba Row told me to write the Secret Doctrine and send to him through you every week what I had written. I promised this to him and will do so....He is going to make notes and commentaries and then the T.S. will publish it...."

> (Source: H.P.B.'s letter to Henry S. Olcott, dated April 11, 1885, and quoted in Boris de Zirkoff, *Rebirth of the Occult Tradition*, p. 7.)

April 13, 1885—H.P.B. reaches Aden.

> (Source: H.P.B.'s letter to Colonel Olcott., April 11, 1885; Lloyd's of London records.)

April 23, 1885—H.P.B. and party reach Naples, Italy.

> (Source: Lloyd's of London records.)

July (end), 1885—H.P.B. leaves Italy for Würzburg, Germany.

>(Source: V. S. Solovyoff, *Modern Priestess of Isis*, 1895 English ed., pp. 132-133.)

August (soon after 12th), 1885—H.P.B. and Bawaji reach Würzburg, Germany and take an apartment at 6 Ludwigstrasse.

>(Sources: Countess Constance Wachtmeister, *Reminiscences of H. P. Blavatsky*, 1893, p. 49; V. S. Solovyoff, *Modern Priestess of Isis*, 1893 Russian ed., pp. 190-91.)

August (after middle), 1885—Vsevolod S. Solovyoff arrives in Würzburg to visit H.P.B. and stays at Hotel Rugmer.

>(Sources: *Letters of H. P. Blavatsky to A.P. Sinnett*, p. 117; V. S. Solovyoff, *Modern Priestess of Isis*, 1895 English ed., p. 144.)

August (late), 1885—H.P.B. writes to her sister Vera de Zhelihovsky in Russia:

>"I am sitting quietly in Würzburg, waiting for Nadya's [H.P.B.'s aunt] promised visit, and won't stir from here. I am writing a new book [*The Secret Doctrine*] which will be worth two such as *Isis*."

>(Source: H.P.B.'s letter to her sister Vera, *The Path*, August, 1895, p. 142.)

September 1, 1885—Miss Francesca Arundale and Mohini M. Chatterji come to Würzburg on a visit from London. H.P.B.'s aunt, Nadyezhda A. de Fadeyev, arrives from Russia to visit her.

>(Sources: *Letters of H. P. Blavatsky to A.P. Sinnett*, p. 119; V. S. Solovyoff, *Modern Priestess of Isis*, 1895 English ed., pp. 172-73.)

September 21 to October 1, 1885—A.P. Sinnett and his wife Patience visit H.P.B. at Würzburg. Mr. Sinnett writes:

> "The 'Secret Doctrine' was still untouched in September 1885, when my wife and I saw her...and some premonitory symptoms indicated that the preparation of the 'Secret Doctrine' might shortly be set on foot."

> (Sources: A.P. Sinnett, *Incidents in the Life of Madame Blavatsky*, 1886 edition, pp. 302-03; A.P. Sinnett, *Autobiography of A.P. Sinnett*, p. 32.)

October (early), 1885—H.P.B. writes to Mr. Sinnett about the Mahatmas helping her with *The Secret Doctrine*:

> "...But Master [Morya] said to me that...He would help and the Mahatma [Koot Hoomi] also, as They are often here now for the Secret Doctrine...."

> (Source: *Letters of H. P. Blavatsky to A.P. Sinnett*, p. 253.)

October (early), 1885—Franz Hartmann, Prof. C. W. Sellin, Dr. William Hübbe-Schleiden, and Mr. and Mrs. Schmiechen visit H.P.B. at Würzburg.

> (Source: *Letters of H. P. Blavatsky to A.P. Sinnett*, pp. 121, 244.)

October (early), 1885—Dr. Hübbe-Schleiden gives the following details of his trip to Würzburg:

> "When I visited her in October, 1885, she [Madame Blavatsky] had just begun to write it [*The Secret Doctrine*]....I remained with her in Würzburg about a week or ten days....While I occupied myself chiefly with Babaji, who was then living with her, she was writing at her manuscript almost all day, from the early morning until the afternoon and even until night, unless she had guests. At that time she wrote articles for *The*

Theosophist as well....For instance [the article titled]: 'Have animals souls?'....But she had scarcely any books, not half a dozen, and I had to procure for her an English Bible, either to quote some text correctly or to control the correctness of some quotation....I...saw her write down sentences as if she were copying them from something before her...."

(Source: Countess Constance Wachtmeister, *Reminiscences of H. P. Blavatsky*, 1893, pp. 112, 111.)

October (early), 1885—H.P.B. writes to Mr. Sinnett:

"Yesterday Franz Gebhard delighted me with his arrival and rejoiced my ears with the following quotation from a letter....

"'Besides the block of Humanity to which we belong, passing round the chain of planets—as correctly described in E[soteric] B[uddhism]—*there are six other similar blocks simultaneously evolving on other parts of the chain.*'

"To this I listened in silent dismay, and would have remained dumb on the subject for ever had not Master's far away tones struck me . . . on the ear coming from the N.W. direction (for a wonder! He must be roaming somewhere in Europe my Boss) and saying: 'Now don't you let Sinnett go off again on the *wrong* track. Explain.' Just as though *I* had led you deliberately on to wrong tracks and not your own . . . vile curiosity! Easy to say 'explain,' I wish *He* would Himself; for if I do and you do not understand me, or—which is as likely I shall not be able to 'explain' so that you should understand, I shall be responsible for it and the only one blamed as usual.

"However, listen, and you may perhaps realise also what led even Mohini *off* the right mechanical track and made him write the unutterable flapdoodle he has in *Man* [an 1885 book written by Mohini M. Chatterji and Laura C. Holloway]—from the simply mechanical-*cosmos*-arrangement standpoint and tolerably correct one, if understood as applying to the 'simultaneous evolution' of the *six races* you are talking about, in a Socrates-like way, with your DAIMON whispering it in your ear. For I don't see *how* you could have got the idea in any other way.

"There are six races besides our own, which makes seven races, if you please. Seven upper ones and seven *nether*, or lower ones which make in all the 14 Brahmanical *lokas* spoken about in the *Vedanta*. This is the *exoteric* text: 'From the *five quintuplated elements* (the five quintuplated Buddhas of Rhys Davids and *exoteric* Buddhism)—proceed or spring, one above the other, the worlds *Bhur, Bhuvar, Swar, Mahar, Janas, Tapas* and *Satya*; and *one below the other*, the nether worlds called Atula, Vitala, Sutala, Rusatala, Talatala, Mahatala and Patala.' Now all the Orientalists have made a worse mess of it than you would, had I not been ordered to come benevolently to your rescue. Wilson makes of it in *Vishnu Purana* (pp. 209, 225 Vol ii) a regular *olla podrida*. Nor shall your great mathematician Elliot do you any good in the calculation of *duration* as you want him for he has not the ROOT number which cannot be given. So 'Boss' says, not I. However.

"What I give you now—please do not use it before it comes out in SECRET Doctrine—for it is from there as Master gave me."

I have only given above the beginning part of H.P.B.'s letter to Mr. Sinnett in which she apparently copies for Mr. Sinnett's benefit a portion of her *Secret Doctrine* manuscript. See complete letter for all the quoted material from the S.D.

This quoted portion from the S.D. manuscript may have been from the portion dealing with cosmogony. Nevertheless, this quoted material is NOT found anywhere in the published *Secret Doctrine*, Volumes I and II (1888) or in Volume III (1897). This material is therefore missing and unaccounted for to the present day.

See also a followup letter that H.P.B. wrote to Mr. Sinnett in which she continues her explanations. In this letter, she writes:

"Well you say you got that 'impression' while reading some matter among the *Secret Doctrine* (in Dharbagiri's writing). I looked over carefully page by page and found nothing in D. N.'s writing, but in Damodar's which you probably mistook. It is about what the Earth (and other planets) does during 'obscuration'? Is it this? For if so, then I can tell you that Damodar wrote it *under dictation*—but you have not understood the meaning quite correctly. It *does* refer to the 'worlds' I speak of and says (restoring it in its *full* sense) the following:—

"'It (the planet) cannot be resting for such a length of time. The fact is, that after our exit from here, the Planet gets ready to receive another group of Humanity coming after us. On the Planetary chain there are *seven groups* of Humanity simultaneously evolving; each Planet receiving *another group*, after one has passed away to the next Planet. These seven are distinct groups and do not intermingle with each other.' (But some of them do with *us* or our planet, as I shall show). Then, he goes on talking of *natural* and artificial Fifth Rounders. Is it this? I take it to be what you found among my papers and as there is nothing else so I shall talk on this.

"No your theory *does not* conflict so far, with facts; but then they must be shown to you in their correct position, not in a fanciful one like Mohini's theory of *Rings* and

Rounds. The conversation you had with me referred in *my* mind only to the *surplus* of Humanity or of the 'family' left over when partial obscuration came, not to the *nature* of that family. I shall try to explain as well as I can. By the bye. Dharbagiri says that he never meant anything but the 14 Brahma lokas."

I will not quote any more from this followup letter but again it appears that we have here material never published by H.P.B.

Both letters from which I have quoted above contain important information and esoteric teaching for readers and students of *The Secret Doctrine.*

(Source: *The Letters of H. P. Blavatsky to A.P. Sinnett*, Letter CXVIII, pp. 244-248; Letter CXIX, pp. 248-254.)

October 10 (est.), 1885—H.P.B. has a bad time with her heart. A doctor is called in to see H.P.B.'s condition.

(Source: *Letters of H. P. Blavatsky to A.P. Sinnett*, p. 133.)

October 28, 1885—H.P.B. writes to Colonel Olcott:

"I have not much time now with the *Secret Doctrine*. I am only at the middle of Part I, but shall in a month or two send you the first six sections.

"I take from *Isis* only facts, leaving out everything in the shape of dissertations, attacks on Christianity and Science—in short, all the useless stuff, and all that has lost its interest. Only myths, symbols, and dogmas explained from an esoteric point of view. It is actually and *de facto* a new work entirely.

"Cycles are explained, along with everything else, from their occult bearings...."

(Source: Henry S. Olcott, *Old Diary Leaves*, Volume III, p. 317.)

November—(sometime during the month), 1885—H.P.B. writes to Mr. Sinnett about her writing of *The Secret Doctrine*:

> "...The thing at N[ew] Y[ork] is repeated—only far clearer and better. I begin to think it shall vindicate us. Such pictures, panoramas, scenes *antediluvian* dramas with all that! Never saw or heard better."

(Source: *Letters of H. P. Blavatsky to A.P. Sinnett*, p. 244.)

November 25, 1885—H.P.B. in a letter to Colonel Olcott tells him:

> "...I have three Chap[ters] ready, the *fourth* nearly finished and the S.D. shall be another, quite another kind of hair-pin than *Isis*....if he [Subba Row] is willing to be looking over the MSS and correct them or add, or take out—then *I am willing by return post* to send what I have to Adyar.
>
> "....Well, say the word—by return post and I shall send what I have already. But you must be very careful that there should be no repetitions in such case as I shall have no MS. to refer to...."

(Source: Letter of H.P.B. to Henry S. Olcott, unpublished letter in Adyar Archives, quoted in Boris de Zirkoff, *The Rebirth of the Occult Tradition*, pp. 10-11.)

November (last part of month), 1885—Countess Constance Wachtmeister joins H.P.B. at Würzburg. She writes:

> "In the month of November, 1885, I went to Würzburg to visit Madame Blavatsky...Madame Blavatsky was settled in comfortable apartments with lofty rooms and

with the quiet surroundings she so much needed for the stupendous work in which she was engaged....

"...It was evening when I reached Madame Blavatsky's lodgings, and as I mounted the stairs my pulse was a little hurried while I speculated upon the reception which awaited me. Madame Blavatsky's welcome was a warm one....

"I remember very well that it was then, on going into the dining room together to take some tea, that she said to me abruptly, as of something that had been dwelling on her mind.

" 'Master says you have a book for me of which I am much in need.' "

" 'No, indeed,' I replied, 'I have no books with me.' "

" 'Think again,' she said, 'Master says you were told in Sweden to bring a book on the Tarot and the Kabbalah.' "

"Then I recollected the circumstances...From the time I had placed the volume in the bottom of my box it had been out of my sight and out of my mind. Now, when I hurried to the bedroom, unlocked the trunk, and dived to the bottom, I found it in the same corner I had left it when packing in Sweden, undisturbed from that moment to this. But this was not all.

"When I returned to the dining room with it in my hand, Madame Blavatsky made a gesture and cried, 'Stay, do not open it yet. Now turn to page ten and on the sixth line you will find the words . . . .' And she quoted a passage.

"I opened the book which, let it be remembered, was no printed volume of which there might be a copy in

H.P.B.'s possession, but a manuscript album in which had been written notes and excerpts by a friend of mine for my own use; yet, on the page and at the line she had indicated, I found the very words she had uttered.

"When I handed her the book I ventured to ask her why she wanted it. 'Oh,' she replied, 'for *The Secret Doctrine*. That is my new work that I am so busily engaged in writing. Master is collecting material for me. He knew you had the book and told you to bring it that it might be at hand for reference.'

"...At this time I learned little more concerning *The Secret Doctrine* than that it was to be a work far more voluminous than *Isis Unveiled,* that it would consist when complete of four volumes....Soon, however, I was entrusted with the task of making fair copies of H.P.B.'s manuscript, and then of course I began to get some glimpses of the subject matter of *The Secret Doctrine*...."

"...Every morning at 6 a.m. she used to rise, having a good hour's work before her breakfast at 8 a.m., then, after having read her letters and newspapers she would again settle to her writing [of *The Secret Doctrine*], sometimes calling me into the room to tell me that references from books and manuscripts had been given to her by her Master with the chapter and page quoted, and to ask me whether I could get friends to verify the correctness of these passages in different Public Libraries: for as she read everything reversed in the Astral Light, it would be easy for her to make mistakes in dates and numbers—and in some instances it was found that the number of the page had been reversed, for instance 23 would be found on page 32, etc."

(Sources: Collated from Countess Constance Wachtmeister, *Reminiscences of H. P. Blavatsky*, 1893, pp. 23, 18; and http://blavatskyarchives.com/wacht1891b.htm)

December (some time after the 5th), 1885—In a letter to Franz Hartmann, H.P.B. writes:

> "The dear Countess Wachtmeister is with me, and copies for me, and does what she can in helping....Now, as you know, I...am occupied with my book....I have written in a fortnight more than 200 pages (of the *Isis* shape and size). I write day and night...I am permitted to give out for each chapter a page out of the Book of Dzyan—the oldest document in the world, of that I am sure—and to comment upon and explain its symbology. I think really it shall be worth something, and hardly here and there a few lines of dry facts from *Isis*. It is a completely new work."

(Source: Letter from H.P.B. to Franz Hartmann, quoted from *The Path*, January, 1896, p. 299.)

December 28, 1885—Countess Wachtmeister writes to Mr. Sinnett:

> "...No news to give you, the days glide away very smoothly and Madame says the *S.D.* goes on wheels. Madame [Blavatsky] would be very glad if Mr. Sinnett would kindly begin to make enquiries about publication [*of The Secret Doctrine*], etc., with prices, she would like the pamphlet to be about the size of the *Platonist*, different from ordinary magazines—there will be two chapters each month every chapter containing about 90 of her written sheets. She wishes the type to be a large and distinct one.
>
> "Madame hopes shortly to send the Preface with 1st Chapter to Mr. Sinnett. I am very glad to be here with Madame for I feel that I am a comfort and of use to her. I also consider it a great privilege to be allowed to witness the marvellous way in which this book is being written."

(Source: Letter from Countess Wachtmeister to A.P. Sinnett, *The Letters of H. P. Blavatsky to A.P. Sinnett*, p. 268.)

December 29, 1885—Again Countess Wachtmeister writes to Mr. Sinnett:

"Watching Madame as I do every day writing her S.D. and seeing how thoroughly absorbed she is in her work, it seems to me a sad pity that anything should come to disturb her....You see Madame must have peace of mind to enable her to write this book and it is only by ignoring or crushing scandals that this can be done.... she is in a calm and peaceful frame of mind and is perfectly happy writing the *S.D.*... Madame supposes that there will be about 100 printed pages every month in the *S.D.*"

(Source: Letter from Countess Wachtmeister to A.P. Sinnett, *The Letters of H. P. Blavatsky to A.P. Sinnett*, pp. 268-269.)

December 31, 1885—"On New Year's Eve," Prof. Sellin comes to visit H.P.B. He brings with him the Society for Psychical Research Report in which H.P.B. is declared a fraud and Russian spy.

(Source: Constance Wachtmeister, *Reminiscences of H. P. Blavatsky*, 1893, p. 25; letter from H.P.B. to H. S. O. dated Jan. 6, 1886.)

1886

January 4, 1886—Countess Wachtmeister writes to Mr. Sinnett:

"Madame is delighted with your proposition about the *S.D.* She thinks it is a most favourable and satisfactory arrangement for herself, but she says the journal must come out every month or if you think it better every three months, for if she lives she believes so much will be given to her that it will last 3 years or more. The size of the Journal you can arrange as you think best. There will be no regular preface, only about 6 or 7 pages addressed to the Reader to give them an idea of what the book will contain, for otherwise they would be plunging wholesale into matter entirely unknown to them.

"Madame will send you shortly the Title pages, and in a week or so the address to the Reader with first two chapters. From this you will be able to judge of the general purpose of the whole work. I wish myself that some clever theologian could be found who would read and criticise before the book is put into print...."

"Thank you very much for sending *Phallicism*. . . . Madame is much interested to find that 'Phallicism' contains a few of the things which she has *already* written out in the *S.D.*, only given in a Jesuitical point of view, and she intends to cut them up finely; it was in reading her manuscripts that I saw the resemblance in some points and so was anxious that she should see the book. Again another curious fact. Madame had written many pages on the signification of numbers, and that the words Jehovah and Cain are simply algebraical numbers, when she receives by post a book from Arthur Gebhard which he has found in America and sends it to her as he thinks it so interesting, it corroborates and confirms all that she has previously written, only from a mathematical point of view. The book is by Skinner...."

(Source: Letter from Countess Wachtmeister to A.P. Sinnett, *The Letters of H. P. Blavatsky to A.P. Sinnett*, pp. 271-72.)

January (early), 1886—Dr. William Hübbe-Schleiden comes on a second trip to Würzburg. He receives on this visit two important letters from Masters K.H. and M., concerning the authorship of *The Secret Doctrine*. Dr. Schleiden writes:

"...I saw...[Madame Blavatsky]...one afternoon and night...early in January, 1886....she had finished about a dozen chapters [of *The Secret Doctrine*]. She was writing at her manuscript almost all day, from the early morning until the afternoon and even until night, unless she had guests....

"...I also saw her write down sentences as if she were copying them from something before her, where, however, I saw nothing....I saw a good deal of the well-known blue K.H. handwriting as corrections and annotations on her manuscripts as well as in books that lay occasionally on her desk.

"...on the night of my last parting from H.P.B., the two...[letters from Masters KH and M] were given to me. At least I found them in my copy of Hodgson's *S.P.R. Report* after I had left her...."

(Source: Constance Wachtmeister, *Reminiscences of H. P. Blavatsky*, 1893, pp. 111, 113.)

January (early), 1886—Master M.'s letter to Dr. Hübbe-Schleiden reads:

"If this can be of any use or help to Dr. Hübbe-Schleiden—though I doubt it—I, the humble undersigned Fakir, certify that the 'Secret Doctrine' is dictated to Upasika [H.P.B.] partly by myself & partly by my Brother K.H."

(Source: *Letters from the Masters of Wisdom,* Volume II, Letters 69 and 70.)

January (early), 1886—Master K.H.'s letter to Dr. Hübbe-Schleiden reads:

"I wonder if this note of mine is worthy of occupying a select spot with the documents reproduced [in Hodgson-

S.P.R. Report], and which of the peculiarities of the 'Blavatskian' style of writing it will be found to most resemble? The present is simply to satisfy the Dr. that 'the more proof given the less believed.' Let him take my advice and not make these two documents public. It is for his own satisfaction that the undersigned is happy to assure him that *The Secret Doctrine* when ready, will be the triple production of M., Upasika and the Doctor's most humble servant [K.H.]."

(Source: *Letters from the Masters of Wisdom*, Volume II, Letters 69 and 70.)

January 6, 1886—H.P.B. writes to Colonel Olcott:

"...[*The*] *Secret Doctrine* is *entirely* new. There will not be there 20 pages quoted by bits from *Isis*. New matter, occult explanations....In *four* Parts—Archaic, Ancient, Mediaeval and Modern Periods. Each Part 12 chapters, with Appendices and a Glossary of Terms at the end.

"Countess [Wachtmeister is] here, and she sees I have almost *no books*. Master [Morya] and Kashmiri [Master Koot Hoomi] dictating [to me] in turn. She copies all....

"Now listen. Secure the help of Subba Row for *Secret Doc*. *Lots* there of Adwaitism or *old* Aryan Religion occult....If he promises faithfully and you think he will do it I shall send you...two or three chapters at once; if not—I begin publishing here. Let him see first five or six chapt[ers] and judge....Answer at once...."

(Source: Letter of H. P. Blavatsky to H.S. Olcott, *The Theosophist*, August, 1931, p. 667.)

January 6, 1886—H.P.B. writes to Mr. Sinnett:

"Now I am here alone with the Countess for witness. I have no books, no one to help me. And I tell you that the *Secret Doctrine* will be 20 times as learned, philosophical and better than *Isis* which will be *killed* by it. Now there are hundreds of things I am permitted to say and *explain*. It will show what a Russian *spy* can do, an alleged *forger plagiarist* etc. The whole Doctrine is shown the *mother stone* the foundation of all the religions including Xty, and on the strength of *exoteric* published Hindu books, with their symbols explained *esoterically*. The extreme lucidity of 'Esoteric Buddhism' will also be shown and its doctrines proven correct mathematically, geometrically logically and scientifically...."

(Source: *The Mahatma Letters to A. P. Sinnett*, Chronological Edition, p. 456.)

January 11, 1886—Countess Wachmeister writes to Mr. Sinnett:

"Not a word has been added to the S[ecret] D[octrine] since the 31st Dec., but if we can only get a few days of calm and quiet I hope Madame [Blavatsky] will be able to begin writing again."

(Source: *Letters of H. P. Blavatsky to A.P. Sinnett*, p. 273.)

January 15, 1886—The Countess writes to Sinnett again:

"...At last Madame has settled down again to [work on] the S.D., *a whole fortnight lost.*"

(Source: *Letters of H. P. Blavatsky to A.P. Sinnett*, p. 273.)

January 19, 1886—Henry Olcott in India writes to H.P.B.:

"You may send the MSS. in installments: Subba Row will go over it with Oakley and it will be returned to you. He asked if he should be free to add or amend, to which I answered of course, it was for that he was requested to edit it. He then consented....Send the S.D. MSS. to Oakley's address, as I sail for Colombo on the 25th and shall be absent 3 months...."

(Source: Letter from Henry S. Olcott to H.P.B., *The Letters of H. P. Blavatsky to A.P. Sinnett*, pp. 326, 328.)

Jan. 27, 1886—Col. Olcott sails for Ceylon [Sri Lanka] on a prolonged lecture tour.

(Source: Henry S. Olcott, *Old Diary Leaves*, Volume III, pp. 351-52).

January, 1886—H.P.B. writes to Mr. Sinnett:

"I will send to you two or three chapters of S.D. before I send them to Subba Row to India. I want you to see and read it for yourself before it [is] passed through the hands of S.R...."

(Source: *Letters of H. P. Blavatsky to A.P. Sinnett*, p. 197.)

March 3, 1886—H.P.B. writes to A.P. Sinnett and tells him that she has finished an "enormous Introductory Chapter" of *The Secret Doctrine*:

"There's a new development and scenery, every morning. I live two lives again. Master finds that it is too difficult for me to be looking consciously into the astral light for my S.D. and so, it is now about a fortnight, I am made to see all I have to as though in my dream. I see large and long rolls of paper on which things are written and I recollect them.

"Thus all the Patriarchs from Adam to Noah were given me to see—parallel with the Rishis; and in the middle between them, the meaning of their symbols—or personifications. Seth standing with Brighu for first sub-race of the Root race, for inst: meaning, anthropologically—first speaking human sub-race of the 3rd Race; and astronomically—(his years 912 y.) meaning at one and same time the length of the solar year in that period, the duration of his race and many other things—(too complicated to tell you now). Enoch finally, meaning the solar year when our present duration was settled, 365 days—('God took him when he was 365 years old') and so on. It is very complicated but I hope to explain it sufficiently clear.

"I have finished an enormous Introductory Chapter, or Preamble, Prologue, call it what you will; just to show the reader that the text as it goes [on Cosmogenesis], every Section beginning with a page of translation from the Book of *Dzyan* and the Secret Book of 'Maytreya Buddha' *Champai chhos Nga* (in prose, not the five books in verse known, which are a blind) are no fiction.

"I was ordered to do so, to make a rapid sketch of what was known historically and in literature, in classics and in profane and sacred histories—during the 500 years that preceded the Christian period and the 500 y[ears] that followed it: of magic, the existence of a Universal Secret Doctrine known to the philosophers and Initiates of every country and even to several of the Church fathers such as Clement of Alexandria, Origen, and others, who had been initiated themselves. Also to describe the Mysteries and some rites; and I can assure you that most extraordinary things are given out now, the whole story of the Crucifixion, etc. being shown to be based on a rite as old as the world—the Crucifixion on the Lathe of the Candidate—trials, going down to Hell etc. all Aryan. The whole story hitherto unnoticed by Orientalists is found even exoterically, in the Puranas and Brahmanas, and then explained and supplemented with what the Esoteric explanations give. How the Orientalists have failed to notice it passes comprehension.

"Mr. Sinnett, dear, I have facts for 20 Vol[umes] like *Isis*; it is the language, the cleverness for compiling them, that I lack.

"Well you will soon [receive] this Prologue, the short survey of the forthcoming Mysteries in the text—which covers 300 pages of foolscap...."

(Source: *Letters of H. P. Blavatsky to A.P. Sinnett*, pp. 194-195.)

March 12, 1886—Countess Wachtmeister writes to Mr. Sinnett:

"In reading the first chapter I got so confused over the 'Stanzas' and the 'Commentaries' that I could make nothing of them. Madame then wrote the former in *red ink*, the latter in *black ink*, and now they are far easier to comprehend as confusion of ideas is avoided...."

(Source: Letter from Countess Wachtmeister to A.P. Sinnett, *Letters of H. P. Blavatsky to A.P. Sinnett*, p. 294.)

March 24, 1886—H.P.B. writes to William Q. Judge:

"...I want you badly for the arrangement of *Secret Doctrine*. Such facts, *such facts*, Judge, as Masters are giving out will rejoice your old heart...."

(Source: Constance Wachtmeister's *Reminiscences of H. P. Blavatsky*, 1893, p. 101.)

April, 1886—William Q. Judge in the very first issue of his new Theosophical journal *The Path* includes the following notice about Madame Blavatsky and her writing of *The Secret Doctrine*:

"...Madame H. P. Blavatsky is now engaged upon this work, in Germany, where she went last year for her health. The subject is interesting, and the result of the author's endeavors will mark an era. It will not only be an amplification and explanation of *Isis Unveiled*, but will contain mines of further information. There will be in it verbatim passages from the Book of Dzyan and Limri [Lam-rim] of Tsong-Kha-pa, and old commentaries, to which, hitherto, access has not been possible, and great attention will be paid to the doctrine of Human Evolution, to Divine or White Magic, and Human or Black Magic. The portion in which the subject of the Divine Hermaphrodite is considered, should be of absorbing interest. It will be divided into four parts: Archaic, Ancient, Mediaeval and Modern, presenting the complete sequences of the development of Occultism and Magic in their religious and anti-religious aspects."

(Source: *The Path* (New York), April 1886, p. 29.)

April (before 20th), 1886—Miss Emily Kislingbury visits H.P.B. at Würzburg.

(Sources: Constance Wachtmeister, *Reminiscences of H. P. Blavatsky*, 1893, p. 59; *Letters of H. P. Blavatsky to A.P. Sinnett*, p. 302.)

May 1 (or a few days before), 1886—Marie Gebhard and Gustav Gebhard come to visit H.P.B. at Würzburg.

(Sources: Constance Wachtmeister, *Reminiscences of H. P. Blavatsky*, 1893, p. 59; *Letters of H. P. Blavatsky to A.P. Sinnett*, p. 207.)

May 5, 1886—H. S. Olcott returns to Adyar after trip to Ceylon and has long talk with T. Subba Row on May 6th. Subba Row is in a very inimical state of mind and objects to H.P.B.'s return to India.

(Sources: Henry S. Olcott, *Old Diary Leaves*, Volume III, pp. 359-60; Josephine Ransom, *Short History of the Theosophical Society*, p. 232.)

May 8, 1886 (estimated)—H.P.B. leaves Würzburg for Ostende, Belgium, accompanied by Miss Kislingbury. Countess Wachtmeister leaves with Marie Gebhard to visit Austria. The Countess plans to return to her home in Sweden.

Having arrived at Cologne, Germany, H.P.B. is persuaded by Gustav Gebhard to go to Elberfeld, Germany, for a visit with the Gebhard family.

(Sources: Constance Wachtmeister, *Reminiscences of H. P. Blavatsky*, 1893, pp. 60-61; *Letters of H. P. Blavatsky to A.P. Sinnett*, p. 302.)

May 10, 1886—H.P.B. slips on the parquet of her bedroom at Elberfeld. She sprains her ankle and hurts her leg.

(Sources: Constance Wachtmeister, *Reminiscences of H. P. Blavatsky*, 1893, p. 61; *Letters of H. P. Blavatsky to A.P. Sinnett*, p. 213; letter from H.P.B. to Olcott, dated Ostende, July 14, 1886, published in *The Theosophist*, May, 1908.)

May (middle), 1886—Vera de Zhelihovsky (H.P.B.'s sister) and her daughter Vera arrive at Elberfeld on a visit.

(Sources: Constance Wachtmeister, *Reminiscences of H. P. Blavatsky*, 1893, pp. 61, 105, 107; *Letters of H. P. Blavatsky to A.P. Sinnett*, p. 213.)

June 3, 1886—Still at Elberfeld, H.P.B. writes Colonel Olcott:

"My foot has turned a more serious matter than was first thought. The sprain has held me already over 3 weeks in bed and armchair motionless and heaven knows whether in a fortnight I will be able to go to Ostende where I mean to settle and try to finish my unfortunate *Secret Doctrine*.

"That it is an *extraordinary* work and revelation I am now sure. A learned Occultist, an Englishman (one who is a man of exact science but whose name I cannot give, though he is known to the Countess and Mme. Gebhard) has proclaimed it a wonderful work, 'full of the most important revelations and secrets'....Moreover, he has not found three words to correct in its English in the two enormous chapters he has seen, and that's *flattering*...."

(Source: Letter of H.P.B. to Henry S. Olcott, dated "Elberfeld, June 3," published in *The Theosophist*, August, 1931, p. 673.)

June, 1886—H.P.B. writes the Countess Wachtmeister:

"My old leg goes a little better, pain gone, but it is entirely helpless, and heaven alone knows when [I] will be able to walk with it even as superficially as I did before.

"Dear Mrs. Gebhard! She does nurse me....

"Manuscript of *The Secret Doctrine* came back from our Revd. friend; he finds it far superior to the introductory—but not even half-a-dozen words corrected. He says it is *perfect*...."

(Source: Letter of H.P.B. to Constance Wachtmeister, quoted in Countess Wachtmeister, *Reminiscences of H. P. Blavatsky*, 1893, p. 49.)

June, 1886—Vera Johnston, H.P.B.'s niece, writes the following about her stay with H.P.B. at Elberfeld, Germany:

"In June, 1886, I stayed with my aunt in Elberfeld and then in Ostend. It was her habit to read out in the afternoon what was written of *The Secret Doctrine* in the preceding night. Not knowing much English then I am sorry to say I was seldom present at these readings and only half understood the conversations that ensued…

"Generally on coming down in the morning from the bedroom I occupied in the house of Madame Gebhard together with my mother, I found my aunt deep in her work. So far as I know, she never wrote at that time in the morning, but carefully went over what was written the previous night. One day I saw evident traces of perplexity written on her face. Not wishing to disturb her I sat down quietly and waited for her to speak. She remained silent a long time with her eyes fixed on some point on the wall, and with a cigarette between her fingers, as was her custom. At last she called out to me:

" 'Vera,' she said, 'do you think you could tell me what is a pi?' "

"Rather astonished at such a question, I said I thought a pie was some kind of an English dish.

" 'Please don't make a fool of yourself' she said rather impatiently, 'don't you understand I address you in your capacity of a mathematical pundit. Come and see this.' "

"I looked at the page that lay before her on the table, and saw it was covered with figures and calculations, and soon became aware that the formula $\pi = 3.14159$ was put down wrongly throughout them all. It was written $\pi = 31.4159$. With great joy and triumph I hastened to inform her of her mistake.

" 'That's it!' she exclaimed. 'This confounded comma bothered me all the morning. I was rather in a hurry yesterday to put down what I saw, and to-day at the first glance at the page I intensely but vaguely felt there was something wrong, and do what I could I could not remember where the comma actually was when I saw this number.' "

"Knowing very little of Theosophy in general and my aunt's ways of writing in particular at that time, I of course was greatly struck with her not being able to correct such a slight mistake in the very intricate calculations she had written down with her own hand.

" 'You are very green,' she said, 'if you think that I actually know and understand all the things I write. How many times am I to repeat to you and your mother that the things I write are dictated to me, that sometimes I see manuscripts, numbers, and words before my eyes of which I never knew anything.' "

"On reading *The Secret Doctrine* several years later I recognised the page. It was one of the pages which discuss Hindu astronomy...."

(Source: Countess Constance Wachtmeister, *Reminiscences of H. P. Blavatsky*, 1893, pp. 107-109.)

July 8, 1886—H.P.B. leaves Elberfeld for Ostende accompanied by her sister and niece. Upon arrival at Ostende, she stays at Villa Nova, 10, Boulevard Van Isgham.

(Source: H.P.B.'s letter to Henry Olcott (dated July 14, 1886), published in *The Theosophist*, May, 1908.)

July (before the 12th), 1886—H.P.B. writes to the Countess Wachtmeister about her arrival in Ostende and also about *The Secret Doctrine*:

"Here I am [in Ostende]....For one night at the Continental [Hotel] I had to pay 117 francs for our rooms. Then in despair my sister rose in the morning and felt herself drawn to a certain part of the Boulevard on the sea shore, and in a side street she found an apartment...three splendid rooms on the left and two on the right of the passage, or five rooms and a kitchen downstairs....Result your legless friend established in a suite of rooms on the left, and my sister has two rooms, a bedroom, an elegant one, and a parlor or dining room on the right side of the passage. When she goes away, which will be in ten days, that suite remains empty.

"But then, perhaps Mr. Sinnett will come....

"Yes, I will try and settle once more at my *Secret Doctrine*. But it is hard. I am very weak, dear, I feel so poorly and legless as I never did when you were there [in Würzburg] to care for me...."

(Source: Letter from H.P.B. to Countess Wachtmeister, quoted in Constance Wachtmeister, *Reminiscences of H. P. Blavatsky*, 1893, p. 50.)

July 12 (est.), 1886—A.P. Sinnett arrives in Ostende to visit H.P.B. Mrs. Patience Sinnett does *not* come with her husband to see H.P.B. Mr. Sinnett writes about this trip as follows:

"We [Sinnett and his wife Patience] spent the...holidays this year at Ventnor...But before joining my wife at Ventnor I...paid a visit to Madame Blavatsky at Ostende whither she had migrated....[A]ssisted by the diary...I find a reference to my departure for Ostende and for the rest, I well remember being for a time with the O[ld]L[ady] at Ostende where she was busy writing the Secret Doctrine...."

(Source: A. P. Sinnett, *The Autobiography of A. P. Sinnett*, p. 33.)

July, 1886—H.P.B. writes another letter to Countess Wachtmeister:

"I am trying to write *The Secret Doctrine*. But Sinnett, who is here for a few days, wants all my attention directed to the blessed Memoirs [Mr. Sinnett's forthcoming book titled *Incidents in the Life of Madame Blavatsky*]. Mrs. Sinnett was unable to come...."

(Source: Letter of H.P.B. to Countess Wachtmeister, quoted in Constance Wachtmeister, *Reminiscences of H. P. Blavatsky*, 1893, p. 51.)

July 14, 1886—Vera de Zhelihovsky and her daughter leave H.P.B. at Ostende and go back to Russia. H.P.B. writes to Henry Olcott in India:

"....on the 8th of July....I had to leave Elberfeld. I did so with my sister and niece....Then as my sister had to go (they have left for [St.] Petersburg this morning) ....The Countess [Wachtmeister] will come I suppose, to pass the winter with me in October or November....

"Well, about the *S.D.*....Of course, Subba Row's advice will be priceless; if you can make him keep the MSS. no longer than a month it will be excellent. But suppose he keeps it an indefinite time....

"Now I will send to *your care* and on *your* responsibility the 'Preface to the Reader' and the 1st chapter of the *Secret Doctrine* proper. There are 600 pages and more of foolscap as an Introductory Preliminary Book, showing the undeniable historically proven facts of the existence of Adepts before and after the Christian period, of the admission of a double esoteric meaning in the two Testaments by Church Fathers, and *proofs* that the real source of every Christian dogma rests in the Aryan oldest MYSTERIES during the Vedic and Brahmanic period, proofs and evidence for it being shown in the exoteric as well as esoteric Sanskrit works.

"This I will send after, if Subba Row approves of Chap. I, which consists of Seven Stanzas taken from the Book of Dzan (Dzyan) and is commented and glossed upon, as in the three glossaries upon it—in Sanskrit, Chinese, and Tibetan. I cannot part with it without having a copy, for, if lost on the way [to India], or otherwise mutilated, I cannot rewrite it. Now I am alone; no one to copy [the remaining S.D. manuscript] or help me.

"In a fortnight I will send you the Preface and 1st Chapter. But you must force S.R. to read and not to put it...aside, leaving it at his leisure and pleasure as he always does...."

(Sources: H.P.B.'s letter to Henry Olcott is dated July 14, 1886 and is published in *The Theosophist*, May, 1908, pp. 753-756; some of this text is also quoted by Boris de Zirkoff in his *Rebirth of the Occult Tradition*, pp. 28-29.)

August (early), 1886—H.P.B. writes again to Colonel Olcott:

"Sinnett has left, after stopping with me three weeks, and Mrs. . . . [possibly Mrs. Mary Emily Bates, the future wife of Elliott Coues] remains for ten days more. She is very kind, and copies for me *The Secret Doctrine*.

"The enormous (volume) of Introductory Stanzas, the first chapter on the Archaic Period and Cosmogony, with numberless appendices, is ready; but how to send it to Adyar? Suppose it is lost! I do not remember one word of it, and so we would be cooked!

"...Z. has read it through twice and begun again for the third time. He has *not found one part to be corrected* in the English, and he is amazed, he says, at the 'gigantic erudition and the soundness of reasoning in its showing of the esotericism of the Bible and its incessant parallels with the Vedas, Brahmanas, etc.' This is a little more wonderful yet than *Isis*. Then you corrected, and [Alexander] Wilder suggested.

"*Now, I am absolutely alone,* with my arm-chair and inkstand before me, and no books to speak of.

"I wrote a whole section and the interpretation of a whole stanza (about 40 pages), without any books around me, and without stopping, for about four hours, simply listening...."

Colonel Olcott writes the following about the above letter:

"...H.P.B. cites the fact of Mr. Z. having sat with her for hours while she was transcribing what was spoken to her clairaudient sense by a Master, invisible to him but seen by herself."

(Source: Quoted from Henry S. Olcott, *Old Diary Leaves*, Volume III, pp. 379 & 383.)

August 26th, 1886—H.P.B. writes to A. P. Sinnett about a visit from Mary Gebhard:

"Mad[ame] Gebhard...is now here with me...."

(Source: *Letters of H. P. Blavatsky to A.P. Sinnett*, p. 219.)

September 21, 1886—H.P.B. writes to Mr. Sinnett about the Secret Doctrine:

"Mme. G[ebhard] is gone [back home to Elberfeld]; I am alone, and I have profited by my isolation to think over a good deal....I saw Them [the Masters] and talked to and with Them, the whole evening and night yesterday....

"...I have sent Vol. I of the S.D. [via Madame Gebhard] to Adyar and am now on Vol. II—the *Archaic*. This alone with the new information in it will be more than you will be able to digest in 25 years with *the explanations promised....*"

(Source: *Letters of H. P. Blavatsky to A. P. Sinnett*, pp. 221-222.)

September 23, 1886—H.P.B. writing to Colonel Olcott says she is sending him First Volume of SD MSS through Madame Gebhard, who had just gone back home to Elberfeld:

"I send you the MSS. of *Secret Doc[trine]* through Mrs. Gebhard who will insure the thing for 3 or 4,000 marks. She took them with her to Elberfeld whither she returned.

"Now I send only 1st volume of *Introduct.* Section, and in a fortnight [I] will send the real pucka *S.D., Archaic* Period [Volume 2 on Cosmogenesis], the 7 Stanzas, from Book of *Dzyan* commented upon.

"There are in the 1st *Introductory* Vol[ume] *Seven Sections* (or Chapt[ers] §.) and 27 Appendices, several App[endices] attached to every *Section* from 3 to 6, etc. Now all this will make either more or at any rate one volume and *it is not the S.D.* [proper] but [only] a Preface to it.

"It [Volume I] is an absolutely necessary one, otherwise if they begin reading [first] the Archaic Vol[ume on Cosmogenesis] the public would get crazy before reading five pages, *too metaphysical.*

"Now, it is so arranged that the Appendices [in Volume I] can either go as attached to the [seven] Sections or be taken out and placed in a *separate Vol[ume]* or at the end of each, but you cannot put the App[endices] from the *Vol[ume]* of Preliminary Sections in Vol. II or Book I the Archaic; I have been careful to mark every page of App[endices] with title, number and to what Sect[ion] or Chap[ter] it belongs to. If you take out the App[endices] then there will not [be] 300 pages printed in Int. Sections, but they will lose in interest.

"Do, however, as you please, but do not lose pages and do not allow the thing to be mutilated. If you or S. Row find anything too much, cross it out lightly; and if you want to add, write the addition on a page and pin it to the page you add to...."

(Source: Letter of H.P.B. to Henry Olcott, dated Sept. 23, 1886, published in *The Theosophist*, March 1925, pp. 789-790, also quoted in Boris de Zirkoff, *Rebirth of the Occult Tradition*, pp. 30-31.)

[Note: **These two manuscripts to be sent (one at a time) to Colonel Olcott in India were *not* the *original* manuscripts in H.P.B's own handwriting but copies made by Countess Wachtmeister, Mrs. Gebhard, and Mrs. Bates.** Of course H.P.B. kept the originals with herself and later in May 1887 took these originals to England.

Furthermore, the "1st volume" manuscript mentioned above by H.P.B. (as the first package going to India) is *only part* of the so-called "Würzburg Manuscript" now preserved in the Archives of the Theosophical Society, Adyar, Chennai, India.

This Volume I of the *extant* Würzburg Manuscript consists of only *five* sections and *one* appendix.

Therefore, this letter from H.P.B. to Olcott indicates that the *extant* Volume I of the Würzburg Manuscript is *incomplete* and probably represents *only a quarter to a third* of the original first volume of *The Secret Doctrine*. In other words, the *extant* Volume I of the Würzburg Manuscript is missing two-thirds to three-quarters of what was sent to Adyar.—D. H. Caldwell]

October (early), 1886—Countess Wachtmeister joins H.P.B. at Ostende. The Countess writes:

> "In October, 1886, I joined H.P.B. in Ostende, and found her settled in comfortable enough quarters....We recommenced our monotonous but interesting life, the thread being taken up from where it was last broken, and I watched with delight how the piles of manuscript for the *S.D.* were increasing. Our near vicinity to England caused people once more to come buzzing round H.P.B., and we received several visitors...."

(Source: Quoted from: http://blavatskyarchives.com/wacht1891b.htm)

October 1886—H.P.B. writes the following to Mr. Sinnett about some of her SD commentaries on the Stanzas of Dzyan:

> "Thanks for . . . Mr. [William] Crookes' chemical speculations. He is a dear man who has all my respect, admiration and sympathy....Mrs. Countess has and says she understands nothing. Nor will I of course; we are ignorant fools she and I...Mr. Crookes...preaches and teaches a very old occult Doctrine. I will of course lay his work and new discovery before the Master [M.] and Mah[atma] K.H. and will let you have Their opinions.
>
> "Meanwhile I am impressed to send you a few pages that I have unhooked from my Book I, Archaic Period [the SD manuscript on Cosmogenesis] the beginning of which you have seen [in Ostende] and beg you to read them carefully....This [part of the SD manuscript] was written at Villa Nova when you left and the Countess has copied it all long ago. Only for mercy's sake do not lose those 8 pages or you will ruin me in time lost and other things. If you find it answers please show to Mr. Crookes; if not—...then send back...those 8 pages...."

The Secret Doctrine Würzburg Manuscript

(Source: *The Letters of H. P. Blavatsky to A. P. Sinnett*, pp. 224-25.)

October (three days later), 1886—H.P.B. writes more to Mr. Sinnett about Professor Crookes and *The Secret Doctrine*. In this letter she also mentions in passing "the Comm[entary] on Stanza VI...."

> "I doubt whether the news I have to give you will be found satisfactory by yourself or Mr. Crookes. I have heard from Master and—Masters. It appears (as I have thought from the first) that he is on the orthodox occult path, in his general method. 'No one went nearer than he did to the laya region' I am told. The laya is the Nirvana of all organic (we have no inorganic) Substance, the zero point or 'neutral centre' where all differentiation ceases....

> "Well today Dj. Khool put in an [astral] appearance...he told me that Master sent in a word for you...: 'Sinnett has evidently forgotten what he had read in the Comm[entaries] on the 7 Stanzas (Book II Archaic period). Otherwise he would have known that out of what is plainly stated there, seven such pamphlets (as about protyle) could be written by Mr. Crookes if he only knew it. No such scientific orthodox terms used in the S.D. but all that can be given out in this century is there and about chemistry and physics more than anything else. If Mr. Sinnett is willing to read those portions to Mr. Crookes—or Mr. Crookes wants to read them himself—send the MSS. to them by all means. . . . Anything that will appear hazy, incomprehensible or too grotesque I (Master) am willing to explain and even to be corrected if I fail to do so.'

> "On my kicking against the idea of sending you the MSS. which I want all the time for reference...—Dj. Khool said that if I had any regard for yourself and

Mr. Crookes I better do so, or else never ask Master to help anyone again....

"It is true that ever since you left [me at Ostende in July], Master has made me add some thing daily to the old [Secret Doctrine] MSS. so that much of it is new and much more that I do not understand myself. So that with God's help you may find in it something to attract the attention of even such an eminent [scientific] man as Mr. Crookes. I never thought he was so learned—till I heard Masters' opinions about him and his aura. Master says...there is no one higher than him in chemistry in England..."

(Source: *The Letters of H. P. Blavatsky to A. P. Sinnett*, pp. 225-226.)

October 18, 1886—Mme. Blavatsky writes to G. Subbiah Chetty in India:

". . . I am generally in poor health and my *Secret Doctrine* absorbs all my attention and takes up all my time. . . . . Please tell Olcott that if as he thinks Subba Row has no time to go through the S.D. I better not send it to Adyar. . . ."

(Source: Boris de Zirkoff, *Rebirth of the Occult Tradition*, pp. 31-32.)

October 21, 1886—Upon receiving a letter from Colonel Olcott, H.P.B. writes the following to him about the *Secret Doctrine* manuscript:

"Just a month ago, I gave to Mme. Gebhard the MSS. of S.D. [Volume I] to post [to India] from Elberfeld—insuring it for 3,000 marks. Well, last night as you wrote to me that it had not been received till now, I telegraphed to her to ask whether she had not sent it....and she answered she *was going to*.

"Well after what you say of S[ubba] R[ow] that he won't look at it even, of course it is better it should be printed without his approbation; for I want to begin [publishing] this spring and will go to London for it. *Have to* [go to London]—because of the proofreading, and the British Museum, and books.

"But now what shall I do for the 2nd Volume [on Cosmogenesis], the beginning of the true Archaic Doctrine—where I have any number of Sanskrit words and sentences, and the esoteric meaning of any number of exoteric Hindu allegories from their Cosmogony and Theogony?

"Can you ask Shrinivas Row and Bhavani Row to help me? Then I could send you the 2nd Vol[ume] consisting of Books 1, 2 and 3. Unless someone helps I do not know what to do. And who will make the glossary? I can't and have no time....Please answer immediately.

"The whole almost is given by the 'old gentleman' [Master Narayan] and Master [Morya] and there *are* wonderful things there I tell you. But someone must see to the Sanskrit and the corrections of the *exoteric* rendering. This book *will* make our future (yours and mine) see if it won't.

"Meanwhile I have written to Mme. Gebhard to send the MSS. of Vol. I back here [to me] and not to send it to Adyar. It does seem useless since Subba R[ow] is no more to be hoped for....

"Rev. A. Ayton is on a visit now here to us and living in a room of mine upstairs, and the Countess takes care of him....

"...I am always thinking how to send to you Bhavani's ring and what I promised to Babula...."

(Source: Letter (dated Oct. 21, 1886) from H.P.B. to Colonel Olcott, quoted in Boris de Zirkoff, *Rebirth of the Occult Tradition*, p. 33.)

November (first part of), 1886—H.P.B., writing to Mrs. Patience Sinnett, says:

"The Countess [Wachtmeister]...[a] few days or a fortnight ago...asked me whether I would not like to go for a week to London with her....I said I would think [about it]; finally [when] she asked again yesterday, I told her decidedly that I had neither time, wish, nor money to travel....Of course I have to go to London and am decided, but in two or three months, when I have matter enough ready and after I find what I need in London in the shape of *a flat*...I need two rooms for myself and a spare bedroom and kitchen.

"I have Louise's husband, a Dane, coming to live with her without wages and promising to do what he can in the house, since she has to support him he being very delicate—simply for board and lodging....

"...What about the 8 pages from S.D. sent by me to Mr. Sinnett. Surely he has read them and either has found therein the spirit of Mr. Crookes' *protyle* or has not. In either case do let him forward them [back] to me...."

(Source: *Letters of H. P. Blavatsky to A. P. Sinnett*, pp. 234-35.)

November (middle of), 1886—H.P.B. writes to Colonel Olcott:

"The Countess [Wachtmeister] who goes for a week to London will send from there three things in a box—

"(1) The Saptapurna ring for Bhawani Rao. It is the seven-leaved mystical leaf, made of seven stones all consecrated to planets and *now* strongly magnetized....

"(2) The Mohur, I had for years, as you know—for Tookaram Tatya as he asks always for something magnetized by Master and myself. I have worn it for years. Please send to him or keep till he comes to Adyar [in December] for [the Theosophical Society] Anniversary....

"(3) A sovereign for poor Babula. It is little but I can give no more, being very poor as you know. If I make money this year with my work then will I give him £5. He is a good boy—give him my blessing and love....

"I will see what I can do to review...Pratt's book. It is very *occult* no doubt, quite esoteric ideas some, yet terribly heretical and materialistic, these 'New Aspects of Life.' I hope the O[ld] Gentleman [Master Narayan] will help me."

(Source: Letter of H.P.B. to Henry Olcott, undated, published in *The Theosophist*, August 1931, pp. 684-85.)

November (middle of), 1886—H.P.B. writes to Mr. Sinnett:

"Please...as soon as Mr. Crookes finishes that archaic stuff...send it back, as I have to send it [S.D.] to Subba Row who seems to lose patience now he is ordered [by Master Morya] to look it over...."

(Source: *Letters of H. P. Blavatsky to A. P. Sinnett*, p. 236.)

November (before the 18th), 1886—H.P.B. writes to Countess Wachtmeister who was then in London for a week:

"I sent a telegram yesterday asking whether I could send you . . . my MSS [of the first volume of *The Secret Doctrine*], as I have to forward it without delay to Madras. It is all splendidly packed up by Louise's husband, corded and sewn in oil cloth, all secure for the journey, so you will have no trouble with it, but [be sure] to have it insured. Please do this yourself. You are the only one in whom I have absolute faith.

"Olcott [now] writes that Subba Row is so anxious about the MSS. that he is enquiring daily when it comes, etc. and Master [Morya finally] ordered him, it appears, to look it over.

"Please send it on by this mail and do insure it for no less than £150 or £200, for if lost—well good-bye!—so I send it to you to-day to your address and do answer immediately [when] you receive it...."

(Source: Letter of H.P.B. to Countess Wachtmeister, undated, quoted in Constance Wachtmeister, *Reminiscences of H. P. Blavatsky*, 1893, p. 66.)

November (latter part of month), 1886—Countess Wachtmeister returns to Ostende from London.

December 10, 1886—Colonel Olcott at Adyar, Madras, India, receives Volume I of *The Secret Doctrine* manuscript that had been mailed to him by Countess Wachtmeister when she was in London for a week in November.

In Olcott's 1886 handwritten diary, the entry for December 10[th] reads in part:

"Rec[eive]d. MSS. of Secret Doctrine, Vol. I...."

In his book *Old Diary Leaves*, Olcott writes:

"By the first week of December [1886]...I received from H.P.B., for reading and revision by T. Subba Row and myself, the MS. of Vol. I of The Secret Doctrine...."

(Source: Henry S. Olcott, *Old Diary Leaves*, Volume III, p. 398.)

Dec. 27, 1886—Colonel Olcott in his Address at the Theosophical Society Annual Convention (Adyar, Madras, India) tells his audience about receiving Volume I of the SD:

"The MSS. of the first volume [of the Secret Doctrine] has been sent to me, and is undergoing revision. It will gratify you to learn that it more than maintains her [H.P.B.'s] reputation for learning and literary ability...."

(Source: *The Theosophist*, January 1887, Supplement, pp. xx-xxi.)

Dec. 28, 1886—Colonel Olcott also mentions receipt of this Volume I in his closing address about the opening of the Adyar Library. He says:

"...permit me...to announce that the entire MSS. of the first of five volumes that Madame Blavatsky is now writing upon the Secret Doctrine is in my hands; and that even a cursory reading has satisfied better critics than myself that it will be one of the most important contributions ever made to philosophical and scientific scholarship, a monument of the learned author, and a distinction to the Adyar Library, of which she is one of the founders."

(Source: *The Theosophist*, January 1887, Supplement, p. xlvii.)

December (last week of), 1886—Countess Wachtmeister at H.P.B.'s request leaves Ostende and goes again to London. The Countess writes:

"One day H.P.B. called me and asked me whether I could go to London to undertake some private business on her behalf. I told her that I would willingly do so, but felt anxious about leaving her alone. So I started for London with a heavy heart, as I thought of the 'old lady's' loneliness and her look of sad yearning as she gave me a farewell kiss...."

(Source: Constance Wachtmeister, *Reminiscences of H. P. Blavatsky*, 1893, pp. 64-65.)

1887

January 4, 1887—H.P.B. answers a letter she has recently received from Colonel Olcott in India. She writes:

"This is the first time I awoke and passed a New Year *quite alone*, as if I were in my tomb. Not a soul the whole day, as the Countess [Wachtmeister] has gone to London and I have no one but Louise [H.P.B.'s Swiss maid] with me in the big house....

"I had been writing [on the *Secret Doctrine*] the whole day....occupied in finishing the Archaic Period....

"...[O]n the morning of the 2nd Jan....I wrote to [Edward Douglas] F[awcett]....We are making very successful experiments with him in thought-reading, and he is amazed at some things, such a success!...

"I am glad Subba Row [has now read and] likes my *Proem* [first volume of *S.D.*]. But it is *only* a *Preliminary* Vol[ume] and the real, original doctrine is in the [second] Volume [on Cosmogenesis that] I will send you when F[awcett] comes [to Ostende to visit me] on the 20th and he will take it to England himself—for I cannot send it or rather *ensure it*, from here.

"So keep the other MSS. till you have read both [volumes] and see what changes to make. Let S.R. do what he likes—I give him *carte blanche*. I trust in his wisdom far more than in mine, for I may have misunderstood in many a point both Master and the Old G[entleman Narayan]. They give me facts only and rarely dictate in succession. I am *no maker* of books you know it. But I know that my facts are all original and new. Wait and see...."

"...Have you received the three gold things I sent? The Countess sent them [to you from London] on the same day as the MSS. [of the first volume of *The Secret Doctrine*]...."

(Source: H.P.B. in a letter dated January 4, 1887 to Colonel Olcott, published in *The Theosophist*, August 1931, pp. 681-683.)

January, 1887—H.P.B. writes to Countess Wachtmeister who is in London at this time:

"...After a long conversation with Master [Morya] ...[e]ither I have to return to India to die this autumn, or I have to form between this and November next a nucleus of true Theosophists, a school of my own, with no secretary, only myself alone, with as many mystics as I can get to teach them. I can stop here [in Ostende], or go to England, or whatever I like...."

"...Because I wrote twice or thrice to Z. [Fawcett] telling him what he did and thought and read on such and such a day, he is crazy and a full blown mystic.

"Well, may the Master inspire and protect you, for you have to play a part in the coming struggle.

"I hear the people who subscribed to *The Secret Doctrine* are getting impatient—[but it] cannot be helped. I, *you know*, work fourteen hours a day.

"The last MSS. [of the first volume of *The Secret Doctrine*] sent [by you] to Adyar will not be back [with comments and corrections] for three months, but then we can begin publishing. Subba Row is making valuable notes, so Olcott tells me [in his latest letter]. ....

"I wish to goodness you would come back quicker. Your room upstairs with stove is ready, so you will be more comfortable. But you do useful work in London...."

(Source: H.P.B.'s letter to Countess Wachtmeister, quoted in Constance Wachtmeister, *Reminiscences of H. P. Blavatsky*, 1893, pp. 66-67.)

January 10, 1887—H.P.B. writes to Mr. Sinnett about *The Secret Doctrine*, etc:

"You want to know what I am doing? Atoning for my sins of having sent to you my *Archaic Doct[rine]* before it was ready. Rewriting it, adding to it, pasting and repasting, scratching out and replacing my notes from my AUTHORITIES. I was told to send you the MS.—but not told when. The Countess [Wachtmeister] who is always on the look out for practical things, wanting to profit through [Bernard] Hamilton going back to London—made me send with him the MS....

"...Fawcett is coming to see me on the 21st. He will be the first human creature I will talk to since the Countess is gone; for even my doctor is sick and I never saw him but once this month. For three weeks I am practicing the Pythagorean 'silence-vow' and see only astrals from morning till night.

"You know, that young Fawcett is my great friend now. A few experiments having succeeded he sees in me a 'Magician'! Only because I saw what he thought one or two nights, and described it to him. Well! I hope his enthusiasm will not evaporate...."

(Source: *The Letters of H. P. Blavatsky to A. P. Sinnett*, pp. 226-227.)

January 21, 1887—Approximate date when Edward Douglas Fawcett comes to visit H.P.B. at Ostende.

(Source: *The Letters of H. P. Blavatsky to A. P. Sinnett*, p. 227).

January (sometime after 21st), 1887—H.P.B. writes again to Countess Wachtmeister who was still in London:

"Remember much as I need you (and I need you badly), as I know through Master that you are doing excellent work in London, please stay a week or more even, if you think it right. I feel very miserable, but I can stand it, never mind.

"Z. [Fawcett] is very young and never gets up till 12 or 1 o'clock, but he is doing me good service, finding me a few quotations and correcting the English in some of the appendices [of The Secret Doctrine]....

(Source: H.P.B.'s letter to Countess Wachtmeister, quoted in Constance Wachtmeister, *Reminiscences of H. P. Blavatsky*, 1893, pp. 65-66.)

February, 1887—Writing to A. P. Sinnett, H.P.B. tells him:

"I have never read Rhys David's *Paranibbana* and therefore do not know how far he blunders. But judging by what I have read by him, I should say he blunders all along the line and to set it as all a blunder is the safest.

"Boar's flesh eaten by Buddha is of course a very transparent symbology. The first form assumed by Brahma when he arose from primal chaos (water in which the earth was formed, see *Ramayana*), and Manu, was that of a boar who raised the earth out of that water.

"The dish of *rice* and *boar's* flesh refers to Brahmanism. The Secret Doctrine explains that the legend of the Adepts of the *Left* Path— (whose descendants are now the *Tantrikas*) —Brahmins, had by magical arts, induced Buddha to eat of a meal of boar's flesh with rice. That rice was, called *tsale rice*—synonymous with the paradise for 'forbidden fruit' or apple....

"I am explaining this symbolism in the *Secret Doctrine* along with other things.

"The explanation of it is simply that *left hand* Brahmanism (instead of the *Right Divine Knowledge*) prevailed. The rice is the 'forbidden fruit' and boar and *pig's flesh* is Brahmanical exotericism—Buddha being vowed to secrecy and having compromised between the whole truth and symbolism as much as he dared—that truth choked him and he died of grief for being unable to explain all....

"There is an extraordinary and awful mystery at the bottom of this ridiculous allegory which none but the initiates know. If it had been simple pork and rice—how is it that Buddha compares the 'pork and rice' or puts it on the same footing as the delicious *Nogana* he ate on the morning of the day when he reached Buddha-ship? And why should he send Ananda to thank the goldsmith's son for the exquisite food and promise him great rewards for it *hereafter* in Brahma-loka.

"I explain it as far as I am allowed in one of the Chap[ters] of *Secret Doctrine* which *grows, grows and grows....*"

(Source: *Letters of H. P. Blavatsky to A. P. Sinnett*, pp. 241-242.)

February, 1887—H.P.B. writes again to Countess Wachtmeister:

"Only a few words, since, thank goodness, I will see you again soon....

"Ever since you went away, I have felt as though either paralysis or a split in the heart would occur. I am as cold as ice and four doses of *digitalis* in one day could not quiet the heart.

"Well, let me only finish my *Secret Doctrine*.

"Last night, instead of going to bed I was made to write till 1 o'clock. The *triple Mystery* is given out...."

(Source: H.P.B.'s letter to Countess Wachtmeister, quoted in Constance Wachtmeister, *Reminiscences of H. P. Blavatsky*, 1893, p. 68.)

February 23, 1887—H.P.B. writes to William Q. Judge in New York:

"...I will be June the 1st in London. If, during this summer you came for a month or two—it would do you good and my S.D. too as I will be reading the proof sheets....

"...today....dear old [Bertram] Keightley [is here].... [he] came from Engl[and] to see me...."

(Source: H.P.B.'s letter to William Q. Judge, published in *The Theosophical Forum*, July, 1932, pp. 224 & 227.)

February (late), 1887—Bertram Keightley is in Ostende visiting H.P.B. He writes later about his trip to Ostende as follows:

"The first I saw of *The Secret Doctrine* manuscript was on a visit paid to H.P.B. at Ostend...[in] 1887. I had gone over to urge upon H.P.B. the advisability of coming to settle in London for the purpose of forming a centre for active work in the cause of Theosophy. There were six of us in all who felt profoundly dissatisfied with the deadness which seemed to pervade the [Theosophical] Society in England, and we had come to the conclusion that only H.P.B. could give efficient aid in restoring the suspended animation of the movement, and initiating active and wisely directed work. Of these six—with H.P.B. the original founders of the first Blavatsky Lodge—two only, alas! now remain active workers in the Society.

"During the few days I then spent at Ostend with H.P.B., she asked me to look over parts of the MSS. of her new work, which I gladly consented to do. Before I had read much it grew plain that *The Secret Doctrine* was destined to be by far the most important contribution of this century to the literature of Occultism; though even then the inchoate and fragmentary character of much of the work led me to think that careful revision and much re-arrangement would be needed before the manuscript would be fit for publication.

"On a second visit a week or two later, this impression was confirmed by further examination; but as H.P.B. then consented to come and settle in or near London as soon as arrangements could be made for her reception, nothing further was done about it at the time."

The Secret Doctrine Würzburg Manuscript

(Source: Countess Constance Wachtmeister, *Reminiscences of H. P. Blavatsky and The Secret Doctrine*, 1893, p. 89.)

February (sometime around the 23th), 1887—H.P.B. writes to Mr. Sinnett about her progress on writing *The Secret Doctrine* manuscript [Volume 3 on Anthropogenesis]:

"...young Fawcett [is] upsetting books and furniture behind me [as I write this.]...

"...I am [writing] on the 4th Race. I have done with the Hermaphrodite Third Race...."

(Source: *The Letters of H. P. Blavatsky to A.P. Sinnett*, pp. 229-230.)

February, 1887—Countess Wachtmeister writes in her book *Reminiscences of H. P. Blavatsky*:

"...I hurried through the remaining work [I had to do in London] as quickly as possible, and was much distressed on arriving at Ostend to find H.P.B. looking so worn and ill. Mr. Z [Fawcett] left, and then we recommenced our usual routine of life, and the writing of *The Secret Doctrine* was carried on strenuously.

"Very rarely was I able to persuade H.P.B. to bask in a bath chair on the esplanade. I thought that the warmth from the sun and the sea air might do her good, but she always seemed dissatisfied when she came in, as if she felt she had done wrong in losing so much valuable time.

"She often said, 'Soon we shall no longer be alone, and then the conditions will be altered, and the currents will be broken, and I shall not be able to work nearly so well.'

"And so she would keep at her desk, no matter what her pains or sufferings were. She just clenched her teeth together and fought her battle bravely."

(Source: Constance Wachtmeister, *Reminiscences of H. P. Blavatsky*, 1893, pp. 68-69.)

March, 1887—Archibald Keightley goes to see H.P.B. at Ostende. He writes:

"In the early months of 1887 there were some few members of the T.S. in London who felt that if Theosophy did not receive some vital impulse, the centre there would be confined to a few individuals only who were pursuing and would continue to pursue their studies. Of course there may have been many who felt the same, but I write here of those with whom I was actually in contact. There were many anxious discussions as to how a vital interest could be awakened in the truths of Theosophy, and how attention should be restored to the ethical philosophy. This was the more necessary, for in the public mind the philosophy had been inseparably connected with the phenomena.

"We all felt that we were working in the dark and that we were ignorant of the real basis upon which the philosophy rested. Obviously we required a leader who might intelligently direct our efforts. We then determined each separately to write to H. P. Blavatsky, who was then in Ostende, laying before the Founder of the T.S. and the Messenger of the Masters the position as each of us saw it. We asked her to reply in a collective letter giving us advice as to what to do. She replied, however, to each individual, writing letters of eight to twelve pages. The result of this was that we all wrote and asked her to come over and direct our efforts.

"She had told us that she was writing the *Secret Doctrine* and must finish that before undertaking other work.

Nevertheless we wrote to her that there was, we believed, urgent need of her directing presence, and that she could finish the *Secret Doctrine* in London as well as or better than in Ostende.

"After receiving her reply, which urged objections, Mr. Bertram Keightley went over to Ostende during the latter part of February or beginning of March and talked matters over with her. She agreed to come to London at the end of April provided we would find a house for her somewhere a little out of London in which she could work in peace. Soon after he returned I went over to Ostende rather unexpectedly myself.

"I naturally went to call after leaving my luggage at the hotel. Madame Blavatsky received me with the greatest kindness, although previously to that occasion I was almost unknown to her. She insisted that I should transfer my things to her house and stay with her while in Ostende. At that time she was occupying the first floor of the house, with a Swiss maid to wait on her and Countess Wachtmeister to keep her company. I was at once introduced to the *Secret Doctrine* with a request to read, correct, and excise, a privilege I naturally did not avail myself of.

"Madame Blavatsky at that time had never ventured out of her rooms since the previous November, and never came from her writing and bed-room into the dining-room until the windows had been closed and the room well warmed. Several attacks of inflammation of the kidneys had warned her that the slightest chill was dangerous to the completion of her work. At the close of my visit I returned to England with renewed assurances of her arrival on May 1st, and under pledge to return and assist Madame Blavatsky on her journey to London."

(Source: *The Path* (New York), November 1892, pp. 245-248.)

March (toward end of month) 1887—H.P.B. becomes seriously ill with a kidney infection. Countess Wachtmeister gives the following account:

> "To my great distress, I now began to notice that she [H.P.B.] became drowsy and heavy in the middle of the day, and often was unable to work [on *The Secret Doctrine*] for an hour together. This increased rapidly, and as the doctor who attended her pronounced it to be an affection of the kidneys, I became alarmed, and sent a telegram to Madame Gebhard to tell her of my apprehensions, and to beg her to come and help me. . . . I was, therefore, thankful when I received a cordial response to my telegram and knew that in a few hours I should see Madame Gebhard.
>
> "When she came, I felt as if a great burden had been lifted off my shoulders. In the meanwhile H.P.B. was getting worse, and the Belgian doctor, who was kindness itself, tried one remedy after another, but with no good result, and I began to get seriously alarmed and anxious as to what course I should adopt. H.P.B. was in a heavy lethargic state, she seemed to be unconscious for hours together, and nothing could rouse or interest her. Finally, a bright inspiration came to me. In the London [Theosophical] group I knew there was a Doctor Ashton Ellis, so I telegraphed to him, described the state that H.P.B. was in, and entreated him to come without delay.
>
> "I sat by H.P.B.'s bed that night listening to every sound as I anxiously watched the hours go by, till at last, at 3 a.m., the joyful sound of a bell was heard. I flew to the door, opened it, and the doctor [Ashton Ellis] walked in. I eagerly told him all her symptoms, and described the remedies that had been applied, whereupon he went to her and made her drink some medicine that he had brought with him. . . .

"The next day there was a consultation between the two doctors. The Belgian doctor said that he had never known a case of a person with the kidneys attacked as H.P.B.'s were, living as long as she had done, and that he was convinced that nothing could save her. . . . Mr. Ellis replied that it was exceedingly rare for anyone to survive so long in such a state. He further told us that he had consulted a specialist before coming to Ostend, who was of the same opinion, but advised that, in addition to the prescribed medicine, he should try massage, so as to stimulate the paralyzed organs. . . .

"The night passed quietly, and several times the following day Mr. Ellis . . . [massaged] her until he was quite exhausted; but she got no better, and to my horror I began to detect that peculiar faint odour of death which sometimes precedes dissolution. I hardly dared hope that she would live through the night, and while I was sitting alone by her bedside she opened her eyes and told me how glad she was to die, and that she thought the Master would let her be free at last. Still she was very anxious about her *Secret Doctrine*. I must be most careful of her manuscripts and hand all over to Col. Olcott with directions to have them printed. She had hoped that she would have been able to give more to the world, but the Master knew best. And so she talked on at intervals, telling me many things. At last she dropped off into a state of unconsciousness, and I wondered how it would all end.

"It seemed to me impossible that she should die and leave her work unfinished; and then, again, the Theosophical Society . . . what would become of it? How could it be that the Master who was at the head of that Society should allow it to crumble away? . . . Still the thought came to me that the Master had told H.P.B. that she was to form a circle of students around her and that she was to teach them. How could she do that if she were to die? And then I opened my eyes and glanced at her and thought, was it possible that she who had slaved, suffered, and striven so hard should be allowed to die in the middle of her work? . . .

"None of those who knew her, really understood her. Even to me, who had been alone with her for so many months, she was an enigma, with her strange powers, her marvelous knowledge, her extraordinary insight into human nature, and her mysterious life, spent in regions unknown to ordinary mortals, so that though her body might be near, her soul was often away in commune with others. . . .

"Such were the thoughts which passed through my mind, as I sat hour after hour that anxious night, watching her as she seemed to be getting weaker and weaker. A wave of blank despondency came over me, as I felt how truly I loved this noble woman, and I realised how empty life would be without her. . . . My whole soul rose in rebellion at the thought of losing her. . . . I gave a bitter cry and knew no more.

"When I opened my eyes, the early morning light was stealing in, and a dire apprehension came over me that I had slept, and that perhaps H.P.B. had died during my sleep—died whilst I was untrue to my vigil. I turned round towards the bed in horror, and there I saw H.P.B. looking at me calmly with her clear grey eyes, as she said, 'Countess, come here.'

"I flew to her side. 'What has happened, H.P.B.—you look so different to what you did last night.'

"She replied, 'Yes, Master has been here; He gave me my choice, that I might die and be free if I would, or I might live and finish *The Secret Doctrine*. He told me how great would be my sufferings and what a terrible time I would have before me in England (for I am to go there); but when I thought of those students to whom I shall be permitted to teach a few things, and of the Theosophical Society in general, to which I have already given my heart's blood, I accepted the sacrifice, and now to make it complete, fetch me some coffee and something to eat, and give me my tobacco box.'"

(Source: Constance Wachmeister, *Reminiscences of H. P. Blavatsky*, 1893, pp. 71-76.)

April 25 or 26, 1887—Archibald Keightley goes again to Ostende. He writes:

". . . In the middle of April Mr. [Bertram] Keightley again went over [to Ostende] and I followed him about the 25th or 26th. We were rather in consternation because Madame Blavatsky said she could not possibly leave in such weather as then prevailed, especially on account of her late serious illness. Her landlord said she must leave, for the rooms were let. Countess Wachtmeister had previously left for Sweden to attend to urgent business affairs there under promise to rejoin Madame Blavatsky in London. Staying in the house with us was a friend of Dr. Ellis who assisted in the removal.

"The fated day came, and in place of being bright but cold, as had been the case two days before, the morning proved to be cold and foggy, with a steady drizzling rain falling and penetrating all it touched, the thermometer being about 40 degrees. We fully expected Madame Blavatsky would decline to move, and thought her justified in doing so. Nevertheless she appeared that morning in full marching order, the trunks were packed, and all was ready. The carriage arrived and Madame Blavatsky was assisted into it, and off it drove to the wharf. It must be remembered that she had not had a window open in her room while she was in it (and would scarcely allow it open while she was out) for six months. She kept her room at a temperature of over 70 deg., believing that anything under that would kill her.

Moreover, she was almost crippled with rheumatism and could hardly walk, and was a constant martyr to sciatica. On getting to the wharf we found the tide low, and in consequence that there was only a narrow gangway leading at a very steep incline to the steamer's deck. Imagine our dismay. Madame Blavatsky, however, said nothing, but simply grasping the rails walked slowly and without assistance to the deck. We then took her to a cabin on deck where she sank on to the sofa and only then betrayed the pain and exhaustion caused by her effort.

"The journey was uneventful so far as Dover, save that for the first time in her life Mme. Blavatsky knew what the preliminary qualms of sea-sickness meant and was much puzzled. At Dover the tide was still lower, and as a result four very stalwart piermen had to carry her to the top. Then came the greatest difficult, for the platform is low and the English railway carriage steps were high. It required the united efforts of all the party (and the piermen as well) to assist Madame Blavatsky in her crippled state into the carriage. The journey to London was uneventful, and with the help of an invalid chair and a carriage she was safely lodged in the house we had secured for her. Secretly I was afraid the journey would have serious results, but, whatever was the reason, she seemed to enjoy better health for some time after her arrival in England then she had for months previously. The day after her arrival she was at work on the *Secret Doctrine* at 7 a.m., and did not appear best pleased because she had been prevented from an earlier start through her writing materials not having been unpacked the previous night."

(Source: *The Path,* November 1892, pp. 246-248.)

May 2 or 3, 1887—Having now settled in England at Mabel Collins' house, Maycot, Crownhill, Upper Norwood, London, H.P.B continues her work on *The Secret Doctrine*.

Bertram Keightley provides the reader *with the following important facts* about *The Secret Doctrine* manuscript that H.P.B. had brought with her to London:

> "A day or two after our arrival at Maycot, H.P.B. placed the whole of the so far completed MSS. in the hands of Dr. [Archibald] Keightley and myself....We both read the whole mass of MSS.—a pile over three feet high—most carefully...and then, after prolonged consultation, faced [H.P.B.]...with the solemn opinion that the whole of the matter must be rearranged on some definite plan....
>
> "Finally we laid before her a plan, suggested by the character of the matter itself, viz., to make the work consist of four volumes...."
>
> **"Further, instead of making the first volume to consist, as she had intended, of the history of some great Occultists, we advised her to follow the natural order of exposition, and begin** [in the 1st volume] **with the Evolution of Cosmos, to pass from that to the Evolution of Man** [in the 2nd volume], **then to deal with the historical part in a third volume treating of the lives of some great Occultists; and finally, to speak of Practical Occultism in a fourth volume should she ever be able to write it.** [Bold added.]
>
> "This plan was laid before H.P.B., and it was duly sanctioned by her.
>
> "The next step was to read the MSS. through again and make a general rearrangement of the matter pertaining to the subjects coming under the heads of Cosmogony and Anthropology, which were to form the first two volumes of the work. When this had been completed, and H.P.B.

duly consulted, and her approval of what had been done obtained, the whole of the MSS. so arranged was typewritten out by professional hands...."

(Source: Constance Wachtmeister, *Reminiscences of H. P. Blavatsky and The Secret Doctrine*, 1893, pp. 78-79; also quoted in Boris de Zirkoff, *Rebirth of the Occult Tradition*, p. 41.)

Bertram's account of 1893 is also confirmed by the following testimony. A report of Bertram Keightley's lecture "Theosophy in the West" to the annual T.S. convention at Adyar, Madras, India, in December 1890, includes the following about *The Secret Doctrine*:

"[In 1887 in England] H.P.B. handed over to him [Bertram Keightley] the manuscript of the 'Secret Doctrine,' with a request that he should read it through. He read through the substance of the two volumes published, and the third still unpublished....what would now be the 3rd volume of the history of Occultism was to have been the first volume, while the treatises on Cosmogony and the Genesis of Man were to form a later series....He then drafted a scheme with the natural and obvious order, namely, the Evolution of the Universe and the Evolution of man, &c. &c. The next thing...was to rearrange...the manuscript according to the [new] scheme."

(Source: *The Theosophist,* July 1891, pp. 586-587.)

May through Summer 1887—Archibald Keightley writes about the work done on The Secret Doctrine during this time-period:

"All through the summer of 1887 every day found her [H.P.B.] at work [on the manuscript of the *Secret Doctrine*] from six to six, with intervals for meals only, visitors being with very rare exceptions denied or told to come in the evening. The evenings were given up to talk and discussion, and only on rare occasions was any writing done.

"All through that summer Bertram Keightley and I were engaged in reading, re-reading, copying and correcting. The last amounted to casting some of the sentences in English mould, for many of them were 'literal translations from the French.' . . .

"Many of the quotations had to be verified, and here we should have been lost if it had not been for a hint from H.P.B. She told us one night that sometimes in writing down quotations, which for the purpose of the book had been impressed on the Astral Light before her, she forgot to reverse the figures—for instance page 123 would be allowed to remain 321 and so on. With this in mind, verification was easier, for one was puzzled on examining all editions in the British Museum to find in several cases that the books did not contain the number of pages. With the reversal, matters were straightened out and the correct places [for the quotations] were found.

"Much of the [*Secret Doctrine*] MSS. was type-written at this period. This was H.P.B.'s opportunity. The spaces were large and much could be inserted. Needless to say, it was. The thick type-MSS. were cut, pasted, recut and pasted several times over [by H.P.B.], until several of them were twice the size of the original MSS.

". . . no work and no trouble, no suffering or pain could daunt her from her task. Crippled with rheumatism, suffering from a disease which had several times nearly proved fatal, she still worked on unflaggingly, writing at her desk the moment her eyes and fingers could guide the pen."

(Source: Constance Wachtmeister, *Reminiscences of H. P. Blavatsky*, 1893, pp. 98-99.)

May 7, 1887—From her new residence in England, H.P.B writes to William Q. Judge:

"MAYCOT, CROWNHILL, UPPER NORWOOD, LONDON, *May 7th*.

". . . Didn't know old H.P.B. was for seventeen days hovering between life and death [at Ostende]; drawn irresistibly by the charm *beyond* the latter, and held by her coat-tails by the Countess [Wachtmeister] and some London Lodges? Nice intuitional friend. Anyhow *saved* once more, and once more stuck into the mud of life right with my classical nose. Two Keightleys and Thornton (a dear, REAL new Theosophist) came to Ostende, packed me up, books, kidneys, and gouty legs, and carried me across the water partially in steamer, partially in invalid chair, and the rest in train to Norwood, in one of the cottages of which here I am; living (rather vegetating) in it till the Countess returns. . . . Very, very seedy and weak; but rather better after the mortal disease which cleansed me if it did not carry me off. Love and sincere, as usual and for ever. Yours in heaven and hell.—'O.L.' H.P.B."

(Source: *The Path,* November 1892, p. 248.)

May 29, 1887—Bertram Keightley writes to W. Q. Judge:

"H.P.B. is fairly well & working away right hard at the Secret Doctrine, which is *awfully good* & I am sure you will be immensely pleased with it. . . . I am staying with H.P.B. at Maycot, Crown Hill, Upper Norwood, S.E. where I expect she will be for the next two or three months. We have got a scheme on foot for establishing H.P.B. in *winter* quarters near London where she can live in peace & gather the real workers in the Society around her...."

The Secret Doctrine Würzburg Manuscript

(Source: Kirby Van Mater's "The Writing of *The Secret Doctrine*," *Sunrise*, November, 1975, pp. 60-61.)

Summer 1887 and later—Bertram Keightley gives the following description of the work done on the *Secret Doctrine* manuscript during these months:

". . . [The new copy of *The Secret Doctrine*] typewritten out by professional hands . . . [was] then re-read, corrected, compared with the original MSS., and all Greek, Hebrew, and Sanskrit quotations inserted by us.

"It then appeared that the whole of the Commentary on the Stanzas did not amount to more than some twenty pages of the present work, as H.P.B. had not stuck closely to her text in writing. So we seriously interviewed her, and suggested that she should write a proper commentary, as in her opening words she had promised her readers to do. Her reply was characteristic: 'What on earth am I to say? What *do* you want to know? Why it's all as plain as the nose on your face! ! !' We could not see it; she didn't—or made out she didn't—so we retired to reflect.

". . . I think the removal [of H.P.B. and the household] to Lansdowne Road [in September 1887 was] effected, before the problem of the Commentary on the Stanzas was finally solved.

"The solution was this:—Each sloka of the stanzas was written (or cut out from the type-written copy) and pasted at the head of a sheet of paper, and then on a loose sheet pinned thereto were written all the questions we could find time to devise upon that sloka. In this task Mr. Richard Harte helped us very considerably, a large proportion of the questions put being of his devising. H.P.B. struck out large numbers of them, made us write fuller explanations, or our own ideas—such as they were—of what her readers expected her to say, wrote more herself, incorporated the little she had already written on that particular sloka, and so the work was done.

"But when we came to think of sending the MSS. to the printers, the result was found to be such that the most experienced compositor would tear his hair in blank dismay. Therefore Dr. Keightley and myself set to work with a type-writer, and alternately dictating and writing, made a clean copy of the first parts of volumes I. and II.

"Then work was continued till parts II. and III. of each volume were in a fairly advanced condition, and we could think of sending the work to press.

"It had originally been arranged that Mr. George Redway should publish the work, but his proposals not being financially satisfactory, the needful money was offered by a friend of H.P.B.'s, and it was resolved to take the publication of *Lucifer* into our own hands. So the Duke Street office was taken, and business begun there, the primary object being to enable the T.S. to derive the utmost possible benefit from H.P.B.'s writings.

" . . . there were months of hard work [still] before us. H.P.B. read and corrected two sets of galley proofs, then a page proof, and finally a revise in sheet, correcting, adding, and altering up to the very last moment:— result: printer's bill for corrections alone over 300 [pounds] . . . .

"Of the value of the work, posterity must judge finally. Personally I can only place on record my profound conviction that when studied thoroughly but not treated as a revelation, when understood and assimilated but not made a text for dogma, H.P.B.'s *Secret Doctrine* will be found of incalculable value, and will furnish suggestions, clues, and threads of guidance, for the study of Nature and Man, such as no other existing work can supply."

(Source: Constance Wachtmeister, *Reminiscences of H. P. Blavatsky,* 1893, pp. 92-95.)

September (early) 1887—Countess Wachtmeister goes to London and joins H.P.B. at Maycot, just prior to H.P.B. moving to Lansdowne Road.

(Source: Constance Wachtmeister, *Reminiscences of H. P. Blavatsky,* 1893, pp. 80-81.)

September 10, 1887—H.P.B. writes to G. Subbiah Chetty in India:

"...Subba Row has even refused through C. Oakley to read or have anything to do [with] my *Secret Doctrine.* I have spent here £30 to have it typed, on purpose to send to him, and now when all is ready, he refuses to look into it. Of course, it will be a new pretext for him to pitch into and criticize when it does come out. Therefore I will defer its publication...."

(Source: Boris de Zirkoff, *Rebirth of the Occult Tradition,* pp. 44-45.)

September (middle), 1887—H.P.B. moves to 17, Lansdowne Road, Holland Park, London.

September 1887 and later—Archibald Keightley writes:

"Then came the time of the founding of *Lucifer.* This work had to be added to that of writing *The Secret Doctrine....*

"In September [1887] came the move to London, to Lansdowne Road...."

"During the greater part of this period in London, H.P.B. had the assistance of E. D. Fawcett, especially in those parts of the second volume [of *The Secret Doctrine* on anthropogenesis] dealing with the evolutionary hypotheses. He suggested, corrected, and wrote, and several pages of his MSS. were incorporated by H.P.B. into her work."

(Source: Constance Wachtmeister, *Reminiscences of H. P. Blavatsky,* 1893, p. 99)

Autumn, 1887—Madame Blavatsky writes to her sister Vera:

"If you only knew . . . how busy I am! Just imagine the number of my daily duties; the editing of my new magazine, LUCIFER, rests entirely with me, and besides that I have to write for it each month from ten to fifteen pages. . . . [Concerning] my *Secret Doctrine*. . . I have to continue the second volume and correct the proofs of the first [volume] two or three times over. And then the visits! . . . . Very often as many as thirty [visitors] a day. . . . Impossible for me to get out of it! . . . . There ought to be a hundred and twenty-four hours in each day. . . ."

(Source: *Lucifer,* April 15, 1895, p. 102.)

December, 1887—At the Theosophical Society's 1887 Annual Convention at Adyar, Madras, India, Colonel Olcott tells his listeners that:

"During the past twelve months she [H.P.B.] has sent me the MSS. of four out of the probable five volumes of the 'The Secret Doctrine' for examination...."

Later in writing about the events of 1887 in his *Old Diary Leaves,* Colonel Olcott gives us additional information about *The Secret Doctrine* manuscripts sent to him:

"....Subba Row [refused] to edit the *Secret Doctrine* MSS., contrary to his original promise, although she [H.P.B.]...had it typed-copied at a cost of £80 and sent [to] me for that purpose...."

(Sources: *The Theosophist*, Vol. IX, Supplement to January, 1888 issue, p. xvii; Henry S. Olcott, *Old Diary Leaves*, Volume IV, p. 23.)

1888

February 24, 1888—H.P.B. writes to Colonel Olcott:

"Now Tookaram writes me a letter. In it he says that S[ubba] R[ow] told him he was ready to help me and correct my *S.D. provided* I took out from it every reference to the Masters!

"Now, what's this? Does he mean to say that I should deny the Masters, or that I do not understand Them and garble the facts They give me, or that he, S.R., knows Master's doctrine better than I do? For it can mean all this. Please take your first opportunity of telling the whole of Adyar as follows:

"...It is *I*, who brought in, the first, the existence of our Masters to the world and the T.S. I did it because They sent me to do the work and make a fresh experiment in this XIX Century and I have done it, the best I knew how. It may not dovetail with S.R.'s ideas, [but] it answers truth and fact....*I either know Them personally as I have ever maintained*; or—*I have invented Them and Their doctrines*...."

(Source: Boris de Zirkoff, *Rebirth of the Occult Tradition*, pp. 47-48.)

April 1888 (estimated)—A notice in *The Theosophist* tells the reader:

> "Mr. Bertram Keightley writes encouragingly from London about the health of . . . [Madame Blavatsky]. He says 'she is much stronger than at the beginning of the year, and, though suffering much from the derangement of the stomach, is wonderfully cheerful.'
>
> "The publication of the 'Secret Doctrine' has been commenced, and as soon as the magnitude and, of course, the cost of the work can be definitely calculated, the price to subscribers will be fixed and a circular sent them...."
>
> (Source: *Supplement to The Theosophist,* May 1888, p. xxxvii.)

April 3, 1888—H.P.B. writes to the Second American Theosophical Society Convention:

> "The MSS. of the first three volumes [of *The Secret Doctrine*] is now ready for the press...."
>
> (Source: H. P. Blavatsky, *Collected Writings*, Volume IX, p. 247.)

May or June, 1888 (estimated)—H.P.B. has a circular issued and sent out from London announcing the forthcoming publication of *The Secret Doctrine* "on or about October 27th, 1888, in Two Volumes, Royal Octavo, of *circa* 650 pp. each."
One important excerpt reads:

> ". . . The first of these [two] volumes contains Book I of the 'Secret Doctrine,' and is concerned mainly with the evolution of Kosmos. It is divided into three parts.
>
> "Part I commences with an introduction explaining the philosophical basis of the system. The skeleton of this

book is formed by seven Stanzas, translated from the Secret Book of Dzyan, with commentary and explanations by the translator. This work is among the oldest MSS. in the world; it is written in the Sacred Language of the Initiates, and constitutes the text-book which was the basis of the oral instructions imparted during the Mysteries...."

"...Book II (forming the second volume) ... treats of the Evolution of Man....Part I contains a series of Stanzas from the Book of Dzyan, which describe the Evolution of Humanity in our cycle...."

A Table of Contents for these two volumes is also given in this circular.

The arrangement of the material as given in this Table of Contents is somewhat different from the final arrangement of the material as found in the First Edition published several months later. A photographic facsimile of this circular as printed in *The Path* can be found at:

http://blavatskyarchives.com/sdprospectus.pdf

In this table, Part II of the first volume is headed with the following significant words:

"*Explanatory Sections on Symbolism and the Eastern Presentation of the Secret Cosmography.*"

This Table of Contents shows that Volume II on Anthropogenesis contained a chapter titled "Nebo of Birs-Nimrod" in the Part II "Chapters on Symbolism." In the final rearrangement of some of the material as issued in the published First Edition, this chapter is *missing*. This "Nebo" article was finally published by Boris de Zirkoff in Volume XIII of H.P.B.'s *Collected Writings* with the following editorial note:

"This manuscript in H.P.B.'s handwriting was in the possession of John M. Watkins, the renowned Publisher and Bookseller, who was a close friend of hers. It is marked XV(a) and covers a little over twelve numbered pages. It may have been intended for *The Secret Doctrine* and later set aside. A few words or brief sentences have remained illegible. It has been transcribed from a microfilm of the original MS. now in the hands of Geoffrey Watkins."

The listing of this "Nebo" chapter in the above circular gives support to Mr. de Zirkoff's speculation that "it may have been intended for *The Secret Doctrine* and later set aside."

(Sources: The above circular was published in *The Path*, July, 1888, pp. 133-136; it was also published in *The Theosophist*, July 1888, pp. 632-635. See "Nebo" chapter in H.P.B.'s *Collected Writings,* Volume XIII, pp. 271-282.)

July, 1888—Madame Blavatsky, in a letter dated Oct. 25, 1888 to Elliott Coues, writes:

"...[Master] K.H....only a few months ago...[was here] in flesh and bones. But He is gone, was in London only eleven days, in July...."

(Source: "The History of a Humbug: The Letters of H. P. Blavatsky to Elliott Coues," *The Canadian Theosophist,* July-Aug. 1985.)

July/August, 1888 (estimated)—At this time, Madame Blavatsky apparently writes and adds a special 41-page section to Volume I of *The Secret Doctrine* correcting certain mistakes in A.P. Sinnett's *Esoteric Buddhism* and giving further esoteric teachings on the Moon chain, the Lunar Pitris, etc. In this added section, letters from Master K.H. are given correcting some of Mr. Sinnett's mistakes.

Archibald Keightley refers to this additional material in a letter to a Mrs. Malcolm:

> "...H.P.B. did not hold back the Secret Doctrine from the Press and delay its printing for a week, so as to write in that part about the lunar Pitris, for nothing. All that part about Sinnett in the first volume was put in in a great hurry at great expense and delay, for a special purpose...."

The material/section referred to apparently covers pp. 151 to 191 of Volume I of the 1888 First edition. H.P.B. decided to insert this additional material between her commentaries on "the 4th Sloka of Stanza VI" and Stanza VI, Sloka 5.

Compare the above material with the two chronological entries about Master K.H. for July and Aug. 22, 1888.

It may be that at this point in time some of the material was rearranged in Volumes I and II of the S.D. The interested reader may want to compare and contrast the Table of Contents as found in the circular mentioned a few entries above with the Table of Contents as published in the First Edition.

> (Source: Archibald Keightley's letter is dated Sept. 24, 1895 and is quoted in: Knoche, Grace F., ed. *Secret Doctrine Centenary, October 29-30, 1988: Report of Proceedings.* Pasadena, California: Theosophical Society, 1989, p. 84.)

August 22, 1888—During his trip to England from India on board the steamship *Shannon*, Colonel Olcott receives in his cabin an important letter from Master Koot Hoomi. The Master tells Olcott:

> "I have . . . noted your thoughts about the 'Secret Doctrine.' Be assured that what she [H.P.B.] has not *annotated* from scientific and other works, we have given or *suggested* to her. Every mistake or erroneous notion, corrected and explained by her from the works of

other theosophists *was corrected by me, or under my instruction.* It is a more valuable work than its predecessor [*Isis Unveiled*], an epitome of occult truths that will make it a source of information and instruction for the earnest student for long years to come. . . ."

(Source: *Letters from the Masters of the Wisdom*, Series I, Letter 19.)

August 26, 1888—Colonel Olcott arrives in London from India. He sends a report of his European visit back to Adyar. A summary titled "The President's European Visit" is given in the *Supplement to the Theosophist:*

"Embarking at Bombay on board the P. and O. mail steamer *Shannon* on the 7th of August, the President [of the Theosophical Society, Henry S. Olcott] reached Brindisi [Italy] on the 23rd, and proceeded overland to London, when he arrived on the 26th. . . .

"The President found Madame Blavatsky in bad health, but working with desperate and pertinacious energy. An able physician told him that the fact of her even being alive at all was in itself a miracle, judging by all professional canons. Her system is so disorganized by a complication of diseases of the gravest character that it is a simple wonder that she can keep up the struggle; any other being must have succumbed long ago. The microscope reveals enormous crystals of uric acid in her blood, and the doctors say that it is more than likely that one hot month in India would kill her.

"Nevertheless, not only does she live, but she works at her writing desk from morning to night, preparing 'copy' and reading proofs for *The Secret Doctrine* and her London magazine, *Lucifer*. Of her greatest work over three hundred pages of each of the two volumes were already printed when Colonel Olcott arrived. . . . From all he heard from competent judges who had read the manuscript, the President was satisfied that *The Secret Doctrine* will surpass in merit and interest even *Isis Unveiled*.

"Madame Blavatsky is living at 17, Lansdowne Road, Holland Park, with three Theosophical friends, among them her devoted guardian, nurse and consoler, the Countess Wachtmeister of Sweden, who has attended her throughout all her serious illnesses of the past three years. The house is a pleasant one, in a quiet neighbourhood, and the back of it looks upon a small private park or compound, common to the occupants of all the houses which surround it.

"Madame Blavatsky's rooms are on the ground floor, she being practically unable to go up and down stairs. Her desk faces a large window looking out upon the green grass and leafy trees of Holland Park; at her right and left hands are tables and book racks filled with books of reference; and all about the room are her Indian souvenirs — Benares bronzes, Palghat mats, Adoni carpets, Moradabad platters, Kashmir plaques, and Sinhalese images, which were so familiar to visitors at Adyar in the old days. . . .

"Clustering around her in London she has several devoted Theosophists who, besides advancing £1,500 to bring out *The Secret Doctrine* and *Lucifer*, have formed a Theosophical Publishing Co. (Limited), to issue at popular prices reprints of articles from *The Theosophist, Lucifer* and *The Path*, and useful tracts of all sorts. The interest in Theosophy increases and deepens in Europe, and still more in America. . . . "

(Source: *Supplement to the Theosophist,* October 1888, pp. xvii-xviii.)

October 20, 1888—On this day the First Volume of *The Secret Doctrine* comes off the press in London. The first printing of 500 copies is exhausted before date of publication. Second Volume comes out towards the end of the year. On the same day, Col. Olcott and Richard Harte leave for India.

A penciled notation in Harte's own copy of Vol. I of the S.D. reads:

> "This is the first copy ever issued. I got it from Printer by special Messenger on the morning of the 20 Oct. '88 as I was leaving the house 17 Lansdowne Road, with Col. Olcott for India....The Second Vol. followed me to India.—R.H."

October-December 1888—H.P.B. writes about the still unpublished third volume of *The Secret Doctrine* in the newly published Volumes I and II of *The Secret Doctrine*:

> "Even the two volumes now issued do not complete the scheme, and these do not treat exhaustively of the subjects dealt with in them. A large quantity of material has already been prepared, dealing with the history of occultism as contained in the lives of the great Adepts of the Aryan Race, and showing the bearing of occult philosophy upon the conduct of life, as it is and as it ought to be. Should the present volumes meet with a favourable reception, no effort will be spared to carry out the scheme of the work in its entirety. The third volume is entirely ready; the fourth almost so." [1: vii]

> "But if the reader has patience, and would glance at the present state of beliefs and creeds in Europe, compare and check it with what is known to history of the ages directly preceding and following the Christian era, then he will find all this in Volume III. of this work.

> "In that volume a brief recapitulation will be made of all the principal adepts known to history, and the downfall

of the mysteries will be described; after which began the disappearance and final and systematic elimination from the memory of men of the real nature of initiation and the Sacred Science. From that time its teachings became Occult and Magic sailed but too often under the venerable but frequently misleading name of Hermetic philosophy. As real Occultism had been prevalent among the Mystics during the centuries that preceded our era, so Magic, or rather Sorcery, with its Occult Arts, followed the beginning of Christianity." [1: xxxix-xl]

"Read by the light of the Zohar, the initial four chapters of Genesis are the fragment of a highly philosophical page in the World's Cosmogony. (*See* Book III., "*Gupta Vidya and the Zohar.*")" [1: 10-11]

"The explanation with regard to the 'Anupadaka' given in the Kala Chakra, the first in the Gyu(t) division of the Kanjur, is half esoteric. It has misled the Orientalists into erroneous speculations with respect to the Dhyani-Buddhas and their earthly correspondencies, the Manushi-Buddhas. The real tenet is hinted at in a subsequent Volume, (see "The Mystery about Buddha"), and will be more fully explained in its proper place." [1: 52n]

"Therefore the meaning of the 'fairy tale' translated by Chwolson from an old Chaldean MSS. translated into Arabic, about Qu-tamy being instructed by the *idol* of the moon, is easily understood (*vide* Book III.) Seldenus tells us the secret as well as Maimonides.... The worshipers of the *Teraphim* (the Jewish Oracles) 'carved images and claimed that the light of the principal stars (planets) permeating these through and through, the angelic VIRTUES (or the regents of the stars and planets) conversed with them, teaching them many most useful things and arts.'" [1: 394]

"If one studies comparative Theogony, it is easy to find that the secret of these 'Fires' was taught in the *Mysteries* of every ancient people, pre-eminently in Samothrace.... There is no space to describe these 'fires' and their real meaning here, though we may attempt to do so if the third and fourth volumes of this work are ever published." [2: 106]

"In Volume III. of this work (the said volume and the IVth being almost ready) a brief history of all the great adepts known to the ancients and the moderns in their chronological order will be given, as also a bird's eye view of the Mysteries, their birth, growth, decay, and final death—in Europe. This could not find room in the present work. Volume IV will be almost entirely devoted to Occult teachings." [2: 437]

"These two volumes should form for the student a fitting prelude for Volumes III. and IV. Until the rubbish of the ages is cleared away from the minds of the Theosophists to whom these volumes are dedicated, it is impossible that the more practical teaching contained in the Third Volume should be understood.

"Consequently, it entirely depends upon the reception with which Volumes I. and II. will meet at the hands of Theosophists and Mystics, whether these last two volumes will ever be published, though they are *almost* completed." [2: 797-8]

1889

April 29, 1889—Archibald Keightley is quoted in an interview in the *New York Times*:

"The third volume of 'The Secret Doctrine' is in manuscript ready to be given to the printers. It will consist mainly of a series of sketches of the great occultists of all ages, and is a most wonderful and fascinating work. The fourth volume, which is to be largely hints on the subject of practical occultism, has been outlined, but not yet written...."

(Source: *New York Times*, April 29, 1889, p. 5.)

November 21, 1889— H.P.B. writes to N. D. Khandalavala in India:

"...[I] have been able to write my *S.D.*, 'Key,' 'Voice,' and prepared two more volumes of the S. Doctrine...."

(Source: *Theosophist,* August 1932, p. 626.)

1890

February, 1890— H.P.B. writes in a letter to her sister Vera:

". . . I must put the third volume of the *[Secret] Doctrine* in order, and the fourth [volume]—hardly begun yet, too."

(Source: *The Path,* December, 1895, p. 268.)

1891

January 7, 1891—Claude Falls Wright writes:

> "H.P.B. has within the last week or so begun to get together the MSS. (long ago written) for the Third Volume of *The Secret Doctrine*; it will however, take a good twelve months to prepare for publication."

(Source: *The Path,* February 1891, p. 354.)

February, 1891—Writing from London, Mrs. Alice Leighton Cleather sends a report to India with the following news about H.P.B.:

> "I am sorry to have to begin my letter with the news of H.P.B.'s ill-health. It is, unhappily, the case that she has been far from well of late again; and we can only hope and trust that, with the disappearance of frost and fog, she may regain somewhat of health and strength.
>
> ".... Another edition of the *Secret Doctrine,* too, is in course of preparation.... Moreover H.P.B. has already started on Vol. III."

(Source: *The Theosophist,* April 1891, p. 438.)

February 18, 1891—Countess Wachtmeister writes in a letter to W. Q. Judge:

> "When Volume 3 [of *The Secret Doctrine*] comes out this summer I expect there will be a fresh demand for the earlier [two published] volumes."

(Source: *Report of Proceedings, Secret Doctrine Centenary, October 29-30, 1988,* 1989, p. 86.)

March 27, 1891—Madame Blavatsky writes to W. Q. Judge:

> "...UNSELFISHNESS AND ALTRUISM is Annie Besant's name, but with me and for me, she is Heliodore, a name given to her by a Master, and that I use with her, it has a *deep*

meaning. It is only a few months she studies occultism with me in the *innermost* group of the E.S. and yet she has passed far beyond all the others. She is not psychic nor spiritual in the least—all intellect, and yet she hears Master's voice when alone, sees His Light, and recognizes his voice from that of *D——*. Judge, *she is a most wonderful woman*, my right hand, my successor, when I will be forced to leave you, my sole hope in England, as you are my sole hope in America."

(Source: Countess Constance Wachtmeister's *H.P.B. and the Present Crisis in the Theosophical Society*, p. 4.)

April, 1891—In her own London journal *Lucifer,* H.P.B. tells the readers in the April 1891 issue about her current work on the *forthcoming* third volume of *The Secret Doctrine*:

"Two years ago, the writer promised in *The Secret Doctrine*, Vol. II, p. 798, a third and even a fourth volume of that work. This third volume (now almost ready) treats of the ancient Mysteries of Initiation, gives sketches—from the esoteric standpoint—of many of the most famous and historically known philosophers and hierophants (everyone of whom is set down by the Scientists as an *impostor*), from the archaic down to the Christian era, and traces the teachings of all these sages to one and the same source of all knowledge and science—the esoteric doctrine or WISDOM RELIGION.

"No need our saying that from the esoteric and legendary materials used in the forthcoming work, its statements and conclusions differ greatly and often clash irreconcilably with the data given by almost all the English and German Orientalists. . . ."

(Source: H.P.B.'s *Collected Writings,* Volume 13, p. 145.)

May 4, 1891—Annie Besant gives testimony in H.P.B.'s legal case against Elliott Coues and the New York *Sun*:

> "There is one other work of hers [H.P.B.'s], which I have seen in manuscript, still unpublished; a third volume of 'The Secret Doctrine' which is now being got ready for the press under my own eyes. Madame Blavatsky has also in preparation a glossary of Sanscrit and Eastern tongues; those are both in preparation; one of them is already in type and the other is nearly ready for type."

(Source: Michael Gomes, ed., *Witness for the Prosecution: Annie Besant's Testimony on Behalf of H. P. Blavatsky in the N. Y. Sun/Coues Law Case,* 1993, p. 23.)

May 8, 1891—H.P.B. dies in London. Laura Cooper writes about H.P.B.'s death:

> "About 11:30 I was aroused by Mr. Wright, who told me to come at once as H.P.B. had changed for the worse, and the nurse did not think she could live many hours; directly I entered her room I realised the critical condition she was in. She was sitting in her chair and I knelt in front of her and asked her to try and take the stimulant....The nurse said H.P.B. might linger some hours, but suddenly there was a further change, and when I tried to moisten her lips I saw the dear eyes were already becoming dim, though she retained full consciousness to the last. In life H.P.B. had a habit of moving one foot when she was thinking intently, and she continued that movement almost to the moment she ceased to breathe. When all hope was over the nurse left the room, leaving C. F. Wright, W. R. Old and myself with our beloved H.P.B.; the two former knelt in front, each holding one of her hands, and I at her side with one arm round her supported her head; thus we remained motionless for many minutes, and so quietly did H.P.B. pass away that we hardly knew the second she ceased to

breathe; a great sense of peace filled the room, and we knelt quietly there until, first my sister [Isabel Cooper-Oakley] then the Countess [Constance Wachtmeister] arrived. I had telegraphed to them and Dr. Mennell—when the nurse said the end was near, but they were not in time to see H.P.B. before she left us. No time was lost in vain regrets, we all tried to think and to do what she would have wished under the circumstances, and we could only be thankful she was released from her suffering."

(Source: Laura M. Cooper, "How She Left Us," *Lucifer*, June 1891, p. 271. Reprinted in *H.P.B.: In Memory of Helena Petrovna Blavatsky by Some of Her Pupils*, London, Theosophical Publishing Society, 1891, pp. 6-7.)

May 8, 1891 (soon after H.P.B. had died)—Countess Constance Wachtmeister writing later about this time testifies:

"...I...searched diligently and minutely for various articles belonging to H.P.B. after her death, thus obeying certain instructions given by her to me....H.P.B.'s property, which I had thus collected, I handed over to Annie Besant on her arrival in England from America....."

Isabel Cooper-Oakley and Laura Cooper added the following to Countess Wachtmeister's words:

"...We, with Mr. Mead, were present when Countess Wachtmeister made the search referred to, and after everything had been carefully examined, all cupboards, drawers and boxes were sealed up in our presence until Mrs. Besant's return...."

(Source: *Lucifer*, April 1895, p. 164.)

May 11, 1891—In an interview given in Australia shortly after Madame Blavatsky had died, Colonel Henry S. Olcott says the following about Madame Blavatsky and her writings to a reporter:

> ". . . she has just completed a glossary of Sanscrit and other Eastern terms for the use of theosophical students. At the time of her death she was engaged upon the third and fourth volumes of The Secret Doctrine. . . ."

(Source: *The Daily Telegraph* (Sydney, Australia), May 12, 1891, p. 5.)

August 1891—Annie Besant writing an editorial notice tells readers of *Lucifer*:

> "In the September issue, the first number of our new Volume—Volume IX—will appear a long and most interesting article from the pen of H. P. Blavatsky entitled, 'The Substantial Nature of Magnetism Demonstrated.' This will be succeeded by other papers from the MSS. left by her [H.P.B.] in my charge, so that *Lucifer*, her own Magazine, will be able for a considerable time to come to regard its Founder as being still its leading contributor."

(Source: *Lucifer*, August 1891, p. 528.)

October, 1891—Isabel Cooper-Oakley writes from London:

> "The H.P.B. Press...is developing into a regular printing office....A new edition of *The Secret Doctrine* is to lead the van, and last but not least the third volume is to be published. This last piece of news will be hailed with joy by all true students."

(Source: *The Path*, December 1891, p. 295.)

October 29, 1891—In a letter addressed to Bertram Keightley in India, Archibald Keightley writes:

> "There is some talk [at London T.S. headquarters] of entirely reprinting 'Secret Doctrine' [Volumes 1 & 2] and of correcting errors when the Third Volume is issued. The plates [of the older edition of the S.D.] are in many cases found to be faulty and the expense of casting is so great as to make this [revised reprinting] worth while...."

(Source: *The Messenger*, January, 1926, p. 166.)

November, 1891—In a notice about the work of the H.P.B. Press in London, readers of *Lucifer* are informed that:

> "...The first two volumes of *The Secret Doctrine* are practically out of print and a new and revised edition has to be at once put in hand. The third volume has also to be brought out...."

(Source: *Lucifer*, November, 1891, pp. 254-255.)

November, 1891—Readers of *Lucifer* are told:

> "IMPORTANT NOTICE: A Revised Edition of the 'Secret Doctrine'
>
> "The second edition of H.P.B.'s masterpiece being exhausted, a third edition has to be put in hand immediately. Every effort is being made to thoroughly revise the new edition, and the editors earnestly request all students who may read this notice to send in as full lists of 'errata' as possible. Verifications of references

and quotations, mis-spellings, errors of indexing, indication of obscure passages, &c., &c., will be most thankfully received. It is important that the 'errata' of the first part of Volume I should be sent in immediately.

ANNIE BESANT
G.R.S. MEAD"

(Source: *Lucifer*, November, 1891, p. 261.)

November 1891—Writing later about this time-period, James Pryse says the following concerning *The Secret Doctrine*, Vols. I and II:

"The first printing [in 1888] of the S.D. was divided into two 'editions,' which are therefore identical save for the words 'second edition' on the title-page. The printing was done from the type, but stereotype matrices were made in case another [edition] should be called for. When that time came [in late 1891], however, we found that the matrices had been accidentally destroyed; and I, for one, was decidedly pleased at their loss, since it made opportune a much needed revision of the text, which arduous labour was undertaken by Mr. Mead and Mrs. Besant. Joyfully I placed copies of the S.D. in the paper-cutter, trimmed off the edges, and had assistants paste the pages on large sheets of writing-paper, to afford wide margins for marking corrections. As Mrs. Besant could spare but little time from her other Theosophical activities, the work of revision was done mostly by Mr. Mead, who was assisted by other members of the staff in verifying quotations and references...."

(Source: "An Important Statement by Mr. J. M. Pryse," *The Canadian Theosophist*, Sept. 1926, pp. 140-141.)

November 13, 1891—Writing to Bertram Keightley in India, G.R.S. Mead says:

> "We find it will be cheaper to reprint it [*The Secret Doctrine*, Volumes 1 & 2] entirely. The moulds [of the older edition of the S.D.] are practically useless . . . ."

(Source: *The Messenger,* January, 1926, p. 166.)

November 27, 1891—G.R.S. Mead writes in a report titled "European Section" and dated "London, Nov. 27, 1891":

> ". . . a revised edition of the latter work [*The Secret Doctrine*, Volumes I and II] is now in the press, and the third volume [of the S.D.] will be undertaken immediately on the completion of the new edition [of S.D. Vols. I & II]."

(Source: *Report of the Sixteenth Convention and Anniversary of the Theosophical Society,* the Head-Quarters, Adyar, Madras, December the 27th, 28th, and 29th, 1891 with Official Documents, p. 36. This report is attached to the Jan. 1892 issue of *The Theosophist.*)

1894

January, 1894—Readers of *Lucifer* are told the following:

> "...The year 1894 also sees the publication of the new edition of H. P. Blavatsky's great work, *The Secret Doctrine* [volumes I & II], revised with much labour and care, and rendered doubly valuable by the addition of an exhaustive index of perhaps a hundred thousand words....the third volume of *The Secret Doctrine* is [now] being type-written from the MS."

(Source: *Lucifer*, January, 1894, p. 354. This quote occurs in the lead article/editorial titled "On the Watch-Tower." Probably written by G. R. S. Mead.)

January, 1894—A notice appears in *The Path*:

"Volume one of the new edition of *The Secret Doctrine* is now ready, and a copy has been sent, charges paid, to all subscribers.... Volume two, it is now thought, can be sent out in January."

(Source: *The Path*, January, 1894, p. 323.)

January 1894—Writing later about this time-period, James Pryse says the following concerning Volume Three of *The Secret Doctrine*:

"When I had finished printing vols. I and II. Mrs. Besant placed the manuscript of vol. iii. in my hands. After reading it, I gave it to my brother John to make a typewritten copy, which he did. It was in an unfinished state, and badly arranged. H.P.B. had rewritten some of the pages several times, with erasures and changes, but with nothing to indicate which copy was the final revision; Mrs. Besant had to decide that as best she might...."

(Source: "An Important Statement by Mr. J. M. Pryse," *The Canadian Theosophist*, Sept. 1926, pp. 140-141.)

1895

May, 1895—Annie Besant writes in *Lucifer* (p. 188):

"The third volume of *The Secret Doctrine* . . . was placed into my hands by H.P.B."

June, 1895—The first pages of Volume III of *The Secret Doctrine* were sent to the printer.

(Source: *Lucifer,* June 1895, p. 271.)

1896

June, 1896—An editorial note appears in *Lucifer* (p. 265):

> "In the course of preparing the third volume of *The Secret Doctrine* for the press, a few manuscripts were found mixed with it that form no part of the work itself, and these will be published in [*Lucifer*]...."

September, 1896—Volume III of *The Secret Doctrine* was completed.

(Source: *Lucifer,* September 1896, p. 271.)

1897

June, 1897—Volume III of *The Secret Doctrine* is published in London. Mrs. Besant wrote in the Preface to this third volume:

> "This volume completes the papers left by H.P.B., with the exception of a few scattered articles that yet remain and that will be published in her own magazine *Lucifer.*"

(Source: *The Theosophist,* September 1897, p. 766.)

The Secret Doctrine Würzburg Manuscript

The Myth of the "Missing" Third Volume of *The Secret Doctrine*

by Daniel H. Caldwell

Part 1

INTRODUCTION

In 1897, Annie Besant published what she called the third volume of *The Secret Doctrine,* which had been announced by H. P. Blavatsky but left unpublished during the author's life. Received opinion at the present time is that what Besant published was not Blavatsky's third volume, but instead something assembled out of various documents left by HPB.

Some examples of the received opinion are as follows:

A spurious 'Third Volume' . . . [was] issued in 1897, six years after the death of H. P. Blavatsky. Compiled from miscellaneous papers found among her effects, this volume forms no part of the original SECRET DOCTRINE written by H.P.B. [Publishers' preface (1947) to the facsimile reprint of the 1888 edition of *The Secret Doctrine* by The Theosophy Company, Los Angeles, California.]

Volume III of The Secret Doctrine. . .was published in London in 1897 with a preface written by Annie Besant. It should be understood, however, that this volume is not *the* third volume contemplated by H.P.B. [Geoffrey A. Barborka, *H. P. Blavatsky, Tibet and Tulku,* 159]

The *real* Volume III...vanished without a trace. [Boris de Zirkoff in H.P.B.'s *Collected Writings,* 7: 226 fn]

The prospective Volume III...never saw the light. [de Zirkoff in SD 1: 679 (*Collected Writings* edition)]

It is possible that H.P.B. had in mind an additional [third] volume of *The Secret Doctrine* which was never actually found among her papers. [de Zirkoff in CW 14: 1]

In volume 1, Blavatsky had promised a third volume and projected a fourth. That promise was repeated at the end of volume 2.... There was some material left over from volume I as she had originally conceived it . . . but relatively little seems to have been actually written down....When Annie Besant tried to find the unpublished material, she was able to locate very little that seemed to belong to what HPB had intended for the continuation of the book. The little which Besant found, she combined with some instructions Blavatsky had written for members of the Esoteric Section...and that material, admittedly a hodgepodge, was published...as the "third volume" of HPB's work. The "third volume" undoubtedly contains some material—that on the lives of famous occultists—which had been rejected from the first volume of the original work. But it also contained a good deal of material which certainly was never intended to be a part of *The Secret Doctrine.* [John Algeo, *Getting Acquainted with The Secret Doctrine: A Study Course,* 1990 ed., 23-4]

H. N. Stokes, editor of *The O. E. Library Critic* (Washington, D.C.), held the view that the real Volume III manuscripts vanished and were never published. He wrote about seventeen articles analyzing the evidence concerning the Volume III manuscripts.

To the list of those holding similar views, we can add many other distinguished names: Alice Cleather, Basil Crump, Charles J. Ryan, Victor Endersby, Walter A. Carrithers, Jr., Kirby Van Mater, Ted G. Davy, Richard Robb, Dara Eklund, and several more.

This received view was also my initial opinion. But after a great deal of study of the Wurzburg MSS of *The Secret Doctrine* and all the other relevant primary source documents (1886-1897) on the subject, I am no longer certain that the Theosophical writers mentioned above are correct in their views concerning Volume III.

In fact, I am inclined to believe that pages 1-430 of Volume III of *The Secret Doctrine* published in 1897 was the real third volume intended by HPB. (Pages 433-594 of that published volume consist of H. P. Blavatsky's esoteric teachings given to members of her Esoteric Section or School during the years 1889-1891 and are not at issue.) The evidence and reasoning to support this position follow.

Part 2

MANUSCRIPT VOLUME ONE
AND THE WURZBURG MANUSCRIPT

Writing only six years after the events he describes, Bertram Keightley tells us that upon her arrival in London in May, 1887, Madame Blavatsky "placed the whole of the so far completed MSS. [of The Secret Doctrine] in the hands of Dr. [Archibald] Keightley and myself....We both read the whole mass of MSS.—a pile over three feet high—most carefully through" (in *Reminiscences of H. P. Blavatsky and The Secret Doctrine*, by Countess Constance Wachtmeister et al., Quest edition, 1976, p. 78; also cited in Boris de Zirkoff's "Historical Introduction" to *The Secret Doctrine*, "Collected Writings" edition, I, 41).

Bertram goes on to say that this original manuscript was divided into three parts or volumes:

- Volume I: History of some great Occultists
- Volume II: Evolution of Cosmos
- Volume III: Evolution of Man

Bertram's reference to "the whole of the so-far completed MSS." is, of course, to the original Secret Doctrine manuscript, written during the period 1884 through April, 1887, which was in HPB's own handwriting.

What were the arrangement and contents of Volume I—the volume dealing with the history of some great occultists, which Bertram and Archibald Keightley read in May, 1887?

In a letter dated September 23, 1886 (only eight months before the Keightleys read the three volumes in London), HPB wrote to Colonel Henry S. Olcott:

I send you the MSS. of *Secret Doctrine*.....Now I send only 1*st* volume of *Introduct.* Section.... There are in the 1st *Introductory Vol. Seven Sections or* Chapt. § and 27 Appendices, several App. attached to every Section from 1 to 6, etc. Now all this will make either more or at any rate one volume and it is not the S.D. but a Preface to it.... Now, it is so arranged that the Appendices can either go as attached to the Sections or be taken out and placed in a *separate Vol.* or at the end of each.... If you take out the App. then there will not [be] 300 pages printed in Int. Sections, but they will lose in interest. [quoted in de Zirkoff, *SD* Intro., 30-1]

This manuscript to be sent to Colonel Olcott was *not* the original manuscript in HPB's own handwriting but a copy made by Countess Constance Wachtmeister and Mrs. Mary Gebhard. This "1st volume" manuscript is part of the "Wurzburg Manuscript" now preserved in the Archives of the Theosophical Society, Adyar, Madras, India.

(For those interested in the Wurzburg Manuscript, most of Volume I of the manuscript was published serially in the pages of *The Theosophist* August 1931 and October 1932 to November, 1933; vol.52, pt.2, pp. 601-7; vol.54, pt. l, pp. 27-36, 140-50, 265-71, 397-401, 538-42, 623-8, and pt. 2, pp. 9-14, 137-43, 263-6, 391-5, 505-9, 633-7; vol. 55, pt. 1, pp. 12-6, 143-6. Also consult the index to CW XIV for more excerpts from the manuscript. The Stanzas of Dzyan as found in Volume II of this manuscript have been published as the "Stanzas in the Wurzburg Manuscript," pp. 514-20 in Volume III of *The Secret Doctrine*, the "Collected Writings" edition, Adyar, 1978; Wheaton, 1993. Also see p. 34 in de Zirkoff's "Historical Introduction" to the *S.D.* for a facsimile of a page from the Wurzburg Manuscript. This page gives one of the Stanzas of Dzyan. Microfilm copies of the "Wurzburg Manuscript" exist; I have consulted the microfilm while researching this subject.)

Volume I of the Wurzburg Manuscript consists of only five sections and one appendix. See the accompanying Table for the contents of Volume I of the Wurzburg Manuscript. HPB's letter to Olcott (quoted above) indicates that the extant Wurzburg Manuscript is incomplete and probably represents only a third of the original first volume of *The Secret Doctrine*.

How does HPB describe the subject matter of her original Volume I? In her letter of July 14, 1886, to Olcott, she gives the following information:

Now I will send to *your care* and on *your* responsibility the *"Preface* to the Reader" and the 1st chapter of the *Secret Doctrine* proper. There are 600 pages and more of foolscap as an Introductory Preliminary Book, showing the undeniable historically proven facts of the existence of Adepts before and after the Christian period, of the admission of a double esoteric meaning in the two Testaments by Church Fathers, and *proofs* that the real source of every Christian dogma rests in the Aryan oldest MYSTERIES during the Vedic and Brahmanic period, proofs and evidence for it. In a fortnight I will send you the Preface and 1st Chapter. [quoted in de Zirkoff, *SD* Intro., 28-9]

In this letter, HPB is describing not only the contents of the original first volume of *The Secret Doctrine* but also the contents of the extant Wurzburg Manuscript. As early as March 3, 1886, in a letter to A. P. Sinnett, HPB described the contents of this same first volume of *The Secret Doctrine*:

I have finished an enormous Introductory Chapter, or *Preamble,* Prologue, call it what you will; just to show the reader that the text as it goes, every Section beginning with a page of translation from the Book of *Dzyan* and the Secret Book of "Maitreya Buddha" *Champai chhos Nga* (in prose, not the five books in verse known, which are a blind) are no fiction.

I was ordered to do so, to make a rapid sketch of what *was* known historically and in literature, in classics and in profane and sacred histories—during the 500 years that preceded the Christian period and the 500 y. that followed it: of *magic,* the existence of a Universal Secret Doctrine known to the philosophers and Initiates of every country and even to several of the Church fathers such as Clement of Alexandria, Origen and others, who had been initiated themselves.

Also to describe the Mysteries and some notes; and I can assure you that most extraordinary things are given out now, the whole story of the Crucifixion, etc. being shown to be based on a rite as old as the world—the Crucifixion on the *Lathe* of the Candidate—trials, going down to Hell etc., all Aryan.

The whole story hitherto unnoticed by Orientalists is found even exoterically, in the Puranas and *Brahmanas,* and then explained and supplemented with what the *Esoteric* explanations give. [*Letters of H.P. Blavatsky to A. P. Sinnett,* ed. A. T. Barker, 195; also cited by de Zirkoff in *SD* Intro., 26]

Boris de Zirkoff and Geoffrey Barborka (SD Intro., 68-70) believe that this March letter describes material no longer extant. There are reasons for a contrary view. De Zirkoff (69) says that HPB in her letter of March 3 describes "an enormous Introductory Chapter" and that "every Section thereof is said to begin with 'a page of translation from the Book of Dzyan.'" This, I believe, is a mistaken interpretation of what HPB wrote and was quoted just above:

> I have finished an enormous Introductory Chapter, or *Preamble*, Prologue, call it what you will; just to show the reader that the text as it goes, every Section beginning with a page of translation from the Book of *Dzyan* and the Secret Book of "Maitreya Buddha" *Champai chhos Nga* (in prose, not the five books in verse known, which are a blind) are no fiction.

The key to understanding this passage is the phrase "the text as it goes," which refers, I believe, to the main text in the second volume of *The Secret Doctrine* (dealing with cosmogony), in which every section begins with a page of translation from the Book of Dzyan. In other words, HPB had written an enormous "Introductory Preliminary Book," "Introductory Chapter, or preamble, prologue, call it what you will" (Volume I) in order to show the reader that the main text in Volume II on cosmogony was "no fiction." Then HPB goes on to explain what was in that original first volume: "I was ordered ... to make a rapid sketch of what was known."

Boris de Zirkoff (in SD Intro., 69) says Geoffrey Barborka points out that HPB's "Prologue" is not the "Introductory" (or any other section) in Volume I of *The Secret Doctrine* as published in 1888. That is true. But what is HPB referring to in her letter? Missing text no longer extant? No, what she is talking about is Volume I of the *Secret Doctrine* manuscript (as described in her letters of 1886, as partially found in the extant Wurzburg Manuscript, and as read by the Keightleys in May 1887). Boris de Zirkoff continues:

It is also important to remember that H.P.B.'s description of this material in her letter to Sinnett does not tally with any of the miscellaneous material gathered together and published in 1897 under the rather misleading title of 'Secret Doctrine, Volume III.'

However, as far as I can ascertain, HPB's description to Sinnett of her "enormous Introductory Chapter" does tally quite well, not only with the 1897 volume, but also with the contents of Volume I of the Wurzburg Manuscript. For example, "the Crucifixion on the Lathe of the Candidate" is covered in the Wurzburg Manuscript [CW 14: 261-2, "The Trial of the Sun Initiate"]. The "lathe" was also specifically mentioned in Volume III, published in 1897, but those pages also contain a gap in the manuscript. Annie Besant says: "There is a gap in H.P.B.'s MS." (Vol. III, 1897 ed., 272). L. H. Leslie-Smith later provided the missing part from the Wurzburg Manuscript [Quest edition of Vol. III, titled *Esoteric Writings*, 466-7]. But what happened to the original page in HPB's handwriting that was missing from the 1897 volume and constituted "a gap"? I suggest that this page somehow got disconnected from the manuscript of the third volume but was found and published as a "Fragment" in *Lucifer*, August 1896 [CW 7: 275-6]. Also the "whole story of the Crucifixion, etc., being shown to be based on a rite as old as the world-the Crucifixion on the *Lathe* of the Candidate-trials, going down to Hell etc.," about which HPB wrote in her letter to Sinnett, is also covered in the 1888 *Secret Doctrine* 1: 543, 559, 558, 560-2.

Therefore, HPB's description of an "enormous Introductory Volume" does not indicate "lost material," as de Zirkoff and Barborka believed. Instead, HPB's description is of her original Volume I manuscript. The same material can be found in Volume I of the Wurzburg Manuscript and in Volume III of 1897.

So far we have determined, based upon HPB's own words, that the original first volume consisted of seven sections and twenty-seven appendices. We have also estimated that the extant Volume I of the Wurzburg Manuscript gives us the text of approximately one-third of the original Volume I that the Keightleys read in May, 1887. Can we determine the contents of the rest of this Volume I?

Following is a partial list of material not extant in the Wurzburg Manuscript but probably to be found in the original Volume I manuscript in HPB's own hand-writing:

1. In *CW* 14: 342, HPB wrote: "turn to the 'Appendix' of this INTRODUCTION and read On Jesuits and their Policy." The *Collected Writings* editors have added a footnote: "Untraced under this title. Possibly re-titled Theosophy or Jesuitism?; see *B.C.W.*, IX."

2. In *CW* 7: 190, HPB wrote: "explained in our Appendices on 'Egyptian Magic' and 'Chinese Spirits' (*Secret Doctrine*)." The *Collected Writings* has two contradictory editorial notes on these two articles (7: 104 and 190-91).

3. In *CW* 7: 226, HPB says: "I have tried to explain and have given the collective and individual opinions thereon of the great philosophers of antiquity in my *Secret Doctrine*." In an editorial note, de Zirkoff says: "By turning to pages 234-240 of the Volume [III] published in 1897. . . the student will find a brief essay on 'The Idols and the Teraphim.'" That essay is precisely the material spoken of by HPB in her comment just quoted.

4. In Volume II of the Wurzburg Manuscript, dealing with the Stanzas of Dzyan and HPB's commentaries thereon, the following reference is found: "(See 'A Mystery about Buddha,' App. to Sect. VI.)" I interpret this to mean that the article "A Mystery about Buddha" was an appendix to section six of the first volume of the Secret Doctrine manuscript of 1886-1887. The original Volume II (dealing with the Seven Stanzas of Dzyan and HPB's commentaries) had numerous appendices, at least seventeen, if not more. These appendices are not extant in the Wurzburg Manuscript but are referred to by HPB in the course of her commentaries. For example HPB wrote: "See Divine Dynasties, App. XII" or "App. VII, 'Primordial Substance'," and so on.

5. Another reference to the contents of the original Volume I is possibly made in Volume II of the Wurzburg Manuscript, where HPB refers to "App. In Prel. Sect. 'Kuan-Shai-Yin'."

All these references give us some indication as to what additional material was in the original Volume I of the Secret Doctrine (1886-1887).

Contents of *The Wurzburg Manuscript, Volume One* Introduction			
CONTENTS OF THE WURZBURG MANUSCRIPT		MS PAGES	PUBLISHED VERSIONS	SD VOLUME III (1897)
To the Readers Chapter I		3-23	*Theosophist*, Aug. 1931, 601-7; CW 14: 462-9	
On Eastern and Western Occult Literature Section I	1. Explanations of the 1st Page of *Isis Unveiled*	25-41	*Theo*, Oct. 1932, 27-36	
	2. Hermetic and Other Books of Antiquity	41-61	*Theo*, Nov. 1932. 140-50	Sec. 2, p. 30; Sec. 3, pp. 36-8. 39 43
Section II	1. White and Black Magic in Theory and Practice	63-73	*Theo*, Dec. 1932, 265-71	Sec. 6, pp. 67-72, 74-5
	2. Hermes and the 32 Ways of Wisdom	73-93	*Theo*, Jan. 1933, 397-401; *Theo*, Feb. 1933, 538-	Sec. 9, pp. 91, 47, 48, 92,

			42; 93- 6 *Theo*, Mar. 1933, 623-4	
Section III	1. Mathematics and Geometry—The Keys to the Universal Problems	95-101	*Theo*, Mar. 1933, 625-7	Sec. 10, pp. 98-104
	2. The Key of the Absolute in Magic—the Hexagon with the Central Point—or the Seventh Key	101-11	*Theo*, Mar. 1933, 628; *Theo*, Apr. 1933, 9-14	Sec. 11, pp. 105-8
Section IV	1. Who Was the Adept of Tyana?	115-23	*Theo*, May 1933, 138-42	Sec. 17, pp. 129-32
	2. The Roman Church Dreads the Publication of the Real Life of Apollonius	123-33	*Theo*, May 1933, 142-3; *Theo*, June 1933, 263-6	Sec. 17, pp. 133-7

Section V	1. Confession and Property in Common	135-59	*Theo,* July 1933, 391-5; *Theo,* Aug. 1933, 505-9; *Theo,* Sep. 1933, 633-7; *Theo,* Oct. 1933, 12-4	Sec. 35, pp. 315-24
	2. What the Occultists and Kabalists Have to Say	159-69	*Theo,* Oct. 1933, 14-6; *Theo,* Nov. 1933, 143-6	Sec. 23, pp. 211-4
	3. The Souls of the Stars— Universal Heliolatry	169-93	CW 14: 33-43	Sec. 37, pp. 332-6
	4. The Mystery "Sun of Initiation"	194-201	CW 14: 269-73	Sec. 30, pp. 277-80
	5. The Trial of the Sun-Initiate	201-23	CW 14: 259-68	Sec. 29, pp. 270-6
Appendix I	The Star-Angel Worship in the Roman Church, Its Re-Establishment, Growth and History	225-41	CW 10: 13-32	

> [Also consult Blavatsky's *CW*, XIV, 471-72, especially the latter page for an outline of the contents of "Volume Two" of the Wurzburg manuscript.]

Part 3

MANUSCRIPT VOLUME ONE BECOMES VOLUME THREE

Returning to Bertram Keightley's account of the editing of *The Secret Doctrine,* he wrote:

> A day or two after our arrival at Maycot [in May, 1887], H.P.B. placed the whole of the so far completed MSS. in the hands of Dr. [Archibald] Keightley and myself....We both read the whole mass of MSS.—a pile over three feet high—most carefully...and then, after prolonged consultation, faced [HPB]...with the solemn opinion that the whole of the matter must be rearranged on some definite plan....
> Finally we laid before her a plan, suggested by the character of the matter itself, viz., to make the work consist of four volumes....
> Further, instead of making the first volume to consist, as she had intended, of the history of some great Occultists, we advised her to follow the natural order of exposition, and begin with the Evolution of Cosmos, to pass from that to the Evolution of Man, then to deal with the historical part in a third volume treating of the lives of some great Occultists; and finally, to speak of Practical Occultism in a fourth volume should she ever be able to write it.
> This plan was laid before H.P.B., and it was duly sanctioned by her.
> The next step was to read the MSS. through again and make a general rearrangement of the matter pertaining to the subjects coming under the heads of Cosmogony and Anthropology, which were to form the first two volumes of the work. When this had been completed, and H.P.B. duly consulted, and her approval of what had been done obtained, the whole of the MSS. so arranged was typewritten out by professional hands.... [in *Reminiscences of H. P. Blavatsky and The Secret Doctrine,* by Countess Constance Wachtmeister et al., Quest edition, 1976, pp. 78-9; also quoted in de Zirkoff, *SD* Intro., 41]

So as Bertram Keightley tells us, the order of the volumes of *The Secret Doctrine* was rearranged. *Volume I became Volume III.*

Were the contents of the new and unpublished Volume III kept completely intact? No. For example, HPB decided to take out one of the appendices ("Star-Angel Worship in the Roman Church") and publish it as an article in *Lucifer (CW* 10: 13-32). Another example: The appendix entitled "Kuan-Shai-Yin" was apparently taken out and published in Volume I of 1888, pp. 470-3. Some other portions of the re-ordered third volume were also incorporated into Volume I as published in 1888: Part of the section "To the Readers" and part of "Explanations of the 1st Page of *Isis Unveiled*" (see the Table for the contents of Vol. 1) were incorporated into the "Introductory" (xvii-xxi and xii-xlvii) of the published Volume I of 1888. But by and large the material that was in Volume I of the original Secret Doctrine manuscript of 1886-1887 remained in the manuscript of what became Volume III.

Part 4

THE THIRD VOLUME FROM 1888 TO HPB'S DEATH

We can now trace the history of the third volume from 1888 to HPB's death in 1891 by citing various published documents.

April 3, 1888—HPB wrote to the Second American T.S. Convention:

The MSS. of the first three volumes is now ready for the press. (CW 9: 247).

1888—HPB wrote about the third volume in Volumes I and II of *The Secret Doctrine* (1888):

Even the two volumes now issued do not complete the scheme, and these do not treat exhaustively of the subjects dealt with in them. A large quantity of material has already been prepared, dealing with the history of occultism as contained in the lives of the great Adepts of the Aryan Race, and showing the bearing of occult philosophy upon the conduct of life, as it is and as it ought to be. Should the present volumes meet with a favourable reception, no effort will be spared to carry out the scheme of the work in its entirety. The third volume is entirely ready; the fourth almost so. [1: vii]

But if the reader has patience, and would glance at the present state of beliefs and creeds in Europe, compare and check it with what is known to history of the ages directly preceding and following the Christian era, then he will find all this in Volume III. of this work.
      In that volume a brief recapitulation will be made of all the principal adepts known to history, and the downfall of the mysteries will be described; after which began the disappearance and final and systematic elimination from the memory of men of the real nature of initiation and the Sacred Science. From that time its teachings became Occult and Magic sailed but too often under the venerable but frequently misleading name of Hermetic philosophy. As real Occultism had been prevalent among the Mystics during the centuries that preceded our era, so Magic, or rather Sorcery, with its Occult Arts, followed the beginning of Christianity. [1: xxxix-xl]

Read by the light of the Zohar, the initial four chapters of Genesis are the fragment of a highly philosophical page in the World's Cosmogony. (*See* Book III., "*Gupta Vidya and the Zohar*") [1: 10-1]

The explanation with regard to the "Anupadaka" given in the Kala Chakra, the first in the Gyu(t) division of the Kanjur, is half esoteric. It has misled the Orientalists into erroneous speculations with respect to the Dhyani-Buddhas and their earthly correspondencies, the Manushi-Buddhas. The real tenet is hinted at in a subsequent Volume, (see "The Mystery about Buddha"), and will be more fully explained in its proper place. [1: 52n]

Therefore the meaning of the "fairy tale" translated by Chwolson from an old Chaldean MSS. translated into Arabic, about Qu-tamy being instructed by the *idol* of the moon, is easily understood (*vide* Book III.) Seldenus tells us the secret as well as Maimonides.... The worshipers of the *Teraphim* (the Jewish Oracles) "carved images and claimed that the light of the principal stars (planets) permeating these through and through, the angelic VIRTUES (or the regents of the stars and planets) conversed with them, teaching them many most useful things and arts." [1: 394]

If one studies comparative Theogony, it is easy to find that the secret of these "Fires" was taught in the *Mysteries* of every ancient people, pre-eminently in Samothrace.... There is no space to describe these "fires" and their real meaning here, though we may attempt to do so if the third and fourth volumes of this work are ever published. [2: 106]

In Volume III. of this work (the said volume and the IVth being almost ready) a brief history of all the great adepts known to the ancients and the moderns in their chronological order will be given, as also a bird's eye view of the Mysteries, their birth, growth, decay, and final death—in Europe. This could not find room in the present work. Volume IV will be almost entirely devoted to Occult teachings. [2: 437]

These two volumes should form for the student a fitting prelude for Volumes III. and IV. Until the rubbish of the ages is cleared away from the minds of the Theosophists to whom these volumes are dedicated, it is impossible that the more practical teaching contained in the Third Volume should be understood.

Consequently, it entirely depends upon the reception with which Volumes I. and II. will meet at the hands of Theosophists and Mystics, whether these last two volumes will ever be published, though they are *almost* completed. [2: 797-8]

These descriptions by HPB of what was in the unpublished Volume III of *The Secret Doctrine* correspond fairly well with what she says in her letters of 1886 in describing the original volume I.

April 29, 1889—Archibald Keightley was quoted in an interview in the *New York Times,* p. 5:

The third volume of 'The Secret Doctrine' is in manuscript ready to be given to the printers. It will consist mainly of a series of sketches of the great occultists of all ages, and is a most wonderful and fascinating work. The fourth volume, which is to be largely hints on the subject of practical occultism, has been outlined, but not yet written....

November 21, 1889—HPB wrote in a letter to N. D. Khandalavala (*Theosophist,* August 1932, 626):

[I] have been able to write my *S.D.,* "Key," "Voice," and prepared two more volumes of the S. Doctrine.

February 1890—HPB wrote in a letter to her sister Vera (*Path,* December 1895, 268):

I must put the third volume of the *[Secret] Doctrine* in order, and the fourth—hardly begun yet, too.

December 1890—A report (*Theosophist,* July 1891, 586-7) of Bertram Keightley's lecture "Theosophy in the West" to the annual T.S. convention at Adyar, Madras, India, included the following:

H.P.B. handed over to him [B. Keightley] the manuscript of the "Secret Doctrine," with a request that he should read it through. He read through the substance of the two volumes published, and the third still unpublished....what would now be the 3rd volume of the history of Occultism was to have been the first volume, while the treatises on Cosmogony and the Genesis of Man were to form a later series....He then drafted a scheme with the natural and obvious order, namely, the Evolution of the Universe and the Evolution of man, &c. &c. The next thing...was to rearrange...the manuscript according to the [new] scheme.

January 7, 1891—Claude Falls Wright wrote (*Path,* February 1891, 354):

H.P.B. has within the last week or so begun to get together the MSS. (long ago written) for the Third Volume of *The Secret Doctrine*; it will however, take a good twelve months to prepare for publication.

February 1891—Alice Leighton Cleather wrote (*Theosophist,* April 1891, 438):

H.P.B. has already started on Vol. III.

February 18, 1891—Countess Wachtmeister wrote in a letter to W. Q. Judge (cited in *Report of Proceedings, Secret Doctrine Centenary, October 29-30,* 1988, 1989, 86):

When Volume 3 [of *The Secret Doctrine*] comes out this summer I expect there will be a fresh demand for the earlier [two] volumes.

April 1891—HPB wrote in *Lucifer* (*CW* 13: 145-6):

Two years ago, the writer promised in *The Secret Doctrine,* Vol. II, p. 798, a third and even a fourth volume of that work. This third volume (now almost ready) treats of the ancient Mysteries of Initiation, gives sketches—from the esoteric standpoint—of many of the most famous and historically known philosophers and hierophants (everyone of whom is set down by the Scientists as an *impostor*), from the archaic down to the Christian era, and traces the teachings of all these sages to one and the same source of all knowledge and science—the esoteric doctrine or WISDOM RELIGION. No need our saying that from the esoteric and legendary materials used in the forthcoming work, its statements and conclusions differ greatly and often clash irreconcilably with the data given by almost all the English and German Orientalists....Now the main point of Volume III of *The Secret Doctrine* is to prove, by tracing and explaining the *blinds* in the works of ancient Indian, Greek, and other philosophers of note, and also in all the ancient Scriptures—the presence of an uninterrupted esoteric allegorical method and symbolism; to show, as far as lawful, that with the keys of interpretation as taught in the Eastern Hindoo-Buddhistic Canon of Occultism, the *Upanishads,* the *Puranas,* the *Sutras,* the Epic poems of India and Greece, the Egyptian *Book of the Dead,* the Scandinavian *Eddas,* as well as the Hebrew *Bible,* and even the classical writings of Initiates (such as Plato, among others)—all, from first to last, yield a meaning quite different from their dead letter texts.

May 4, 1891—Annie Besant gave testimony in HPB's case against Elliott Coues and the New York *Sun* (Michael Gomes, ed., *Witness for the Prosecution: Annie Besant's Testimony on Behalf of H. P. Blavatsky in the N. Y. Sun/Coues Law Case,* 1993, 23):

There is one other work of hers [HPB's], which I have seen in manuscript, still unpublished; a third volume of "The Secret Doctrine" which is now being got ready for the press under my own eyes. Madame Blavatsky has also in preparation a glossary of Sanscrit and Eastern tongues; those are both in preparation; one of them is already in type and the other is nearly ready for type.

May 8, 1891—H. P. Blavatsky died in London.

From the above 1890-1891 statements (either written by HPB herself or by her London students) a reasonable conclusion can be drawn that HPB had finally decided to publish the third volume of *The Secret Doctrine* and was, in fact, working on the third volume manuscript during the months preceding her death.

In light of this conclusion, it is difficult to understand what Boris de Zirkoff meant when he wrote (in *SD* Intro., 71) that "no outright positive or negative answer can be made to the oft-repeated question whether a completed Manuscript of Volumes III and IV ever existed."

Setting aside de Zirkoff's reference to Volume IV, there is no reason to doubt that a manuscript of Volume III existed during the last years of HPB's life. Furthermore, had she lived, HPB would probably have added and deleted material from the manuscript; she would probably have rewritten and reedited the material even more. But at the time of her death, this manuscript was as "complete" as HPB could make it. What more could be expected?

In the twentieth century, many Blavatsky students have chosen to believe that the real unpublished Volume III manuscript of 1887-1891 (the former Volume I of 1886-1887) somehow vanished. Some have suggested that the manuscript was either destroyed by HPB before her death, or—after HPB's death—suppressed by Besant, "dematerialized" by the Masters, or otherwise disappeared.

Part 5

THE THIRD VOLUME FROM HPB'S DEATH TO 1897

Let us now follow the history of the third volume of *The Secret Doctrine* from May 1891 to its publication in June-July 1897.

October 1891—Isabel Cooper-Oakley wrote (*Path,* December 1891, 295):

The H.P.B. Press...is developing into a regular printing office....A new edition of *The Secret Doctrine* is to lead the van, and last but not least the third volume is to be published.

October 29, 1891—Dr. Archibald Keightley wrote in a letter to Bertram Keightley (cited by C. Jinarajadasa in "Dr. Besant and Mutilation of the Secret Doctrine," *Messenger,* January 1926, 166):

There is some talk of entirely reprinting *Secret Doctrine* [Volumes I and II] and of correcting errors when the Third Volume is issued.

December 1891—A notice was published in *The Path, The Vahan,* and *The Theosophist* by Annie Besant and G. R. S. Mead:

The second edition of H.P.B.'s masterpiece being exhausted, a third edition has to be put in hand immediately. Every effort is being made to thoroughly revise the new edition, and the editors earnestly request all students who may read this notice to send in as full lists of ERRATA as possible....It is important that the ERRATA of the first part of Volume I should be sent in IMMEDIATELY.

January 1894—A notice appeared in *The Path* (323):

Volume one of the new edition of *The Secret Doctrine* is now ready, and a copy has been sent, charges paid, to all subscribers....Volume two, it is now thought, can be sent out in January.

January 1894—A statement was published in *Lucifer* (354):

The third volume of *The Secret Doctrine* is being typewritten from the MS.

May 1895—Annie Besant wrote in *Lucifer* (188):

The third volume of *The Secret Doctrine*...was placed into my hands by H.P.B.

June 1895—The first pages of Volume III went to the printer (*Lucifer,* June 1895, 271).

June 1896—An editorial note appeared in *Lucifer* (265):

In the course of preparing the third volume of *The Secret Doctrine* for the press, a few manuscripts were found mixed with it that form no part of the work itself, and these will be published in *[Lucifer]*....

September 1896—Volume III was completed (*Lucifer,* September 1896, 271).

June 1897—Volume III of *The Secret Doctrine* was published (*Theosophist,* September 1897, 766).

Part 6

CONCLUSIONS AND REFLECTIONS

Is Volume III of *The Secret Doctrine* as published in 1897 the same (more or less) as the manuscript originally known as Volume I in 1886-1887 and later reordered and known as Volume III from 1887 to 1891?

A most telling piece of information to help us answer this question concerns the extant Volume I of the Wurzburg Manuscript.

Most of the material in this extant Volume I is also to be found in Volume III of 1897. And the material from Volume I of the Wurzburg Manuscript left out of Volume III of 1897 either was incorporated into Volume I of *The Secret Doctrine* as published in 1888 or was published in the pages of *Lucifer* during HPB's lifetime or soon after her death.

Furthermore, since it was discovered from primary source documents of 1886 that the original Volume I contained the articles "Egyptian Magic," "The Idol and the Teraphim," and "A Mystery About Buddha," is it not of some significance that these three articles also turn up in Volume III of 1897?

But what happened to the two sections of essays and twenty-six appendices (missing in the extant Wurzburg Manuscript) but certainly an integral part of HPB's original Volume I manuscript of 1886-1887?

If most of the extant Volume I Wurzburg Manuscript ended up in Volume III of 1897, is it not reasonable to suggest that the remaining two sections and twenty-six appendices (with several exceptions) probably also ended up in Volume III of 1897?

Also consider the following fact. Both H. P. Blavatsky and Bertram Keightley described the third volume as dealing with the lives of great occultists. A considerable amount of material in Volume III of 1897 deals with the lives of Simon Magus, St. Paul, Peter, Apollonius of Tyana, St. Cyprian of Antioch, Gautama the Buddha, and Tsong-kha-pa. And one of the essays in Volume III of 1897 is entitled "Facts underlying Adept Biographies."

Let us review two of HPB's descriptions of the contents of the third volume. First, in *The Secret Doctrine* (1888, 2: 437), HPB wrote:

In Volume III. of this work . . . a brief history of all the great adepts known to the ancients and the moderns in their chronological order will be given, as also a bird's eye view of the Mysteries, their birth, growth, decay, and final death—in Europe. This could not find room in the present work.

Also in *The Secret Doctrine* (1888, 1: xl), HPB pens the following:

371

In that [third] volume a brief recapitulation will be made of all the principal adepts known to history, and the downfall of the mysteries will be described; after which began the disappearance and final and systematic elimination from the memory of men of the real nature of initiation and the Sacred Science. From that time its teachings became Occult, and Magic sailed but too often under the venerable but frequently misleading name of Hermetic philosophy. As real Occultism had been prevalent among the Mystics during the centuries that preceded our era, so Magic, or rather Sorcery, with its Occult Arts, followed the beginning of Christianity.

With those lists of content, compare the descriptions given by HPB in her letters of 1886, cited above, with the most relevant parts recapitulated here:

...the undeniable historically proven facts of the existence of Adepts before and after the Christian period, of the admission of a double esoteric meaning in the two Testaments by Church Fathers, and *proofs* that the real source of every Christian dogma rests in the Aryan oldest MYSTERIES during the Vedic and Brahmanic period, proofs and evidence for it being shown in the *Exoteric* as well as Esoteric Sanskrit works. [July 14, 1886, to Olcott]

...a rapid sketch of what *was* known historically and in literature, in classics and in profane and sacred histories—during the 500 years that preceded the Christian period and the 500 y. that followed it: of *magic,* the existence of a Universal Secret Doctrine known to the philosophers and Initiates of every country and even to several of the Church fathers such as Clement of Alexandria, Origen, and others, who had been initiated themselves. Also to describe the Mysteries and some rites; and I can assure you that most extraordinary things are given out now, the whole story of the Crucifixion, etc. being shown to be based on a rite as old as the world—the Crucifixion on the *Lathe* of the Candidate—trials, going down to Hell etc. all Aryan. The whole story hitherto unnoticed by Orientalists is found even exoterically, in the Puranas and *Brahmanas,* and then explained and supplemented with what the *Esoteric* explanations give....[March 3, 1886, to A. P. Sinnett]

These various excerpts from HPB describe fairly well some of the material in Volume III of 1897 as the title headings of the following essays from that volume show:

3. The Origin of Magic
4. The Secrecy of Initiates
5. Some Reason for Secrecy
13. Post-Christian Adepts and Their Doctrines
14. Simon and his Biographer Hippolytus
15. St. Paul—The Real Founder of Present Christianity
16. Peter—A Jewish Kabalist, not an Initiate
17. Apollonius of Tyana
18. Facts Underlying Adept Biographies
19. St. Cyprian of Antioch
28. The Origin of the Mysteries
30. The Mystery "Sun of Initiation"
31. The Objects of the Mysteries
32. Traces of the Mysteries
33. The Last of the Mysteries in Europe
34. The Post-Christian Successors to the Mysteries
43. The Mystery of Buddha
44. "Reincarnations" of Buddha
49. Tsong-kha-pa; Lohans in China

The *focus* of this paper has been on *primary source* documents (various letters, articles, and the Wurzburg Manuscript) written during the years 1885-1897.

Most of these testimonies were given either during the same time HPB was writing and editing *The Secret Doctrine* or within several years of the events narrated, when we would still expect the participants to remember accurately various details and the true course of events.

An attempt has also been made to present the evidence *in chronological order* so that the reader might discern *the natural flow of events related to the writing and editing* of "The Secret Doctrine" manuscript.

The reader should also be aware that there are testimonies that give accounts conflicting with the ones cited in this article. Most of the contrary evidence was given either by individuals who were not directly involved in the writing and editing of the *SD* manuscript or by witnesses writing in the 1920s and 1930s (some thirty or forty years after the actual events).

It is not surprising that a person's recollection of events several decades earlier would contain contradictions and inconsistencies. The reader who would like to examine these conflicting accounts should consult Boris de Zirkoff's "Historical Introduction" to *The Secret Doctrine* (especially pp. 61, 63-6, 71) as well as his survey of the third volume (1897) in CW XIV (especially pp. xxxi-xxxii, xxxiv-xl). See also the Appendix to this paper.

One correspondent, reading the first draft of this article, wrote to me in reply:

In view of the inconsistency of the statements made by those who were familiar with HPB's work at the time; also the contradictory—even self-contradictory—nature of some of them, I do not see how it is possible to reach a conclusion on Vol. III on the strength of these statements, as you and Boris [de Zirkoff] have attempted to do.

In reply, I would ask what historical event of any importance does not involve contradictory and inconsistent testimonies?

Consider the contradictory (pro and con) statements of people who knew HPB personally and made statements about her psychic powers and the existence of her Masters. Emma Coulomb, Richard Hodgson, Vsevolod Solovyov, Hannah Wolff and others gave very different, contradictory, and negative accounts about HPB compared to those of Henry Olcott, Constance Wachtmeister, William Judge, Annie Besant, and others who testified to the genuineness of HPB's claims.

Do these contradictions mean that one cannot reach a reasonable conclusion concerning the genuineness or not of HPB's psychic powers and the existence of her Masters? Historical research is undertaken, at least in part, to try to sift through the evidence (pro, con, and neutral) of an event or series of events, to scrutinize the primary sources, to weigh the evidence (including contradictions), and to attempt to reach reasonable conclusions as to what most probably happened or did not happen.

Another topic not considered in this article has been the 'editing' of HPB's manuscript of the third volume for publication. Annie Besant in her preface to the third volume clearly stated:

With the exception of the correction of grammatical errors and the elimination of obviously un-English idioms, the papers are as H.P.B. left them, save as otherwise marked. In a few cases I have filled in a gap, but any such addition is enclosed within square brackets, so as to be distinguished from the text.

Nevertheless, some students of HPB's writings have voiced concern about how much Besant and her assistants may have edited the manuscript. James M. Pryse in a review of the third volume of *The Secret Doctrine* (*Theosophy*, New York, September 1897, 314-6) wrote:

If it had been printed as H.P.B. wrote it, then Theosophists generally would have prized it; but Mrs. Besant and others having edited it, they will regard it with a just suspicion.

(It should be noted that, some thirty years later, Pryse reversed his view on this subject.)

Another personal student of HPB's, Alice Leighton Cleather (*H.P. Blavatsky: A Great Betrayal*, 1922, 75), testified:

It so happens that while it [Volume III] was being set up [for publication] I was able actually to peruse one or two of the familiar long foolscap sheets which H.P.B. always covered with her small fine hand-writing. They were mutilated almost beyond recognition, few of her sentences remaining intact; and there were 'corrections'.

More recently, Nicholas Weeks, who helped in the preparation of the manuscripts of volumes 13, 14, and 15 of HPB's *Collected Writings,* has expressed similar concerns to me (private correspondence):

When we were working on BCW 14 we found many differences or changes between the "First Draft" [the Wurzburg Manuscript] and "SD III" [1897]. Some of the most radical are included in the Index to 14, see "Wurzburg MS Interpolations." On pp. 104 & 266-67 of BCW 14 are two examples of HPB's typically sharp criticisms of the Roman Catholic Church that *did not* appear in "SD III" [1897]. I find it impossible to believe that HPB deleted them, or approved of their removal. Thus the question arises, how many other "corrections" and "innovations" were made that HPB would not have permitted? . . . Without the "Wurzburg MS" there would have been not even a clue as to any tampering having occurred.

The issue of the editing of the manuscript of Volume III (1897) needs to be carefully researched in the future.

Returning to my thesis, I conclude this section with a relevant quotation from a letter of Bertram Keightley (written from Lucknow, India on December 6, 1922 and addressed to Charles Blech, a French Theosophist):

As regards the matter intended by H.P.B. for future volumes—besides the two first published under her own supervision—*all* this material has been published in the *third* volume which contains absolutely *all* that H.P.B. has left in manuscript. [quoted in *The O. E. Library Critic*, July 4, 1923]

If any Theosophist was knowledgeable about the contents of HPB's third volume, it was Bertram Keightley.

For the various reasons outlined in this paper, I am inclined to believe that Volume III of *The Secret Doctrine* as published in 1897 was the *real* Volume III intended by HPB during her lifetime.

Part 7

SELECTED BIBLIOGRAPHY

(Item with asterisk indicates important source for quotations of primary materials.)

Anonymous. *The Unpublished Secret Doctrine, Volumes Three and Four: Some Observations for the Negators of Vol. III & IV of the Secret Doctrine.* No publisher; no date (1995?). 8 pp. Compiled by U.L.T. student in Sweden.

Blavatsky, H.P. *The Letters of H.P. Blavatsky to A.P. Sinnett.* London: T. Fisher Unwin, 1925; Pasadena, California: Theosophical University Press, 1973. xv + 404 pp.

Cleather, Alice Leighton. "The Third Volume S.D." *The Canadian Theosophist*, December 1937, 300-303.

Crump, Basil. "New Evidence About Vols. III. and IV. of 'The Secret Doctrine'." *The Canadian Theosophist*, April 1939, 39-40.

_____. "The Missing S.D. MSS. Mystery." *The Canadian Theosophist*, September 1939, 214-216.

_____. "More Light on S.D.Vols. III and IV." *The Canadian Theosophist*, September 1939, 216-218.

de Zirkoff, Boris. "Facts and Fiction [on *The Secret Doctrine*, Volume III]." *American Theosophist* (Wheaton, Illinois), June 1962, 127-8.

*_____. "Historical Introduction: How 'The Secret Doctrine' Was Written." In the "Collected Writings" edition of *The Secret Doctrine 1:* [1-76]. Adyar, Madras, India: Theosophical Publishing House, 1978; Wheaton, Illinois: Theosophical Publishing House, 1993 (paperback edition). A valuable source for quotations of primary materials.

*_____. "The Secret Doctrine—Volume III As Published in 1897: A Survey of Its Contents and Authenticity." In H. P. Blavatsky's *Collected Writings,* XIV: xxv-xliv. Wheaton, Illinois: Theosophical Publishing House, 1985. Another valuable source for quotations of primary materials.

Eklund, Dara. "Notes on the Wurzburg Manuscript." In *Symposium on H. P. Blavatsky's Secret Doctrine held at San Diego, California, July 21-22, 1984, 42-5.* San Diego: Wizards Bookshelf, 1984.

Jinarajadasa, C. "More About Vol. III. S.D." *The Canadian Theosophist*, March 1936, 19-20.

Pryse, James Morgan. "An Important Statement by Mr. J.M. Pryse." *The Canadian Theosophist*, September 1926, 140-41.

_____. "The Third Volume of *The Secret Doctrine*." *The Canadian Theosophist*, August 1927, 113-15.

_____. "No Missing Volume of *The Secret Doctrine*." *The Canadian Theosophist*, May 1939, 73-77.

*Ransom, Josephine. "How *The Secret Doctrine* Was Written." In *The Secret Doctrine*, Six-volume edition, 1: 18-36. Adyar, Madras, India: Theosophical Publishing House, 1938.

*Ryan. Charles J. "Some Notes on *The Secret Doctrine* Especially in Regard to the So-called 'Third Volume.'" *Theosophical Forum* (Covina, California), March 1945, 97-112.

Stokes, H. N. "The Lost (?) Volumes of 'The Secret Doctrine.'" *The O. E. Library Critic* (Washington, DC), September 27, 1922, 5-8 and October 25, 1922, 3-6.

_____. "On the Missing Volumes of 'The Secret Doctrine.'" *The O. E. Library Critic*, January 1930, 7-8.

_____. "Is 'Secret Doctrine, Vol. III' Genuine?" *The O. E. Library Critic,* June 1938, 7-11.

_____. "The Mystery of Vols. III and IV, 'Secret Doctrine': A Defense of Madame Blavatsky." *The O. E. Library Critic,* June 1939, 3-8.

Van Mater, Kirby. "The Writing of *The Secret Doctrine*." *Sunrise* (Pasadena, California), November 1975, 54-62. Reprinted in *An Invitation to The Secret Doctrine*, 1988.

*Wachtmeister, Constance. *Reminiscences of H.P. Blavatsky and The Secret Doctrine*. London: Theosophical Publishing Society, 1893; Wheaton, Illinois: Theosophical Publishing House, 1976. xiv + 141 pp.

www.ingramcontent.com/pod-product-compliance
Lightning Source LLC
Chambersburg PA
CBHW021957160426
43197CB00007B/166